Cases of the Reincarnation Type

Volume IV

Twelve Cases in Thailand and Burma

Cases of
the Reincarnation Type

Volume IV

Twelve Cases in Thailand
and Burma

Ian Stevenson, M.D.

University Press of Virginia

Charlottesville

Published with the assistance of the Neill M. Coney, Jr., Memorial Fund

The University Press of Virginia

First published 1983

Library of Congress Cataloging in Publication Date (Revised)

Stevenson, Ian.
  Cases of the reincarnation type.

  Includes indexes.
  Contents: v. 1. Ten cases in India.—v. 2. Ten cases
in Sri Lanka.—v. 3. Twelve cases in Lebanon and
Turkey.—v. 4. Twelve cases in Thailand and Burma.
  1. Reincarnation—Case studies. I. Title
[DNLM: 1. Parapsychology—Case studies. BL 518 S847c]
BL515.S746   133.9′01′3   74-28263
ISBN 0-8139-0602-4 (v. 1)
ISBN 0-8139-0624-5 (v. 2)
ISBN 0-8139-0816-7 (v. 3)
ISBN 0-8139-0960-0 (v. 4)

Printed in the United States of America

Contents

Contents

Acknowledgments

A S WITH THE PREVIOUS VOLUMES of case reports that I have published, many persons have assisted me in the investigation of the cases reported here and in the preparation of this book for publication. The following persons have special claims on my gratitude.

Thailand

My investigations in Thailand were made possible only by the extraordinary exertions of Dr. Chien Siriyananda, Chief, Medical Division, Juvenile Court, Bangkok, who arranged for interpreters and other assistance both in Bangkok and in other cities and towns of Thailand where I investigated cases.

Col. Chalor Utogapachana and Mr. Ed na Pompejra also contributed important assistance in arrangements for the investigations.

For cases that I investigated out of Bangkok, Mr. Tem Suvikrom was my principal interpreter during the several years before his death in 1973. He also greatly assisted the late Francis Story in the investigation of cases.

In 1969 Miss Orathai Srihong assisted me as interpreter in the investigation of several cases, including that of Ampan Petcherat of this volume.

Mr. Chou Niyomvan, Mr. Seri Prakitrittanon, and Capt. Yod Pengsritong also acted as interpreters at different times in cases investigated in the area of Bangkok.

Dr. Sophon Nakphairaj made arrangements for my first two visits in connection with the investigation of the case of Bongkuch Promsin and also acted as interpreter on these occasions. Dr. Sophon also read a draft of the report of Bongkuch's case.

I am no less indebted to the Ven. Sayadaw U Sobhana, who accompanied me on four of my five visits to study Bongkuch's case in the area of Tha Tako, and who was my sole interpreter for that case in 1971. (He is also the subject of a case in this book.)

In Chiang Mai, Miss Penchai Sirorasa made arrangements for my investigation of the case of Hair Kam Kanya. Mr. R. R. Boonyoros of the

Department of Philosophy, Faculty of Humanities, Chiang Mai University, helped me as an interpreter for this case both in 1969 and in 1971. Mr. Boonyoros also read the introductory chapter for the cases in Thailand and gave me suggestions for its improvement.

Professor Kloom Vajropala, Department of Biology, Chulalongkorn University, Bangkok, aided in several aspects of these investigations. After the untimely death of Mr. Tem Suvikrom, who had acted as my interpreter for the investigation of the case of Ratana Wongsombat, Professor Kloom willingly undertook a careful reading of a draft of the report of that case and corrected some errors. He assisted with information bearing on the case of Ampan Petcherat. He also interpreted for me during follow-up interviews for the cases of Bongkuch Promsin and Ratana Wongsombat.

Dr. Thavil Soonthararaksa assisted me in the investigation in Surin Province of Chaokhun Rajsuthajarn's case and acted as my interpreter for interviews concerning the case.

Dr. Sunthorn Na-Rangsi and Mr. Cerm Jumketu have also assisted me in the investigation of cases in Thailand. Mr. Cerm accompanied me as an interpreter for my visit to Bongkuch Promsin in February 1977. Dr. Sunthorn read and gave helpful comments for the chapter introducing the cases of Thailand.

Mrs. Nasib Sirorasa has assisted me for many years as an interpreter in southern Thailand. She was my principal interpreter for my investigation of the case of Pratomwan Inthanu. In addition, she assisted me during follow-up interviews with Ratana Wongsombat and Bongkuch Promsin in 1980.

Burma

U Win Maung has worked indefatigably as my Research Assistant and interpreter in Burma from early 1971 to the present. With extraordinary zeal and effectiveness he has obtained a mass of information on a large number of cases. The number of cases—about four hundred—that we have under investigation in Burma exceeds that in any other single country. Difficulties of traveling to and within Burma have prevented me from studying most of these cases as thoroughly as I would like. Nevertheless, U Win Maung and I have managed to bring the investigation of a number of them to a point that warranted publication of a report.

Many persons have contributed to the investigation of cases in Burma or have notified U Win Maung and me about cases of which we had not previously heard. Among these persons I particularly wish to thank Dr. R. L Soni, Miss Sujata Soni, U Tin Tut, Maung Aye Kyaw, Daw Tin Tin Myint, and U Nu.

An earlier version of the report of the case of Ampan Petcherat was published in the *Journal of the American Society for Psychical Reseach* (67:361–80, 1973). Although I have revised the report for publication in this book and added some information from a follow-up visit, the report is not greatly altered from its earlier form. I am grateful to the American Society for Psychical Research for permission to reprint the report (with the mentioned revisions) in this book.

An earlier version of the report of the case of Ma Tin Aung Myo was published in the *Journal of Nervous and Mental Disease* (165:201-208, 1977). The report published here has been revised and brought up to date. I am nevertheless grateful to the editor and publisher of the *Journal of Nervous and Mental Disease* for permission to use material previously published.

My Research Assistants, Ms. Carolee Werner and Mrs. Emily Williams Cook, have continued to give me valuable—more accurately, indispensable—aid in various matters concerned with both the investigations themselves and the preparation of my reports based on them.

Thanks are extended also to Mrs. Irene Dunn and Miss Betsy Byrd for typing of high quality in the revision of numerous drafts.

Finally, I gratefully renew my thanks to the following foundations for the support of my research: The Bernstein Brothers Parapsychology and Health Foundation, the John E. Fetzer Foundation, and the McDonnell Foundation, Inc.

The Cases in
Thailand

Introduction to Cases in Thailand

THE CASES IN THAILAND that I shall present in this volume all occurred among Theravada Buddhists. Theravada Buddhism is the official state religion of Thailand, and approximately 94 per cent of the population adhere to it (Kusalasaya, 1965). In the second volume of this series (Stevenson, 1977), I described the beliefs concerning reincarnation among the Sinhalese Buddhists of Sri Lanka, who are also Theravadins, and I shall therefore make briefer remarks about the belief in reincarnation among the Thais.[1]

Buddhism first reached Thailand in the third century B.C. during the reign of the Emperor Asoka of India (Kusalasaya, 1965; Sumitra, 1968). (Asoka was also responsible through his son, Mahinda [or Mahendra], for the conversion of the Sinhalese to Buddhism [Rahula, 1966].) Subsequently, in the eighth century A.D., missionaries of the Mahayana (or northern) branch of Buddhism came to Thailand from Srivijaya in what is now Sumatra, Indonesia. They had considerable influence, especially in the area of what is now southern Thailand. But in the eleventh century A.D., King Anuruddha of Burma, who controlled the territory of present northern and central Thailand down to Nakhon Pathom and Lopburi, promoted the development of Theravada Buddhism in these regions. This branch gained additional strength in Thailand when, in the thirteenth century A.D., King Ram Kamhaeng invited Sinhalese monks from Nakhon Sri Thammaraj to come to Sukhothai, which was then the capital of Thailand. From this time, Theravada Buddhism has been the domi-

---

[1]Readers wishing more information about Buddhism in Thailand will find this in the works of Kaufman (1960), Ling (1979), Suksamran (1977), Tambiah (1970, 1976), Wells (1960), and Young (1955). But these authors concerned themselves little or not at all with the belief in rebirth among the Thais. More pertinent in this respect is a much older work, that of Alabaster (1871/1972). Part I of this book is entitled "The 'Modern Buddhist,' or the Ideas of a Siamese Minister of State on His Own and Other Religions." (The book, incidentally, includes a brief summary of the case of a young child who remembered a previous life, some details of which were verified.) I also recommend Na-Rangsi's (1976) work on the Buddhist concepts of *karma* and rebirth. Na-Rangsi writes about Buddhism supranationally, not with special reference to Thailand; but I mention his book here because he is a Thai scholar who, writing in English, has summarized the essential teachings of Buddhism about karma and rebirth.

I

nant sect in Thailand, although a few Mahayana temples and monks persist to this day.

Brahmanism and animism preceded Buddhism in Thailand, and, as in Sri Lanka, Buddhism has not entirely displaced them. What we may call the everyday religion of the average Thai blends Theravada Buddhism, as transmitted through the Pali Canon and interpreted by modern monks, with residues of Brahmanism and animism (Kaufman, 1960; Tambiah, 1970; Young, 1955). I think, however, that other beliefs and practices have diluted Theravada Buddhism less in Thailand than in any other country. Thailand seems to have preserved the traditions and prescribed conduct of the *Sangha* (order of monks) better than other Buddhist countries. In Sri Lanka many monks engage in education, medicine and politics. No one should condemn their participation in such activities as inherently harmful, and indeed it may have valuable results; but these activities necessarily distract an aspirant from the single-minded effort of attaining *Nirvana*, for which the Buddha instructed the *bhikkhus* (monks) to strive with all their attention. The wearing of yellow or ocher robes is supposed to distinguish those persons (the monks) whose main vocation is the effort to reach Nirvana from other persons who have different aims in life. The distinction becomes blurred when monks also engage in traditionally secular activities. In contrast to the monks of Sri Lanka, those of Thailand, despite their important role in education, do not participate extensively in other professions or in traditionally lay activities, such as politics.[2] They restrict themselves, for the most part, to their voluntarily assumed task of "getting off the wheel of rebirth."

I make no claim to having a profound knowledge of religious practices, but I have had occasion to notice them informally in a wide variety of countries. Therefore, I venture to comment that the gap between precept and practice seems to me narrower in the religion of the Thais than in that of any other country where I have made relevant observations. Buddhism seems to penetrate deeply the life of the Thai people. Many Thai laymen practice meditation, and most men join the Sangha at some time or other, even if only for a brief period. It is unusual for a Thai man not to have spent at least a few weeks or months of his life in a *wat*, as the Buddhist temples of Thailand are called. During such a period, he wears a monk's robe and observes all the rules of the Sangha. Since monks must live primarily on charity, often from family members who can ill afford the expense, many leave the wat to earn their own living. Others find life there more exacting and less rewarding than expected. Occasionally monks are asked to disrobe for misconduct, but the majority of those who

---

[2]Piker (1973) and Morgan (1973) have reviewed some of the conflicts in Thai Buddhism between the traditional vocation of the Buddhist monks and the demands placed upon them by the political and economic changes of the modern world.

leave the Sangha do so honorably, and some return later for another period of meditation or other learning.

The Concept of Reincarnation Among Thai Buddhists

As I have already indicated, the belief in reincarnation[3] among Thai Buddhists closely resembles that among Sinhalese Buddhists. When a person dies, a new personality is born. According to Buddhism, immediate rebirth in a new terrestrial body may occur; more often, however, the first rebirth after a physical death is into a nonterrestrial plane of existence—of which there are thirty, having many gradations of suffering and bliss. A person's previous deeds, misdeeds, and other actions (*karma*) determine the conditions, circumstances, and duration of the life in the intermediate plane of existence. The personality reborn in this (nonterrestrial) realm rarely makes any progress there toward further spiritual development; that can usually happen only during a physical life. A new terrestrial rebirth eventually occurs when the merit (or demerit, as the case may be) of the previous personality runs out. The circumstances of this new earthly existence are also determined by the actions of the previous personalities in this series of lives.

Thai Buddhists, like Sinhalese Buddhists, subscribe to the doctrine of *anatta* (no soul). According to this concept, personality is not an enduring entity; nor does it develop upon the ground of such an entity. Instead, it constantly changes as one condition gives rise to another in a ceaseless series. At the death of one personality, a new one comes into existence. The concept of rebirth thus includes continuity, but not persistence of identity.[4]

Some students of the concept of anatta, including some Theravada Buddhists, find this principle difficult to reconcile with the idea of karma. If a new personality arising after the death of an old one is not the

[3]Buddhists prefer the term *rebirth* to *reincarnation*. In their judgment, the former word does not imply an enduring soul that passes from one physical body to another, as does the word *reincarnation*. For a further discussion of this point, see the chapter introducing the cases in Sri Lanka in the second volume of this series. Since Western readers are more familiar with the word *reincarnation*, and since most are unfamiliar with the distinction drawn by Buddhists, I shall use the two words more or less interchangeably.

Buddhists also use the word *rebirth* when referring to the transition after physical death into another (intermediate) plane of existence. This is a type of rebirth, but the word *reincarnation* would not describe it appropriately.

[4]For a further discussion of the concept of anatta and the distinction between it and the concept of the *atman* in Hinduism, see Stevenson (1977).

Horner (1970) questioned whether the Buddha himself taught the doctrine of anatta. I have not hesitated, however, to mention the doctrine as an important ingredient of modern Theravada Buddhism. It certainly is generally believed and taught today by Theravadins. Whether or not it should be believed and taught (assuming Buddhists should believe only what the Buddha himself taught) seems to me quite another matter.

"same," why should it be expected to pay for the failings of the preceding personality? And how can it be expected to profit from the mistakes of the predecessor? Since I have already alluded to this dissonance elsewhere (Stevenson, 1977), I shall not elaborate on the topic here. Moreover, I wish to describe the various beliefs about rebirth held by different peoples without discussing their respective merits.

The belief in anatta entails the creation of a new physical body under the influence of the effects of the deceased personality in the same series of lives. It follows that a person whose life someone else later remembers should die before that person (for example, the subject of one of these cases) is born, or even conceived. Cases in which a subject is born before the concerned previous personality dies (for example, that of the Ven. Chaokhun Rajsuthajarn in this volume) do not accord with these concepts and pose some difficulty for Buddhist theologians.

Thai Buddhists believe that rebirth continues inexorably until a personality arising from a linked series of lives achieves Nirvana. The successive terrestrial lives in a series may occur in bodies of different sexes; they may also occur in the bodies of subhuman animals.

Characteristics of Cases of the Reincarnation Type in Thailand

My colleagues and I have investigated thirty-eight cases of the reincarnation type in Thailand. This small sample allows me to make only tentative remarks about the characteristics found in Thai cases. (Data on some features are missing for a number of the cases, so that for these features the sample is even smaller.)

These cases in Thailand have occurred over a wide geographical area. I have personally investigated cases in the areas of Nakhon Sri Thammaraj (in the south), Chiang Mai (in the north), Rajburi (in the southwest), Surin (in the east), and Udon Thani (in the northeast). Numerous cases have occurred in and around Bangkok. In short, there seems no discernible concentration of the cases in particular geographic areas of the country.

Most of the subjects are the children of poor villagers or humble urban dwellers; this is to be expected, since the majority of Thai people still belong to these groups, even though Thailand has developed further economically than its neighbors in Southeast Asia. The subjects of some cases, however, come from middle- or upper-class families with educated members working in professional or governmental positions. The cases are therefore apparently not confined to specific socioeconomic classes.

Announcing dreams[5] were reported in thirteen of the thirty-eight cases. The subject's mother had the dream in twelve instances, the father in one. Among nine dreams that informants could place temporally, one occurred during the pregnancy, the other eight before the subject's conception. This tendency for the dreams to occur before conception agrees with the Theravada Buddhist belief that a connection becomes established at conception between the residues of the previous personality and the new physical body activated by its karma. According to this teaching, one would not expect the previous personality (as a discarnate entity) to be "heard from" after this time, whether in a dream, as an apparition, or in a mediumistic communication.

Of the thirty-eight subjects of these cases, twenty-two were males and sixteen females.

Four of the subjects claimed to remember previous lives as members of the opposite sex. (I have included a report of the case of one of these subjects, Ampan Petcherat, in this volume.) In a fifth case, one of little evidential value, a girl was identified as the reincarnation of a deceased boy mainly on the basis of an announcing dream; she had no imaged memories of the boy's life. With this case included, five (13 per cent) of the cases were of the "sex change" type. This incidence is higher than that of most other cultures, where cases of this type comprise 5 per cent or fewer of the total number of cases. No cases of the sex change type have been found among the Druses of Lebanon and Syria, the Alevis of Turkey, the Tlingit of southeastern Alaska, or the Haida of Alaska and British Columbia. On the other hand, 28 per cent of 230 cases in Burma are of this type. And Slobodin (1970) has reported an even higher incidence (50 per cent) of such cases among the Kutchin of the Canadian Northwest Territories.

In thirty-five (92 per cent) of the cases, a particular previous personality was identified. Three (8 per cent) of the cases remain "unsolved," that is, no deceased person corresponding to the subject's statements has been identified. Among the thirty-five identified previous personalities, twenty-four (69 per cent) were males and eleven (31 per cent) were females. Among the three unsolved cases, one male subject indicated that he had been a man in the previous life he claimed to recall, and two female subjects indicated that they had been females in theirs. Thus none of these unsolved cases was of the sex change type.

[5]By the phrase *announcing dream*, I mean a dream experienced by a woman, or sometimes by one of her close relatives or friends, in which, as it seems to the dreamer, a deceased person communicates his or her wish or intention to be reborn as that woman's baby. For examples of such announcing dreams, see my article summarizing the cases among the Tlingit of Alaska (Stevenson, 1966). The reports of several Turkish cases (Stevenson, 1980) include some examples of announcing dreams. Further examples will be found in the reports of all of the Burmese cases in this volume.

In twenty-two (69 per cent) of the thirty-two cases for which we have information about the previous connections between the two families concerned, the subject and the previous personality were members of the same immediate or extended family. In three other cases (9 per cent) the families were acquainted, and in seven cases (22 per cent) the families were total strangers before the development of the case.[6] In this relatively high incidence of biological relationships between subjects and concerned previous personalities, the cases in Thailand resemble those of the Burmese and the Tlingit.

Among twenty-eight cases in which the cause of death of the concerned previous personality was verified, the death was violent in twelve (43 per cent) and natural in sixteen (57 per cent).[7]

Birthmarks and deformities occurred in twenty (53 per cent) of the cases in Thailand. Not all the birthmarks corresponded to fatal wounds of the related previous personalities. Some derived from the "experimental" marking of a deceased child; in Thailand, as in some other countries, grieving relatives may mark the body of a deceased person so that they may identify the person if a baby is later born with a birthmark in the same location. The case of Ampan Petcherat (in this volume) illustrates this practice; her case is an unsatisfactory example, however, because of an informant's blurred memories. I intend to enlarge on the topic of experimental birthmarks in a volume now in preparation.

Claims of memories of previous lives as subhuman animals occur rarely in Thailand, much less commonly than the widespread belief in animal rebirth would lead one to expect.

Twenty-one (55 per cent) of the cases in Thailand included reports by the subject of experiences he claimed to have had between his death in the previous physical life and his birth in the present one. This incidence of such reports is much higher than that in other cultures, most of whose subjects say they remember nothing of the "intermission" period between death and presumed rebirth.

Three features commonly occur in accounts of such intermission experiences. First, many of the subjects say that after they died, they saw their physical bodies, observed the funeral rites for these, or became aware of other terrestrial events occurring in their families.

Second, many of the subjects say they remember encountering a "man

[6]In one case (that of Pratomwan Inthanu, reported in this volume), the two families concerned were apparently not acquainted before the development of the case. After the two families met, they learned that they were distantly related. This case has been counted here as one in which the families were not acquainted before the development of the case.

[7]For a comparison with data on this feature from cases of other cultures, see Table 15 in Stevenson (1980).

in white," a sagelike person wearing white robes.[8] This figure often welcomes the recently deceased person as he arrives at the plane of his discarnate sojourn; he acts as his guide and companion there and may subsequently direct him to the home of his next birth. These "men in white" do not appear to influence the *choice* of the home for the next birth; they only lead the subject to it, somewhat as an airline agent at an airport may read one's already prepared ticket and guide one to the proper gate for boarding an airplane to a previously selected destination.

Third, many of the subjects report that just prior to rebirth, the "man in white" or perhaps some other figure offered them food, usually fruit, to eat. Eating this fruit supposedly erases memories of the previous life, and informants occasionally refer to it as the "fruit of forgetfulness."[9] Subjects who remember previous lives sometimes claim that when offered this fruit, they managed not to eat it by, for example, surreptitiously disposing of it when the "man in white" was not looking. They may attribute the preservation of their memories to this successful disobedience.[10]

[8]Since Theravada Buddhists regard the ocher-robed monks as the persons closest to Nirvana, one may ask why these discarnate sages are dressed in white instead of in ocher. Francis Story gave me an answer in a letter of August 1, 1969, in which he pointed out that, according to Buddhist teaching, there is no Sangha in the intermediate realms of existence. A monk who does not attain Nirvana becomes in these realms a layman—although, to be sure, one in a more advanced state than others. The inhabitants of these planes (who, as I said earlier, can make little or no progress there toward Nirvana) are all laymen. And white is the traditional color of dress for the devout Buddhist layman. It is worn by the *Upasakas* and the *Anagarikas*, devotees who have committed themselves to the Buddhist way of life without taking all the vows of the Buddhist monk.

[9]These reports of eating the "fruit of forgetfulness" resemble the ancient Greek tradition of drinking the water of Lethe before being reborn. Plato's (1935, p. 325) description of such a scene includes the following passage: " . . . then all [the souls to be reincarnated] proceeded . . . to the plain of Lethe where grew no plants nor any trees. At last they encamped by evening by the river of Forgetfulness, whose water no pitcher may hold. All had to drink a certain measure of this water, but those who were not preserved by wisdom drank more than the measure. Each as he drank it forgot everything." Er, the narrator of this scene, which he claimed to have witnessed during what we should today call a "near-death experience," said that "he himself had been forbidden to drink of the water." One infers that he thereby retained his memories when he recovered consciousness in his physical body, which, by the time he awoke, had been placed on a pyre ready for its cremation.

[10]None of the subjects of the seven Thai cases included in this volume reported avoiding the "fruit of forgetfulness." I have, however, investigated other Thai cases in which the subjects have made such a claim. I shall include a report of one of these cases, that of Phra Som Pit, in a later volume.

Lê Quang Hu'o'ng (1972) published a remarkably similar account narrated by the subject of a case in Vietnam. The subject claimed to recall that he had been offered a food—in his case soup, not fruit—to promote amnesia before his rebirth, and that he had succeeded in not eating it, thereby preserving his memories of the previous life. The subject stated that he had clandestinely passed his portion of the "soup of forgetfulness" to his (also discarnate) dog, who was accompanying him in this realm. According to the traditional belief, disposing of the soup in this way would have deprived the dog of the ability to remember *his* previous life. Lê Quang Hu'o'ng subsequently sent me accounts of two other Vietnamese cases that he investigated. In each of them, the subject said that he (or she) had been offered the "soup of forgetfulness" just prior to rebirth, but had managed to avoid eating it.

Our ignorance should restrain conjectures about why the subjects of Thai and Burmese cases have (on the average) so much more to tell about experiences during the intermission period than have subjects of other cultures.

For thirty-two of the thirty-eight Thai cases, data concerning birth and death dates were sufficiently reliable for calculating the median interval between the death of the concerned previous personality and the subject's birth. This median interval was sixteen months, a duration somewhat shorter than the corresponding intervals for cases in Sri Lanka (eighteen months) and Burma (twenty-one months), both of which are also predominantly Buddhist countries. Claims to remember experiences during the period between death and rebirth occur rarely in cases in Sri Lanka, but they occur frequently in Burma (in 23 per cent of the cases). The differences between the three countries in this respect cannot be readily explained by the difference between the median intervals between death and presumed rebirth. Table 1 gives the median interval for all the countries from which data have been analyzed to date.

The age at death of the concerned deceased person was known or could be estimated with reasonable accuracy in thirty-three Thai cases. The median age was eighteen years.

Notes on the Romanization of Thai Names and Terms Used in Buddhism

Some readers may notice inconsistencies in the romanizations I have adopted for Thai names. This derives from my having had different interpreters who have sometimes suggested different English spellings for Thai names.

Although Pali is the original language of the scriptures of Theravada Buddhism, I have used the Sanskrit spelling of many words, such as dharma, karma, and Nirvana, that are familiar to Western readers. The glossary provides some of the corresponding Pali words.

Note on Thai Honorifics and Usages Concerning Proper Names

Nai is a general honorific for men in Thailand; it corresponds roughly to Mr. in English. Nang is the corresponding honorific for women. Khun is a more respectful honorific, which may be used in addressing both men and women.

Phra is a general honorific for junior Buddhist monks in Thailand. More senior monks receive the honorific Phra Kru and the most senior ones that of Chaokhun.

Chee means "nun" in Thai. Mae means "mother." Most Buddhist nuns in Thailand are addressed with a double honorific of Mae Chee.

TABLE 1. *Median Interval in Months between Death of Previous Personality and Birth of Subject*

	Tlingit (23 cases)	Burma (122 cases)	Thailand (32 cases)	Sri Lanka (17 cases)	India (95 cases)	Turkey (63 cases)	Lebanon (34 cases)
Median interval in months	48	21	16	18	16	9	6

Buddhist monks are usually referred to with the honorific *Venerable,* but when I have occasion to refer to a particular monk frequently, I have sometimes omitted this honorific; and similarly, I have sometimes referred to Buddhist nuns without preceding their names with Mae Chee.

Family names are not used as much in Thailand as they are in Western countries. It is thus common practice to refer, for example, to Professor Kloom Vajropala as Professor Kloom and to Dr. Chien Siriyananda as Dr. Chien.

References

Alabaster, H. 1972. *The wheel of the law: Buddhism.* Varanasi and Delhi: Indological Book House. (First published in 1871.)

Horner, I. B. 1970. Atta and anatta. *The Middle Way: Journal of the Buddhist Society* 45:66–69.

Kaufman, H. K. 1960. *Bangkhuad: A community study in Thailand.* Monographs for the Association for Asian Studies. New York: J. J. Augustin.

Kusalasaya, K. 1965. *Buddhism in Thailand: Its past and its present.* Kandy: Buddhist Publication Society.

Lê Quang Hu'o'ng. 1972. Histoires viêtnamiennes de réincarnation. *Message d'Extrême-Orient* 2, no. 7, 535-39.

Ling, T. 1979. *Buddhism, imperialism and war: Burma and Thailand in modern history.* London: George Allen & Unwin.

Morgan, F. B. 1973. Vocation of monk and layman: Signs of change in Thai Buddhist ethics. *Contributions to Asian Studies* 4:68–77.

Na-Rangsi, S. 1976. *The Buddhist concepts of karma and rebirth.* Bangkok: Mahamakut Rajavidyalaya Press.

Piker, S. 1973. Buddhism and modernization in contemporary Thailand. *Contributions to Asian Studies* 4:51–67.

Plato. 1935. *The republic.* Translated by A. D. Lindsay. London: J. M. Dent and Sons.

Rahula, W. 1966. *History of Buddhism in Ceylon.* 2d ed. Colombo: M. D. Gunasena and Co.

Slobodin, R. 1970. Kutchin concepts of reincarnation. *Western Canadian Journal of Anthropology* 2:67–79.

Stevenson, I. 1966. Cultural patterns in cases suggestive of reincarnation among the Tlingit Indians of southeastern Alaska. *Journal of the American Society for Psychical Research* 60:229–43.

———. 1977. *Cases of the reincarnation type.* Vol. 2, *Ten cases in Sri Lanka.* Charlottesville: University Press of Virginia.

———. 1980. *Cases of the reincarnation type.* Vol. 3, *Twelve cases in Lebanon and Turkey.* Charlottesville: University Press of Virginia.

Suksamran, S. 1977. *Political Buddhism in Southeast Asia.* London: C. Hurst and Company.

Sumitra, L. 1968. *Theravada Buddhism of Thailand.* Bangkok: Buddhist Association of Thailand.

Tambiah, S. J. 1970. *Buddhism and the spirit cults in northeast Thailand.* Cambridge: Cambridge University Press.

_____. 1976. *World conqueror and world renouncer: A study of Buddhism and policy in Thailand against a historical background.* Cambridge: Cambridge University Press.

Wells, K. E. 1960. *Thai Buddhism: Its rites and activities.* Bangkok: The Christian Bookstore.

Young, J. E. de. 1955. *Village life in modern Thailand.* Berkeley: University of California Press.

1.   The Case of Ratana Wongsombat

Summary of the Case and Its Investigation

RATANA WONGSOMBAT was born in Bangkok on May 3, 1964. She was the daughter of Surapol Suwansit and his wife, Sunisa. Ratana had some older siblings, but I do not know her order of birth in her family. Her parents were unhappily married, and her mother did not want another child. She and her husband separated around the time of Ratana's birth or soon after. (I shall refer to Ratana's mother hereafter as Sunisa Sutaputra.) Since Ratana's maternal grandmother, Charoon Sri Wongsombat, and her second husband, Samnuan Wongsombat, a practicing lawyer, had no children, they asked to have Ratana even before she was born, and they formally adopted her about a month after her birth. During part of Ratana's childhood, including the period in 1969 when I first became acquainted with her family, her mother lived in the Wongsombat household, as did some other children. These were, I think, Ratana's older siblings, but I did not learn their exact relationship. From 1971 on, Ratana was the only child living with her adoptive parents.

Ratana learned to speak early. Samnuan Wongsombat said she could articulate the Thai word for "yes" at seven months and could speak well at eleven months. At that age, Ratana began asking him to take her for merit-making [1] to Wat Mahathat. (This is a well-known wat in Bangkok on the other side of the city from where the Wongsombats lived.) He thought her too young at that time, but a few months later, when she was fourteen months old, he did take her to Wat Mahathat, and there she showed an unexpected knowledge of the buildings and of the proper gestures and offerings for Buddhist worship.

After returning from the wat in the evening, Samnuan Wongsombat asked Ratana where she had been before this life. Ratana said: "Which part shall I tell about?" He asked her to tell him first about Wat Mahathat. Ratana replied that she [2] had been in a green hut [3] meditating, had been

[1] Merit-making includes, among other acts, listening to expositions of the Buddha's life and teachings *(dharma)* and making donations *(dana)* to monks, nuns, and beggars. Thus visiting temples provides abundant opportunities for merit-making in Buddhism.

[2] I would like to make a disclaimer here similar to the one that I made in the first volume of this series (p. 47). The use of the third person pronoun without quotation marks in referring to the previ-

driven from it, and had moved to Banglampoo (a district of Bangkok). Ratana further said that she had become ill and had returned to her old home in Sri Racha, where she had an operation and died.[4] To this account Ratana added some details about her experiences after death and before her birth, which I shall describe later. At about this time, Ratana also said that her name in the previous life had been Kim Lan.

When Ratana was a little more than two years old, Samnuan Wongsombat again took her to Wat Mahathat. On this occasion they passed a hut in the wat compound, and Ratana said: "That is my house." (Samnuan Wongsombat told Francis Story that this recognition occurred during Ratana's first visit to the wat; he told me that it occurred at this later visit.) They also passed a large group of nuns, one of whom Ratana seemed to recognize. Ratana shouted at her: "Mai Chan." The nun thus addressed paid no attention to the small child, and the group passed on. Ratana said she had once lived with that nun.

Some days later Samnuan Wongsombat went back to Wat Mahathat and there located a nun called Mae Chee Chan Suthipat.[5] Mae Chee Chan confirmed to Samnuan Wongsombat that she had once shared a meditation hut with a woman called Kim Lan. Her full name had been

---

ous personality implies no judgment concerning how the subject acquired his (or her) information about the previous personality. I am recording what he (or she) said (or was said to have said) about what seemed to him (or her) memories of events experienced in a previous life.

[3]In addition to temples and other buildings available for religious services and teaching, the wats of Thailand often have small houses or huts that are used for meditation. The Thai word *kuti* applied to these places is imperfectly rendered by "hut" in English. Some of these buildings may be correctly described as huts and have just enough room for a monk or nun to meditate, but not to live in them. Others are more substantial, with one or two rooms, and may serve as both living quarters and places for meditation. Such a small building, known as the *kuti kheo* ("green hut") at Wat Mahathat, was occupied residentially by the previous personality of this case and figures in the evidence that I shall present.

[4]Readers may find it difficult to believe that a child of this young age could communicate so many details. Ratana's adoptive parents, however, gave independent and agreeing statements concerning her precocious ability to speak. I am not saying that Ratana, when she was a young child, spoke the exact words that her adoptive parents later used in telling me what she had said. For example, I do not believe that she herself used the word *operation*. Samnuan Wongsombat told me that she used to point to her abdomen and thus somehow communicate the idea of having been cut there. He also told Francis Story (who began the investigation of the case) that Ratana had said: "The doctor put the knife beside my heart and made me die." Similarly, it is unlikely that Ratana used the word *hospital* when she was young; but she was somehow able to let her family know that a doctor had cut her and that this had occurred in a building where such a cutting was done. For further comments on subjects' abilities to express their thoughts when young, see the General Introduction in the first volume of this series (p. 47). For examples of other subjects who had difficulty in expressing their apparent memories when first trying to do so, see the cases of Imad Elawar (I. Stevenson, *Twenty Cases Suggestive of Reincarnation* [Charlottesville: University Press of Virginia, 1974]; hereafter referred to as *Twenty Cases*), Kumkum Verma (first volume in this series), Ruby Kusuma Silva, and Sujith Lakmal Jayaratne (second volume).

[5]I have not verified that Ratana shouted directly at Mae Chee Chan; the most I can say on this point is that Ratana thought she recognized Mae Chee Chan among the group of nuns who passed by when she was at the wat.

Kim Lan Prayoon Supamitr, and she had died in Sri Racha less than two years before Ratana's birth. Mae Chee Chan was also able to verify some of Ratana's other statements about the previous life.

About a week later, Ratana was taken again to Wat Mahathat, where she successfully picked out Mae Chee Chan from among a group of four nuns who were lined up for a test of her ability to recognize her. Unfortunately, she was asked to say which one was Mae Chee Chan and the glances of the knowledgeable bystanders may well have guided her.[6] On this and subsequent visits to Wat Mahathat, Ratana spoke about and recognized various monks of the wat and the particular places inside its precincts where they stayed. She made comments about gifts she had given to this wat and to another one.

In its issue of July 31, 1967, the *Bangkok Times* published a summary of the case up to that time. Capt. Yod Pensritong, a correspondent of Francis Story and myself, sent me a copy of the newspaper (published in the Thai language) and a translation of the article. At this time Ratana was a little more than three years of age. I do not know the stimulus prompting the newspaper to publish an account of the case when it did, which was about a year after Ratana had met Mae Chee Chan but before she had met members of Kim Lan's family.

In September 1968, Francis Story was in Bangkok, and he interviewed Ratana, her adoptive parents, Mae Chee Chan, and another nun, Mae Chee Anong Khaopongpaitoon.

Ratana expressed a wish to go to Sri Racha, and when a monk known to the family said he had gone there, Ratana reproached him for not taking her to visit her previous daughter. Eventually, early in March 1969, Samnuan Wongsombat took Ratana to Sri Racha to visit Kim Lan's daughter and to let Ratana see and perhaps recognize other persons and places there. His wife and a monk, the Ven. Chaokhun Suvimol Thammajan, accompanied them to Sri Racha.

In the middle of March 1969, I was in Bangkok and began my investigation of the case there. I had several interviews with Samnuan Wongsombat and talked also with his wife and with Ratana. Ratana was extremely shy and it would be more accurate to say that I saw her rather than I talked with her. I also interviewed, at Wat Mahathat, the two nuns, Mae Chee Chan and Mae Chee Anong Khaopongpaitoon, as well as two of the monks and another resident of the wat. Then I went to Sri Racha, where I had two interviews with Anan Suthavil Prayoon Supamitr, the only daughter of Kim Lan Prayoon Supamitr, and interviews with three other informants of that area.

In 1970 I returned to Thailand and resumed the investigation of the

---

[6]I was given discrepant statements about when this second recognition of Mae Chee Chan occurred. Samnuan Wongsombat said Ratana was then twenty-six months old, which would have placed the event in the middle of 1966. Mae Chee Chan, speaking with me in March 1969, said the meeting occurred "two years ago," which would mean early in 1967.

case. I met Ratana and her adoptive parents again. I also went a second time to Sri Racha to check certain details once more with Anan Suthavil. During this period of the investigation, I first met Dr. Sukri Suebsanguan, the surgeon of Sri Racha who had operated on Kim Lan before her death, and obtained his testimony.

In November 1972, I was in Bangkok again and visited Ratana's family once more. Ratana was away on a visit to Chiang Mai, but I had a long talk with her adoptive parents about her further development.

On November 16, 1974, I again met Ratana and her adoptive parents in Bangkok. Prof. Kloom Vajropala accompanied me. We met Ratana and her adoptive mother, Charoon Sri Wongsombat, at their home and her adoptive father, Samnuan Wongsombat, at his office. In this way I obtained independent opinions from Ratana's adoptive parents about her later development.

In 1977, 1978, and 1980, I visited Ratana and her adoptive parents again. In 1978 Ratana and her parents went with Professor Kloom and me to Sri Racha, where we met Anan Suthavil and her family again.

Persons Interviewed during the Investigation

In Bangkok I interviewed:

Ratana Wongsombat
Charoon Sri Wongsombat, Ratana's maternal grandmother and adoptive mother
Samnuan Wongsombat, Ratana's stepgrandfather and adoptive father
Mae Chee Chan Suthipat, nun of Wat Mahathat and friend of Kim Lan
Mae Chee Anong Khaopongpaitoon, nun of Wat Mahathat
Ven. Chaokhun Suvimol Thammajan, senior monk of Wat Mahathat
Ven. Phra Kru Sorn Wichai, monk of Wat Mahathat
Chee Nai Kaisan, member of the management committee of Wat Mahathat

In Sri Racha I interviewed:

Anan Suthavil Prayoon Supamitr, Kim Lan's daughter
Boonyium Suthavil, Anan Suthavil's husband and Kim Lan's son-in-law
Prakeb Sirikool, Anan Suthavil's chauffeur
Ven. Phra Kitti Vudho, monk of Wat Banglamoong
Dr. Sukri Suebsanguan, surgeon who had operated on Kim Lan at Somdet Memorial Hospital in Sri Racha

The first five persons in the above list were interviewed also (in Bangkok) by Francis Story in September 1968.

*Relevant Facts of Geography and Possibilities for Normal Means of
Communication between the Two Families*

Sri Racha is a seaside town on the Gulf of Siam about 120 kilometers
south of Bangkok. Anan Suthavil, the only daughter of Kim Lan Prayoon
Supamitr, was the manager there of the Sri Racha branch of the Bangkok
Bank. She came into Bangkok rather often on banking business, but said
she had no previous acquaintance with Samnuan Wongsombat and his
family. She was familiar with Wat Mahathat, where she had often visited
her mother during the last few years of her life. And she knew Mae Chee
Chan, the nun Ratana had recognized, who had been her mother's room-
mate at the wat.

In 1969 Samnuan Wongsombat lived on a side road off Sukhumvit
Road in a part of Bangkok about 8 kilometers from Wat Mahathat.
Earlier, he had lived closer to the wat. Wat Mahathat is one of the largest
and best-known temples of Bangkok. When Samnuan Wongsombat was
young, he had stayed some time in it as a monk. In later life he took up
meditation again, and in about 1962 he began going to Wat Mahathat for
meditation practice once a week. He said he had never met Kim Lan or
Mae Chee Chan before Ratana began talking about them. He knew some
of the monks at Wat Mahathat, but not all of them, since there were more
than 300 there. He did, however, know two of the monks mentioned or
pointed out by Ratana; these were the Ven. Chaokhun Suvimol
Thammajan and the Ven. Phra Kitti Vudho.

Of the monks known to both Kim Lan and Samnuan Wongsombat,
only the Ven. Phra Kitti Vudho seems to have known Kim Lan well.
However, he appears not to have been a close acquaintance of Samnuan
Wongsombat. For this statement my evidence is his not having met
Ratana (although he knew about her case) up to the time of my meeting
with him (on April 2, 1969). On the other hand, the Ven. Chaokhun
Suvimol Thammajan was a friend of Samnuan Wongsombat, and I once
met him at the latter's house. But he did not know Kim Lan well. He said
he was aware of who she was, and had seen her walking in the compound
of Wat Mahathat. He had not attended the burial ceremony for her
ashes; and he did not know that her ashes had been scattered, not buried,
until Ratana asserted this to be a fact. He was surprised when she turned
out to be correct.

Mae Chee Chan said she had never met Samnuan Wongsombat or his
family before he sought her in the wat, when he began to verify Ratana's
statements.

In summary, the two families had no personal acquaintance whatever,
so far as the informants could remember, before the verification of
Ratana's statements. Nevertheless, Samnuan Wongsombat undoubtedly

knew persons who had had at least some acquaintance with Kim Lan. Kim Lan had spent three years in Wat Mahathat as a meditator. She had been a wealthy woman and a notable benefactress of the wat, and her ashes were deposited there. It is therefore conceivable that Samnuan Wongsombat had picked up some information about her without realizing that he had done so.

The Life, Death, and Character of Kim Lan Prayoon Supamitr

My information about the life, death, and personality of Kim Lan was obtained chiefly from her daughter, Anan Suthavil, and to a lesser extent from her companion at Wat Mahathat, Mae Chee Chan, and other informants.

Kim Lan Prayoon Supamitr was born in Bangkok in 1894. Her father was Chinese, her mother half Thai and half Chinese. I know nothing of her early life. She married and was, or became, prosperous and indeed wealthy. She had only one child, a daughter, Anan, of whom she was extremely fond, as she was of Anan's husband, Boonyium Suthavil. Although Kim Lan and her daughter were devoted to each other, they sometimes quarreled, and Anan thought that her mother actually liked her son-in-law more than herself. Anan and Boonyium had one son, Kim Lan's only grandchild, and Kim Lan was much attached to him also.

At the age of forty-three, Kim Lan underwent three abdominal operations. There was some difficulty in translating the Thai words for the causes of the operations into English for me, but eventually, with the help of Dr. Sukri Suebsanguan, it became clear that an ovarian tumor necessitated at least one of these operations. Otherwise Kim Lan's health remained fairly good until shortly before her final illness, operation, and death.

Kim Lan was unhappily married. For many years she and her husband occupied the same house, but barely spoke to each other. They seem to have quarreled over Kim Lan's objections to her husband's extravagance in giving money away, as she saw the matter. But Kim Lan herself was extremely liberal, especially to religious persons and foundations. She generously supported temples, monks, and nuns. She made a substantial donation for rooms at the Somdet Memorial Hospital in Sri Racha. She also gave to crippled beggars, although rarely to healthy ones.

Religion was the dominant interest of her life, at least in her later years. At night, Kim Lan always prayed and prostrated herself before a Buddha image before going to sleep. She meditated assiduously.

In addition to her private religious practices, Kim Lan entered enthusiastically into the public services at wats. When the congregation responded to the utterances of the presiding monk, Kim Lan spoke first and loudest. People stared at her, and her daughter, when she was present, wanted to shrink into invisibility from embarrassment over her mother's loud voice. She scolded her mother for shouting, but Kim Lan thought Anan's objections foolish. At the same time, she said she would have a sweet (but still loud) voice in her next life.

She also often expressed a wish to be reborn as a man, so that she could become a monk.[7]

Ascetic in dress and eating, she bought cheap clothes for herself and avoided expensive foods. When her daughter brought her costly food, she would sometimes give it away to other persons. In order to neutralize this tendency, Anan would lie to her mother about the price of food. She would also cut open good fruit, such as durians, so it would spoil if not eaten. In addition, Anan bought silk clothes for her mother, who, although wealthy, would have dressed herself in cotton only.

With all her generosity to others and her stinting herself, Kim Lan was nevertheless a shrewd purchaser. She knew prices well, and no one could cheat her.

She ate seafood, chicken, and pork, but not beef. She was a strict vegetarian only during Buddhist periods of fasting. She restricted her eating of crabs and shrimp to those species that die when removed from the sea.[8] Although her family background was mostly Chinese, she seems not to have been particularly fond of Chinese foods. Her favorite foods were soup and vegetables, however, and these are important foods among the Chinese.

Toward the end of her life, Kim Lan separated completely from her husband, and in about 1958, she entered Wat Mahathat as a meditator. (I feel entitled to conjecture that a wish to escape from her unhappy marriage contributed importantly to her decision to take up the religious life full time.) At Wat Mahathat she lived in a meditation hut with one of the nuns, Mae Chee Chan, for three years. She then had some disagreement with a new abbot of the wat, who wanted her to leave so that he could assign her hut to a monk. She left Wat Mahathat and, although she was now about sixty-seven years old, she moved to a house in the Bangkok

[7]Buddhism generally accords women a lower status than men. They can attain enlightenment, but it is more difficult for them to do so since they are not allowed to become monks, who have greater opportunities for spiritual advancement. For this reason, and also because of the generally inferior social status of women in Asia, they often wish to be reborn as men.

[8]A Buddhist precept enjoins killing and devout Buddhists will not kill animals. But Buddhists are not, or need not be, vegetarians. (It is said that the Buddha himself ate some pork on the day he died.) Meat is plentifully available in Buddhist countries, but the butchers and fishermen are usually Moslems.

Kim Lan could satisfy a taste for seafood so long as the animals were not deliberately killed for her. Since removing the animals from the sea was fatal to them, this may seem a quibble; but it was not so for Kim Lan, and she drilled her daughter on the distinction.

For further information about Buddhism and meat-eating, see the chapter on this subject in F. Story, *The Buddhist Outlook,* (Kandy: Buddhist Publication Society, 1973).

district of Banglampoo and continued meditating there. Then her health
began to fail. A few months after moving to Banglampoo, she attended a
ceremony connected with the opening of a new wing at the hospital in Sri
Racha; this wing contained some rooms she had donated. The king of
Thailand was present and gave Kim Lan a medal. Kim Lan's daughter,
Anan, then noticed that she looked ill and, instead of allowing her
mother to return to Banglampoo, had her admitted to the hospital in Sri
Racha.[9]

Examination showed that Kim Lan had a mass in her right upper abdomen and a gall stone. Kim Lan pleaded for an operation to relieve her
discomfort, and the director of the hospital, Dr. Sukri Suebsanguan,
eventually agreed to operate. Anan wished the operation to take place on
an astrologically auspicious day, but Kim Lan did not care about that; she
wanted to have it as soon as possible. She wanted to live longer so that she
could again see her grandson, who was then abroad. She concealed from
her daughter the actual day chosen for the operation. On the other hand,
she was also resigned to die, and the day before the operation she made
out her will.

The operation was seemingly a success, and Kim Lan was recovering
when, a few hours later, she hemorrhaged and was taken back to the
operating room. She died on the operating table.

I discussed Kim Lan's operation with Dr. Sukri, who had operated on
her. She urged him to operate, and he twice refused to do so, but eventually consented. As she was taken to the operating room she handed Dr.
Sukri a letter, which turned out to be a kind of will in which she be-
queathed her body for the use of medical students and directed that her
remains were to be deposited under the Bo Tree at Wat Mahathat. During the operation, he performed a cholecystectomy. The mass in her
right upper abdomen proved to be her liver, somewhat enlarged with cir-
rhosis. The liver disease had diminished the clotting capacity of her
blood, so that she bled uncontrollably, and loss of blood was the immediate cause of her death.

I verified in the Municipal Office of Sri Racha that Kim Lan died on
September 12, 1962, at the age of sixty-eight years.[10]

[9]In 1978 Anan Suthavil said that she had kept her mother at home in Sri Racha for about *two years*
after she became no longer able to stay in Banglampoo and before she was admitted to the hospital
with her terminal illness. I do not understand this discrepancy, which I did not notice until after my
last meeting with Anan. It could be due to slips in the translation into English of Thai words for
intervals of time, such as *years* and *months*. Anan and I communicated in English, but she does not
speak it well. I think her earlier account of the sequence of events, which she gave in 1969, more
likely to be correct than her later one.

[10]Anan Suthavil told me that her mother was approximately sixty-seven years old when she died.
This discrepancy seems unimportant. The younger age is as likely to be correct as the older one,
since the latter was presumably derived originally from Kim Lan's family, either directly after her
death or indirectly from the records at Somdet Memorial Hospital.

Anan Suthavil tried to follow her mother's wishes in the matter of burial of her ashes, but found too many roots at the base of the Bo Tree at Wat Mahathat; she therefore simply scattered the ashes around the base of the tree.

Statements and Recognitions Made by Ratana

In Table 2 I have listed all the statements and recognitions attributed to Ratana by informants of the case. I have placed the statements together first, followed by the recognitions. I am not certain of the chronological order in which Ratana made the statements and recognitions, but I believe that the following order is approximately correct. Items 1–7 were stated to Samnuan Wongsombat before or soon after Ratana's first visit to Wat Mahathat. For two of these items (items 3 and 5), Ratana later made the same or similar statements to other informants. Items 8–23 were made after Ratana's first visit to Wat Mahathat. Items 24–26 were made during Ratana's first visit to Sri Racha in March 1969. Items 27–28 occurred on the occasion of Ratana's first visit to Wat Mahathat, when she was about fourteen months old. Items 29–30 occurred on the occasion of Ratana's second visit to Wat Mahathat, when she was about twenty-six months old. Items 31–35 probably occurred during Ratana's second or later visits to Wat Mahathat. Items 36–40 occurred during Ratana's first visit to Sri Racha, in 1969. Item 41 occurred during Ratana's second visit to Sri Racha, in 1970.

I have included in Table 2 a small number of items stated by Ratana to Francis Story in 1968. Ratana was so shy, however, that she answered questions or made statements only to her (adoptive) mother, Charoon Sri Wongsombat, who then relayed them to the interpreter.

The statements and recognitions made by Ratana cluster around events in the last few years of Kim Lan's life, which she mostly passed as a meditator at Wat Mahathat. But Ratana had one memory, that of Anan Suthavil's change of name, relating to an event that had occurred about fifty years earlier.[11] She talked much of her (previous) daughter, but never, before going to Sri Racha, of her (previous) husband. Even after returning from Sri Racha, she referred to him only once, and then in terms of repugnance that I shall describe later. This different emphasis in Ratana's statements accords with the widely different degrees of affection Kim Lan felt for her daughter and her (Kim Lan's) husband.

---

[11]For other instances of subjects remembering events that occurred many years before the deaths of the related previous personalities, see the cases of Kumkum Verma (first volume of this series), Lalitha Abeyawardena (second volume), Zouheir Chaar, Rabih Elawar (third volume), the Ven. Chaokhun Rajsuthajarn, and the Ven. Sayadaw U Sobhana (this volume).

In Sri Racha, Ratana failed to make some recognitions that she might have been expected to make. For example, her recognition of Kim Lan's daughter, Anan, was doubtful. Anan thought that Ratana had recognized her and that Ratana had pointed her out to Anan's chauffeur, who was with Samnuan Wongsombat's party after they reached Sri Racha. But the chauffeur, Prakeb Sirikool, did not remember this; since I talked with him less than ten days after Ratana's first visit to Sri Racha, it is doubtful that Ratana specifically indicated Anan Suthavil. But Prakeb Sirikool did say that Ratana came and sat close to Anan Suthavil and seemed happy to be in Sri Racha.

Ratana also failed to recognize Boonyium Suthavil, Anan's husband, of whom Kim Lan had been extremely fond. And she failed to recognize a photograph of Kim Lan that was shown to her.

I should also mention a recognition attributed to Ratana by Samnuan Wongsombat that was incorrect. In 1974 he said that Ratana, at the time of her second visit to Sri Racha (in 1970), had claimed that she had built the fences around the meditation center there. Although title to the land on which the meditation center was built had belonged to Kim Lan (see item 41, Table 2), the center itself and the fences surrounding it had not been erected until after Kim Lan's death. (I learned this from Anan Suthavil in 1979.) It is possible that Ratana made some other comment about the fences, which, from the perspective of Kim Lan, would have been new to her. Samnuan Wongsombat may have then misunderstood Ratana to be claiming that she (in the previous life) had built them.

Ratana's Statements about Events Occurring after Kim Lan's Death and before Her Birth. Ratana, when still less than two years old, spoke in some detail about events that she claimed to remember after the death of Kim Lan and before her own birth.[12] Samnuan Wongsombat's account in 1968 to Francis Story of what Ratana had said about these events differed slightly from what he told me in 1969. Ratana made some statements on the subject to Francis Story in 1968.

Ratana's remark about how Kim Lan's ashes had been scattered around the Bo Tree at Wat Mahathat instead of being buried there as directed in her will (item 18, Table 2) seems especially impressive to me.

Ratana also said, according to Samnuan Wongsombat's 1968 account:

[12]For other examples of subjects of these cases who have claimed to remember events between the death of the concerned previous personality and the subject's birth, see the cases of Wijeratne *(Twenty Cases)*, Gopal Gupta, Puti Patra, Veer Singh (first volume of this series), Disna Samarasinghe (second volume), the Ven. Chaokhun Rajsuthajarn, and the Ven. Sayadaw U Sobhana (this volume).

TABLE 2. *Summary of Statements and Recognitions Made by Ratana*

Item	Informants	Verification	Comments
1. She had been a Chinese woman.	Samnuan Wongsombat, Ratana's stepgrandfather and adoptive father	Anan Suthavil, daughter of Kim Lan Prayoon Supamitr	Kim Lan's father was Chinese, her mother half Thai and half Chinese.
2. Her name had been Kim Lan.	Samnuan Wongsombat Ratana (1968)	Mae Chee Chan Suthipat, nun of Wat Mahathat and friend of Kim Lan Anan Suthavil	
3. She had stayed at Wat Mahathat.	Samnuan Wongsombat Mae Chee Anong Khaopongpaitoon, nun of Wat Mahathat	Mae Chee Chan Anan Suthavil	Kim Lan spent three years learning and practicing meditation at Wat Mahathat.
4. She had lived in a green hut.	Samnuan Wongsombat	Mae Chee Chan Anan Suthavil	Ratana referred to this hut as the "kuti kheo," which literally means "green hut." As I saw when I visited Wat Mahathat, the hut is definitely blue, and I was told that it had not been repainted. Samnuan Wongsombat told me that the hut had been painted green, but its color had afterward faded to the blue I saw. I have also found that Thai speakers sometimes use the word *kheo* when they mean to indicate blue, not green. In any event, Mae Chee Chan remembered that Kim Lan had called this particular hut "kuti kheo."

| 5. She had built a [meditation] hut at Wat Mahathat. | Samnuan Wongsombat
Chee Nai Kaisan, member of management committee of Wat Mahathat
Ven. Phra Kitti Vudho, monk of Wat Banglamoong | Samnuan Wongsombat stated in 1969 that Ratana had said that she (in the previous life) had built the "kuti kheo," but a few days later he said that she had not said this. His first statement about the item may have been based on secondhand information. It is of doubtful value as evidence that Ratana made such a statement before any of her statements had been verified.
Chee Nai Kaisan said Ratana had said that she had built a hut at Wat Mahathat and, according to him, Kim Lan had in fact built a hut there. But he did not specify which hut Ratana had referred to, or which Kim Lan had built. The Ven. Phra Kitti Vudho was the only informant who said that Kim Lan had built the *green* meditation hut at Wat Mahathat that was known as the "kuti kheo." Mae Chee Chan said that Kim Lan had not built the "kuti kheo" in which she and Kim Lan had been roommates. Anan Suthavil said her mother had built a meditation hut at a place in Lopburi |
| | Chee Nai Kaisan | |

NOTE: In this and similar tables, the *Informants* column lists the witnesses of what the subject did or said related to the previous life. The *Verification* column lists the informants for information verifying the accuracy of what the subject said or did with regard to the previous personality. In citing recognitions, I have usually left the *Verification* column blank, since the person who was the informant for the recognition (nearly always himself a witness of this recognition) either knew that the recognition was correct at the time it occurred or later verified its accuracy. Whenever possible, I have asked a person who was recognized by the subject about the details of the recognition, including circumstances, other persons present, and whether there were leading questions put or simply requests to name the person to be recognized. I have included information on these matters under *Comments*, in the right-hand column. This column also contains some other information or explanatory material. Unless specifically noted to the contrary, the statements and recognitions made by the subject were verified as being correct or appropriate for the previous personality.

TABLE 2. (cont.)

Item	Informants	Verification	Comments
			Province. She did not mention that her mother had built one at Wat Mahathat. I therefore consider this item somewhat doubtful as to its verification.
6. She had lived with Mae Chan.	Samnuan Wongsombat	Mae Chee Chan	It appears that Ratana called the nun only "Mae Chan," but this was appropriate enough; Mae Chee Chan said that Kim Lan, as well as other persons, sometimes called her "Mae Chan."
7. She had only one daughter, who lived in Sri Racha.	Samnuan Wongsombat	Anan Suthavil	
8. Her daughter brought her necessities when she was living in the wat.	Samnuan Wongsombat	Anan Suthavil	Every week Anan Suthavil went from Sri Racha to Bangkok on banking business. She visited her mother at Wat Mahathat and brought her food.
9. She had been driven from the wat.	Samnuan Wongsombat	Mae Chee Chan	The hut Kim Lan was living in was needed for a monk, and as the nuns and lay meditators have a lower priority, she was asked to leave. *Driven* seems rather strong language. One can imagine, however, that a wealthy woman who had donated generously to the wat would feel irritated when asked to vacate a meditation hut. The Ven. Phra Kitti Vudho told

Statement	Informants Who Gave Statement	Verification	Comments
			me that Kim Lan had had a disagreement with the new abbot of Wat Mahathat, and that he made her so uncomfortable that she left. The abbot's view was that she had left of her own accord.
10. She had left Wat Mahathat and gone to live at Banglampoo.	Samnuan Wongsombat	Anan Suthavil	Kim Lan remained in Banglampoo for only a few months before she returned to Sri Racha.
11. She had left a bundle of clothes at Wat Mahathat when she left there.	Samnuan Wongsombat	Unverified	Mae Chee Chan could not remember any bundle of clothes left behind by Kim Lan when she departed from Wat Mahathat.
12. She became ill at Banglampoo.	Samnuan Wongsombat	Anan Suthavil	
13. She had lived at Sri Racha.	Samnuan Wongsombat Ratana (1968)	Anan Suthavil	This was one of a few statements made by Ratana herself to Francis Story in 1968. In 1969 Samnuan Wongsombat told me that Ratana had said that (in the previous life) she had gone from Wat Mahathat to Banglampoo, after which, because of illness, she had gone back to Sri Racha. Anan Suthavil verified this order of moves for the last year of Kim Lan's life.
14. She had been operated on at Sri Racha Hospital.	Samnuan Wongsombat	Anan Suthavil Dr. Sukri Suebsanguan, surgeon of Somdet Memorial Hospital (Sri Racha), who operated on Kim Lan	In 1968 Samnuan Wongsombat told Francis Story that Ratana had said she was operated on in Chonburi Hospital. In 1969 he told me that she had said she was operated on in the Sri Racha hospital. The second statement was verified as correct. Sri Racha, however, is in Chonburi Province.

TABLE 2. (cont.)

Item	Informants	Verification	Comments
15. She had an abdominal operation.	Samnuan Wongsombat	Anan Suthavil Dr. Sukri Suebsanguan	Kim Lan had been operated on successfully and was recovering when an abdominal hemorrhage occurred. She was taken back to the operating room and died during an operative attempt to stop the hemorrhage.
16. She died during the operation.	Samnuan Wongsombat	Anan Suthavil Dr. Sukri Suebsanguan	
17. Her daughter's name had the sound *lee* in it.	Samnuan Wongsombat	Anan Suthavil	Samnuan Wongsombat said Ratana was only fourteen months old when she communicated this item. Ratana had said she had a daughter (in the previous life) and he asked the daughter's name. Ratana then replied that it was like the last part of his mother's name. Samnuan Wongsombat's mother was called Samlee, so this gave the syllable *lee*. In fact, the first name given to Anan Suthavil was "Malee." Samnuan Wongsombat's testimony on this item was slightly inconsistent in that in 1969 he said Ratana had not been able to recall the name of the previous daughter; but in 1971 he told me that Ratana had remembered a part of it, as described in this item.

Item			Comment
18. Her ashes were scattered, not buried.	Ven. Chaokhun Suvimol Thammajan, senior monk of Wat Mahathat	Ven. Chaokhun Suvimol Thammajan Anan Suthavil	This item relates to Kim Lan's desire, expressed in her will, that her ashes be buried under the Bo Tree at Wat Mahathat. Buddhists venerate Bo Trees because the Buddha attained Enlightenment while sitting under one. They consider it desirable to have one's ashes buried under such a tree. When trying to carry out Kim Lan's wishes, Anan Suthavil found that there were so many roots at the base of the trunk that it was infeasible to bury the ashes there; she therefore scattered them around the tree. The Ven. Chaokhun Suvimol Thammajan did not know that the ashes had not been buried. He was surprised when, upon enquiring, he found that Kim Lan's ashes had been scattered, and not buried as she had directed.
19. A place where nuns lived in the wat had formerly been a kitchen.	Mae Chee Anong Khaopongpaitoon	Mae Chee Anong Khaopongpaitoon	Ratana made this statement during one of her early visits to Wat Mahathat, when she met Mae Chee Anong Khaopongpaitoon. She pointed to a place where nuns were staying and said that a kitchen had been there before. I do not know if the alteration was made before or after Kim Lan's death, but in any case it certainly was made after her departure from the wat.
20. She had bought a microphone for the wat.	Samnuan Wongsombat	Chee Nai Kaisan Ven. Phra Kitti Vudho	Samnuan Wongsombat said Ratana even mentioned the price Kim Lan had paid for the

TABLE 2. (cont.)

Item	Informants	Verification	Comments
			microphone, but I did not verify that Ratana had been correct in this detail.
21. She had given an electric plant to Wat Pho.	Chee Nai Kaisan	Chee Nai Kaisan	Wat Pho is a well-known wat in Bangkok. I did not learn more about the electric plant, but presume it was an electricity generator to be used to supplement the main current supply of electricity or, in an emergency, to replace it.
22. Mae Chong Khin was her friend.	Mae Chee Anong Khaopongpaitoon	Unverified	This was testimony obtained by Francis Story in 1968. Mae Chee Chong Khin had died before then.
23. She had known Phra Kitti Vudho.	Samnuan Wongsombat Ratana (1968)	Ven. Phra Kitti Vudho	Kim Lan had known the Ven. Phra Kitti Vudho well. He appears to have divided his time between Wat Mahathat (in Bangkok) and Wat Banglamoong (near Sri Racha), where I met him in 1969. He was then going once a week to Wat Mahathat.
24. She had known Chaokhun Suvimol.	Mae Chee Anong Khaopongpaitoon	Ven. Chaokhun Suvimol Thammajan	The Ven. Chaokhun Suvimol Thammajan had not known Kim Lan well, but he had seen her walking in the temple compound.
25. She had built the hotel in Sri Racha.	Samnuan Wongsombat	Anan Suthavil	Samnuan Wongsombat seems to have been a secondhand witness for this item. He said Ratana

made the statement to Anan Suthavil's chauffeur, Prakeb Sirikool, but the latter could not recall the remark.

The accuracy of this item depends upon the interpretation of the word *built*. The building in question had been a residence built by the whole family, principally Anan Suthavil and her husband. Kim Lan had contributed many ideas for its construction but none of the money for it. Kim Lan and her husband had lived there with their daughter and son-in-law.

After Kim Lan's death, the building was converted into a hotel, and Anan Suthavil and her husband moved to a new house.

Anan Suthavil

When Anan Suthavil was a child of about four or five, she became ill, and advisors suggested a change of name. (Thais sometimes attribute illness in a child to incorrect naming and recommend a change of name as therapy.) The changing of Anan's name was known only to Kim Lan, her husband, and Anan Suthavil herself. The name first given to Anan was "Malee." Ratana did not recall this name at Sri Racha; she simply said that Anan was not the first name given her daughter. Earlier she had recalled a syllable of the first name. (See item 17.)

Anan Suthavil
Samnuan Wongsombat

26. Anan was not the first name given to her daughter.

TABLE 2. (cont.)

Item	Informants	Verification	Comments
27. Recognition at Wat Mahathat of the building where the Buddha's relics are kept	Samnuan Wongsombat		Ratana said she wanted to go to this building and led the way to it without guidance. This occurred when she was fourteen months old, at the time of her first visit to Wat Mahathat.
28. Recognition of the Ven. Phra Kru Palad Ganha	Samnuan Wongsombat		When Ratana saw the Ven. Phra Kru Palad Ganha, she addressed him familiarly with the words: "Hello, *Achan* ("teacher"), just as Kim Lan had done. Samnuan Wongsombat verified the appropriateness of Ratana's greeting. I did not meet the Ven. Phra Kru Palad Ganha, who was in Sri Lanka in 1969.
29. Recognition of Mae Chee Chan	Samnuan Wongsombat Mae Chee Chan		At Wat Mahathat Ratana pointed to a nun and said: "Mae Chan." Later, Samnuan Wongsombat returned to the wat and, upon enquiring there, learned that Kim Lan had lived with a nun called "Mae Chee Chan." Mae Chee Chan herself did not hear Ratana make this recognition. It occurred when Ratana was a little more than two years old. Samnuan Wongsombat then arranged for a formal test to see if Ratana could pick out Mae Chee Chan from a group of nuns. There were four nuns together, and Ratana was

asked to point out Mae Chee Chan, which she did correctly. She then went up to Mae Chee Chan and said: "Do you remember me? I am Kim Lan."

30. Recognition of the Ven. Phra Kitti Vudho	Samnuan Wongsombat	This recognition occurred at Wat Mahathat. The Ven. Phra Kitti Vudho was a monk who spent some time at Wat Mahathat. When Ratana saw him, she called him by name. Samnuan Wongsombat knew him before Ratana's recognition. The Ven. Phra Kitti Vudho was not aware that Ratana had recognized him.
31. Recognition of the place in Wat Mahathat where the Ven. Phra Kitti Vudho lived	Samnuan Wongsombat	Since Samnuan Wongsombat knew the Ven. Phra Kitti Vudho before Ratana recognized him, I presume that he also knew the house in the wat where the Ven. Phra Kitti Vudho stayed before Ratana pointed it out.
32. Recognition of the Ven. Phra Kru Sorn Wichai	Samnuan Wongsombat	The Ven. Phra Kru Sorn Wichai was a monk and meditation teacher of Wat Mahathat. Samnuan Wongsombat did not know him before Ratana pointed him out and called him by name. The Ven. Phra Kru Sorn Wichai was not a witness to Ratana's recognition of him, which must have occurred outside his hearing.

TABLE 2. (cont.)

Item	Informants	Verification	Comments
33. Recognition of the place in Wat Mahathat where the Ven. Phra Kru Sorn Wichai stayed	Samnuan Wongsombat		
34. Recognition of Chee Nai Kaisan	Samnuan Wongsombat Chee Nai Kaisan		Samnuan Wongsombat did not know Chee Nai Kaisan before Ratana pointed him out. According to Chee Nai Kaisan, Ratana only smiled at him. He did not hear her give his name, but Samnuan Wongsombat said that he heard her give the name.
35. Recognition of the meditation hut ("kuti kheo"), in which Kim Lan had stayed at Wat Mahathat	Mae Chee Anong Khaopongpaitoon Samnuan Wongsombat		Ratana pointed to the hut and said that she had once lived there. This probably occurred at Ratana's second visit to Wat Mahathat, when she was about two months more than two years old. Samnuan Wongsombat had told Francis Story in 1968 that Ratana had recognized the "kuti kheo" at the time of her *first* visit to the wat; but he told me in 1969 that on the occasion of her first visit to the wat he had not taken her to the "kuti kheo."
36. Recognition of the room where Kim Lan had slept in her house at Sri Racha	Anan Suthavil		Ratana was asked to say where Kim Lan had slept in the house, and she pointed to the correct

37. Recognition of addition of bathroom to Kim Lan's former bedroom	Samnuan Wongsombat Charoon Sri Wongsombat, Ratana's maternal grandmother and adoptive mother	Ratana remarked that a bathroom connected to Kim Lan's bedroom at the time of Ratana's visit had formerly been elsewhere. This was correct. When the building had been turned into a hotel, a bathroom had been built with a connection to the room formerly occupied by Kim Lan. I did not obtain independent verification from Anan Suthavil of the changes to which Ratana drew attention. Samnuan Wongsombat said Anan had told them that Ratana had been correct in her comments about the new bathroom.
38. Recognition of Kim Lan's husband	Anan Suthavil	This recognition occurred at Anan Suthavil's new house, not the former residence that had been converted to a hotel. Kim Lan's husband was still staying in this house with their daughter and son-in-law. Ratana went into a room of the house where Kim Lan's husband was sitting. She stared at him, and he smiled at her. Ratana then came out of the room and said: "That was Gong in there." *Gong*, which means "grandfather," in Chinese, was the name by which everyone in the household referred to Kim Lan's husband.

room. This recognition occurred at the house that had been turned into a hotel. (See item 25.)

TABLE 2. (cont.)

Item	Informants	Verification	Comments
39. Recognition of the rooms at Somdet Memorial Hospital in Sri Racha that were donated by Kim Lan	Prakeb Sirikool, Anan Suthavil's chauffeur		At the hospital, Ratana broke away from the group and ran upstairs to the rooms donated by Kim Lan. She spontaneously said that she had given them to the hospital. I saw these rooms at the hospital. One had become an operating room. The name "Prayoon Supamitr" was written on the door, but there was nothing to indicate specifically that she had given the room. (Prayoon Supamitr was Kim Lan's surname.) At the time of this visit, Ratana was just beginning to read, and it is unlikely that she could have read these words.
40. Recognition of the coffee shop at Somdet Memorial Hospital	Anan Suthavil		Ratana again broke away from the group she was with and ran ahead to the hospital coffee shop. This coffee shop had been a favorite place of Kim Lan, and she had frequented it even when she was not a patient in the hospital. She enjoyed drinking black coffee there and had done so on the day of her operation.

This recognition occurred in 1970, when Ratana was invited to the opening ceremony of a meditation center that Anan Suthavil had donated to a wat in Sri Racha. Ratana insisted that the land on which the center was built had been hers (in the previous life).

Anan Suthavil confirmed to me that the title to the property in question had been in her mother's name, although she had not actually invested any money at the time of its purchase.

41. Recognition of land   Samnuan Wongsombat
Kim Lan had owned

The doctor put the knife beside my heart and made me die. When I died, a *deva* [a minor god] came with a carriage and took me to heaven. There I tried to find you [Samnuan Wongsombat], but could not. Then I came down from heaven. The descent was like one breath. Then I went straight to the green house [the "kuti kheo" meditation hut in Wat Mahathat is meant] because I had forgotten something there. But unfortunately a monk was living there,[13] so I could do nothing. After coming out of the hut I found my uncle [Ratana apparently meant Samnuan Wongsombat, her stepgrandfather and adoptive father; a slip in translation probably occurred here] walking in meditation.

In 1969 Samnuan Wongsombat mentioned that Ratana had said:

"There were many levels of heaven . . . She asked the deva to go to the highest level of heaven. The deva took her to pay respects to the Buddha's relics. [Presumably the relics in Wat Mahathat are meant.] She did not find me [Samnuan Wongsombat] [there]. Later she found me meditating at the wat [Mahathat]. Ratana further said that she "walked with me and sat with me there [at the wat]."

Ratana said that she had wanted to come to Samnuan Wongsombat's wife, but could not do so,[14] and so came to her daughter. This was Sunisa Sutaputra, Ratana's mother, who even before Ratana's birth had consented to let her mother and stepfather adopt the child.

Ratana further said (when about fourteen months old) that she had been a daughter of Samnuan Wongsombat in two previous lives.[15]

Ratana's Behavior Related to the Previous Life

Circumstances and Manner of Ratana's Speaking about the Previous Life. Ratana was especially close to her stepgrandfather and adoptive father, Samnuan Wongsombat. She spoke more to him than to other persons about the previous life and seemed extremely reluctant to talk directly about it with anyone else. She would not do so with Francis Story in 1968 or with me in 1969. In 1968 she did answer some questions put to her (by the interpreter) through her adoptive mother. In 1969 she objected to

---

[13]The ostensible reason for getting Kim Lan out of Wat Mahathat in 1962 was that her meditation hut was needed for a monk. I do not know just when the former nuns' huts were taken over for monks, but when I was at the wat in 1969 a monk was living in the "kuti kheo." The nuns of the wat were then living in a nearby building.

[14]Charoon Sri Wongsombat had had at least one child, Ratana's mother, by her first husband. But she and Samnuan Wongsombat had no children, and at the time of Ratana's birth in 1964 were unable to have any. Charoon was probably beyond childbearing age by then.

[15]If this was true, these lives would have occurred before the birth of Kim Lan in 1894 and therefore during at least one previous life of Samnuan Wongsombat, who was born in 1905.

her adoptive father's even discussing her case with me. She neverthemonitored the confrom time to time about our discussing her memories. In 1971 Samnuan Wongsombat told me that Ratana had explained that when she thought about the previous life, the memories of her daughter made her cry; for this reason she did not want anyone to talk about the previous life.

Ratana talked most about the previous life at night, after she prayed and before she went to sleep.[16] During these times, her demeanor changed so that she seemed more mature than during the daytime, when she behaved for the most part like an ordinary child.[17]

Unlike some other subjects of these cases, Ratana expressed no strong emotion when talking about the previous life. She did, however, importune her parents to take her to Wat Mahathat when she was quite young, and later she besought them to take her to Sri Racha. When she reached Sri Racha, she expressed a strong desire to stay there—so strong, in fact, that her adoptive mother said she had to be brought back almost by force. She cried and said that she wanted to stay with Anan Suthavil. She left only after being promised a return visit at the end of the school year. (Ratana was then in the first grade of school.)

Both Samnuan Wongsombat and Anan Suthavil indicated that Ratana showed considerable assurance in talking about the previous life. Anan told me that, at Sri Racha, Ratana had corrected her adoptive father if he made any error in narrating details of her memories to her (Anan Suthavil). And when Ratana was in the houses at Sri Racha—the old one that had been turned into a hotel and the newly built one—she walked around them quite familiarly, as if she owned them. (Although the second house had been built after Kim Lan had died, this did not seem to inhibit Ratana's sense of proprietorship.) Samnuan Wongsombat said that Ratana remarked: "I have come to my house. I will not go back to Bangkok, because this is my old house."[18]

Ratana's Relationship with the Persons and Places of the Previous Family. As already mentioned, when Ratana went to Sri Racha, she showed pleasure

[16]For other examples of subjects who have shown a tendency to talk about the previous life more at one time of day than another, see the cases of Prakash Varshnay (*Twenty Cases*), Kumkum Verma (first volume of this series), Gamini Jayasena, Shamlinie Prema, Indika Guneratne, Disna Samarasinghe, Wijanama Kithsiri (second volume), Suleyman Andary (third volume), Bongkuch Promsin, and Ornuma Sua Ying Yong (this volume).

[17]For other examples of adult behavior on the part of subjects of these cases (when they were young children), see the cases of Sukla Gupta, Swarnlata Mishra, Parmod Sharma (*Twenty Cases*), Kumkum Verma (first volume of this series), Disna Samarasinghe, Lalitha Abeyawardena (second volume), Suleyman Andary (third volume), Bongkuch Promsin, and Hair Kam Kanya (this volume).

[18]For other examples of subjects who showed a sense of ownership with regard to the property of the concerned previous personality's family, see the cases of Jagdish Chandra, Sunil Dutt Saxena (first volume of this series), Gamini Jayasena (second volume), İsmail Altınkılıç, and Süleyman Zeytun (third volume).

in being with Kim Lan's daughter, Anan Suthavil. Her rapid attachment to Anan particularly impressed Samnuan Wongsombat, who said that Ratana ordinarily rarely left him, but that in Sri Racha she showed pleasurable excitement and affection toward Anan. He was impressed by Ratana's obvious contentment in being with Anan Suthavil and her strong wish to remain in Sri Racha, which developed into a struggle when it came time for Ratana's family to take her back to Bangkok.

Anan Suthavil remarked that Ratana spoke to her more like an adult addressing a small girl than the reverse, which would have seemed appropriate considering their actual sizes and relationship. Ratana even ordered Anan around as a mother might have behaved toward a daughter.

Her attitude toward Kim Lan's husband, "Gong," was quite different. She smiled at him and commented that he had smiled at her. But she showed no interest in staying with him. And after the first visit to Sri Racha, although Ratana asked to be taken back there to see her daughter, she specifically said she did not want to see "that guy" (meaning Kim Lan's husband), and added that she did not like him.

Anan Suthavil was much taken with Ratana and was rather strongly convinced that she was her mother reborn. Although Samnuan Wongsombat did not ask her for any financial assistance, she offered to give some to Ratana. The two families even talked of having Ratana educated in Sri Racha; but nothing came of this proposal, and, to the best of my knowledge, Anan Suthavil has given Ratana's family no money for her.

Other Behavior of Ratana Related to the Previous Life.   Ratana's most singular behavior, in which she stood out sharply from other children known to her adoptive parents, was her knowledge of religious practices and her interest in them. She showed this on her first visit to Wat Mahathat, when she was barely fourteen months old. The following account derives from the statements made by Samnuan Wongsombat to Francis Story in 1968 and to me in 1969.

There are numerous beggars at Wat Mahathat, and one meets them sitting or standing in a row almost as soon as one passes into the compound through the main entrance. Ratana gave 50 *satang* to the crippled ones and 25 satang to the healthy ones, disbursing altogether 8 *baht*.[19] Before giving to the beggars, Ratana saluted them with folded palms. Then, without anyone instructing her to do so, she went to buy flowers, candles, and incense sticks at a stall. When the party reached the temple, where Samnuan Wongsombat had wished to go, he said: "This way." But Ratana said they must first worship the Buddha's relics, which were in another building. She then went ahead of them while they watched her,

[19]The Thai baht (or *tical*) is worth approximately U.S. $.05, or 100 satang.

and found this building by herself. There she paid respects to the Buddha image in the manner of an adult, by folding her hands and kneeling down. She placed a handkerchief on the floor and put the flowers on it. She knew where to put her offerings and how to put money in the box available for donations. Since this was the first time Ratana had ever been in a wat, her seemingly experienced manner of behaving there astonished her family.

After leaving the building that held the Buddha's relics, Ratana said: "Now we can go to the main temple." In this building, she went straight to where the incense sticks are placed and positioned them correctly. She then prostrated three times and returned to her family. She did not know any *gathas* (Buddhist scriptural verses), but seemed to be murmuring something in the temple.

The family stayed through some chanting, and a priest then expounded the precepts of Buddhism. A woman nearby who had noticed Ratana asked her how many precepts she wanted to keep. Ratana replied: *"Pancha sila."*[20] The woman then asked her how many her father kept, and Ratana replied: "Probably eight."

---

[20]The pancha sila ("five precepts") are the five more elementary precepts of Buddhism kept by laymen who are, so to speak, beginners in Buddhism. An additional three precepts are added to make eight that together are somewhat more advanced in difficulty.

The five precepts enjoin the follower:

1. From killing anything that breathes;
2. From taking what is not given;
3. From sexual misconduct;
4. From speaking falsehood;
5. From liquor that causes intoxication and thoughtlessness.

The additional three precepts further enjoin the follower:

6. From untimely eating;
7. From dancing, singing, music, unseemly entertainments, and the use of garlands, perfumes, beauty creams, and other personal embellishments;
8. From luxurious beds and couches.

A person following the eight precepts, as many laymen do on special days, such as days of the full moon and new moon, modifies the third precept and avoids sexual relations even with his or her own spouse.

For an exposition of the five precepts and the eight precepts, see Piyadassi Thera. 1964. *The Buddha's Ancient Path*. London: Rider and Co.

In *The Light of Asia*, Sir Edwin Arnold beautifully expressed the five precepts in verse:

More is the treasure of the Law than gems;
  Sweeter than comb its sweetness; it delights
Delightful past compare. Thereby to live
  Hear the *Five Rules* aright:—

Kill not—for Pity's sake—and lest ye slay
The meanest thing upon its upward way.

After the exposition of the precepts, Ratana said she wanted to go to the Relic Shrine and meditate there. They let her go while the rest of the family listened to the sermon. After the sermon, Samnuan Wongsombat went to the Relic Shrine and discovered Ratana in the half-lotus position surrounded by a surprised crowd. She had been in this position for half an hour. A nearby woman said Ratana had assumed it without anyone telling her to do so. Samnuan Wongsombat said Ratana had never seen this meditation posture before, meaning at her home before this first visit to the wat. Certainly she could have seen other persons at the wat sitting in the posture for meditation. Nevertheless, her behavior in imitating them, if that is what she did, remains remarkable for a child of her age.[21]

According to Samnuan Wongsombat, he observed all the foregoing behavior on the occasion of Ratana's first visit to Wat Mahathat. But on subsequent visits and at other times she continued to show precocity in her attitudes and behavior in religious observances.

One of the monks of the wat, the Ven. Phra Kru Sorn Wichai, whom Ratana said she remembered from the previous life, told me Ratana had prostrated herself before him and given him offerings exactly as an old lady paying respects to a monk would do. Ratana, at least up to age five

---

Give freely and receive, but take from none
By greed, or force, or fraud, what is his own.

Bear not false witness, slander not, nor lie;
Truth is the speech of inward purity.

Shun drugs and drinks which work the wit abuse;
Clear minds, clean bodies, need no Sôma juice.

Touch not thy neighbour's wife, neither commit
Sins of the flesh unlawful and unfit.

[E. Arnold, *The Light of Asia* (London: Kegan Paul, Trench, Trübner and Co., 1911), pp. 153–54.]

[21]A colleague who read a draft of this case report expressed incredulity at the claim that a child of fourteen months could show such knowledge of religious practices. She rebuked me for expecting my readers to believe the account. The stated age of Ratana, fourteen months, does not derive from an error of translation. Of that I can be certain, because the same age is given for Ratana with regard to this visit to Wat Mahathat in the newspaper report of the *Bangkok Times* (1967), in the notes of Francis Story (1968), and in my own notes (1969). It is possible that Samnuan Wongsombat remembered Ratana's age incorrectly at first and later repeated his error. I do not myself, however, believe that he made a mistake about Ratana's age or, at any rate, not a mistake of more than one or several months at most. My experience with these cases has convinced me that some of the subjects are indeed markedly precocious.

Persons unfamiliar with the wats in Thailand may also wonder that a child of fourteen months would be allowed to go alone from one building to another. I should mention, therefore, that the wats—even the largest of them—are enclosed by walls with gates and have no vehicular traffic passing through their compounds. Although the wat compounds are often crowded with worshipers, a small child can move around within the compound quite safely.

(the time of my first interviews in Bangkok), worshiped regularly and bowed to an image of the Buddha every night before sleeping. The other children of the Wongsombat household did not worship at all. This contrast is important, because Samnuan Wongsombat is himself a devout Buddhist from whom Ratana might have picked up habits of religious worship; but if she did, why did none of the other children of the household do so also?

Ratana had some of the attitudes of a rich person, which were noticeably inappropriate in the extremely modest circumstances of the Wongsombats. She frequently asked for money to give to the poor, such as needy friends at her school. She also asked for good food and fine clothes for herself. If allowed to select, she would choose the best of anything.[22] She also knew prices and values well. Whenever she became ill, Ratana gave another indication of assuming herself to be wealthy: she called for injections. Such medical treatments were then still largely available only to wealthy people in Thailand, and thus requesting an injection would be a sign of expecting the best medical care available.

Ratana's food preferences to some extent coincided with those of Kim Lan. Ratana preferred Chinese food, especially (Chinese) soup and vegetables. (Kim Lan, it will be recalled, was three-quarters Chinese.) She was not a vegetarian and enjoyed roast duck and chicken.

Samnuan Wongsombat said that Ratana had a loud voice, which he thought was characteristic of Chinese women. Anan Suthavil, as I have already mentioned, complained about her mother's loud voice.

On two occasions, Ratana used Chinese words. Once, when Ratana was two, she said a few words Samnuan Wongsombat recognized as Chinese. And about three years later, on her first visit to Sri Racha, when she saw Kim Lan's husband, she referred to him as "Gong," which is the Chinese word for "grandfather." (In fact, everyone in Kim Lan's household had called her husband "Gong" because he was the oldest male member.) Anan Suthavil (but not Samnuan Wongsombat) heard Ratana call him "Gong." To Samnuan Wongsombat, Ratana referred to Kim Lan's husband (in Thai) as "that guy" or "the old Chinese man."

In contrast to many of the children subjects of these cases, Ratana showed no desire to be called Kim Lan, the name of the previous person-

---

[22]Since Kim Lan was rather austere with regard to spending money on herself, Ratana's requests to have good clothes and food may appear somewhat incongruous with what would have been expected of Kim Lan. The difference becomes less surprising, however, when one remembers that Kim Lan would have anticipated that the merit she had earned during her life would assure her of having wealth again in the next life. Ratana could be considered as simply trying to "cash in" or "collect" what she thought she had saved in the previous life. Most Buddhists would consider such expectations acceptable, but not laudable. They rank lowest in their scale of meritorious actions any deed, including almsgiving or other charities, that has the motive of earning a reward in the next life. For a discussion of Buddhist ethics, see R. F. Gombrich; *Precept and Practice: Traditional Buddhism in the Rural Highlands of Ceylon* (London and New York: Oxford University Press, 1971).

ality,[23] although she had mentioned the name and introduced herself as such to Mae Chee Chan, perhaps to jog the latter's memory.

In Table 3, I have summarized the correspondences between the important behavioral traits reported for Kim Lan and for Ratana.

Evidence of Extrasensory Perception on the Part of Ratana

Samnuan Wongsombat told me of several incidents that seemed to show that Ratana had some powers of extrasensory perception. The following are examples of such episodes.

When Ratana was two years old, Samnuan Wongsombat brought to the house a girl intended as a servant. Ratana clearly indicated that she distrusted the girl, but he hired her anyway. Later this girl tried to murder someone in the family.

When Ratana was just over two and a half years old, Samnuan Wongsombat ran into his nephew, quite by accident, away from home. He returned home immediately afterward, and Ratana told him he had met this nephew.

Once, when Ratana was only fourteen months old, she told Samnuan Wongsombat that his brother and another person were coming to visit. It was then already 9:00 P.M., and Samnuan Wongsombat thought such a visit impossible at that late hour, but five minutes later his brother and nephew arrived.

When Ratana was three and a half years old, Samnuan Wongsombat went unexpectedly to the temple. When he returned home, Ratana asked him if he had gone to the temple and given food to the monks, which he had done.

Ratana showed such instances of apparent extrasensory perception especially at night after worshiping—the same time of day when she was particularly likely to talk about the previous life.

Ratana had these experiences of apparent extrasensory perception not only with Samnuan Wongsombat, but with other persons as well. She seems, however, to have had many more incidents with him than with any other person. She had none with Anan Suthavil, Kim Lan's daughter.

Comments on the Evidence of Paranormal Processes in the Case

Although no written record was made in this case before Ratana's family began verifying her statements, Francis Story and I began studying it soon after its main events occurred. Francis Story made a preliminary investigation of it in September 1968, when Ratana was about four and a

---

[23]For examples of subjects who insisted on being called by the name of the person whose life they remembered, see the cases of Prakash Varshnay *(Twenty Cases)*, Rabih Elawar, İsmail Altınkılıç, Cevriye Bayrı (third volume of this series), and Ma Than Than Sint (this volume).

TABLE 3. *Correspondences in Behavior between Ratana and Kim Lan*

Ratana	Kim Lan
1. A precocious interest in religion and enthusiasm for it	Extremely interested in religion; spent last three years of her life in meditation centers
2. A loud voice	A loud voice
3. Favorite foods included soup and vegetables	Favorite foods included soup and vegetables
4. Expected good clothes and food for herself	Rejected good clothes and food for herself*
5. Generous to others	A generous philanthropist who gave much money to monasteries and hospitals
6. Gave money to crippled beggars, less to healthy ones	Generous to crippled beggars, but rarely gave money to healthy ones
7. Showed strong attachment to previous personality's daughter, but coolness toward her husband	Unhappily married, but devoted to her daughter

*See n. 22, above, for a possible interpretation of this difference.

half years old. By that time Samnuan Wongsombat had verified some of Ratana's statements from the nun Mae Chee Chan and other persons of Wat Mahathat; but Ratana had not yet gone to Sri Racha or met members of the previous family. Unfortunately, we were unable to witness this occasion, which took place early in March 1969. However, I began work on the case later that month and interviewed informants within about ten days of Ratana's first visit to Sri Racha. The informants for this case were therefore being asked to recall events that had happened—some of them at least—just a few weeks before my interviews.

It seems to me unlikely that Ratana could have acquired her detailed knowledge of the life and death of Kim Lan through normal means. I was unable to trace any source, such as mutual acquaintances, that could have imparted so much information about Kim Lan to Ratana without her family being aware of it. In this case, however, there certainly exist some persons—for example, some of the monks and nuns of Wat Mahathat—from whom Ratana might have telepathically received information about the life of Kim Lan. In communications of this type, her adoptive father might have acted as a telepathic link ("psychometric object"),[24] since he regularly visited Wat Mahathat. The evidence of extra-

[21]For other examples in which a person or persons who had some contact with the previous personality of a case might have acted as a telepathic link ("psychometric object") between the previous personality, or surviving members of his family, and the subject, see the cases of Sukla Gupta, Jasbir Singh, Parmod Sharma, Imad Elawar (*Twenty Cases*), Disna Samarasinghe, and Indika Guneratne (second volume of this series). For a definition of *psychometry* as used in parapsychology, see the glossary.

since he regularly visited Wat Mahathat. The evidence of extrasensory perception on the part of Ratana offers support for this explanation.

As with other cases of this type, however, we must also account for the unusual behavior Ratana showed, especially her intense religious attitudes and her precocity in religious practices. Samnuan Wongsombat was himself a diligent Buddhist, and he certainly found agreeable the keen interest of his adoptive daughter in Buddhist worship and precepts. But it seems unlikely that he would have wished or been able to impose on a small child the religious fervor that Ratana demonstrated at an early age. According to him, Ratana showed her interest in Buddhist worship and unexplained precocious knowledge of its rituals when she was only about fourteen months old. I am bound to say, however, that in the present case the subject's adoptive parents had stronger motives for encouraging their child to personate the previous personality than I can discern in most other cases. In some of them the previous personality had had various unlovable traits, or had even been a miscreant. One can only understand with difficulty why any parent would want to encourage a child to identify with such persons. But Kim Lan was a woman of obvious virtue, and the worst fault anyone imputed to her was a loud voice. A previous personality of a devout and generous Buddhist lady might enhance the reputation of a family in Thailand. This case may therefore provide support for the hypothesis that the subjects of these cases obtain information about deceased persons through extrasensory perception, after which their parents encourage their identification with these persons.

Ratana's Later Development

An apparent fading of the memories began unusually early in this case. At the age of four and a half (in September 1968), Ratana had already begun to talk less of the previous life, a change that Charoon Sri Wongsombat attributed to her beginning school. And in March 1969, Samnuan Wongsombat told me Ratana did not want to talk much of the previous life, even with him and his wife. As we shall see, however, Ratana was showing reticence, not amnesia, at this stage.[25]

[25]Ratana's family put no pressure on her to stop talking about the previous life. Her reluctance to talk about it may have derived from the painful feelings accompanying memories of Kim Lan's daughter, which I mentioned above. Perhaps Kim Lan's piety also contributed to Ratana's unwillingness to talk about her memories, especially with strangers. Earnest Buddhists consider preoccupation with psychical experiences, such as memories of previous lives, a seductive and harmful distraction from their main goal of getting off "the wheel of rebirth" and reaching Nirvana. To illustrate this attitude, I shall mention an episode that happened during one of my investigations in Thailand. I asked a Buddhist monk if he would make a statement about a recognition reported to have been made by a subject, to which he had been an eyewitness. He bluntly refused even to discuss the matter. He apparently regarded my investigation as spiritually corrupting. Ratana may have had a similar attitude. (I should add, however, that nearly all the Buddhist monks whom I have asked for

I met Ratana again in March 1971, at which time she was not yet seven. She was then attending school, and Samnuan Wongsombat said she was doing well in her work there.

Ratana continued to be intensely interested in religious practices and meditated every day. When asked why she meditated, Ratana told Charoon Sri Wongsombat that the mind needs meditation the way the body needs food. Before sleeping, she would chant and then prostrate herself in front of the Buddha image.

According to Samnuan Wongsombat, by 1971 Ratana was no longer showing any evidence of extrasensory perception. She was still, however, talking spontaneously about the previous life and still tended to do so especially at night, after chanting and before going to sleep.

She also continued to have a strong desire to go to Sri Racha. Samnuan Wongsombat said: "She always asks to go." But her family had not taken her there since the previous year. They had some concern that she might want to remain in Sri Racha, and she had gone there only twice. She first went there early in March 1969. About a year later, early in 1970, Ratana's adoptive father took her back to Sri Racha, and she then met some other relatives of Kim Lan. (Anan Suthavil said Ratana made no new recognitions on this occasion.) During this second visit, Ratana again wanted to be near Anan Suthavil, and again did not want to return to Bangkok. Anan Suthavil had not been to see Ratana in Bangkok.

Ratana was continuing in 1971 the generosity to beggars she had shown when younger, and she also wanted to give monks better food than she herself ate.

Ratana's behavior toward me in 1971 contrasted markedly with her attitude in 1969. She was friendly and affable. Instead of objecting to the conversation I was having with her adoptive father, she often made comments. For example, when I asked Samnuan Wongsombat whether Ratana still wanted to go to Sri Racha, she interjected "yes" for herself.

During a visit to Bangkok in November 1972, I called on Ratana's family again. Ratana was in Chiang Mai staying with relatives, but her adoptive parents gave me some further news about her.

Ratana was then about eight and a half years old. She was in the fourth class at school and stood fourth among thirty-nine pupils, although she was the youngest girl in the class.

Ratana's memories seemed not to have faded, according to the judgment of Samnuan Wongsombat. He said that she continued to speak frequently to him about the previous life, but did not mention it to other

---

assistance, as informants or otherwise—and they have been numerous—have helped me most amiably.)

For a discussion of the difficulty of distinguishing apparent from real fading of memories, see the chapter on follow-up interviews in *Twenty Cases.*

persons. She still had the tendency to speak of the previous life after meditating. And at such times she seemed to him to have the manner of an old woman rather than that of a young girl. Samnuan Wongsombat was encouraging her to talk about the previous life by asking her questions about it from time to time. He showed a degree of pride in reporting that her memories had not faded.

According to Samnuan Wongsombat, Ratana's references to the previous life included discussion of what she said she remembered about practicing meditation in the previous life. She spoke "always" of Kim Lan's daughter (Anan Suthavil) and sister. (I had not learned earlier that Ratana had referred to a sister of Kim Lan.) She never referred to Kim Lan's husband. She continued to ask to go to Sri Racha, but she had not been taken there again, and Anan Suthavil had not visited her.

Ratana continued to be just as assiduous in her religious practices as she had been before. She was adhering strictly to the pancha sila. For example, she would not kill insects, but merely drove them away.

Samnuan Wongsombat said that Ratana exhibited familiar behavior toward the Ven. Phra Kitti Vudho, a monk whom Kim Lan had known and supported. (See item 30 of Table 2.) When Ratana met him, she called him by his name, as though she was on familiar terms with him, instead of addressing him by the title *achan* ("teacher"), as might have been expected in the relationship between a small girl and a monk.

Samnuan Wongsombat told me about a precognition Ratana had had when he and she were visiting Chiang Mai together in the spring of 1972.[26] Samnuan Wongsombat had gone there principally for business connected with his law practice. When the time came for him to return to Bangkok, he asked Ratana to come with him, but she at first refused. A little later, however, she changed her mind and said she was ready to accompany him, adding that if she did not do so he would lose his life. They then got on a bus leaving Chiang Mai for Bangkok. Two or three hours out of Chiang Mai Ratana said there would be an accident and warned Samnuan Wongsombat to be careful. Shortly afterward, the bus ran into some water buffaloes on the road and overturned. Samnuan Wongsombat was seriously injured and required hospitalization for forty days. Eventually he made a good recovery that was almost complete by the time of my visit to him in November 1972. From my own experiences on the highways of Thailand, I can comment that the first part of Ratana's forecast has much more value as a precognition than the statement she made in the bus itself. She could have sensed normally that the bus driver was driving too fast for the road conditions (as many drivers do in Thailand) and was therefore liable to have an accident.

---

[26]This seems to have been an exception to Samnuan Wongsombat's earlier statement of 1971 that Ratana was no longer showing any evidence of extrasensory perception.

When I met Ratana and her adoptive parents in November 1974, she was ten and a half years old. She was then studying in the sixth class at school, where she ranked second among twenty-five pupils. Her health, in general, was good, but she had some myopia.

Her adoptive mother said that Ratana no longer spoke spontaneously about the previous life. Ratana herself said that she did not remember much about it. But when I put questions to her, she quickly showed that she still remembered such details as the names of the previous personality (Kim Lan), her daughter (Anan), and the place where Kim Lan had lived (Sri Racha). She also recalled living in the "kuti kheo" at Wat Mahathat, practicing meditation, and dying at the hospital in Sri Racha after a stomach operation. She did not remember the names of any of the nuns that Kim Lan had known in the wat, but she did recall the name of Chaokhun Suvimol. It is naturally difficult to say to what extent Ratana was telling us about original imaged memories and to what extent she was repeating what others had told her she had earlier remembered. However, visits between the families concerned had not sustained her memories, because there had been no further meetings between Ratana and Anan Suthavil since Ratana's last journey to Sri Racha in 1970.

Ratana's adoptive parents concurred in saying that she still seemed to them to be more religious than the average child of her age. She liked reading religious books, continued to be generous to the poor and to her friends, and always worshiped before sleeping.

Samnuan Wongsombat described further episodes of Ratana's foretelling the arrival of unexpected visitors. And he mentioned an occasion (in January 1974) when Ratana had irrationally said she wished to remain home from school on a particular day so that she could accompany him to the hospital. He was feeling well that morning, but he indulged her, and she stayed home. Later that day he had a heart attack, and Ratana was able to go with him to the hospital. Samnuan Wongsombat outlined the symptoms of angina pectoris and showed me his nitroglycerine tablets; thus, the illness, which reached a symptomatic level on the particular day designated by Ratana, was genuine and not faked as an act of compliance with her on his part.

In 1974 Ratana was most friendly with Prof. Kloom Vajropala and me. Considering the aloofness and even distrust with which, in 1969, she had first met me—or rather refused to meet me—I think we had improved our relationship markedly since then.

In February 1977, I visited Ratana and her family, again with Prof. Kloom Vajropala. Ratana, although a little surprised to see us, greeted us cordially. She was then nearly thirteen years old and was studying in the first of the five grades of secondary school.

There had been no further meetings with Anan Suthavil, and the two families had lost touch with each other.

Samnuan Wongsombat said that Ratana no longer spoke spontaneously about the previous life; he had to ask her questions if he wished to discuss it with her.

Ratana herself said that her memories of the previous life had undergone no further fading since our last visit of 1974, but said that she took no interest in the previous life at this time. Apparently her school studies and associated activities absorbed most of her time and attention. She had given up meditating because she had no time for it. Charoon Sri Wongsombat told us that Ratana still seemed exceptional, compared with other children of her age, in her interest in religion. For example, she still showed an unusual interest in giving food to monks, a trait that was perhaps the last behavioral residue of her memories of the previous life.

In March 1978, I was again in Bangkok, and at that time Khun Prasit Karoonyavanich, a banker of Chonburi who is a member of the American Society for Psychical Research and keenly interested in these cases, told me that Anan Suthavil, with whom he was acquainted, had expressed a wish to meet Ratana again. This was easily arranged. Ratana and her adoptive parents accompanied Professor Kloom and me to Sri Racha, where we had a long meeting with Anan Suthavil and her husband. Ratana and Anan Suthavil seemed happy to see each other, but I observed no signs of affection between them. I asked Ratana whether the meeting had stimulated any memories of the previous life, and she said that it had not.

My last meeting with Ratana before publication of this book occurred in Bangkok on March 8, 1980. Readers will easily understand that I had become fond of Ratana and liked to visit her, even though I did not by this time expect to generate new information about her case. Ratana was in good health apart from some trouble with her vision. She was studying in the eleventh grade of secondary school. She said she then had no memories of the previous life and no interest in it. She was tired of her "story" and of talking about it. (Samnuan Wongsombat had recently published an account of Ratana's case in Thai, and its composition might have contributed to Ratana's sense of tedium concerning her case.) Then too, she was almost sixteen years old and had the normal preoccupations of young persons. It seemed to me, however, that her manner was graver and more mature than that of most persons of her age.

2. The Case of Ampan Petcherat

Introduction

THE PRINCIPAL INTEREST of this case lies in the claim of the subject, a girl, to remember details of the life of a boy and in her showing, when she was young, a number of definitely masculine traits.[1] The case is also somewhat unusual because the subject claimed to remember the previous life of a young child who was only about four when he died.[2]

Summary of the Case and Its Investigation

Ampan Petcherat was born in Song Klong sometime in March 1954. She was the daughter of Yod "Ngoi"[3] Petcherat and his wife, Kim Suan. Ampan was Kim Suan's third child. Her parents later separated, and Ampan stayed with her mother. The family had earlier lived at Song Klong, but in 1966 Ampan and her mother were living in the town of Klong Darn, which is 7 kilometers north of Song Klong and about 30 kilometers southeast of Bangkok.[4]

When Ampan was about a year old, she began to tell her mother that she had another mother and father at Klong Bang Chag near Klong Bang Plee. She said she had been a boy in the life with those parents. She described a house and objects in it, and also narrated how she had drowned after being bitten by a snake. Ampan would cry in talking about the previous home and ask to be taken to it. She repeated the story of her

---

[1] For other cases in which the subject remembered a previous life as a member of the opposite sex, see those of Paulo Lorenz, Gnanatilleka Baddewithana *(Twenty Cases)*, Dolon Champa Mitra (first volume of this series), Ruby Kusuma Silva (second volume), and Ma Tin Aung Myo (this volume).

[2] For other examples of subjects who remembered the previous lives of young children, see the cases of Rajul Shah and Veer Singh (first volume of this series).

[3] *Ngoi* is a nickname meaning "lame."

[4] Readers will find this case easier to understand if I explain now that this part of Thailand has numerous connected *klongs* ("canals") running through it. The klongs actually have some sluggish current; they resemble the bayous of southern Louisiana. Formerly they provided the chief routes of transport in the area, and even today, although many roads have been built, they are still much used for travel and transport. Towns and villages along the klongs often have the same names as the klongs on which they are located, as do some of the wats. Thus the village of Bang Chag is located on Klong Bang Chag.

drowning from time to time. She gave no names of the previous family, only that of the place where she said she had lived.

Every year at harvest time, Ampan's mother used to paddle in a boat over to the area of Klong Bang Chag, which is about 20 kilometers from Klong Darn. When Ampan was still an infant, her mother began taking her in the boat on these trips. When Ampan was between one and two years old, she recognized—on one of these trips—the village of Bang Chag (which her mother would have known anyway); but they did not attempt at that time to trace the previous family Ampan was talking about. As to why she did not look for the previous family earlier, Kim Suan said later that Ampan expressed fear of a ghost that she said was in the village of Bang Chag.

In 1961, when she was seven, Ampan spontaneously recognized a woman on the street of Klong Darn,[5] whom she addressed as "my aunt." This woman was later identified as Joy Ruang Gun, a maternal aunt of the child whose life Ampan was remembering. It seems that on the first occasion of seeing this woman, Ampan merely pointed to her and said to her mother: "That is my aunt." On a later occasion, when they passed on the road, Ampan addressed her as "aunt"; this time Joy Ruang Gun stopped and asked Ampan how she knew her. Ampan then said: "You are my mother's older sister." She was in fact the older sister of Tong Bai Puang Pei of Bang Chag, who had lost a son, Chuey, by drowning in 1950.[6] Impressed by this and other statements Ampan made to her (see Table 4), she took Ampan and her mother to Klong Bang Chag to meet Chuey's family. At Klong Bang Chag, Ampan made some additional statements about the previous life and recognized some people and places connected with Chuey. Later, she was taken to Wat Bang Plee Noi, where she recognized Chuey's older brother, Chuan, and one of his cousins. Ampan's statements fitted closely facts in the life and death of Chuey Puang Pei, who was a boy of about four when he drowned at Klong Bang Chag in 1950.

The case came to my attention in 1963, when a correspondent in Bangkok, T. Magness, sent me some preliminary information about it, which he had obtained from a newspaper report. I was unable to investigate the case until July 1966, when I spent several days interviewing members of both families. Francis Story participated in this phase of the investigation. In March 1969, I returned to the area and interviewed several of the main informants again, as well as two new ones. In the meantime, Ampan and her mother had moved south to Sattahib, about 250 kilometers south of Bangkok. In March 1971, I returned to the area once

[5]The three informants for this meeting, Ampan, Kim Suan, and Joy Ruang Gun, differed concerning where it had taken place. I discuss this discrepancy in the testimony later (see item 21, Table 4).

[6]Dates for birth and death in this case are approximate only.

more and had further interviews with members of the previous family. I have not met Ampan and her mother again since I saw them in 1969.

Persons Interviewed during the Investigation

In Klong Darn I interviewed:

Ampan Petcherat
Kim Suan Petcherat, Ampan's mother
Ladda Lak Yam, Kim Suan Petcherat's cousin

In Song Klong I interviewed:

Yod "Ngoi" Petcherat, Ampan's father
Ben Ja Gauchainiem, an acquaintance of Ampan

At Wat Bang Plee Noi I interviewed:

Ven. Phra Chim Dhamma Choti, abbot of Wat Bang Plee Noi
Ven. Phra Thong Yoi Uttamo, monk of Wat Bang Plee Noi

In Bang Chag I interviewed:

Tai Puang Pei, Chuey's father
Tong Bai Puang Pei, Chuey's mother
Tong Puang Pei, Chuey's paternal great-aunt
Klah Puang Pei, Chuey's paternal uncle
Chuan Puang Pei, Chuey's older brother
Joy Ruang Gun, Chuey's maternal aunt (Tong Bai Puang Pei's older sister)
Pad Ruang Kham, Chuey's maternal aunt (older sister of both Tong Bai Puang Pei and Joy Ruang Gun)

Of the above informants, I have set aside the testimony of two as being largely worthless. Ampan's father, Yod "Ngoi" Petcherat, said that he did not remember much about the case, and in comparison with other informants, his testimony showed an unusually large number of discrepancies. He did not, however, discredit the case. Ben Ja Gauchainiem was a young woman about twenty years of age who, in 1969, helped me to trace Ampan and her mother at their new home in Sattahib. She expressed doubts about the case and impugned the veracity of Kim Suan Petcherat. When I questioned her about her knowledge of the case, however, I found that she herself had never talked with Ampan about it and (almost certainly) had never talked with Kim Suan Petcherat either. She also reversed some of her statements about the case and, in my opinion, disqualified herself as a reliable informant.

The testimony of the remaining informants hung together well. The accounts of the members of the two families concerned agreed in all substantive matters.

In 1966 I did not interview the Puang Peis independently of Ampan and her mother, who came along in the boat to Bang Chag to show us the way. But they were not with me in 1969 or in 1971, when I returned to Bang Chag and went over many of the details with the Puang Peis again. And the Puang Peis were present when I saw Ampan and her mother again in Sattahib in 1969.

Two of the interpreters who worked with me on the case in 1966 were not adequately qualified, and some of the discrepancies in the testimony are due, I believe, to faults of translation. The testimony of this case includes more discrepancies than does the average case of this type, but these discrepancies seem to me to be about details rather than about the main facts and events reported.

Relevant Facts of Geography and Possibilities for Normal Means of Communication between the Two Families

Song Klong, where Ampan was living with her mother up to the time the two families met in 1961, is 37 kilometers south of Bangkok and about 15 kilometers from Klong Bang Chag and the village of Bang Chag, which is on this klong. In those days, the only feasible way of traveling between these two places was by boat on the klongs. The main highway south from Bangkok runs through both Klong Darn and Song Klong. Since they are marketing towns, persons from the smaller villages, such as Bang Chag, are likely to visit them often. In 1971 a new highway going south came close to Wat Bang Plee Noi, although I still had to reach Bang Chag by boat along Klong Bang Chag.

Both the families concerned in the case said that they had had no acquaintance with each other before Ampan was brought to Bang Chag by Chuey's maternal aunt in 1961. I believe this claim is additionally supported by the failure of Kim Suan to look up Chuey's family on her annual visits to Klong Bang Chag between 1955 and 1961. Ampan's fear of a ghost probably did not deter her; I think that if she had had any knowledge of a family who had lost a boy by drowning, she would have gone to them to verify Ampan's statements.

The Death of Chuey Puang Pei

Chuey's parents were not present when he drowned, and thus they were not firsthand informants as to how this drowning occurred. The two firsthand informants I interviewed were Chuey's paternal uncle, Klah Puang Pei, and his older brother, Chuan Puang Pei. Their accounts of the event, which they were remembering many years later, differed in some respects, but they agreed that no one really knew exactly how Chuey had happened to drown.

Chuan was himself a boy of not more than eight or nine when Chuey drowned. He said that he (Chuan) and a cousin, Sa Ing, had been playing in and around the water, but he did not think that Chuey had been in the water, although he was nearby. According to Chuan, Chuey could not swim, and so only walked in shallow water. (This disagrees with the statement of Klah Puang Pei, who said that Chuey could swim well.) So far as Chuan remembered, Chuey had been sitting on the bank, and they paid no attention to what he was doing until somehow Chuan noticed that Chuey was missing. Chuan told me that he pulled Chuey's body out of the water; Klah Puang Pei said that he, and he alone, pulled the body out of the water. (I have not considered this a serious discrepancy since it is very likely that Chuan in some way helped his uncle to retrieve Chuey's body.)

Since children often drown in the klongs of Thailand, the accident was regrettable and saddening, but not regarded as unusual. No one considered the possibility that Chuey had been bitten by a snake, and so no one examined his body for evidence of a snakebite. That a snake had bitten Chuey was at no time suspected by his family until Ampan's first visit to them in 1961.

There are poisonous snakes in the klongs of Thailand. But even if Chuey had been bitten by one, it is unlikely that death would have occurred so quickly from the venom. It is more probable that the small boy was startled and frightened by the bite (if it occurred) and then began to aspirate water and to sink. Therefore, I believe that Chuey died from drowning, even though he may have been bitten by a snake just before drowning. It is also possible that Chuey was bitten by a snake while sitting on the bank and then, after being bitten, rolled or jumped into the water and drowned.[7]

[7]North American readers familiar with the prominent local reactions produced at the site of a bite by a pit viper, such as a rattlesnake, may find almost incredible the failure of Chuey's family to notice on his body marks or other signs of a snakebite, if one occurred before he drowned. It is important to understand, however, that the hematoxic venoms of the vipers produce much more local reaction at the site of the bite than do the neurotoxic venoms of snakes such as cobras and other members of the *Elapidae* family. "The bitten part shows little local reaction in the case of neurotoxic venoms but is swollen, discolored and painful when infiltrated by the hematoxic type" (T. T. Mackie, G. W. Hunter, and C. B. Worth, *A Manual of Tropical Medicine*, 2d ed. [Philadelphia: W. B. Saunders Co., 1954], p. 620).

Since we do not know that Chuey was bitten by a snake, it is perhaps idle to speculate about what species of snake might have bitten him. But an important candidate would be the Monocled Cobra *(Naja naja kaouthia)*. It is quite common in the area with which we are here concerned, and many cases of snakebite occur there each year, although in most of them the person bitten is on land. These cobras are good swimmers, however, and can remain underwater for a considerable time. Cobras usually bite only in self-defense, but may strike if stepped upon inadvertently.

In the case of Chuey, if a snake had bitten him, local reaction at the site of the bite would have been further reduced, because he died from drowning immediately after the bite.

Klah Puang Pei said that Chuan had playfully pulled Chuey's leg before the drowning, but the family did not think this had contributed to the drowning in any way. Chuan denied to me, however, that Chuey had been playing in the water. Since "leg-pulling" at the time of the drowning figured in Ampan's memories, the point is of some importance, but I cannot decide whether Chuan or his uncle had the more accurate memory of exactly what happened. Considering that Chuan was a young boy at the time, I am inclined to credit the version of his uncle over his own, but not with firm confidence.

Chuey's paternal great-aunt, Tong Puang Pei, put a spot of red ocher[8] on the upper chest of Chuey's body before it was cremated. Unfortunately, in 1966 she did not remember on which side of the chest she had made the mark. Chuey's body was taken to the nearby wat at Klong Bang Plee Noi and cremated.

In 1966 Chuey's father indicated that Chuey had been about four years old when he died. In 1969 Chuey's mother said he was between three and four years old. In 1971 she changed her estimate and suggested that he was about five years old. His brother, Chuan, put Chuey's age at death as between four and six. I think it is safe to conclude that Chuey was about four years old when he died, certainly not much less and probably not much more.

Statements and Recognitions Made by Ampan

In Table 4 I have listed in approximate chronological order all the statements and recognitions made by Ampan. Statements 1–19 were made before the two families met. (The time of occurrence of item 4 is doubtful; it may not have taken place until Ampan went to Bang Chag.)

The recognition of item 20 also occurred before the two families met. Items 21–25 occurred at the time of Ampan's meeting with Joy Ruang Gun in Klong Darn. Items 26–31 occurred at the time of Ampan's first visit to Bang Chag. Items 32–33 occurred at Wat Bang Plee Noi.

I have included a few statements made to me by Ampan herself in 1966 and one she made in 1969. In 1966 her memories had faded considerably, but she said she still remembered some details. I have not, however, listed any item for which she was the sole informant. She was twelve in

---

[8]Such marks are sometimes made on dead bodies in the belief that the mark will be reproduced on the next body in which the person reincarnates and that in this way the person can be identified. The practice is fairly widespread in Burma, Assam (India), and Nigeria, as well as in Thailand, where I have studied other cases of the type. Mi Mi Khaing (*Burmese Family* [Bloomington: Indiana University Press, 1962]) has described the practice in Burma, and N. E. Parry (*The Lakhers* [London: Macmillan and Company, 1932]) gave an account of the custom (as it may fairly be called) in Assam. In a later volume I shall be publishing accounts of other cases of this type that I have investigated.

1966, and her memories were probably beginning to fade. This may account for some discrepancies between what she said and what other informants said she had said earlier.

Item 4 requires some particular comment. Ampan's father, Yod "Ngoi" Petcherat, quoted her as saying that one of her brothers *was a monk.* Chuey's older brother, Chuan, was about eight or nine in 1950 when Chuey drowned. Many young Thai men, perhaps most, spend several months or a year in a wat at some time in their lives. Chuan joined a monastery, Wat Bang Plee Noi (near Klong Bang Chag), when he was about twenty. But he decided to become a monk only about a m onth before he actually entered the monastery, just a few months before Ampan's first visit to Bang Chag in 1961. He was a monk at the wat when Ampan was taken there to see if she could recognize him. At the end of his eight months in the monastery, he disrobed, became a farmer, and married. If Ampan had really said that Chuey's brother was a monk, she could have been showing apparent extrasensory perception of the *present* circumstances of the previous family. But I think that Yod "Ngoi" Petcherat may have been a secondhand informant for this item. Chuey's mother, Tong Bai Puang Pei, told me Ampan said that Chuey had had a brother who *was going to be* a monk. It is quite possible that even a boy as young as Chuan was when Chuey died could have expressed a wish or intention to become a monk. Many Thai boys in their teens or younger enter the monasteries as *samaneras* ("novices"). I have no evidence that Chuan expressed any such intention when Chuey was alive, but if my surmise that he did is correct, then Ampan's remark that she (in the former life) had a brother "who was going to be a monk" may derive from a memory from Chuey's life. The item contributes little to the evidence of paranormal processes in the case, since nearly all young men in Thailand become monks for a time. Of any older boy or young man, it could be easily predicted normally that he would become a monk.

Seven of the items (13–19) in Table 4 relate to Chuey's death. Ampan had insisted that she (as Chuey) had been bitten by a snake (item 14) and had then drowned (item 15). This has not been verified and, as I have already said, was not even conjectured by Chuey's family until Ampan mentioned it to them more than ten years later. Discrepancies occurred in the testimony for item 17. I cannot resolve them completely, and I think that at least some of them are due to faulty translation. Both of Ampan's parents seem to have formed the idea that she was blaming Chuey's brother for the drowning by saying that he had pulled Chuey's leg. Klah Puang Pei, Chuey's uncle, stated that there had been some leg-pulling in the water, and I imagine the usual horseplay of boys swimming. Chuan denied to me in 1971 that there had been any leg-pulling between himself and Chuey before Chuey drowned, although he

TABLE 4. *Summary of Statements and Recognitions Made by Ampan*

Item	Informants	Verification	Comments
1. She had a house at Klong Bang Chag near Klong Bang Plee.	Yod "Ngoi" Petcherat, Ampan's father; Kim Suan Petcherat, Ampan's mother	Tai Puang Pei, Chuey's father; Tong Bai Puang Pei, Chuey's mother	Both informants said Ampan had mentioned both names. Bang Plee is not so much the name of a klong as of a fairly large area. Klong Bang Plee Noi runs through it and past the temple called Wat Bang Plee Noi. Ampan seems not to have given the full name with "Noi" at the end.
2. She had another mother and father.	Kim Suan Petcherat	Tai Puang Pei, Tong Bai Puang Pei	
3. She had two older brothers.	Kim Suan Petcherat	Tong Bai Puang Pei	Chuey had only one older brother, Chuan, who was about eight or nine years old when Chuey drowned. Ampan may also have been counting Chuey's cousin, Sa Ing, as a "brother." A slip in translation may also have occurred here. Chuey also had an older sister, Mio. (She died the same year Chuey drowned.) If Ampan used the Thai word *pee*, which can refer to either brothers or sisters, she would have correctly said that she had two older siblings.
4. One brother was going to become a monk.	Tong Bai Puang Pei, Yod "Ngoi" Petcherat	Unverified	Ampan may not have made this statement until after the two families met. Tong Bai Puang Pei said that Ampan told her she had had a

Statement	Informants	Verification	Comments
5. She had an uncle.	Kim Suan Petcherat	Klah Puang Pei, Chuey's paternal uncle	brother who was going to be a monk. This is also what Tong Bai Puang Pei said (as a secondhand informant) that Ampan had told Chuey's aunt (Joy Ruang Gun). Yod "Ngoi" Petcherat attributed to Ampan the statement: "One brother was a monk." If Ampan did make such a statement, either she was incorrect or she had apparent paranormal knowledge of the present circumstances of Chuey's family. It is possible, however, that Yod "Ngoi" Petcherat was confused about this statement, for which he may have been a secondhand informant. See the text for a fuller discussion of this item.
6. She had an aunt.	Kim Suan Petcherat	Tong Bai Puang Pei Joy Ruang Gun, Tong Bai Puang Pei's older sister and Chuey's maternal aunt	Joy Ruang Gun was the aunt Ampan recognized in Klong Darn.
7. She had one younger sister.	Kim Suan Petcherat	Tong Bai Puang Pei	Chuey had had a younger sister called Khao.
8. There was a red dog where she lived.	Kim Suan Petcherat Joy Ruang Gun	Tong Bai Puang Pei	The dog had died by the time Ampan visited Klong Bang Chag.

NOTE: Although I have used the pronouns *she* and *her* in reference to Ampan's statements, readers should remember that she (Ampan) was referring in these statements to Chuey and to places and events in his life. To avoid confusion, I have sometimes used Chuey's name in describing what Ampan said, although she herself does not seem to have mentioned the name to anyone when she was first talking about the previous life. Later, she said that she had remembered the name Chuey.

TABLE 4. (cont.)

Item	Informants	Verification	Comments
			This item is in no sense specific, since it seems to me that about a quarter of all dogs in Thailand are reddish or rust brown in color. Joy Ruang Gun said Ampan had mentioned two red dogs at the house, and she confirmed that two such dogs had lived there. But her sister Tong Bai said that there was only one red dog.
9. There were three buffaloes.	Kim Suan Petcherat Joy Ruang Gun	Tong Bai Puang Pei	The Puang Pei family had two adult buffaloes and one baby buffalo during Chuey's lifetime. Joy Ruang Gun said that Ampan mentioned only two buffaloes, a statement she said was correct, perhaps thinking only of the adult ones.
10. Red trousers belonging to her were hanging on the second floor.	Kim Suan Petcherat	Tong Bai Puang Pei	Some red cloth for a sarong, not for trousers, was hanging up in the house when Chuey drowned. The sarong was Chuey's.
11. She was a boy in the previous life.	Kim Suan Petcherat	Tong Bai Puang Pei	Chuey Puang Pei was a boy of about four when he drowned.
12. The house looked like a stable.	Kim Suan Petcherat	Doubtful	The house, which I visited in 1966 and 1969, was elevated on stilts like most houses along the klongs in Thailand. Animals could sometimes get under the floor of the upper part, but I would not

Item	Informants	Verification	Comments
			have described this house as resembling a stable.
13. Before she died, she had been playing hide-and-seek and swimming.	Kim Suan Petcherat	Unverified	I did not learn at what the children had been playing before going into the water. Chuan Puang Pei and another boy, Sa Ing, had been playing together in the water.
14. She had been bitten by a snake.	Kim Suan Petcherat Ladda Lak Yam, Kim Suan Petcherat's cousin	Unverified	See the text for a full discussion of Chuey's drowning. Ampan said the snake bit her on the right leg while she was in the water. See the following item.
15. She then fell into the water and drowned.	Kim Suan Petcherat Ampan (1966)	Klah Puang Pei	Ampan herself said in 1966 that she (Chuey) had been in the water when bitten by the snake.
16. Her two brothers were there when she drowned.	Kim Suan Petcherat Ampan (1969)	Chuan Puang Pei, Chuey's older brother Tai Puang Pei	Chuan was nearby when Chuey drowned. One other child, a cousin, Sa Ing, who could be loosely called a "brother," was present also. In 1969 Ampan said that, in addition to her (Chuey's) brother, another boy was present. She did not give his name, but referred to him as *pee-nawng*, which can be used in Thai to refer to a brother, sister, or cousin. Since Tai Puang Pei was away from the house when Chuey drowned, he was (for this item) a secondhand witness only.
17. One of her brothers pulled her ankle and held her under the water.	Kim Suan Petcherat Yod "Ngoi" Petcherat	Unverified	In 1966 Ampan herself gave discrepant testimony on two different days, and both of her statements differed from what her

TABLE 4. (*cont.*)

Item	Informants	Verification	Comments
			mother reported she had said earlier.
			Yod "Ngoi" Petcherat's account of what Ampan had said also differed from that of his wife. According to him, Ampan had said that her brother had drowned her by putting his foot on her neck.
			Klah Puang Pei, Chuey's uncle, thought Chuey and Chuan had been playing together in the water and that Chuan had pulled Chuey's leg, although he did not think this had anything to do with Chuey's drowning. But Chuan said he had been playing in the water only with the other boy, Sa Ing, before they noticed that Chuey was missing.
18. Her older brother took her out of the water, but she was already dead.	Ladda Lak Yam	Doubtful	Klah Puang Pei said he alone removed Chuey's body from the water. But Chuan said that he had pulled Chuey's body from the water. Perhaps they helped each other. In 1966 Ampan herself denied that she (as Chuey) had seen Chuey's body being pulled from the water.
19. Her body was taken to Wat Bang Plee for cremation.	Kim Suan Petcherat Ampan (1966)	Tong Bai Puang Pei	Ampan did not give the full name of Wat Bang Plee Noi. She said that Chuey's father had taken the

Item	Informants	Comments and Verification
		body to the wat for cremation. She did not claim to remember seeing the cremation.
20. Recognition of Bang Chag	Kim Suan Petcherat	Ampan repeatedly asked her mother to take her to the place of her previous life. Consequently, Kim Suan took Ampan along when she had occasion to paddle over to Klong Bang Chag. On one of these occasions, Ampan recognized the village of Bang Chag, where Chuey had lived. But she and her mother did not approach Chuey's house or family at that time.
21. Recognition of Chuey's aunt, Joy Ruang Gun	Joy Ruang Gun Kim Suan Petcherat	Kim Suan Petcherat was with Ampan when Ampan saw Joy Ruang Gun in Klong Darn and said: "That is my aunt." Ampan seems not to have talked with Joy Ruang Gun on this first occasion of seeing her. Later, however, she passed her on the street again and called her "aunt." Joy Ruang Gun heard her, stopped, and asked Ampan how she knew her. Ampan then said that she (Joy Ruang Gun) was her mother's older sister. Joy Ruang Gun then asked Ampan: "Who are your parents?" and received the answers reported in items 22 and 23. Kim Suan Petcherat varied in her accounts of what Ampan had called the strange woman they saw in the street. On one occasion she said Ampan had referred to her

Table 4. (cont.)

Item	Informants	Verification	Comments
			as "aunt," but in a later discussion she said Ampan had used a word that means "mother." (This discrepancy may have arisen from a difficulty in translation, because Ampan later left no doubt that she had thought of the woman recognized as her previous aunt.) Ampan and her mother said she recognized Chuey's aunt at Song Klong, but Joy Ruang Gun said she met Ampan first at Klong Darn. This discrepancy may derive from faulty memory, or the two incidents mentioned above may have happened at different towns.
22. Her father was called Tai.	Joy Ruang Gun	Tai Puang Pei	
23. Her mother was called Bai.	Joy Ruang Gun	Tong Bai Puang Pei	Ampan made this remark and that of the next item when she met Chuey's aunt; she was trying to establish her previous identity with her.
24. There was a bamboo tree in front of the house.	Joy Ruang Gun	Joy Ruang Gun	
25. There were two red jars at the house.	Joy Ruang Gun Tong Bai Puang Pei	Tong Bai Puang Pei	Joy Ruang Gun said Ampan had told her, before she came to Bang Chag, that there were two red jars at the house, which Joy Ruang

Gun and Tong Bai Puang Pei said was correct.

Ampan also made a similar remark at Bang Chag, but at that time mentioned only one red jar. When I visited the Puang Pei home in 1966, they still had a large red jar. If one had been there in 1961, when Ampan visited, she might have seen it, although her remark was mentioned to me as an indication of her knowledge of objects around the house in Chuey's time. But even if Ampan had not seen a red jar at the house, the item is not at all specific since perhaps half the houses along the klongs of Thailand have drinking water kept in red jars. (The other jars are nearly all a kind of bistre brown.)

This recognition occurred at Bang Chag. Ampan went to Tong Bai Puang Pei, embraced her tightly, and said: "Mother." But Ampan knew she was going to Bang Chag and naturally expected to meet the previous mother and father there.

When Ampan and her mother arrived at Bang Chag, Chuey's father was not at home, but he later arrived with two other men. While they were sitting in the boat before landing, Ampan was asked to say which was her previous father. She correctly pointed to

26. Recognition of Chuey's mother, Tong Bai Puang Pei

Tong Bai Puang Pei
Ladda Lak Yam
Kim Suan Petcherat

27. Recognition of Chuey's father, Tai Puang Pei

Ladda Lak Yam
Tai Puang Pei

TABLE 4. (cont.)

Item	Informants	Verification	Comments
			Tai Puang Pei. Attempts were made to mislead her, but she insisted on the identification she had made.
28. There were banana and coconut trees at the house.	Tong Bai Puang Pei	Tong Bai Puang Pei	Ampan made this remark when she went to Bang Chag. These trees were no longer standing at the time of Ampan's visit. This is not at all a specific item, but it is not without some value, since the trees were no longer there.
29. There had been two houses where she lived.	Tong Bai Puang Pei	Tong Bai Puang Pei	Ampan made this remark when she went to Bang Chag. One of the houses had been removed by the time of Ampan's visit there.
30. Recognition of the site where Chuey drowned	Tong Bai Puang Pei Ladda Lak Yam		This recognition is of doubtful value. Ampan pointed to a place in the water near the house. She did not indicate the exact spot where Chuey had drowned. Children would obviously swim near the boat dock on the klong, and so this is the most likely site for a drowning.
31. Recognition of Chuey's sister, Khao	Kim Suan Petcherat		Ampan pointed at Khao and said: "Sister," but did not give Khao's name.

32. Recognition of Chuey's brother, Chuan

Kim Suan Petcherat
Ven. Phra Thong Yoi
  Uttamo, monk of Wat
  Bang Plee Noi
Chuan Puang Pei
Ampan (1966)

This recognition occurred at Wat Bang Plee Noi, where Chuan was then living as a monk. Chuan was among a group of other monks variously estimated as ten and thirty in number.

Chuan Puang Pei said that Ampan had picked him out of the group of monks sitting together at the wat. But he wavered on the question of whether she had indicated him spontaneously and said: "You are my brother," or whether someone had asked her to pick out her brother from the group.

According to Ampan in 1966, she had been asked to say which of the monks was her previous brother and had pointed to Chuan correctly. The testimony of the other two informants indicated that the recognition had been more spontaneous.

Ampan wept when she met Chuan and he also, according to Kim Suan Petcherat, was moved to tears.

33. Recognition of Chuey's cousins, Sak and Sa Ing

Joy Ruang Gun
Chuan Puang Pei

Sak was another young monk sitting in the group at Wat Bang Plee Noi. According to Joy Ruang Gun, Ampan indicated him and said: "This monk is the son of Nang Pad." Sak was Nang Pad's son; Nang Pad was the older sister of both Tong Bai Puang Pei and Joy Ruang Gun.

TABLE 4. (cont.)

Item

Informants

Verification

Comments

Chuan Puang Pei did not say that
Ampan had mentioned Sak's
name, but said she had
spontaneously pointed to two
other monks (Sak was one and Sa
Ing the other) and said they were
Chuey's cousins, which was
correct. It would have been
improper for Ampan to have
mentioned a monk's own name.

said he had been playing around in the water with Sa Ing. In 1966 Ampan seemed to preserve some rather clear memories of Chuey's death, although her testimony about it varied on two days. I think, however, that the discrepancy was due to poor translation of what she said. In her clearest statement, she described how Chuey had been playing at pulling legs with his brother before he was bitten by the snake and drowned; but she said that Chuey had not been with Chuan when he actually drowned. I suppose that Ampan had given her parents a somewhat similar account of the events earlier and that they had interpreted this incorrectly as implying that she blamed the drowning on Chuan. But Ampan's parents further said that when Ampan met Chuan (in 1961 at Wat Bang Plee Noi), she scolded him for drowning Chuey. The Ven. Phra Thong Yoi Uttamo, who was present at the wat when Ampan met Chuan, remembered no such comment. Nor did Chuan, who said that he and Ampan did not discuss the drowning when they met at the wat. Ampan's mother said that her husband was not present at the monastery when Ampan first met Chuan, and so his testimony, not very reliable to begin with, was secondhand on this point. It is odd, however, that Kim Suan Petcherat, who appeared to be a reliable informant, was the only firsthand witness who remembered that Ampan had made reproaches about the drowning to Chuan. Possibly Ampan muttered these in a low voice that her mother could hear when the others present could not.

In my effort to understand the discrepancies and incorrect items of this case, it occurred to me that perhaps Ampan, or other informants, had mixed up memories of leg-pulling, if this occurred, before Chuey drowned with those of the pulling of Chuey's body out of the water *after* the drowning. Ampan described how Chuey's body was taken to Wat Bang Plee Noi for cremation. This event happened after the recovery of the body from the water, and she may also have had partially distorted memories of the body being removed from the water. Indeed, Ladda Lak Yam said that Ampan had described how Chuey's body had been taken from the water, and it is quite probable that Ampan did make such a statement, even though in 1966 she no longer included this event among her persisting memories. (See item 18, Table 4.)

In 1966 Ampan told me that she had remembered the name of the previous personality, Chuey, but had not told anyone the name earlier because "there was no one to tell." This seemed a strange remark, since she had told her mother a number of details about the previous life. Her mother, not a person of keen intellect, probably expressed little interest in the matter and did not seem to have encouraged Ampan to relate more details. But neither did she suppress her. Ampan's father was out of the house (and I think out of the household) during much of Ampan's early years.

Ampan's Statements about Events Occurring after Chuey's Death and before Her Birth.   As indicated in item 19 of Table 4, Ampan said she remembered that, after Chuey's drowning, his body was taken to Wat Bang Plee for cremation. (Ampan herself did not then use the full name, Wat Bang Plee Noi.) But she said she had no memory of the cremation itself. She did, however, have a few apparent memories of other experiences after Chuey's death and before her birth. She described these to me in 1966.

She said that a man took her to another place where there were dead persons and introduced her to the "head man" of that place. She then went with another man up a ladder to heaven. There she met yet a third man, of large size and black complexion, who was dressed in white. This man was kind to her. Eventually the man who had escorted her to heaven brought her back to the first man she had met at the "place of dead persons." She was then given fruit to eat; she ate it and was reborn.[9]

The Birthmark on Ampan's Chest

Ampan had a birthmark on the upper left chest below the clavicle. In 1966 it consisted of a circular area of darker pigment about 12 millimeters in diameter. It had the appearance of a pigmented, flat nevus. This birthmark may correspond in location to the red ocher mark that Chuey's great-aunt, Tong Puang Pei, had placed on his body before its cremation. Unfortunately, since she had forgotten on which side of his chest she had placed the mark, we cannot be positive about this correspondence. I learned about the birthmark before I knew that a member of Chuey's family had put red ocher on his upper chest before the cremation of his body.

Ampan said that Chuey had been bitten on the right leg by a snake in the water. No one seems to have examined her legs to see whether she had a birthmark corresponding to a snakebite wound on the body of Chuey.

Ampan's Behavior Related to the Previous Life

Circumstances and Manner of Ampan's Speaking about the Previous Life. Ampan's mother said that she first spoke about how she died in the previ-

---

[9]Ampan's narration includes the "man in white" and the "fruit of forgetfulness," to which I referred in the Introduction to Cases in Thailand. Since she had memories of a previous life, however, one can conjecture that the fruit was ineffective as an obliterator of such memories.

Readers should remember that Ampan was twelve years old in 1966, when she made these statements, and by that age she had probably absorbed much about Thai beliefs concerning events during the interval between death and presumed rebirth. These may have influenced her statements even if they did not provide the sole basis for them.

ous life while she was playing in the water with her "brothers."[10] This situation seems to have reminded her of the circumstances of the death of Chuey, who had been playing in (or near) the water with his "brothers" just before he drowned.

A boat trip with her mother on Klong Bang Chag also stimulated Ampan's memories, for she then recognized the area of Bang Chag where Chuey had lived.

Before Ampan visited the previous family, she apparently had a strong desire to see its members and cried when she expressed this wish. When, at the age of seven, she spontaneously recognized Chuey's aunt Joy Ruang Gun, she embraced her and asked to be taken to her (Chuey's) family. When Ampan first met Chuey's mother, Tong Bai Puang Pei, she also embraced her tightly. Kim Suan Petcherat and Chuan Puang Pei both said that Ampan wept when she met Chuan at Wat Bang Plee Noi. (Kim Suan said that Chuan wept also, but Chuan did not mention this to me himself.)

Ampan distinctly rejected Yod "Ngoi" Petcherat as her father during these early years. According to her mother, she said: "Nai Yod is not my father." The absence of Yod "Ngoi" Petcherat from the home could well have stimulated such rejecting remarks; but Ampan made similar comments about her mother, saying that Kim Suan was not her mother and that she had another mother.

Masculine Traits in Ampan. According to her mother, Ampan had definitely masculine interests and inclinations when she was a child. In 1966 her mother said that Ampan liked to dress as a boy and wear trousers or pants. And she liked boys' games, such as boxing. (Boxing is widely considered to be a man's sport; but it is probably regarded as a genteel ladies' activity even less in Thailand than anywhere else, because the rules of Thai boxing permit the participants to use their elbows, knees, and feet.) Ampan told me (in 1966) that she would prefer to be a boy because boys have a freer life than girls. At that time, she impressed me as being rather boyish in her dress (she was wearing shorts) and in her gait. She seemed to me to have a boyish way of swinging her arms as she walked.

When I saw Ampan again, in March 1969, she was fifteen years old. She had begun to menstruate just three or four months before this date, which (I was told) was late for Thai girls. Ampan's mother said that Ampan had only "learned to dress" in girls' clothes two years earlier, that is, at the age of thirteen. By this expression I think she meant to say that Ampan had then begun to dress in girls' clothes voluntarily, without being pressured or forced to wear them.

[10]Since Ampan had only one brother (actually a stepbrother), I believe that here, as often happens in Asia, the word *brother* was used loosely to mean cousins or other children of the neighborhood as well as biologically related siblings.

In appearance, Ampan seemed in 1969 to be less masculine, and her figure was filling out into feminine proportions. She was beginning to use makeup. But her mother said that she chose her friends among tomboy girls and had little interest in boys. On the other hand, an American soldier from the nearby base at Sattahib had taken an interest in her, and she showed me his photograph.

Ampan said she still liked boxing and still engaged in it herself. She also said she would still prefer to be a boy, since she would be freer as a boy than as a girl.

I offered Ampan a choice between a boy's knife and a bottle of perfume as a gift, and she chose the latter.

To explore her sexual orientation a little further, I asked her to take an extended Draw-a-Person Test.[11] Her first (free choice) drawing was of a boy; her second drawing (after directions to draw a member of the sex opposite to that of the first choice) was of a girl; and her third (free choice) drawing was of a girl. But the figure of this third drawing seemed to me extremely masculine. The hair was short, and the person was wearing what seemed to be a shirt with buttons down the center. I thought Ampan had drawn another boy or man until she told me the drawing was supposed to be of a girl.

In summary, Ampan showed more masculine traits when younger than do most girls of her age. And at the age of fifteen she still showed some definitely masculine traits and preferences and continued to express the wish to be a boy.[12] At the same time, however, she had moved noticeably toward the feminine side in her overall sexual orientation.

Other Behavior of Ampan Related to the Previous Life.   Because Chuey had died of drowning, I wished to learn whether Ampan had manifested any fear of the water. Both Ampan and her mother positively asserted that she had never shown any such fear. She enjoyed swimming from a fairly early age.

Ampan said that she did have a dislike for snakes that persisted up to 1966; but this later receded, and in 1969 she said that she liked snakes

---

[11]L. Whitaker, Jr., "The Use of An Extended Draw-a-Person Test to Identify Homosexual and Effeminate Men," *Journal of Consulting Psychology* 25(1961):482–85. For applications of this test in other cases of the sex change type, see the cases of Paulo Lorenz *(Twenty Cases)*, Ruby Kusuma Silva (second volume of this series), and Ma Tin Aung Myo (this volume).

[12]Ampan's expressed desire to change sex should be considered in the light of other facts and circumstances. First, she was a fifteen-year-old girl, not a grown woman, when she made the remark. Second, Asian women (particularly those of Buddhist countries) express a wish to be men more often than do Western women. Women in other parts of the world may also express a wish to be men, but I believe that such a wish is more often and more strongly expressed by women in Asia than it is by women in Europe and North America. This difference derives, I think, from the generally inferior social status of women in Asia and, in Buddhist countries, from the lower status accorded women with regard to possibilities for spiritual development. I discussed this point above in the report of the case of Ratana Wongsombat.

and enjoyed playing with small ones. I do not think that Ampan ever had a marked phobia of snakes, because in 1969 her mother could not remember that she had ever been afraid of them.

Comments on the Evidence of Paranormal Processes in the Case

I cannot exclude in this case the possibility that the two families may have had some slight, casual contact at some time prior to the development of the case. The Puang Pei family would certainly have gone into the larger towns of Klong Darn and Song Klong along the highway, and it was on one such visit of Chuey Puang Pei's aunt that Ampan recognized her. But this did not happen until Ampan was seven, and if the Puang Peis had frequently visited the area of Song Klong (which is not a large town), where Ampan first lived, one might have expected that she would have recognized one of them earlier. I am confident that the two families had no significant contact with each other prior to Ampan's first statements. Each family denied any previous familiarity with the other, and I see no reason to doubt their statements on the matter.

Both families were of approximately equal social and economic status. Ampan and her mother had nothing to gain from her attaching herself to some not very well-to-do farmers in a village about 15 kilometers away.

In this case extrasensory perception, at least between Ampan and living persons, seems a less plausible interpretation than it may be for some other cases. For one thing, Ampan showed knowledge of conditions of the house and family as they were during the lifetime of Chuey. That is, she remembered a house that had been taken down, a red dog that was no longer there, and trees that had been removed. If she obtained all this information through extrasensory perception, she must have done so by reaching into the past. It was a past known to surviving members of the family, to be sure, but nonetheless it was their *past* situation rather than their present one.

Ampan's recognition of Chuan (item 32, Table 4) may be evidence of extrasensory perception. Chuan was eight or nine when Chuey died and about twenty when Ampan was said to have recognized him at Wat Bang Plee Noi. Although it is conceivable that unusual features of his face—I did not notice any—could have persisted throughout the interval of ten or eleven years, it seems more likely that Chuan's appearance had changed greatly; the years concerned are those of rapid growth. A recognition of him would almost need to derive from some process outside Chuey's memories.[13]

[13]For other examples of subjects who have been reported to recognize someone after many years, see the cases of Gnanatilleka Baddewithana, Swarnlata Mishra *(Twenty Cases)*, and Suleyman Andary (third volume of this series).

Ampan's Later Development

In 1966 Ampan, who was then twelve, spoke freely about her memories of the previous life, which seemed then still fresh. Three years later she said that most of her memories had faded, but not all. She still recalled, and reviewed with me, details of Chuey's drowning. It therefore seems that the memories faded in Ampan at a later age than is usual in these cases.

After the first meeting of the two families in 1961, they continued to exchange visits at least until 1966, when Ampan and her mother were living in Klong Darn. Chuan visited Ampan in Klong Darn, and Ampan went to Bang Chag from time to time. She and her mother accompanied me there in 1966. After Ampan and her mother moved to Sattahib, visits between the two families became more difficult; but in 1971 Chuey's mother said she had seen Ampan the previous year at Klong Darn, presumably when members of both families were visiting there. The visits between Ampan and the previous family may have contributed to the persistence of her memories.

Ampan dropped out of school at the end of the third year, which would have been at the age of about eight years. But she was by no means a recluse and seemed to be leading a normal social life (apart from inattendance at school) for a girl of her age both in 1966 and in 1969.

On March 20, 1978, I returned to Klong Darn in the hope of tracing and meeting Ampan again. I learned that Ampan's mother, Kim Suan, had died two years earlier, but Kim Suan's brother, sister-in-law, and niece were all living in Klong Darn in the area where I had first met Ampan in 1966. Ampan's cousin, Ratana Nimsomboon, told me that Ampan had married an American soldier stationed at Sattahib and had moved to California. She did not know Ampan's address in the United States. I have tried unsuccessfully to locate Ampan through Thai groups in the United States.

On June 13, 1981, Nasib Sirorasa went to Klong Darn in the hope of learning Ampan's address in the United States or obtaining further information about her. She met Ratana Nimsomboon, who told her that Ampan had had a child, a girl. Ampan had not raised her child herself, however; she had let her mother (Kim Suan) do this until Kim Suan had died. Ratana had met Ampan when Ampan had returned to Thailand in about 1978, and she had noticed that Ampan still had some masculine mannerisms. But she said that Ampan was dressing well and looked healthy and attractive.

3.   The Case of Hair Kam Kanya

Introduction

THIS CASE, THE only one that I have investigated in northern Thailand, is not rich in details of imaged memories and recognitions. It also has the weakness that both the personalities concerned in it belonged to the same extended family. It does, however, contain observations of unusual behavior on the part of the subject that, according to the informants, corresponded to behavior shown by the related previous personality. Thus I attach more importance to the reports of the subject's behavior as evidence of some paranormal process than I do to the details of what she claimed to remember (as imaged memories) about the previous life.

The most important informant for the case was an officer of the Royal Thai Army, Major (later Lieutenant Colonel) Pongdet Vilasri. Like many educated Thais, Pongdet Vilasri was a nominal Buddhist, but at the time this case developed, he had little interest in his religion and did not believe in rebirth. His observations in the present case convinced him that its best explanation was the rebirth of his own mother as the subject, Hair Kam Kanya.

Summary of the Case and Its Investigation

Hair Kam Kanya was born on July 8, 1961, in Tung Mah Niew, a village northeast of Chiang Mai. Her parents were Hai Kanya and Tha Kanya. Hair Kam was their third child. During her infancy, her family obtained—by a kind of mediumistic process that I shall describe later—indications that Hair Kam had been a woman called Sukanta Vilasri in her previous life. Sukanta Vilasri was the sister of Tha Kanya's mother, Chansom Tachapang, and she was therefore Hair Kam's maternal great-aunt. Sukanta Vilasri had died on June 29, 1945. In this case, therefore, the interval—sixteen years—between the death of the previous personality and the birth of the subject was much longer than one finds in most Asian cases of the reincarnation type.[1]

---

[1] For other examples of Asian cases with a long interval between the previous personality's death and the subject's birth, see the cases of Wijeratne (*Twenty Cases*), Suleyman Andary (third volume in

Sukanta Vilasri's favorite son, Pongdet Vilasri, lived just outside Chiang Mai in Ban Sanklang. When he heard that Hair Kam was supposed to be his mother reborn, he at first treated the report with great skepticism. Subsequently, however, he began to think more about Hair Kam. He visited Tung Mah Niew from time to time and saw her there. On November 13, 1966 (he remembered the date distinctly), he felt an urge to go to Tung Mah Niew and see his aunt, Chansom Tachapang; thus, he and his wife drove out there. When they arrived at the village, the other children ran away, but Hair Kam remained and stared at Pongdet Vilasri with great intentness. Pongdet Vilasri then asked Hair Kam's grandmother to ask her whether she wished to come and live with him. (He apparently did not want to approach the girl directly himself because of a fear of frightening her.) To his surprise and pleasure, Hair Kam said: "I wanted to live with them [the Vilasris] a long time ago." Hair Kam's mother gave her consent, and Pongdet Vilasri and his wife then took Hair Kam and her grandmother, Pongdet Vilasri's aunt, back to Chiang Mai.[2]

At the Vilasris' home, Hair Kam settled down comfortably. I shall later describe her behavior there in detail. At the end of a week, Hair Kam's grandmother had to return to her village, and Pongdet Vilasri and his wife took her and Hair Kam back to Tung Mah Niew, uncertain whether Hair Kam would afterward return to Ban Sanklang with them or not. But when they got ready to leave the village, Hair Kam led the way to their car, returned with them to Ban Sanklang, and remained there contentedly. Subsequently, Pongdet Vilasri and his wife, who had no children of their own, adopted Hair Kam. She was about five and a half years old at the time she came to live with them.

During her early years in Tung Mah Niew, Hair Kam had not spoken of a previous life. After she moved to Chiang Mai, however, she made a small number of statements and a few recognitions indicating memories of the life of Sukanta Vilasri. These remarks and recognitions, combined with behavior that Pongdet Vilasri said reminded him of his mother, convinced him that Hair Kam was his mother reborn. In April 1967, he pub-

this series), and Bongkuch Promsin (this volume).

In the case of Gopal Gupta (first volume of this series), the corresponding interval was a few month's more than eight years. Gopal, however, claimed to have lived an intermediate terrestrial life during this period, although it remains completely unverified. In the case of Bongkuch Promsin (later in this volume), the corresponding interval was just under eight years; Bongkuch did not claim that he had had an intermediate terrestrial life during this period.

[2]Western readers may consider this a rather casual gift of a child. Asian parents, however, are less possessive of children than are Western ones, without being less affectionate toward them. It is not uncommon for Asian parents with several children to let one go and live with relatives who have none. In the present instance, the poverty of Hair Kam's family contrasted with the comparative affluence of Pongdet Vilasri, who was an army officer, and this difference added the motive of allowing Hair Kam to grow up in a more prosperous family that might provide an education for her.

lished a short report of the case in a Buddhist magazine in Chiang Mai.[3] An assistant in Thailand gave me a copy of the magazine, and in this way I learned of the case.

In 1969 I spent two days in Chiang Mai and the surrounding area investigating the case. In 1971 I spent another day in the area of Chiang Mai and a day in Bangkok interviewing additional witnesses and checking certain points again. During my second visit to Chiang Mai, I was able to meet Hair Kam and her adoptive parents again, and I learned of her further development up to that time. During both of my visits to the area of Chiang Mai, R. R. Boonyoros assisted me as an interpreter.

Between 1971 and 1980 I obtained some additional information by correspondence with R. R. Boonyoros. He put certain questions about details to Pongdet Vilasri and his wife for me, and he also wrote me about Hair Kam's later development.

Persons Interviewed during the Investigation

In Ban Sanklang, on the outskirts of Chiang Mai, I interviewed:

Hair Kam Kanya
Major (later Lieutenant Colonel) Pongdet Vilasri, Royal Thai Army,
    Hair Kam's adoptive father and Sukanta Vilasri's younger son
Ratana Vilasri, Pongdet Vilasri's wife and Hair Kam's adoptive mother

In Buagped I interviewed:

Mae On Kampong, friend of Sukanta Vilasri

In Chiang Mai I interviewed:

Suchint Vilasri, Sukanta Vilasri's older son
Jessada Vilasri Onla-Or, Suchint Vilasri's daughter and Sukanta
    Vilasri's granddaughter
Chiradej Vilasri, Suchint Vilasri's son and Sukanta Vilasri's grandson
Mae Ma Kampira, friend of Sukanta Vilasri
Mae Kam Viriyasingh, friend of Sukanta Vilasri
Ven. Phra Kru Sri Thammakoon, distant relative and friend of
    Sukanta Vilasri

---

[3]Pongdet Vilasri's article was entitled "Mother Ta Comes Back to Live Another Life." It was published in the April 1967 issue of the Thai magazine *Chow Buddh* (15, no. 6:80–85). R. R. Boonyoros furnished me with an English translation, which I have used in the preparation of this report. *Ta* is a short form for the name "Sukanta."

In Tung Mah Niew I interviewed:

Tha Kanya, Hair Kam's mother
Chansom Tachapang, Sukanta Vilasri's sister, Pongdet Vilasri's mater-
    nal aunt, and Hair Kam's maternal grandmother
Sa Mai, maternal niece of Sukanta Vilasri and Chansom Tachapang

In Bangkok I interviewed:

Nipa Vilasri Pongpanit, Sukanta Vilasri's second daughter
Sityan Vilasri Sirisap, Sukanta Vilasri's youngest daughter

Relevant Facts of Geography and Possibilities for Normal Means of Communication between the Two Families

As I have already mentioned, the two families in this case were related,
although they lived a considerable distance apart. (Tung Mah Niew lies
27 kilometers northeast of Chiang Mai.) They had some contact with
each other from time to time. Pongdet Vilasri went out to the village of
Tung Mah Niew to see his relatives, and occasionally he brought one of
his nieces or nephews from the village into Chiang Mai to stay with him
for a while. These contacts between the two families provided opportunities for information about Sukanta Vilasri to pass back and forth. In addition, Sukanta's sister, Chansom Tachapang (who was Hair Kam's maternal grandmother), lived in Tung Mah Niew, and she naturally knew all
the important facts in the life of Sukanta. She could and may have told
some of these to Hair Kam. Moreover, the members of Hair Kam's immediate family believed from her infancy that she was Sukanta reborn.
There were thus motives and opportunities for the members of Hair
Kam's family to promote her identification with Sukanta. That Hair Kam
had a strong identification with Sukanta will become sufficiently obvious
from the details I shall report below. We shall have to decide whether
family influences that may have encouraged this identification can account completely for Hair Kam's related behavior.

The Life, Death, and Character of Sukanta Vilasri

Sukanta Vilasri seems to have been a somewhat unusual Thai woman.
She was born in 1895 in the village of Buagped, which is about 13 kilome-
ters northeast of Chiang Mai, about halfway between Chiang Mai and
Tung Mah Niew. When she grew up, Sukanta married Mo Vilasri and

they had five children. She and her husband were fond of children and were gentle and generous to them. They sold property so that their children could have an education, with the result that they themselves lived afterward in modest circumstances. Sukanta Vilasri could not read at all, although her husband could.

To supplement her husband's income, Sukanta raised vegetables and domestic animals like pigs and fowl, which she sold. She enjoyed trading and selling her vegetables in the markets of the city. Through her generosity (and that of her husband) her younger son, Pongdet Vilasri, was able to become an officer in the Royal Thai Army. Two of her daughters and her other son became schoolteachers. A third daughter, Tun-Keow, remained in the home unmarried and died (in 1965) after her parents' deaths.

The consensus of my informants, who included four of Sukanta Vilasri's five children, was that Pongdet Vilasri had been her favorite child. Pongdet Vilasri seems to have been a more studious and more obedient child than his siblings, and this may have contributed to his becoming his mother's favorite.

Sukanta Vilasri was also close to her sister Chansom Tachapang, and after their marriages they remained on affectionate terms, although living (for northern Thailand) far apart. During Sukanta's terminal illness, Chansom nursed her with loving attention, and the informants of Chansom's village, Tung Mah Niew, think this was why Sukanta, as they believe, was reborn there rather than in Chiang Mai.

Sukanta derived enjoyment from her family and from her business as a market trader. Religious activities provided her other main source of happiness. She went often to the temples and to religious festivals. Her son Suchint Vilasri said that she never missed attending the temple on special religious days; she would make some contribution of money to the temple even when she had little herself. My informants differed as to whether or not Sukanta should be considered more religious than the average Thai woman. Summing up the various accounts given to me, I am inclined to think that she was somewhat more religious than the average Thai woman, but rather less so than, for example, Kim Lan, the previous personality in the case of Ratana Wongsombat. Sukanta was not known to have practiced meditation—not extensively, at any rate.

Sukanta enjoyed attending a type of musical folk drama called *Likai*, which is popular in northern Thailand. The Likai plays are based on the history and legends of Thailand; some of them, but not all, have religious themes derived, for example, from incidents in the life of the Buddha.

Sukanta had a strong aversion to meat, especially beef. This seems not to have been part of vegetarianism based on religion or attitudes toward cows.[4] Rather, she appears to have had an allergy to beef, or possibly a strong conditioning from some other source, so that when she ate it even in small quantities, she would become ill with headaches and vomiting. Since she could not even eat beef fat, her food was cooked in a pot separate from that of other members of her family. (One of her daughters, Nipa Pongpanit, had a similar reaction to beef.) Although she ate absolutely no beef, Sukanta did eat sparingly of other meats. Her favorite foods were *namphrik*[5] and boiled vegetables.

Sukanta seems to have had little interest in the details of housekeeping, such as cooking, which she left to others while she went out to enjoy trading in the markets.

When she was about fifty years old, Sukanta became ill with a severe intestinal infection and died of this within ten days or so. Her death was attributed to cholera, an epidemic of which was occurring in Chiang Mai at that time. Pongdet Vilasri was away on duty in the army when she first became ill, but he returned and was with his mother when she died. Informants recalled that during her last illness Sukanta lay on her side, although ordinarily she slept on her back.[6] Her death greatly affected Pongdet Vilasri. As she was dying, he told her that he had not paid his debts to her and asked her please to return. His sister Sityan Sirisap overhead him make this remark. She recalled that he said to their mother: "If you die, you should be reborn and come to live with me." This remark contradicts Pongdet Vilasri's assertion to me that he did not believe in rebirth before the development of the case; I am unable to decide whether his grief over the imminent death of his mother revived momentarily a belief in rebirth that she had undoubtedly inculcated in him when he was a child or whether he later exaggerated the extent of his earlier skepticism.

Sukanta Vilasri died on June 29, 1945,[7] in Chiang Mai. Her body was cremated, and the ashes were placed in a pagoda in Wat Chatupon. A few months later, on October 1, 1945, her husband, Mo Vilasri, died. Their

---

[4]Some Thai people who keep cattle for plowing, pulling carts, or other farm work do not like to eat beef because it seems to them a violation of the friendship they have developed with their animals. This has nothing to do with Buddhism, which, although it disapproves of killing, is not opposed to meat-eating as such. For a further discussion of Buddhist attitudes toward the eating of meat, see the case of Ratana Wongsombat (earlier in this volume).

[5]Namphrik is a spiced paste made with fish and sometimes shrimp.

[6]Most of the informants at this point attributed Sukanta's lying on her side during her last illness to physical discomfort occurring when she tried to lie on her back. Mr. Tem Suvikrom, who helped me as an interpreter with numerous cases in Thailand, suggested that Sukanta's wish to keep her eyes on a Buddha image as she died may have induced her to lie on her side. Buddhists, like Hindus, attach much importance to the last thoughts before dying, believing them to be influential for the next life. For further comments on this topic, see the chapter introducing the cases in India in the first volume of this series.

[7]I obtained this date from the pagoda containing her ashes in Wat Chatupon, Chiang Mai. The pagoda inscription also gave information about the deaths of Sukanta's husband and daughter.

unmarried daughter, Tun-Keow, died on July 10, 1965. The ashes of both Sukanta's husband and her daughter were placed in the pagoda that already contained her ashes.

The Early Years of Hair Kam's Life

As already mentioned, Hair Kam's parents lived at the poverty level in the rather remote village of Tung Mah Niew. Sukanta Vilasri's sister Chansom Tachapang lived in this village, and Hair Kam was born to her daughter, Tha Kanya. Tha Kanya did not recall having any announcing dream during her pregnancy with Hair Kam. During the eighth month of the pregnancy, she fell and injured herself in the abdomen; although she was afraid she had hurt the baby, Hair Kam was born uneventfully at about the ninth month of the pregnancy.

About two months after her birth, Hair Kam became unwell and cried almost continuously. Every means of calming her failed, and eventually her family decided to ask discarnate spirits to reveal who Hair Kam had been in her previous life.[8] Such information might, it was thought, enable Hair Kam to be put into relationships with persons to whom she had been linked in her previous life, who would help her again. Chansom Tachapang was the medium for this communication, and it stated that Hair Kam should be "adopted" by another member of the family, Sa Mai. The latter was the daughter of Sa, who was a sister of Sukanta and Chansom. The communication said that Sa Mai was the reincarnation of Mae Chum, who had been the mother of Sukanta, Chansom, and Sa. It further indicated that Hair Kam was the reincarnation of Sukanta. From this it appeared, therefore, that if Sa Mai formally "adopted" Hair Kam as her daughter, they would have the same relationship that Mae Chum and Sukanta had had when they were living. Consequently, Sa Mai "adopted" Hair Kam. The communication had instructed Sa Mai to tie a coin on the wrist of Hair Kam with a thread as the symbol of her "adoption" of the child. The "adoption" was purely ceremonial and symbolic, since Hair Kam continued to live with her parents. After the ceremony of "adoption," Hair Kam's health improved and she remained well. I do not know how quickly after the "adoption" she recovered.

---

[8]The method used by the villagers of northern Thailand for trying to communicate with spirits resembles automatic writing practiced in the West; but the instruments are different. I observed a séance of this type when I was at Tung Mah Niew. Dry rice is spread in a layer about 5 millimeters thick on a large, flat wicker tray. A rather long pointed stick is attached firmly to a pot. Two persons, of whom one or both could be the medium, then hold the pot with the protruding stick over the tray of dry rice. The pot and stick dip down, under whatever mental influences and motor impulses come into play, and write the communications on the rice. After each brief message or portion thereof, participants shake the tray with the dry rice so that the letters spelled in the rice by the stick become "erased," and the rice is ready to receive another word or phrase.

The ceremonial "adoption" of Hair Kam by Sa Mai expressed the complete acceptance by members of the family of the apparent spirit communication. It implied also the family's belief that Hair Kam was Sukanta reborn just as Sa Mai was believed to be Mae Chum reborn. In view of these convictions about the previous personalities of Hair Kam and Sa Mai (as daughter and mother respectively in their previous lives), we should interpret cautiously the statement Sa Mai made to me at Tung Mah Niew to the effect that she and Hair Kam had strong positive feelings for each other; they thought of each other before other persons and they exchanged gifts. Such closeness could have derived from the roles they felt assigned to play after the mediumistic communication, whatever its provenance. On the other hand, it is also compatible with the carry-over of affections they may have had for each other in previous lives.

Hair Kam began to speak when she was one year and three months old, at which age she had not yet begun to walk. As I have mentioned, she did not talk of a previous life when living in Tung Mah Niew. She seemed rather precocious intellectually and in her other behavior. She did not play with the other children, but remained aloof from them.[9]

After the mediumistic communication convinced the family at Tung Mah Niew that Hair Kam was Sukanta reborn, Chansom Tachapang told this to her nephew Pongdet Vilasri. As already mentioned, he came out to the village several times, mainly, it seems, to visit his aunt; but according to Tha Kanya, he also came to see Hair Kam. On these visits, however, he expressed serious doubts concerning the claim that Hair Kam was his mother reborn. He said that since his mother had been dead about twenty years, the presumed identification of Hair Kam with his mother, Sukanta, must have been incorrect.[10] His skepticism did not completely extinguish his interest in Hair Kam; he continued to come out to the village, but he also maintained his disbelief that she was his mother reborn. During these years, because he and his wife were childless,

[9]The parents and other observers of the children subjects of these cases often describe the children as being more serious and "adult" in their manner, preferring the company of adults and sometimes refusing outright to play with other children. For other reports of such behavior, see the cases of Sukla Gupta, Swarnlata Mishra, Parmod Sharma (*Twenty Cases*), Kumkum Verma (first volume of this series), Disna Samarasinghe, Lalitha Abeyawardena (second volume), Suleyman Andary (third volume), Ratana Wongsombat, and Bongkuch Promsin (this volume). It is perhaps not surprising that a child who says he remembers vividly that he was married and had children of his own should find ordinary childish play of little interest. This seems especially natural when he uses the present tense and says, for example: "I *have* a wife and children."

[10]Pongdet Vilasri's reason for his skepticism provides another example of a tendency that observers of these cases easily develop—that of thinking that a common occurrence must express a rule, exceptions to which fall under suspicion of being inauthentic. It is true that in most Asian cases the interval between the death of the related previous personality and the birth of the subject is much shorter than it is in this case. But in other Asian cases of good authenticity, the interval is even longer, although such cases are admittedly rare. I have already mentioned several examples, including the case of Wijeratne, in which the interval was more than eighteen years (*Twenty Cases*).

Pongdet Vilasri invited and took to stay at his home near Chiang Mai some other children of Tung Mah Niew. None of them was happy in his home, and all returned to the village. For example, Pongdet Vilasri once brought Hair Kam's older sister to stay in his home; she remained a month, but cried every day and had to be returned to Tung Mah Niew.

When Hair Kam was a little less than five and a half years old, Pongdet Vilasri went again to Tung Mah Niew, ostensibly to see his aunt. I have already described this visit of November 13, 1966. Earlier Hair Kam herself had announced to her family that if Pongdet Vilasri came again, she would go to live with him. As I have mentioned, Hair Kam readily agreed to go to Chiang Mai with the Vilasris and said she had "wanted to live with them a long time ago." Hair Kam's family was far from eager to have her leave, but she seemed determined to go with Pongdet Vilasri, and they posed no serious objection.

Pongdet Vilasri invited Chansom Tachapang, Hair Kam's grandmother, to accompany Hair Kam during her first week at his house near Chiang Mai. At her village Hair Kam had been in the habit of sleeping with her grandmother instead of with her mother. On the first night at Pongdet Vilasri's house, however, she would not sleep with Chansom Tachapang, but insisted on sleeping with Pongdet Vilasri. She came to his room and caressed his face for about five minutes. She then lay down and went to sleep.

Not long after Hair Kam came to stay with Pongdet Vilasri and his wife, they adopted her legally. Hair Kam did not ask to return to her original family in the village of Tung Mah Niew; indeed, whenever Pongdet Vilasri jokingly proposed this, she became markedly disturbed at the suggestion.[11]

The headman of Tung Mah Niew had originally chosen the name Hair Kam for the baby. For some reason Pongdet Vilasri later wanted to change the name and began calling her "Suri Pong." But she became seriously ill after this change, and eventually Pongdet Vilasri reverted to using the original name. After this change, Hair Kam recovered her health.[12]

Statements and Recognitions Made by Hair Kam

As already mentioned, Hair Kam made no statements suggestive of memories of a previous life while she was living with her parents at Tung Mah Niew. After her move to the home of Pongdet Vilasri, she made a

[11]As will be seen, Hair Kam did later (about 1974) return to her immediate family at Tung Mah Niew.

[12]For another example of the belief in Thailand that faulty naming may lead to illness that can be cured by correcting the name, see the case of Ratana Wongsombat earlier in this volume.

The Eskimos also believe that mistakes in naming a child may lead to illness of the child.

small number of statements about the life of Sukanta, as well as a small number of recognitions.

I have listed in Table 5 the statements and recognitions attributed to Hair Kam. All of them were made within a year of Hair Kam's coming to live with Pongdet Vilasri and his wife. I have grouped the items according to topics, but they are also in approximate chronological order, except for items 7 and 8. These remarks, having to do with Hair Kam's memories of Sukanta's trading, occurred in Bangkok when Hair Kam and Pongdet Vilasri were visiting Sukanta's daughters there. I am not sure of the exact chronological order of some other items, particularly item 16.

Hair Kam's statements during and after the visit to Wat Chatupon (items 14–17) require some special comment. A rather large group accompanied Hair Kam to Wat Chatupon. It included Pongdet Vilasri, his wife, Ratana, Sukanta's two daughters Nipa Vilasri Pongpanit and Sityan Vilasri Sirisap, and Pongdet Vilasri's nephew and niece, Chiradej Vilasri and Jessada Vilasri Onla-Or. It happened, however, that only Chiradej Vilasri and Jessada Vilasri Onla-Or were present in front of the pagoda when Hair Kam made her remarks there.

Jessada Vilasri Onla-Or (whom I interviewed in 1971, about four years after the event) recalled that Hair Kam had said she had "lived" in the pagoda (item 15). She also recalled that on the way to or from Wat Chatupon they had passed the place where Sukanta had lived, and Hair Kam had commented: "This is my old house" (item 14). Jessada Vilasri Onla-Or did not, however, remember the other two remarks (items 16 and 17) made by Hair Kam at the time.

Chiradej Vilasri (also interviewed in 1971) said that he did not remember any remark made by Hair Kam at the pagoda. He did not at first even remember the visit to the wat, but eventually, after the circumstances were described to him, he said that he did remember it. He seemed reluctant to talk and even surly. Pongdet Vilasri and the Ven. Phra Kru Sri Thammakoon (a distant relative of Sukanta) independently of each other narrated to me item 16, which they said they had heard at the time from the firsthand witnesses. Pongdet Vilasri included this item in his published account of the case, written less than two months after the event. The Ven. Phra Kru Sri Thammakoon distinctly remembered Chiradej's telling him that Hair Kam had said she had stayed in the pagoda "with Mo" (Vilasri, Sukanta's husband). He attributed Chiradej Vilasri's failure to "remember" to unwillingness to talk to foreigners, an attitude sometimes found, he said, among Thai villagers.[13]

[13]This is probably the correct explanation of Chiradej's apparent lapse of memory. But I must say that I have rarely encountered any reluctance to talk with me in villages of Asia, especially Southeast Asia. I have occasionally found elderly Druse women (and less often men) in Lebanon and Syria hesitant about talking with me; some of them disapprove of discussing the Druse religion with per-

Assuming that Hair Kam actually did make the remarks attributed to her when she was standing in front of the pagoda or as she left the wat, we need to consider further whether she might have read the inscription on the pagoda. I visited and photographed the pagoda, and R. R. Boonyoros, who was interpreting for me, translated the inscription. All the facts stated by Hair Kam are on the inscription, and, if we allow that she might have read the inscription, there is nothing paranormal in her remarks. But at that time Hair Kam was only six, had not started school, and could not read. Possibly she somehow heard the older people talking about whose pagoda they were going to visit. Ratana Vilasri, however, denied this; she said they had gone to the wat for a religious ceremony with no intention of visiting Sukanta's pagoda and no mention of it beforehand. Even if Hair Kam had been able to read the inscription on the pagoda, or otherwise knew whose ashes it contained, her remarks would still have significance for the confidence they showed of her identification with Sukanta Vilasri.

Hair Kam never described the death of Sukanta or made any remarks about events that took place in the period just before it. In this she was exceptional, since the great majority of subjects of these cases have something to say about the mode of death of the previous personality or about events occurring in the last few days or weeks of the previous life.

According to Pongdet Vilasri's report of the case, he thought of Hair Kam's recognition of Sukanta's two daughters in Bangkok (item 13, Table 5) as particularly impressive. The daughters had both moved to Bangkok in 1957, about ten years before Hair Kam was taken there early in 1967. Their appearance in 1967 was unfamiliar to the villagers in Tung Mah Niew among whom Hair Kam had spent her childhood. Thus, they were not in a position to have prepared her to recognize Sukanta's daughters, even if they had wished to do so. And Pongdet Vilasri, who conceived the trip to Bangkok as a test of Hair Kam, certainly did not do so.

Hair Kam's Statements about Events Occurring after Sukanta's Death and before Her Birth. As mentioned in the preceding section, Hair Kam believed that she had spent the period between the death of Sukanta Vilasri and her own birth at the pagoda in Wat Chatupon. She said that both her husband and daughter of the previous life had also been "at" the pagoda. Since both of them died after Sukanta did, these remarks suggest—if we believe that Hair Kam did not read the inscription on the pagoda—some

sons who are not Druses. This is a residue of the days when the Druses, much persecuted by their neighbors, maintained their religion secretly. (For further information on this topic, see the Introduction to Cases in Lebanon in the third volume of this series.) With exceedingly rare exceptions, the villagers of Thailand from whom I have sought information have furnished it most cordially.

TABLE 5. *Summary of Statements and Recognitions Made by Hair Kam*

Item	Informants	Verification	Comments
1. She had been called "Mae Ta."	Ratana Vilasri, Hair Kam's adoptive mother	Pongdet Vilasri, Sukanta Vilasri's son and Hair Kam's adoptive father	Hair Kam seems never to have said directly that her name in the previous life was Sukanta. But once she said: "Mae Ta has been reborn." *Mae* means "mother," and *Ta* is a short form for "Sukanta."
2. She traded at the market.	Pongdet Vilasri	Pongdet Vilasri Sityan Vilasri Sirisap, Sukanta Vilasri's youngest daughter	
3. She left home early in the morning with empty baskets.	Pongdet Vilasri	Pongdet Vilasri	Sukanta would set off toward the market from her home early in the morning, make purchases along the way, and resell what she had bought at the market.
4. She sold chilies, eggs, and mangoes.	Pongdet Vilasri	Mae Kam Viriyasingh, friend of Sukanta Vilasri Nipa Vilasri Pongpanit, Sukanta Vilasri's second daughter	In his published report of the case, Pongdet Vilasri mentioned also that Hair Kam had said that she (in the previous life) sold tamarind leaves, which was correct. In this report he did not mention mangoes.
5. She raised pigs.	Pongdet Vilasri	Mae Kam Viriyasingh Nipa Vilasri Pongpanit	
6. She fed her pigs vegetables and a sticky yellow liquid.	Pongdet Vilasri	Pongdet Vilasri	This item is taken from the published report of Pongdet Vilasri. The "sticky yellow liquid" was a type of yeast that Sukanta obtained from a local distillery.

Informants	Verification
Pongdet Vilasri	
Sityan Vilasri Sirisap	

Item	Informants	Verification
7. She enjoyed being a trader very much.	Sityan Vilasri Sirisap	
8. Her daughter Sityan accompanied her to the market when she sold.	Sityan Vilasri Sirisap	
9. Recognition of coins saved by Sukanta Vilasri	Ratana Vilasri Pongdet Vilasri Sityan Vilasri Sirisap	

The day after coming to Pongdet Vilasri's home, Hair Kam saw some coins that Sukanta had collected and said: "Oh, do you still have these *satangs* [small coins]?" Ratana Vilasri answered: "Yes, why did you keep the satangs?" To this Hair Kam replied: "For *dana* [merit-making through charity]."

On a later occasion, when Sukanta's daughter Sityan Vilasri Sirisap was visiting Chiang Mai, Hair Kam took her by the hand and showed her the coins. She said then that the coins were old ones that she had collected long ago. It was true that some of the coins, satangs dating back to the time of World War II, were no longer in use in Thailand.

Pongdet Vilasri seems to have been a secondhand witness of this item. His published report quoted Hair Kam as saying to his wife, after leading her to a cupboard in which the coins were kept: "Do you still have these coins?" He added that Hair Kam said they were saved "to give away in charity," that is, in almsgiving. Sukanta had valued these coins highly. During air raids on Chiang

TABLE 5. (cont.)

Item	Informants	Verification	Comments
			Mai (at the time of World War II), she took them with her to the air raid shelter.
10. She had two daughters living in Bangkok.	Pongdet Vilasri	Sityan Vilasri Sirisap Nipa Vilasri Pongpanit	Hair Kam asked to be taken to Bangkok soon after she came to live with the Vilasris. Sukanta's daughters had moved to Bangkok in 1957. I have given here the oral statement Pongdet Vilasri made in 1969. In his published account of the case, he did not make this item so specific. He stated that Hair Kam had asked him several times to take her to Bangkok. (He was surprised that she even knew the word *Bangkok*; although it is the capital of Thailand, it might not be known to a child in such a remote village as Tung Mah Niew.) When he asked Hair Kam: "What for?" she replied: "To see them." He then thought of his two sisters who lived in Bangkok.
11. Mae On had been her friend.	Ratana Vilasri	Mae On Kampong, friend of Sukanta Vilasri	When she met Mae On Kampong, Hair Kam said: "We have been friends. Why did you not recognize me?" Mae On did not remember hearing Hair Kam make this remark. For a discussion of possible reasons why some informants fail to confirm a claimed recognition, see the General Introduction in the first volume of this series.

12. Recognition of place where Sukanta Vilasri was born	Pongdet Vilasri	This recognition took place at the village of Buagped. Hair Kam had asked to be taken there. At the village Hair Kam looked around and, indicating a place nearby, said: "This is where I was born." The house in which Sukanta had been born had been destroyed by that time, but Hair Kam was correct about the general area of Sukanta's birthplace. Before Pongdet Vilasri and his wife took Hair Kam to Buagped, they had not asked her why she wanted to go, and there seems no reason to believe anyone had told her that Sukanta had been born there.
13. Recognition of Sukanta's daughters at the Bangkok railway station	Pongdet Vilasri Nipa Vilasri Pongpanit Sityan Vilasri Sirisap	Pongdet Vilasri took Hair Kam to Bangkok to meet his sisters (Sukanta's daughters) Nipa Vilasri Pongpanit and Sityan Vilasri Sirisap. Hair Kam knew they were in Bangkok. At the railway station a group that included Sukanta's daughters met the party from Chiang Mai. One member of the group asked Hair Kam whom she had come to see. Hair Kam then pointed to the two daughters of Sukanta (who were in the group, but standing together) and said, as she pointed: "This one and this one." She did not give their names, but went to them, touched their hands, and said she was glad to see them. There were eight persons in the group that met them at the railway station, including four women.

TABLE 5. (cont.)

Item	Informants	Verification	Comments
14. Recognition of place where Sukanta Vilasri had lived in Chiang Mai	Jessada Vilasri Onla-Or, Sukanta Vilasri's granddaughter Sityan Vilasri Sirisap		This recognition occurred on the day Hair Kam was taken to Wat Chatupon. As the car passed the place where Sukanta had lived, which was not far from the wat, Hair Kam pointed to the area of Sukanta's house and said: "This is my house." The house inhabited by Sukanta had been taken down at the time, and so Hair Kam recognized the area, rather than a building.
15. Recognition of pagoda where ashes of Sukanta Vilasri had been placed	Jessada Vilasri Onla-Or		According to Jessada Vilasri Onla-or, Hair Kam pointed to the pagoda and said: "I used to live here." She made this remark when she was in front of the pagoda. Ratana Vilasri recalled Hair Kam as saying, as she touched the pagoda: "I was lying here a long time." I visited Wat Chatupon and saw the pagoda where the ashes of Sukanta, her husband, Mo, and her daughter Tun-Keow had been placed. Hair Kam was about six when she made this recognition. She had not yet begun school and could not have read the inscription on the pagoda. Pongdet Vilasri (a secondhand informant for this item) said that Hair Kam had tapped the pagoda, presumably for emphasis, as she

Item	Informants	Verification	Comments
			said: "Here is where I lived for a long time."
16. She had stayed in the pagoda with Mo.	Ven. Phra Kru Sri Thammakoon, a distant relative and friend of Sukanta Vilasri Pongdet Vilasri	The pagoda inscription states that Mo Vilasri died on October 1, 1945, thus about three months after Sukanta. It also states that his ashes are in the pagoda as well as those of Sukanta and their daughter Tun-Keow.	This remark refers to the deposit of ashes in the pagoda. According to Thai belief, a discarnate spirit may remain with or near the ashes of its previous physical body until it is reborn. The Ven. Phra Kru Sri Thammakoon and Pongdet Vilasri were both secondhand witnesses of this item. Pongdet Vilasri, in his published account of the case written less than two months after the event, stated that his nephew, Chiradej Vilasri, asked Hair Kam with whom she had stayed in the pagoda after the group had left the monastery. To this Hair Kam had replied: "Po Mo." (Po is the Thai word for father.) Chiradej Vilasri, however, could not remember (when I interviewed him in 1971) what Hair Kam had said during and after the visit to Wat Chatupon. See text for a possible interpretation of this discrepancy.
17. Her husband and daughter were in the same pagoda.	Pongdet Vilasri		Pongdet Vilasri was a secondhand witness of this item. He reported Hair Kam as having said at the pagoda: "Now father and daughter are left lying here."
18. Recognition of clothes worn by Sukanta	Ratana Vilasri		To test Hair Kam, the Vilasris mixed up two pieces of clothing that Sukanta had been wearing at the time of her death with other clothes. Hair Kam correctly identified the two items that had belonged to Sukanta.

apparently paranormal knowledge on her part of events taking place between the time of Sukanta's death (in 1945) and Hair Kam's visit to Wat Chatupon early in 1967.

During my first visit to Chiang Mai in 1969, some students from Chiang Mai University accompanied me and their teacher, R. R. Boonyoros, to one of my interviews with Pongdet Vilasri. They engaged Hair Kam in conversation while I took down the testimony of Pongdet Vilasri and his wife. One of the students afterward said that Hair Kam had told them that she had gone from the pagoda (in Wat Chatupon) to her new mother.

On an earlier occasion, Hair Kam made a cryptic remark to Pongdet Vilasri that is perhaps related to this topic. She said she had not wanted to be born as the daughter of Ratana Vilasri, but had had to go to be born "with her mother's daughter." It happens that Ratana Vilasri has not been able to have *any* children, and so Hair Kam, at least according to expectations based on medical grounds, could not have been born to her even if the discarnate Sukanta had wished this. Hair Kam, however, would have had no normal means of knowing that Ratana Vilasri was barren, although this would be a natural conjecture (in Thailand) from knowing that she and her husband had no children. The phrase "her mother's daughter" presumably refers to Chansom Tachapang (Hair Kam's grandmother), who was Sukanta's sister and therefore the "mother's daughter" of the previous life. If any reader thinks this regrettably indirect, I agree; but I do not see any other meaning we can attach to Hair Kam's remark. And it makes sense if we interpret the case as one of reincarnation. Since, however, Hair Kam later showed herself eager to leave her village and to go into Chiang Mai with Pongdet Vilasri and his wife, I do not understand why she said that she had not *wanted* to be born to Ratana Vilasri and had *had* to go to Tung Mah Niew.[14]

Hair Kam gave some further evidence of knowledge of events that happened after the death of Sukanta when she said that she had two daughters living in Bangkok whom she wanted to visit. These two daughters, Sityan Vilasri Sirisap and Nipa Vilasri Pongpanit, had moved to Bangkok in 1957, twelve years after Sukanta's death. They were married, but also worked as teachers in Bangkok.

Hair Kam's Behavior Related to the Previous Life

Circumstances and Manner of Hair Kam's Speaking about the Previous Life. As many other children subjects of these cases have done, Hair Kam made a

[14]I thought an error in translation might have occurred here, but, on checking the remark again in 1971, I was given the same translation. R. R. Boonyoros (who read a draft of this report) assured me that the translation was correct. He conjectured that Sukanta did not wish to be born as the daughter of her own son; and yet a maternal feeling for Pongdet Vilasri (apparently derived from the previous life) led Hair Kam to wish to be near him and live in his house.

number of her remarks about the previous life when stimulated by the sight of some object or place that had been important to the person whose life she was remembering. Examples occurred in her remarks about the coins Sukanta had collected, the place where she had lived, and the place where she had been born; and her remarks at Wat Chatupon seem to have been stimulated by seeing the pagoda where Sukanta's ashes were deposited.

According to Hair Kam's family, she did not seem more likely to talk of the previous life at one particular time of day than at others. But her adoptive mother, Ratana Vilasri, did observe that she seemed to be sadder than usual when she talked about the previous life. Ratana Vilasri gave no reason for this and does not seem to have questioned Hair Kam herself about it. So far as I could learn, Sukanta had had a happy life, and Hair Kam herself was in a favorable situation, giving and receiving much love with her adoptive parents. She was not, therefore, in the position of some of the children subjects of these cases, who remember a previous life with a longing for its material luxury, which they think they no longer enjoy. Nor was Hair Kam in the situation of some other subjects who crave to be reunited with the members of the previous family they remember; she was already with hers. Possibly the sense of being in a child's body saddened her. She had a vivid sense of still being a mature woman and the mother of Sukanta Vilasri's children, and this may have made her dislike being in the body of a small child and at least physically liable to the dominance of persons whom she regarded as her juniors. But this is only conjecture; neither Pongdet Vilasri nor his wife had ever heard Hair Kam complain of being in a small body, as some subjects of these cases have done.

Other Behavior of Hair Kam Related to the Previous Life.   The characteristic of Hair Kam most commonly mentioned by the major informants for this case was her adult, maternal attitude. Hair Kam remained aloof from other children and would rarely play with them. This behavior began in the village of Tung Mah Niew, where she lived until the age of a little less than five and a half, and it continued after she moved to Chiang Mai and was adopted by the Vilasris. She complained that other children were dirty. She did not have or want any dolls, and said that a big girl should not play with them. As she grew older, Hair Kam played with other children if they asked her, but she never took any initiative to play with them, such as by inviting other children to her home. She was quite happy if alone or with her adoptive parents. When, at the age of about five and a half, Hair Kam was visiting Sukanta Vilasri's daughters in Bangkok, one of them, Sityan Vilasri Sirisap, tried to encourage Hair Kam to play at trading with her daughter who was about Hair Kam's age. Hair Kam said: "No. It should be real trading. Do you not remember that we went together to the market to sell something?"

Toward Sukanta Vilasri's children Hair Kam showed to a considerable extent the attitudes of a mother toward her children. For example, on the same visit to Bangkok, she interrogated Sityan Vilasri Sirisap rather as a mother would when visiting a daughter, asking her: "How long have you been here [that is, in Bangkok]?" "How do you feel living here?" and "Are you not thinking of going back to Chiang Mai?" Nipa Vilasri Pongpanit said that when Hair Kam was alone with her, she behaved like Sukanta. She also noted that Hair Kam seemed to walk and sit like Sukanta.

When her visit in Bangkok ended, Hair Kam told Sityan Vilasri Sirisap: "Do not forget to pay respects on *Songkran* Day."[15] Sityan Vilasri Sirisap queried Hair Kam: "Why? What do you want me to do?" Hair Kam replied: "*Dum hua.*" This is a particular Thai custom in which children give their parents perfumed water with which the parents are to wash their hair. The ritual has become attenuated to a symbolic gesture, but it evidently retained importance for Hair Kam. Her understanding of it, and her application of it to Sityan Vilasri Sirisap, provided for the latter the most impressive evidence that Hair Kam was her mother, Sukanta, reborn.

The following April, Sukanta's daughters did journey from Bangkok to Chiang Mai for the Songkran Festival. Hair Kam received them graciously and blessed them in the manner of an older woman greeting young persons. She asked them what they had brought her as a gift, indicating a natural expectation that they had brought one to her as their mother.

When mealtime came, Hair Kam called Sukanta's daughters to eat with her. When Sityan Vilasri Sirisap was leaving Chiang Mai after her visit to Hair Kam and her family, Hair Kam asked her in a maternal way if she had gone to take leave of Suchint, Sityan's brother and Sukanta's other son. (Suchint lived in Chiang Mai, but not near the Vilasris.) She also said to Sityan: "Come to see me often, even if not to pay respects." By this remark she meant that she did not want them (Sukanta's daughters) to come to Chiang Mai only for the annual Songkran Festival.

Hair Kam's conduct with Pongdet Vilasri was, if possible, even more maternal than her behavior with Sukanta's daughters. I have already mentioned how, on her first night at his home, she caressed him and slept in the same room with him. Her attachment to him had continued just as strong up to the time of my second visit, in 1971, when she was about ten years old. If Pongdet Vilasri became ill, she would come and stroke his head or back. In the tones of a mother she would ask how he felt and

[15]The Songkran Festival, which is held in April, is an important occasion in Thailand, when children pay their respects to parents and try, if possible, to visit them. It somewhat resembles Mother's Day in the United States.

whether he had taken his medicine. Sometimes he pretended to be ill in order to test this behavior and found that she became solicitous of him. He also pretended to be taking her back to the village (Tung Mah Niew) where she was born, and this greatly troubled her.

Hair Kam was pleased when Pongdet Vilasri called her "mother." At times she called him "son." She did not insist, however, on being called "mother," and she generally called him "father." Pongdet Vilasri stated (in his written report) that once when he was leaving the house to go to work, Hair Kam pointed at him and said: "There goes my son to work." He did not hear her make this remark himself, but learned about it from his father-in-law when he returned from work later that day. When Pongdet Vilasri was away from home, Hair Kam became lonely and asked: "When is my son coming home?" Hair Kam also liked being called "Mae Ta" (a familiar way of saying "Mother Sukanta"), but she never insisted on this.[16]

Early in 1969, when Hair Kam was about seven and a half years old, Pongdet Vilasri went away on a trip. Before he left, his father-in-law tied a thread around his wrist according to the custom in Thailand by which older people wish younger ones well on a forthcoming journey. When Hair Kam saw her (adoptive) grandfather do this, she herself also tied a thread around Pongdet Vilasri's wrist. Since this custom is something older persons (usually parents) do to younger ones in Thailand, Hair Kam was clearly expressing her conviction that she was older than Pongdet Vilasri.

On another occasion Pongdet Vilasri was punishing Hair Kam for some misdemeanor, and he made a gesture as if he was going to kick her, but without doing so or actually intending to do so. At this Hair Kam said: "No. You must not do that to me, your mother. You are sinning." Her remark accorded with the important Buddhist precept against injuring one's parents.

A particularly impressive expression of Hair Kam's conviction of her identity with Sukanta occurred on the visit (already mentioned) to Wat Chatupon when she was about six years old. The Thais have a custom of offering food to monks in the name of a particular deceased person. The monk may then pour some water into a glass and place the glass on the ground in front of the pagoda containing the ashes of that person. Ordinarily, such water will not be taken by any living person, but when an offering of this kind was made for Sukanta and a glass of water placed in front of her pagoda, Hair Kam picked up the glass and drank it. In this

---

[16]For examples of subjects of these cases who did insist on being called by the name of the person whose life they remembered, see the cases of Prakash Varshnay *(Twenty Cases)*, Rabih Elawar, İsmail Altınkılıç, Cevriye Bayrı (third volume of this series), Ratana Wongsombat, and Ma Than Than Sint (this volume).

way she communicated her conviction that she was Sukanta and therefore had the right to drink the water offered to her.

Pongdet Vilasri stated that, on another occasion, Hair Kam said: "Now
that you all know I have been reborn, you ought to tell your relations
about this." He asked her whom she meant and she pointed in the direction of the village where Sukanta had been born. This remark and gesture surprised the other members of the household. On more than one
occasion Hair Kam complained that many of her (Sukanta's) friends were
still alive and did not recognize her.[17]

In view of these examples of Hair Kam's unusual behavior, one feels
no surprise at a remark of Ratana Vilasri, who said Hair Kam seemed to
have no sense of having died. She evidently considered herself still to be
exactly the person Sukanta was.

Hair Kam was unusually religious for a girl of her age in Thailand.
Chansom Tachapang told me that when she (Chansom) would pray and
do homage to a Buddha image, Hair Kam would imitate her spontaneously, quite in contrast to the other children, who had to be told to do
this. Hair Kam was also particularly fond of the folk drama called Likai.
She had a large repertoire of Likai stories that she knew and could retell
with pleasure. When she watched Likai plays, she became involved in the
drama to the point of weeping at appropriate places, again reminding observers of Sukanta, who had also wept when attending performances of
Likai plays. Hair Kam had no interest in other types of plays. One of
Sukanta's daughters, Sityan Vilasri Sirisap, once invited Hair Kam to go
with her to a moving picture show. Hair Kam said she would prefer to see
a performance of Likai, a remark Sityan said was characteristic of
Sukanta.

Sometimes Hair Kam heard her adoptive parents planning to offer
food to monks on a certain day. When the day approached, Hair Kam
would remind them of this promise of an offering, as a mother talking to
her children would do.

Hair Kam was generous toward other persons, and she was noticeably
gentle in her manner.

Hair Kam did not show any interest in household work, a trait that accorded with Sukanta's lack of interest in it; Sukanta bought and ate prepared food and did no cooking herself.

Hair Kam dressed in plain clothes and sometimes showed a preference
for the dresses worn by older women in northern Thailand. Sukanta's
daughter, Nipa Vilasri Pongpanit, remarked that Hair Kam dressed like
her mother.

---

[17]For examples of other subjects who have expected relatives or friends of the person whose life
they remembered to recognize them, see the cases of Rabih Elawar, Zouheir Chaar, İsmail
Altınkılıç (third volume of this series), and the Ven. Chaokhun Rajsuthajarn (this volume).

Hair Kam also differed from other children of her age in her food habits. She was almost a vegetarian. Up to the age of six she ate only vegetables and namphrik. She never ate meat in any form. After joining the Vilasri family, she began to eat buffalo meat, but continued to refuse beef or ox meat; and she would not eat pork or fowl. Her dislike of beef amounted to a strong aversion. Before she ate a dish, she often asked if it had beef in it. And if she began inadvertently to eat some food that contained beef and then learned about this, she would stop eating the food.

The villagers of Tung Mah Niew were poor and could afford very little meat of any kind. It was confidently expected that when Hair Kam moved to the prosperous family of Pongdet Vilasri (where all meats were eaten freely), she would begin taking meat, as do nearly all Thai children of her age whose families can afford to give it to them. That she did not do so occasioned much surprise. Sukanta's other son, Suchint, told me that in trying to evaluate the case, he was impressed by the identical food preferences—for namphrik and vegetables—of his mother and Hair Kam. He thought Hair Kam foolish not to be eating better food, meaning meat, when it was available.

Hair Kam's favorite sweet was a preparation of coconut called *khanom krok,* which had also been the favorite sweet of Sukanta Vilasri.

Hair Kam had the habit of sleeping on her side with her hand under her cheek, as had Sukanta Vilasri during her terminal illness. Most Thais sleep on their backs, and Sukanta had done so also until her final illness. (I have earlier described the possible reasons for Sukanta to have changed her sleeping habit at that time.)

According to Pongdet Vilasri, Hair Kam showed another habit characteristic of his mother, that of standing with her hands linked behind her back. He also said that both Hair Kam and Sukanta were concerned about cleanliness. (I mentioned above Hair Kam's disapproval of the dirtiness of other children.)

In Table 6 I have summarized the correspondences in the traits reported for Sukanta Vilasri and Hair Kam. The traits I have listed in Table 6 are not at all specific, individually or collectively, for elderly Thai women, or even for young Thai girls. But they impressed Hair Kam's adoptive parents as being unusual for a girl of her age, and they are all harmonious with what I could learn about the personality of Sukanta Vilasri.

Other Relevant Behavior of Hair Kam

Hair Kam's family had not observed any evidence of extrasensory perception in her, apart from her remarks and behavior related to the previous life.

TABLE 6. *Correspondences in Behavior between Hair Kam and Sukanta*

Hair Kam	Sukanta
1. Above average interest in religion	Above average interest in religion
2. Particular fondness for the folk dramas called Likai	Particular fondness for the folk dramas called Likai
3. Gentle and generous toward other persons	Gentle and generous toward other persons
4. Marked maternal attitude toward the children of Sukanta Vilasri	A devoted, self-sacrificing mother to her children
5. Lack of interest in housework	Lack of interest in housework
6. Almost a vegetarian, eating no beef and preferring to eat namphrik and vegetables	Almost a vegetarian, eating no beef and preferring to eat namphrik and vegetables
7. Favorite sweet: khanom krok	Favorite sweet: khanom krok
8. Slept on side instead of on back	Slept on side instead of on back during terminal illness
9. Habit of linking her hands behind her back	Habit of linking her hands behind her back
10. Unusually clean	Concerned about cleanliness
11. Preference for plain clothes and dresses preferred by older women	An older woman who preferred plain clothes

Comments on the Evidence of Paranormal Processes in the Case

Even if this case contained more statements and recognitions than it does, I do not think we could regard it as strong with regard to its informational elements. The two families concerned in it were related and knew each other well. We certainly cannot exclude the possibility that Hair Kam heard her maternal grandmother, Chansom Tachapang, talking about her deceased sister Sukanta. We know, moreover, that from Hair Kam's infancy, her family generally believed that she was Sukanta reborn on the strength of the "spirit communication" they thought they had received about her previous personality.

One minor informant for the case, Mae Kam Viriyasingh, suggested that because Hair Kam's parents were extremely poor, they might have invented the case so that Hair Kam would be adopted and brought up by Pongdet Vilasri. But she offered no evidence for this conjecture, which alleged fraud and seems to me improbable for the following reasons. In the first place, there was almost no case at all until after Hair Kam moved to the Vilasri home near Chiang Mai when she was about five and a half years old. This is not to say that Hair Kam had no memories before then;

but no one claimed that she had ever talked of them, if she did have some, before she went to the Vilasris' home. More important than that, however, is Hair Kam's strong identification with Sukanta, about which all the major informants agreed. Hair Kam obviously behaved as if she believed she was Sukanta. Whatever may be the correct interpretation of the case, it includes much more than invention of informational details on the part of Hair Kam's immediate family.

This strong identification of Hair Kam with Sukanta provides for me the main strength and value of the case. Hair Kam's sense of not merely having been Sukanta, but of still being her, seemed so strong that it carried conviction to other observers, some of whom, like Pongdet Vilasri, said they initially had been skeptical concerning the interpretation of the case as one of reincarnation. It may be said that, since Hair Kam's family believed she was Sukanta reborn, they imposed on her the role of being Sukanta. We cannot easily set aside the possibility that unconsciously they trained her to believe she was Sukanta because they believed it themselves, and no doubt they sometimes talked in front of Hair Kam about Sukanta and about their belief that she was Sukanta reborn. I do not, however, believe that much was made of the supposed identification of Hair Kam with Sukanta until after she had moved to live with Pongdet Vilasri and his wife. It seems likely that after the initial "spirit communication" and formal "adoption" of Hair Kam by Sa Mai, no one thought much about who Hair Kam might have been in a previous life. Poor Asian villagers have many more important things to think about.[18] It was Pongdet Vilasri who kept the subject alive by coming out to Tung Mah Niew from time to time to see Hair Kam. Until November 1966, however, he expressed doubts about the beliefs held by Hair Kam's family that she was Sukanta reborn.

Nevertheless, this belief certainly persisted in the village. We need to assess then the power of such a belief and corresponding talk, if it occurred, to impose a particular personality on a child. I think we shall have to study many cases of this kind before we can presume to answer this question confidently. As of now, however, I believe that it would take a considerable amount of drill (especially when applied unconsciously) to influence a child to the extent that the personality of Sukanta seemed to permeate that of Hair Kam. Furthermore, even supposing something like this to have happened, such a grafting of another personality could not alone account for the small number of recognitions attributed to Hair Kam, such as her recognition of Sukanta's clothes when mixed with others, or her recognition of Sukanta's two daughters when they were in a

[18]R. R. Boonyoros confirmed the probability of this conjecture from memories of his own childhood in a Thai village. When adults became convinced that a child was a particular person reborn, they left it at that, and had no interest in making a "case" in the Western sense.

group of eight people at the Bangkok railway station. In the General Introduction in the first volume of this series, I emphasized that the recognitions attributed to the subjects are (in general) the least substantial of the different types of evidence in these cases. That, however, is because the recognitions are usually poorly observed or spoiled by leading questions or other cues guiding the child. In principle, recognitions made by the subjects could provide some of the strongest evidence of paranormal processes that we could have in these cases. In the present case it is difficult for me to see how anyone close to Hair Kam, either at the village of Tung Mah Niew or in her adoptive family, could have primed her for the recognitions of Sukanta's daughters in Bangkok. If we nevertheless suppose that this actually happened, then we must believe that at the moment of the previously prepared recognitions, an also previously learned emotional response occurred. I refer to Hair Kam's embracing Sukanta's daughters after she recognized them. This incident provides an excellent example of the interplay between the informational and other behavioral features of a subject's conduct. I believe that the facts of each case must be considered together as a whole. It seems to me unreasonable, except in rare instances, to interpret informational features of the case, such as recognitions, as due, say, to extrasensory perception, and the accompanying emotional responses of the child as due to an imposed identification.

Comments on the Paucity of Hair Kam's Imaged Memories

If the case is best interpreted as one of reincarnation, we may ask ourselves why Hair Kam did not have more abundant imaged memories. But first we should narrow the question. It is true that imaged memories did not come through copiously, but what I call behavioral memories manifested quite strongly, and more so in this case than in those of many other children who have had more numerous imaged memories. I believe that separate factors may govern the "penetrance" of imaged memories and behavioral memories. If reincarnation occurs, behavioral memories probably depend on the strength of habits formed in a particular lifetime, or perhaps during several lifetimes. It is well known that older people are more rigid or, as we sometimes say, more "set in their ways" than are younger persons. And we are beginning to find that the strongest evidences of behavioral memories in the cases we have studied occur in children who remember previous lives in which the previous personalities died in mature or older adulthood. When the previous personality died in childhood or youth, his habits were more soluble, so to speak, and in such cases the subject as a general rule shows fewer unusual behavioral traits related to the previous personality.[19]

One informant for the present case, the Ven. Phra Kru Sri Thammakoon, conjectured that Hair Kam's imaged memories would have been more abundant if she had been born sooner after Sukanta's death than she was. On this point the empirical evidence needs further analysis. I have an impression that, in general, the longer the interval between the death of the previous personality and the birth of the subject, the fewer the subject's imaged memories. From the analysis of a large number of cases now under way, we may eventually construct a graph showing this relationship. If we find a general rule, however, we shall also note important exceptions to it. I have studied some cases with a short interval between death and presumed rebirth in which the subjects had few imaged memories; and I have studied others with relatively long intervals in which the subjects had abundant imaged memories.

The preservation of imaged memories seems to depend, at least in part, on the intensity of the experiences the previous personality has undergone. I believe this explains why so many of the subjects remember the previous lives of persons who died violently. (We do not yet know, however, whether the intensity of feeling usually accompanying violent deaths, or some other factor associated with them, makes lives ending in this way especially memorable.) Sukanta died naturally, although after a rather brief illness. Her life had little more remarkable to remember than her death. The cases of Tibetan *tulkus* (to which I refer briefly in the General Discussion in the third volume of this series) suggest that piety may clarify one's mind and thereby enhance memory, including the ability to remember a previous life. This quality, carried over from Sukanta's to Hair Kam's mind, may have enabled Hair Kam to remember what she did of Sukanta's life.[20]

---

[19]The case of Rajul Shah (first volume of this series), who remembered a previous life as a very young girl, illustrates this point. The absence of unusual behavior corresponding to behavior in the previous personality of her case contrasts with the abundant eccentricities displayed when they were small children by Sunil Dutt Saxena, Kumkum Verma (first volume of this series), Disna Samarasinghe (second volume), Ratana Wongsombat (this volume), and Hair Kam. All these latter subjects showed markedly unusual behavior related to the previous lives of persons who had died in middle or late adulthood. On the other hand, Veer Singh (first volume) provided an exception, because he remembered the previous life of a young Brahmin child and showed an intransigent attitude of caste superiority toward the members of his family. Ampan Petcherat (this volume) was another exception; she recalled the previous life of a boy who died at the age of about four, and yet she showed some distinctly masculine traits.

[20]For other examples of subjects who remembered the lives of devout persons who died natural deaths, see the cases of Disna Samarasinghe (second volume of this series), Ratana Wongsombat, the Ven. Chaokhun Rajsuthajarn, and the Ven. Sayadaw U Sobhana (this volume).

Hair Kam's Later Development

On the two occasions when I met Hair Kam, she impressed me as being a rather grave, dignified child who was much more mature than the average girl of her age. In 1969 she stayed somewhat away from R. R. Boonyoros and me. But in 1971 (perhaps because we were more familiar to her then, and she was older) she associated with us more. She was evidently pleased with this second visit. She had gracious manners and again a rather serious demeanor, but not a sad one. Unlike many children of her age, she did not try to draw attention to herself, although she knew our visit concerned her. She answered questions if asked directly, but otherwise remained silent, although attentive to what we were saying and doing.

In March 1971, Hair Kam was nearly ten years old and was attending school in the third class. This meant that in school she was at about the same level as other girls of her age group. R. R. Boonyoros and I thought she was a child of superior intelligence. She could read easily a passage of rather difficult Thai that R. R. Boonyoros showed her and that he said contained advanced words and phrases.

At the time of my first visit in 1969, when Hair Kam was almost eight years old, her memories were already fading. Pongdet Vilasri attributed this to her beginning school. He said: "Since she has gone to school, she has begun a new life and is forgetting the old one." At the time of my second visit, in 1971, he said Hair Kam no longer talked spontaneously about the previous life. Her family never asked her about it, and so Pongdet Vilasri was unable to say whether she had completely forgotten it or simply never spoke about it. They did not think it wise to "stir up her memories."

I have not met Hair Kam or her family since 1971. In 1974 I asked R. R. Boonyoros to visit her and her adoptive family in order to learn about her later development. He was unable to meet Hair Kam or Pongdet Vilasri; the family in the meantime moved to Pitsanulok, a city of central Thailand about halfway between Bangkok and Chiang Mai. Later in the same year, however, he learned that Hair Kam had left Pongdet Vilasri's home, dropped out of school (after completing the sixth class), and gone back to live with members of her own immediate family in Tung Mah Niew. Why Hair Kam left Pongdet Vilasri's home is not clear. An influence from members of her immediate family was conjectured, but not confirmed. Some puzzling changes in Hair Kam's behavior also developed at about the time she left the Vilasris. She apparently became much less clean, diligent, and concerned about other people than she had been before. One could suppose that she had reverted to a "village type," but this seems simplistic, and, considering that we have no recent firsthand account of either her personality or the reasons for her leaving her adoptive family, I forbear from further comment.

In 1980 R. R. Boonyoros tried to obtain later news of Hair Kam. In November he wrote me to say that he had not been able to trace her. Since 1974 she had lived with different relatives in Tung Mah Niew and in Buagped (Sukanta's native village), but had then moved away from the area of Chiang Mai, and her whereabouts were unknown to Mr. Boonyoros's informants. In the meantime, her mother (Tha Kanya) and grandmother (Chansom Tachapang) had both died.

4. The Case of Bongkuch Promsin

Summary of the Case and Its Investigation

B ONGKUCH PROMSIN WAS born in the town of Tha Tako on February
12, 1962. His parents were Pamorn Promsin and his wife, Sawayi.
Bongkuch was the tenth of their eleven children. The Promsin family
lived in the village of Don Kha, 3 kilometers from Tha Tako. Pamorn
Promsin was headmaster of a school near Don Kha. His wife had gone to
her sister's home in Tha Tako for her confinement at the time of
Bongkuch's birth.

Bongkuch's mother said that he began to speak when he was one year
and four months old. Soon after that, when he was about one year and
eight months old, he began talking about a previous life. After awakening
from sleep, he would say that he wanted to go home and add: "This is not
my home." He kept repeating that he was not at "his" home and wanted
to go to it, although he never actually tried to leave or run away from
home. When he was about two, he told his mother and father of the previous life he was remembering and said his own name had been Chamrat.
Later, he described various possessions he had owned and how he had
been murdered by two men while attending a fair in the town where he
said he had lived, Hua Tanon.

Bongkuch's parents had never heard of a person or family corresponding to his statements. His father had acquaintances in Hua Tanon, but he
did not know a family who had lost a son in the circumstances described
by Bongkuch. Eventually, word of Bongkuch's statements reached a family in Hua Tanon whose son, Chamrat Pooh Kio, had been murdered
there on April 8, 1954. In June 1964, and again in the following September, the parents of this young man went to visit Bongkuch and his family,
and they verified nearly all that Bongkuch had been saying about the life
and death of Chamrat.

The newspaper *Pim Thai* published a report of the case on March 9,
1965. Two days later, on March 11, 1965, another newspaper, *Thai Rat*,
also published a report of the case. A correspondent in Thailand sent a
copy of the first of these reports (with a translation) to me and a copy of
the second one (also with a translation) to Francis Story in Ceylon (now
Sri Lanka). This was how I learned about the case.

In 1965 three physicians of Nakhon Sawan Province, the province of the communities mentioned above, investigated the case and wrote a report of their observations. These were Dr. Sophon Nakphairaj (Director of Sawan Pracyarak Hospital, Nakhon Sawan), Dr. Suthat Thanaped, and Dr. Sompod Phanpreuk. I have made use of their informative report in my study of the case. It presented a three-page summary of the facts that they had elicited, but reached no definite conclusion as to the authenticity and interpretation of the case. The report recommended that the case be studied further.

In 1966 I began my own investigation of the case and spent three days interviewing informants. Dr. Sophon acted as interpreter for me on this occasion and again in 1969, when I returned for follow-up visits and to study further details. In 1966 Francis Story assisted in the investigation, and the Ven. Sayadaw U Sobhana, of Wat Bodharama in Nakhon Sawan, accompanied me during the investigation that year and also in 1969. In 1971 the Ven. Sayadaw U Sobhana acted as interpreter for the interviews.[1]

On November 15, 1974, I made another visit to Don Kha and had a lengthy talk with Bongkuch and his father, Pamorn Promsin. On this occasion, the Ven. U Sobhana again accompanied me from Nakhon Sawan, but Professor Kloom Vajropala acted as interpreter. On February 27, 1977, Professor Kloom and I again visited Bongkuch and his family at Don Kha. I met Bongkuch again (with Nasib Sirorasa) on March 9, 1980, in Nakhon Sawan, where he was staying in student lodgings while he studied at a school there. On the same day I had earlier met his parents at Don Kha.

Persons Interviewed during the Investigation

In Don Kha I interviewed:

Bongkuch Promsin
Pamorn Promsin, Bongkuch's father (in 1966 I interviewed him in Tha Tako; in later years I interviewed him in Don Kha)
Sawayi Promsin, Bongkuch's mother
Supit Tha, Bongkuch's older sister
Sompet, Bongkuch's older sister
Kio Lipthep, neighbor of the Promsin family

---

[1]The Ven. Sayadaw U Sobhana is a native of Burma who has been a resident of Thailand for many years. He belongs to the community of Wat Bodharama in Nakhon Sawan, where he teaches meditation. He is himself the subject of a case in this volume. In addition, he has taken a helpful interest in my investigations of other cases in central Thailand.

Ven. Maha Tong Suk Saung Bundit, abbot of Wat Don Kha
Ploi Chantri, niece of Sawayi Promsin and neighbor of the Promsin
    family

In Hua Tanon I interviewed:

Achan[2] Man Pooh Kio, Chamrat's father
Sa Aht, Chamrat's younger sister
Moun Pooh Kio, Chamrat's older stepbrother
Thien Boon Sim, Chamrat's girl friend

In Tha Tako I interviewed:

Phu Thiman, police sergeant
Learn Wong Kum Harn, police sublieutenant
Pra Yoon Jeen Moeng, police officer
Tong You Srichot, friend of the Promsin family
Bua Kob Buakrie, barber

Chamrat's mother, Siri Nuan, had died in 1965, before my investigation began. Another potentially valuable informant, Saat Chantri, Ploi
Chantri's husband and a friend of the Promsin family, had been murdered before I reached the case in 1966.

Relevant Facts of Geography and Possibilities for Normal Means of Communication between the Two Families

Tha Tako is a district town approximately 45 kilometers due east of
Nakhon Sawan, the provincial capital. (Nakhon Sawan is in central
Thailand about halfway between Bangkok and Chiang Mai.) Hua Tanon,
where Chamrat Pooh Kio lived, is about 6 kilometers west of Tha Tako
on the road toward Nakhon Sawan, and Don Kha is about 3 kilometers
east of Tha Tako. Thus, Hua Tanon and Don Kha are about 9–10 kilometers apart. The highway running through Hua Tanon divides it into
two parts: the southern section of the town is inhabited mainly by people
native to central Thailand; the northern section, chiefly by people from
northeastern Thailand and Laos. These latter residents, or their fore-
bears, migrated from northeastern Thailand, which is dry and agricul-
turally unproductive, in the hope of finding better work and living conditions in the great central valley of Thailand. They spoke Laotian
primarily, although many also spoke Thai.

---

[2] *Achan* is an honorific meaning "teacher." Mah Pooh Kio acquired this title when he was a monk in a wat, and he continued to be called by it after he disrobed and took up farming.

The two families concerned said they had not known each other before the development of the case. Both families would naturally have gone into the district town of Tha Tako for shopping and other business, but Chamrat's father, Achan Man Pooh Kio, said he had never been to the village of Don Kha before the case developed. Bongkuch's parents had both visited Hua Tanon. His father, Pamorn Promsin, had some acquaintances in Hua Tanon, but these did not include Chamrat's family, and he said that he had never heard of Chamrat's death, nor even of his family, prior to the beginning of Bongkuch's statements about a previous life. Bongkuch's mother, Sawayi Promsin, went to Hua Tanon and the area around it to collect bamboo shoots, but she said she had never been into the lane where the Pooh Kio family lived in Hua Tanon. A friend of Bongkuch's family, Tong You Srichot, who lived in Tha Tako, had heard of Chamrat's death, but she did not know him.

It is to be expected that a murder in this part of Thailand would be well known all over the district in which it occurred. One of the police officers who remembered Chamrat's murder told me that it had been much talked about in the area at the time. There were, however, about thirty to forty murders a year in the district, and as Chamrat was just a young man of eighteen, his murder probably received less attention than the average one. There were no newspapers in the area. I should mention also that an interval of almost eight years elapsed between the death of Chamrat and the birth of Bongkuch, and therefore ten years or more had passed between Chamrat's murder and Bongkuch's first talking about it. It remains possible that his parents had heard something about the murder when it occurred but had afterward forgotten this.

A niece of Sawayi Promsin, Ploi Chantri, had married Saat Chantri, a man from Hua Tanon, and they had settled in Don Kha. From Saat Chantri's information, Bongkuch's older sister Supit Tha had verified some of Bongkuch's statements about the previous life. I do not know whether she did this before or after the two families met. Unfortunately, this potentially valuable witness (Saat Chantri) was murdered—although not by an opponent of these investigations, I am sure—before I reached the case in 1966. It is possible that he might have talked about Chamrat's life and death in front of Bongkuch without his parents being aware of this; but I think this unlikely in view of the early age at which Bongkuch began talking of the previous life, an age at which he would rarely have been out of his mother's presence or at least away from her surveillance.

I was able to meet and interview Ploi Chantri in 1971. Although she was originally from Don Kha and was living there again in 1971, she had been living in Hua Tanon when Chamrat was killed. She had relatives in Hua Tanon and had known Chamrat. She had gone to view his body after the murder. But she considered herself an acquaintance rather than a friend of his. She said that she had never discussed Chamrat's murder with Bongkuch's family.

Thus, although Saat Chantri and his wife, Ploi Chantri, knew both families, and Ploi Chantri was related to Bongkuch's mother, it seems improbable that they had been the intermediaries for normal communication of information about Chamrat to Bongkuch.

In 1971 I also questioned Chamrat's older stepbrother, Moun Pooh Kio, about any acquaintance between the two families, a topic I had already discussed with his father in 1966. He stated that his family had no relatives in Don Kha and had had no connections, including mutual acquaintances, with Bongkuch's family prior to the development of the case. He said that he had not known Ploi Chantri. (I failed to ask whether he had known Saat Chantri.)

Pamorn Promsin told me that a mutual friend of his and of Chamrat's family had conveyed to him an offer on the part of Chamrat's family to sell fields and "buy Bongkuch back." (I shall discuss this offer further below.) From what Pamorn Promsin told me of his lack of acquaintance with Chamrat's family, I do not believe that he was aware, before the development of the case, that he had a friend who was also acquainted with Chamrat's family. But I did not question him specifically on this point. All he had said was that he did not know Chamrat's father and had not heard of Chamrat's murder or even of his family before the development of the case.

I believe it almost certain that there was no direct contact between the two families before the case developed. I feel sure that if Bongkuch obtained his information about Chamrat and his family normally, Bongkuch's parents were not the intermediaries for the transmission of such knowledge. I also think it unlikely that anyone else was.

The Life, Death, and Character of Chamrat Pooh Kio

Chamrat's family is of Laotian origin, but his father, Achan Man Pooh Kio, was born in Ubol Rajastani Province in eastern Thailand. He had emigrated from there to Nakhon Sawan Province in his thirties. At the time of the development of the case he had lived in Nakhon Sawan Province for about thirty years. He had spent many years in monasteries as a monk and teacher and had been an abbot of a wat for a time. Eventually he disrobed and became a farmer. He had finally settled in the village of Hua Tanon in Tha Tako District of Nakhon Sawan Province.

Achan Man Pooh Kio had had two wives (successively) when he lived in Ubol Rajastani Province, and had separated from them both. After moving to Hua Tanon he had married again. His third wife, Siri Nuan, was a native of Hua Tanon. They had four children, three sons and a daughter. The oldest was Chamrat, who was born in Hua Tanon in 1936.

Chamrat had one stepbrother, Moun Pooh Kio, about six years his senior. If he had other stepsiblings, I did not learn about them.

Chamrat's family lived in the northern section of Hua Tanon, which was predominantly inhabited by people of Laotian origin.

Chamrat was educated up to the fourth class of school and thereafter helped his father in farming and other work. According to his younger sister, Sa Aht, he had been the favorite son of the family. By the time of his death, his father had already given him one field and two cattle.

Chamrat had rather strong inclinations toward the religious life and had expressed the intention of becoming a monk. At the same time, he was interested in girls and had a girl friend, Thien Boon Sim, with whom he was friendly enough to be considered almost engaged.[3]

Chamrat had also registered for military service in the Royal Thai Army, but had not actually begun his service at the time of his death. Like other young men wishing to join the Sangha, he could not have done so until after he had completed military service.

My informants depicted Chamrat as a gentle, harmless person. He was rather timid, and his father actually applied the adjective *cowardly* to him. He did not like to cross over to the Thai side of Hua Tanon unless accompanied by Laotian friends.

Chamrat was just eighteen years old when he was murdered, for motives that remain obscure. One of the murderers, Nai Maa (who confessed during the police interrogation), had worked for the Pooh Kio family as a laborer, but had not been employed by them for two months prior to the murder. The other suspect, Nai Ban, was thought to have been a friend of Chamrat. The murderers were both Laotians. On the day of the murder, Nai Maa asked Chamrat to go with him that night to the Thai side of the village, where there was a religious fair with a presentation of the Thai folk drama, Likai. Chamrat must have thought himself safe with this Laotian companion. Somehow Chamrat and his companion (or companions) became separated from the main crowd at the fair, and he was stabbed to death. (There were apparently no witnesses to the crime.) The murderers then dragged his body to a nearby field, where they abandoned it. The murder occurred on April 9, 1954, a date I obtained from the official police records at the police station in Tha Tako.

Chamrat's sister, Sa Aht, said that Chamrat and Nai Maa had had a fight about five days before the murder. She surmised that a desire for

[3]Attractions in the apparently opposite directions of marriage and the monastic life occur commonly in Thailand, as elsewhere in the world. Theravada Buddhist monks must be completely abstinent in sexual matters, in contrast to the marriages permitted to monks in some of the northern branches of Buddhism. As I explained in the Introduction to Cases in Thailand, many young Thai men enter wats for some months or years on a trial basis to make what progress they can on the religious path. Some of them later disrobe and resume secular life.

revenge emanating from this quarrel provided the motive for the murder. Phu Thiman, one of the police officers who investigated the murder, had also heard of a quarrel between Chamrat and one of the murderers; he thought they had quarreled over a girl, although he was not positive of this. But, as I have mentioned, Chamrat must have been completely unsuspecting of the dangers of any residue from this dispute; otherwise he would not have gone with Nai Maa to the Thai side of the village to attend the fair.

The murderers took Chamrat's neck chain and wristwatch after killing him, but these thefts seem to have been afterthoughts and not a prime motive for the murder.

I did not obtain a report of an autopsy (if there was one) of Chamrat's body. The police officers and members of Chamrat's family who saw his body furnished the only details known to me about the location of his wounds. It must be remembered that these persons were all recalling events that had happened twelve years earlier in 1954. The police officers had not undressed the body and so had to judge the location of the wounds from what they could see of the exposed parts of the body or could infer from tears and stains in the murdered youth's shirt. According to the testimony I obtained, Chamrat received deep wounds in the back and one in the front of his chest, but my informants disagreed about the location of the latter wound. The wounds in the back were apparently the fatal ones. He also received wounds around the face and neck, but these were relatively minor and probably occurred when the murderers were hastily trying to get Chamrat's neck chain from his body before they fled.

Statements and Recognitions Made by Bongkuch

In Table 7 I have listed the main statements and recognitions that the informants attributed to Bongkuch. I have grouped these according to topics rather than in the chronological order of their occurrence, about which I am uncertain with regard to some items.

So far as I know, Bongkuch made all his statements about the previous life (items 1-34) before the two families met, with the following exceptions. Items 8, 19, 21, and 22 were probably first stated at the time of the first meeting or meetings between the two families. Chamrat's mother spoke in Bongkuch's presence about the clothes Chamrat was wearing when he was murdered; her remarks stimulated Bongkuch to intervene and correct her, at which time he apparently mentioned details of Chamrat's clothing (on the day of his death) for the first time (items 21 and 22). Items 13 and 33 were probably first stated after the two families had met; and Items 7 and 34 were definitely stated after they had met.

Chamrat's father and mother do not figure in the list of recognitions attributed to Bongkuch. Bongkuch was friendly to them and quickly established cordial, even affectionate, relationships with them. This behavior could be considered a kind of recognition, since when Chamrat's family first met Bongkuch, they were total strangers to him; nevertheless, no informant claimed that he specifically named them or otherwise identified them. Perhaps it was just taken for granted by all concerned that he knew who they were, and no questions were asked. Bongkuch recognized Chamrat's parents indirectly in his remark: "Clean up the niece." (See item 36, Table 7.)

In some cases of the reincarnation type, the informational features outweigh the behavioral ones in number and importance. In the present case, however, the behavioral features seem more prominent than the informational ones.[4] Bongkuch stated eight names of persons and places concerned in the previous life; but he showed little knowledge about events in the life of Chamrat. Chamrat's father questioned him about such events without success. His information about the life of Chamrat seemed almost circumscribed to Chamrat's possessions and the details of how he was murdered. On these matters, however, Bongkuch was quite authoritative, and would correct his mother or other persons if they gave information he considered false. He intervened when I was interviewing his mother in 1966.

Bongkuch's Statements about Events Occurring after Chamrat's Death and before His Birth. Several of the events included among Bongkuch's statements in Table 7 occurred during or just after Chamrat died. Bongkuch told his mother that he did not die immediately and said that he did not actually leave his body until after the murderers cut his throat, apparently during their effort to remove his neck chain hastily. He then watched (from another point of view) while the murderers carried his body into the field where it was later found near a bamboo tree.

Bongkuch said that he stayed "over the bamboo tree" for seven years. His mother asked him if he got hungry during this time, and he said that he did not.

Bongkuch told his mother further that one day (after the seven years had passed) it was raining and a bamboo shoot scratched him. He tried to go to his (Chamrat's) mother, but got lost in the market. Then he saw Bongkuch's father and returned with him (to his home) in the bus. Bongkuch's father had attended a meeting in Hua Tanon on a rainy day in the month when his wife became pregnant with Bongkuch.

---

[4]This is also true in the preceding case of this volume, that of Hair Kam Kanya. In the report of her case, I discussed one possible cause for a subject's having "stronger" behavioral memories than imaged memories: a deeply entrenched set of habits of the related previous personality.

TABLE 7. *Summary of Statements and Recognitions Made by Bongkuch*

Item	Informants	Verification	Comments
1. His name was Chamrat.	Sawayi Promsin, Bongkuch's mother Supit Tha, Bongkuch's older sister	Achan Man Pooh Kio, Chamrat's father	
2. He lived at Hua Tanon.	Sawayi Promsin Pamorn Promsin, Bongkuch's father	Achan Man Pooh Kio	I visited and talked with the Pooh Kio family in Hua Tanon.
3. His father was called Chan Man.	Pamorn Promsin	Achan Man Pooh Kio	Bongkuch, as he was just learning to speak, said "Chan," instead of "Achan." (*Achan* is an honorific meaning "teacher.") Achan Man Pooh Kio had spent many years in monasteries, where he had been a teacher, and when he left the Sangha he retained the title Achan.
4. His mother was called Siri Nuan.	Pamorn Promsin Sawayi Promsin Supit Tha	Achan Man Pooh Kio	Siri Nuan Pooh Kio died in 1965.
5. He was a Laotian.	Sawayi Promsin	Moun Pooh Kio, Chamrat's older stepbrother	Achan Man Pooh Kio was born in the eastern province of Ubol Rajastani, his forebears being originally from Laos. He had lived in Nakhon Sawan Province for thirty years, but would still be considered "Laotian," as would his children.
6. He had a girl friend called Thien.	Sawayi Promsin	Thien Boon Sim, Chamrat's girl friend	Chamrat and Thien had been courting for five months when Chamrat was killed.

Item			Comments
7. He had a black red bicycle.	Pamorn Promsin Sawayi Promsin	Achan Man Pooh Kio	On the second visit of Chamrat's mother to Bongkuch's family, she saw the green bicycle owned by Bongkuch's father and asked Bongkuch if he (meaning Chamrat) had a bicycle. Bongkuch replied: "Yes, and it is better than this one; it is black red." He used the words *black red* to mean maroon. The family still had this maroon (and red) bicycle at the time of my visit in 1966, when I saw it in Hua Tanon.
8. He had a knife in a crack in the wall.	Pamorn Promsin	Achan Man Pooh Kio	This item is not specific, since many Thai boys in villages have knives that they stick in cracks in walls when not using them.
9. He had a pencil.	Sawayi Promsin	Moun Pooh Kio	Another item that is not specific. Bongkuch saw his sister using a pencil and said that he used to use a pencil and had one at the other house.
10. He was eighteen.	Sawayi Promsin	Moun Pooh Kio	Bongkuch used the present tense in saying: "I am eighteen." Chamrat was born in 1936 and was murdered in 1954.
11. He used to buy supplies at Tha Tako.	Sawayi Promsin	Moun Pooh Kio	Another item that is not specific, since Tha Tako is the district town and the principal shopping center of the area.
12. His nickname was Bachwan.	Sawayi Promsin Kio Lipthep, neighbor of the Promsin family	Unverified	No member of Chamrat's family could verify this, although according to Moun Pooh Kio, Chamrat was sometimes called

TABLE 7. (cont.)

Item	Informants	Verification	Comments
			"Bachrat" within the family. *Bach* means "Mr." in Laotian, but I do not know what *wan* means. Nor do I know why Chamrat would have had this nickname, if he did. It may have been a private name used by his close friends and not known to his father or older stepbrother.
13. He intended to be a monk.	Sawayi Promsin	Moun Pooh Kio	Bongkuch expressed this thought obliquely by saying that he (Bongkuch) was going to be a monk in two years. This would be a reasonable thing for a young man of eighteen to say, but absurd for a boy of about two, as Bongkuch was when he began talking about the previous life. The stated interval of two years is appropriate; Chamrat had turned eighteen and registered for military service, and he could become ordained only after he had completed this, that is, in two more years. He had often expressed the intention of becoming a samanera of the Sangha. Chamrat's father had opposed his doing this because he needed him at home for the farm work.

14. His house had a metal roof.	Sawayi Promsin	I saw the galvanized iron roof of Achan Man Pooh Kio's house in Hua Tanon.	This roof had special significance for Chamrat, since he had built it himself. The house was new, and the family had only just moved into it on the day Chamrat was killed. When Bongkuch made this remark, in order to indicate clearly what he meant he pointed to the part of the roof on the Promsin house that was made of metal, the remainder being thatched.
15. He had two cows.	Sawayi Promsin	Achan Man Pooh Kio	Bongkuch's family had no cows, only a buffalo. Chamrat's father had six cattle and had given two of them to Chamrat. Although the interpreter (Dr. Sophon) here used the word *cows* in translating this item, *cattle* would have been the proper word, because one of the animals was in fact a bull. See the next two items.
16. One cow was red.	Sawayi Promsin	Achan Man Pooh Kio	This animal was one of two cattle given to Chamrat, and it was actually a bull. See the preceding and following items.
17. The red bull had been castrated.	Sawayi Promsin	Sa Aht, Chamrat's younger sister	
18. One cow was white with a black patch on the neck.	Sawayi Promsin	Incorrect	Achan Man Pooh Kio remembered the second of the cattle that he had given Chamrat as having been cream colored and without a spot. Sa Aht thought that the second one given to Chamrat had also been a bull, red

TABLE 7. (cont.)

Item	Informants	Verification	Comments
			with many white spots. Neither informant recalled a white cow with a black patch, but Sa Aht remembered that they had had a red bull with a black patch on the neck.
19. On the day he was killed, he had gone to the fair on the Thai side of the village.	Sawayi Promsin	Sa Aht	The occasion was a celebration connected with the ordination of a priest. *Fair* seems the best English translation for this event.
20. He was murdered by Bach Ban and Ai Su Maa.	Sawayi Promsin Pamorn Promsin	Achan Man Pooh Kio Learn Wong Kum Harn, police sublieutenant of Tha Tako	*Bach* is a somewhat derogatory Laotian expression for "Mr." *Ai* is a word often used in rural areas as a form of address. Here it also has a derogatory connotation and could be translated as "that guy." Pamorn Promsin observed Bongkuch beating a post and saying: "Bach Ban and Bach Maa, I am going to kill you." The police records at Tha Tako stated that Nai Maa confessed to the murder, but at his trial he was acquitted for lack of evidence. The other suspect, Nai Ban, fled and was not arrested.
21. He was wearing short khaki pants [at the time of his death].	Sawayi Promsin	Achan Man Pooh Kio Sa Aht Learn Wong Kum Harn Pra Yoon Jeen Moeng, police officer of Tha Tako	This item illustrates the sort of discrepancy that occurs in testimony about details after the passage of time, in this case after twelve years. Chamrat's father and

Item	Affirmed by	Verified by	Comments
		Phu Thiman, police sergeant of Tha Tako	one of the police officers, Phu Thiman, said that at the time of the murder Chamrat had on short pants that were dark-colored or khaki. The other two police officers said Chamrat was wearing long pants. Chamrat's sister said he owned khaki short pants, but was actually wearing white short pants when he was killed.
22. He was wearing a white short-sleeved shirt.	Sawayi Promsin	Achan Man Pooh Kio Sa Aht Phu Thiman	Discrepant testimony also occurred for this item. Achan Man Pooh Kio said Chamrat was wearing a long-sleeved shirt without the sleeves rolled up, but Sa Aht and Phu Thiman, the only one of the police officers who recalled the shirt, both said it was white and short-sleeved. Bongkuch's mother reported that Chamrat's mother said he had had on a long-sleeved green shirt, but this was probably wrong. See discussion of this item in text.
23. He was first hit on the side of the head, neck, and face, and fell down.	Sawayi Promsin	Unverified	This statement is plausible, although unverified. However, Chamrat had a wound in the back of his chest (see text for details), and so he may first have been stabbed from behind.
24. One of the murderers held his hands while the other stabbed him.	Sawayi Promsin	Unverified	See Comment for preceding item.
25. He was stabbed in the front.	Sawayi Promsin Pamorn Promsin	Sa Aht Achan Man Pooh Kio	Sawayi Promsin pointed to her own lower left chest in showing the place where Bongkuch would

TABLE 7. (cont.)

Item	Informants	Verification	Comments
			indicate he had been stabbed. In the translation of the report by Dr. Sophon and his colleagues, Bongkuch was said to have said that he was stabbed in the abdomen, and to have pointed to his abdomen as he said this. This would indicate a lower area of the body and be incorrect according to the memories of informants about the sites of the wounds on Chamrat's body. Sa Aht, Chamrat's sister, said that he had a big wound in the back and one under the breast in front. She could not recall on which side the one in the front had been. Chamrat's father said he was wounded on the right side of the chest. One of the police officers I interviewed, Pra Yoon Jeen Moeng, remembered a wound on the anterior part of the axilla, but did not recall on which side this wound was located. One informant, Kio Lipthep, an elderly neighbor of the Promsin family, gave discrepant testimony in saying that Bongkuch had claimed that he had been "shot and killed" (in the previous life). Her testimony otherwise accorded with that of Bongkuch's family,

Statement	Informant	Verification	Comments
			but I think she was clearly wrong with regard to this detail.
26. The murderers took his neck chain.	Sawayi Promsin	Achan Man Pooh Kio	Robbery was one presumed motive for the murder of Chamrat. Chamrat's neck chain and wristwatch had been removed from his body when it was found.
27. In getting off the neck chain, they cut his neck.	Sawayi Promsin	Sa Aht Phu Thiman	There were stab wounds around the mouth and neck. It seems probable that one of the murderers, after killing Chamrat, had impatiently tried to cut the neck chain with his knife and in doing so inflicted further wounds on the body around the neck.
28. The murderers could not get his ring off.	Pamorn Promsin Sawayi Promsin	Unverified	Pamorn Promsin stated this item as I have given it. However, according to Sawayi Promsin, Bongkuch said: "I had two rings; they took one off." Chamrat's father and sister said the murderers had not taken any rings. His father said there were three rings still on his son's body when it was found. The police officers remembered that there were one or two rings; quite likely they paid little attention to how many there were. Since theft was one presumed motive for the crime, it seems possible that the murderers had tried to remove the rings but, meeting resistance, had abandoned the effort.
29. They took his wristwatch.	Sawayi Promsin	Achan Man Pooh Kio	

TABLE 7. (*cont.*)

Item	Informants	Verification	Comments
30. He was killed near a bamboo tree.	Sawayi Promsin	Sawayi Promsin Phu Thiman	Sawayi Promsin verified this item from Chamrat's mother, Siri Nuan. Phu Thiman said Chamrat's body was found 20 meters from a bamboo tree. This does not verify that he was killed where the body was found. See next item.
31. After the murderers killed him, they carried his body into a field.	Sawayi Promsin	Achan Man Pooh Kio	Achan Man Pooh Kio said Chamrat's body was found in a field. Since Chamrat had been attending the fair in the village, the murderers presumably attacked him in the dark and afterward carried his body into a field, hoping to hide it or to delay discovery until they could get away. But it is also possible that Chamrat had strayed or been enticed into a field outside the village and had been murdered there.
32. He was born again eight years after being killed.	Achan Man Pooh Kio Sawayi Promsin	The actual interval between Chamrat's death and Bongkuch's birth was two months less than eight years.	To his mother, Bongkuch said he had been in a bamboo tree for seven years. (See text for Bongkuch's statements about events after Chamrat's death.) If we add nine months for Sawayi Promsin's pregnancy (which Theravada Buddhists would do, based on their belief that the reincarnating personality enters

Item			Comments
33. He was registered [for military service].	Moun Pooh Kio	Sawayi Promsin	This statement may have been made after the two families met. Men in Thailand are registered for military service at eighteen. Chamrat was eighteen and had been registered before he was killed.
34. His father had given him a rice field.	Moun Pooh Kio	Sawayi Promsin	This statement was made after the two families met. Moun Pooh Kio did not mention specifically that Chamrat's father had given him a *rice* field, but said he had given him a field.
35. Recognition of Chamrat's younger sister, Sa Aht		Pamorn Promsin Sa Aht	When Chamrat's mother came to Don Kha (with her daughter) to visit Bongkuch, she asked Bongkuch if he remembered Chamrat's sister and could give her name. Bongkuch said he did remember her, but could not give the name then. He said in Laotian that he was "thinking." His father did not understand this Laotian word. Two days later Bongkuch told his mother (his father was a secondhand witness for this part) that he remembered the girl's name. She was, he said, his younger sister, Sa Aht. Sa Aht corroborated the first part of this episode, and said that Bongkuch's mother had asked him whether he knew who she was, without indicating to him that Sa Aht was

the new body at conception), the two statements would not be discordant.

TABLE 7. (cont.)

Item	Informants	Verification	Comments
36. Recognition of Chamrat's three-year-old niece	Sawayi Promsin Achan Man Pooh Kio Supit Tha Sa Aht		Chamrat's sister. I have no record in my notes of direct testimony from Sawayi Promsin for this recognition. In 1974 Bongkuch's father repeated his earlier (1966) account of the episode, with no important variations except that he stated that Bongkuch had described Sa Aht as his *older* sister (in the previous life), instead of his younger sister. Sa Aht was in fact Chamrat's younger sister. This child, actually younger than Bongkuch, was brought with Chamrat's parents on the occasion of their first visit to Bongkuch's family. The little girl was dirty, and Bongkuch said to Chamrat's mother, Siri Nuan: "Clean up the niece." The child was in fact Chamrat's niece, but she was not born until about nine years after his death. He could not have recognized her from Chamrat's memories. He may, therefore, have identified her by inference after first recognizing the persons with whom she came. They, however, had not introduced themselves, because they wanted to study what Bongkuch was saying without

their identities being known. They did explain who they were before they left.

Bongkuch's mother said that no one had mentioned the identity of the niece before Bongkuch made his remark. Bongkuch's allusion to "the niece" of Chamrat constituted an indirect recognition by him of Chamrat's mother, Siri Nuan. Of interest is the fact that immediately after making the remark Bongkuch fell asleep. He may already have been in a drowsy state that perhaps facilitated his statements relating to the previous life.

Supit Tha corroborated the remark, but said Bongkuch made it to the niece's mother, not her grandmother. She was wrong on this detail, because the child's mother was not in the group. Sa Aht was a secondhand witness of the episode, having heard about it from her (and Chamrat's) father. Extrasensory perception is not excluded as the process whereby Bongkuch recognized the niece.

Item		Informants
37. Recognition of Chamrat's bicycle	Achan Man Pooh Kio showed Bongkuch two bicycles and asked him which one was Chamrat's. Bongkuch chose the maroon and red bicycle that had belonged to Chamrat. He said this was the one his (previous) father had bought for him (see item 7).	Achan Man Pooh Kio
38. Recognition of Chamrat's girl friend, Thien Boon Sim	Thien Boon Sim went to visit Bongkuch when he was in Hua Tanon, and when he saw her, he	Thien Boon Sim Achan Man Pooh Kio

TABLE 7. (cont.)

Item	Informants	Verification	Comments
			spontaneously called out her name. A crowd was present on this occasion, but both the informants thought that no one had indicated Thien's identity before Bongkuch spontaneously said her name. On the other hand, Dr. Sophon and his colleagues, in their report of the case, suggested that someone in the crowd had called out to Thien to come and meet Bongkuch, in which case Bongkuch might have imitated the person who had called out the name Thien; but Dr. Sophon and his colleagues did not themselves witness the meeting between Bongkuch and Thien, as did my informants.
39. Recognition of Chamrat's stepbrother, Moun Pooh Kio	Moun Pooh Kio		On the occasion of Bongkuch's second visit to Chamrat's family, he was playing with some other children (Sa Aht's) when Moun Pooh Kio walked up to the group. Someone asked Bongkuch: "Who is that?" and he said: "Older brother." So far as Moun Pooh Kio knew, no one had indicated who he was.

The above account includes three items—the body being carried into a field, the body being placed near a bamboo tree, and his (Bongkuch's) father being in Hua Tanon on a rainy day near the time of his conception—for which Bongkuch seems to have had paranormal knowledge of events that occurred after the death of Chamrat and before Bongkuch's birth, or, for that matter, before his conception.

A Possible Announcing Dream

When Sawayi Promsin was six months pregnant with Bongkuch, she had a dream in which a man dressed in white[5] appeared to her and told her she would have a boy called Bongkuch.

Apart from the prediction of the sex, there was no indication in this dream of who was being reborn, as occurs in most announcing dreams. They usually tell who the personality that is being reborn was in his previous life. In this case, the pregnant woman was given only a future name, not a previous one. And the dream almost certainly influenced the selection of the child's name by his parents.

Bongkuch's Behavior Related to the Previous Life

Circumstances and Manner of Bongkuch's Speaking about the Previous Life. Many children subjects of reincarnation cases talk spontaneously about the previous life, sometimes almost as if under internal pressure to do so, and some are heard talking to themselves about it.[6] In contrast, Bongkuch said relatively little about the previous life spontaneously. According to his father, he answered questions if asked, but did not say much about it otherwise. His gesture (mentioned in item 20, Table 7) of beating a post with a stick and saying he would kill the murderers of Chamrat was one important exception to this pattern, and there were some others.

Bongkuch was particularly likely to talk of the previous life when going to sleep or when awakening.[7] The first occasion of his speaking about the previous life occurred when (at the age of approximately one and a half

[5]For further observations and comments about the "man in white" who figures so often in claimed memories of the discarnate state in cases in Thailand, see the Introduction to Cases in Thailand and also the reports in this volume of the cases of Ampan Petcherat and the Ven. Sayadaw U Sobhana.

[6]For examples of such children, see the cases of Sukla Gupta, Wijeratne (*Twenty Cases*), Sunil Dutt Saxena, Kumkum Verma (first volume of this series), and Nasır Toksöz (third volume).

[7]For other examples of subjects who seemed to recall previous lives more at these times than at others, see the cases of Prakash Varshnay (*Twenty Cases*), Kumkum Verma (first volume of this series), Gamini Jayasena, Shamlinie Prema, Sujith Lakmal Jayaratne, Wijanama Kithsiri (second volume), Suleyman Andary (third volume), Ratana Wongsombat, and Ornuma Sua Ying Yong (this volume).

years) he awoke and said he wanted to go home. Later Bongkuch would wake up and call his mother, telling her that he had dreamed of his father and mother. When she asked which ones, he replied that he had been dreaming of his other father and mother. On another occasion, he woke up during the night and told her he was not her son, but was grown up. This episode seems to have included what I have called an "attack of adulthood," which I shall describe further below.

Bongkuch's statements about the previous life were often stimulated by his seeing something that reminded him of some object or event in it. For example, when he saw his older sister using a pencil, he said that he had used one and had owned one.

On the occasion of a visit the family paid to Chamrat's family at Hua Tanon, the Promsins noticed Bongkuch looking intently at the roof of the Pooh Kios' house. His staring at the roof impressed them so much that they asked Chamrat's parents if they could explain it. It then turned out that Chamrat himself had built the roof of the house, and the family had only just moved into it on the day of his murder. Bongkuch had earlier referred to the metal roof on the house of Chamrat's family (item 14, Table 7).

Bongkuch often used the present tense in referring to the previous life, saying, for example: "I *am* Chamrat," "I *am* eighteen years old," "I *am* a Laotian, not a Thai," and "My parents *live* in Hua Tanon." At other times he would use the past tense in referring to the fact, as he saw it, that he had been killed and reborn.

Bongkuch showed a definite assurance in the accuracy of his own memories. His mother said that on the occasion of one of the visits of Chamrat's mother to Don Kha, she (Chamrat's mother) began to comment on the clothes Chamrat had worn on the evening when he was murdered. She said he had worn long pants and a green long-sleeved shirt. Bongkuch (then about two and a half years old) was nursing at his mother's breast, but attending enough to the conversation to interrupt and correct Chamrat's mother with a firm statement about just what clothes Chamrat had been wearing when he was killed. The informants who tried to remember the clothes Chamrat wore on the evening of his murder disagreed about the details of these clothes (see items 21 and 22, Table 7), and I cannot positively assert that Bongkuch was right and Chamrat's mother (as reported by Bongkuch's mother) wrong in their memories of what Chamrat wore. But, on the whole, the consensus of other informants supported Bongkuch's memories of the clothing rather than Chamrat's mother's. (No other informant, for example, said Chamrat's shirt was green.) I mention this episode, however, not to assert that Bongkuch was necessarily right, although I think he was, but to draw attention to the complete confidence with which he made statements about the previous life.

Bongkuch talked in the most natural manner and at a very early age of what seemed to him the obvious fact of his rebirth. When he asserted that his parents were really "Chan" Man and Siri Nuan of Hua Tanon, his mother asked him why he talked like that since he had parents at Don Kha. Bongkuch replied that he "had died and been reborn." When his mother asked him why he had died, he said that he had been killed. And when she asked by whom, he said: "Bach Ban and Ai Su Maa" (items 20, Table 7).

Bongkuch's Attitude toward Chamrat's Family and Town.　Many children subjects of these cases request that their parents take them to the family they claim to have lived in before. Bongkuch showed such desires—one could say demands in his case—more strongly than do most subjects. Although he did not actually threaten to run away, he asked repeatedly to be taken to Hua Tanon. Pamorn Promsin said in 1966 that Bongkuch had said, when he was younger, that he wanted to go to stay in Hua Tanon; but in 1971 he denied that Bongkuch had expressed a wish to remain with Chamrat's family and said that he had simply wished to visit them. There is no doubt, however, about the insistent pressure exerted by Bongkuch on his parents to take him to Chamrat's family when he was between the ages of two and four.[8]

On one occasion, before Bongkuch had said much about the previous life, his father was taking him to a place called Patnampo, and they happened to pass through Hua Tanon. Bongkuch demanded to get out at Hua Tanon and cried when they continued the trip without acceding to this request. There was another struggle on the return journey, when Bongkuch again wanted to stop at Hua Tanon to see his "father and mother."

On another occasion of passing through Hua Tanon, Bongkuch showed a different attitude. His father said that he looked around and seemed to be anxious. Pamorn Promsin asked him what the trouble was and he said: "I am afraid." Bongkuch's father did not question him further and never observed such fear on other occasions when they visited Hua Tanon together.

Bongkuch's parents were slightly more prosperous than Chamrat's, and they certainly seemed to love and care for him as much as Chamrat's parents had cared for him. Nevertheless, Bongkuch seems to have had a pervasive feeling that life was better in Hua Tanon.

Various visitors who came to see Bongkuch after the reports about his

---

[8]For examples of other subjects who showed a strong desire to go to the family of a previous life, see the cases of Prakash Varshnay, Gnanatilleka Baddewithana (*Twenty Cases*), Jagdish Chandra, Veer Singh (first volume of this series), Shamlinie Prema, Gamini Jayasena, Indika Guneratne, Wijanama Kithsiri (second volume), Süleyman Zeytun, Rabih Elawar (third volume), and Ratana Wongsombat (this volume).

memories of a previous life had appeared in *Pim Thai* and *Thai Rat* gave him small sums of money. These added up to about 300 baht ($15.00) by 1965, and his parents planned to save the money to spend later on his education. In that year Chamrat's mother, Siri Nuan, died, and when Bongkuch heard this news he wanted to go immediately to Chamrat's family; he proposed to give them the entire 300 baht. It was too late to go to Hua Tanon on the evening of their hearing the news of the death, and so his parents decided to take Bongkuch there the next day. He did not sleep well that night, and the next morning he was up early, dressed and ready to go to Hua Tanon. He had not cried upon hearing the news in Don Kha; he had simply remained quiet. But in Hua Tanon he wept.

Bongkuch reacted similarly when Chamrat's father died in 1967. Chamrat's younger brother Somjit came to Don Kha with this news. (Somjit was three or four years old when Chamrat died; he and Bongkuch became good friends, and Bongkuch talked of giving Somjit the field that Chamrat's father had given to Chamrat. Bongkuch evidently thought that because he was Chamrat reborn, the field was his to dispose of.) When Bongkuch heard of Achan Man Pooh Kio's death, he cried and then got dressed to go to Hua Tanon. He asked his mother to take him there, saying he would go alone (the distance was about 9 kilometers), if she did not want to go. His mother did take him, however, and they accompanied Somjit back to Hua Tanon, where Bongkuch again wept.

By 1966, when Bongkuch was four and a half, he had stopped insisting on going to Hua Tanon, but he still wished to visit there. By 1969 he had stopped even wanting to go there to visit, which was hardly surprising since by then both Chamrat's parents had died.

Bongkuch's Attitude toward Chamrat's Murderers. Bongkuch showed an unforgiving attitude toward the murderers of Chamrat. When he was three years old, he took a stick and beat a post, saying: "I will kill you." At the same time, he cried out the names Bach Ban and Bach Maa. Bongkuch's father observed him beating a post in this fashion several times.

On another occasion, one of Bongkuch's sisters saw him sharpening a knife and asked him what he was doing. He said he was going to kill someone. The sister tried to warn him about cutting himself with the knife, and he threw it at her. This incident occurred some time—I do not know just how long—before my first interviews with the family in 1966. Although she was not the sister at whom Bongkuch threw the knife, Supit Tha had witnessed this episode, and she told me about it in 1966. She said then that he was still rather bad-tempered and easily angered.

Bongkuch's revengeful anger at Chamrat's murderers continued strong, at least until 1966. At the time of my first visit, he said he wanted a

real gun so that he could kill "those two men." He said to us: "I am going
to kill them when I grow up." He also said he was afraid they were going
to kill him.

By 1969, however, his anger had abated and his mother said that he
then talked of revenge only at night when going to sleep. (This had continued to be a time when he was most likely to talk of the previous life.)

Bongkuch's Adult Behavior.   Bongkuch had phases in which he clearly
thought of himself as an adult.[9] I do not think my phrase "attacks of
adulthood" too strong to describe his behavior on these occasions. At
such times he would say, for example, that he was eighteen, that he
wished to be shaved (after a haircut), and that he was soon going to be a
monk. On such days he would brush his teeth like an adult. (The children
of his family would not ordinarily brush their teeth.) Also at these times
he would not play with the other children, but would sit down like an
adult. When asked when he was born, he would give the year of
Chamrat's birth—1936.

The most remarkable feature of Bongkuch's adult behavior was his
sexual aggressiveness. This behavior was still prominent in 1969.
Bongkuch was then saying that he was not interested in small girls, only
big ones. He went up to grown girls and attempted to fondle their
breasts. He tried to touch girls who were going to the well. (He did not do
this with his sisters.) One girl visitor, who had planned to stay longer with
the family, left abruptly after Bongkuch disturbed her with his advances
during the night.[10] (Chamrat had been well developed in heterosexual
behavior and had had a steady girl friend [Thien Boon Sim] whom he
was courting regularly.)

Despite his tendencies to be forward with older girls, Bongkuch also
showed a shyness with them rather typical of adult Thai males. Sometimes he asked for a cloth to wear while taking a bath. (Baths are taken
publicly at the village well, and adults wear a cloth while bathing.)

Bongkuch also showed adult behavior in saying that he intended to become a monk. (This had been an unrealized wish of Chamrat.) He asked
his mother to dress him like a monk. In 1966 there was an ordination
ceremony at Wat Don Kha, and Bongkuch asked his mother for a hat
similar to those worn by the monks at such ceremonies. (His mother

---

[9]For other examples of adult behavior on the part of subjects of these cases (when they were young
children), see the cases of Sukla Gupta, Swarnlata Mishra, Parmod Sharma (*Twenty Cases*), Kumkum
Verma (first volume of this series), Disna Samarasinghe, Lalitha Abeyawardena (second volume),
Suleyman Andary (third volume), Ratana Wongsombat, and Hair Kam Kanya (this volume).

[10]The sort of intimate behavior Bongkuch showed toward older girls in actually touching them is
much more remarkable in Thailand than it would be in Europe or North America. In Thailand, at
least until recently, a boy rarely touched a girl until after they were married.

For another example of precocious sexual behavior in the subject of one of these cases, see the
report of the case of Imad Elawar (*Twenty Cases*).

bought him one.) After this he continued dressing like a monk from time to time. He did not insist on using yellow or ocher cloth such as Buddhist monks wear, but would use any colored cloth, which he would then shape into something like a monk's robe. He had done this two or three times in 1969 before my second visit.

Bongkuch's mother said that his "attacks of adulthood" were less frequent in 1969 than they had been earlier. I did not learn of any circumstances that precipitated these attacks, although, as I have already mentioned, sleep seemed to revive or intensify his memories of the previous life.

Prominent among Bongkuch's remarks were comments on the differences between his parents' house and "his own house." I believe his wish to go to Hua Tanon derived from a sense of estrangement from his present situation, both domestic and corporeal. At some times he thought of himself as a young man of eighteen who shaved, rode a bicycle, and had a girl friend; but at other times he felt that he was imprisoned in a small body[11] and was living in a strange house with the wrong parents.

Bongkuch's Laotian Behavior. Bongkuch's parents commented on two other aspects of his behavior that were unusual in his family and that they considered characteristic of Laotian rather than of Thai people.

First, he had certain dietary cravings, such as a fondness for sticky or glutinous rice, noodles, and namphrik with fermented fish.[12] These foods are not eaten much by Thais, but are popular among Laotian people. Thais usually eat "ordinary rice" rather than sticky or glutinous rice. When they do eat the latter type of rice, they take it as a dessert; but Bongkuch wanted to eat sticky rice with fermented fish or shrimp paste. Once when Bongkuch's mother reproached him for his unusual (for their family) dietary habits and asked him why he did not eat sticky rice with sugar as the other members of the family did, he said: "I am not a Thai. I am a Laotian." (His father was a secondhand informant for this remark.)

During her pregnancy with Bongkuch, Sawayi Promsin had a special craving for noodles with soup and tamarinds, which she had to have every day. Bongkuch also showed a special fondness for noodles with soup

---

[11]Some other children subjects of these cases have also seemed to remember having been "big" in a previous life. For examples, see the cases of Marta Lorenz, Parmod Sharma (*Twenty Cases*), and Rabih Elawar (third volume of this series). Bongkuch, however, experienced more than an imaged memory of being an adult; he seemed actually to have the feelings of a young adult, aged eighteen.

[12]Namphrik is prepared somewhat differently in different regions of the country. The Laotians and Thais of the northeastern part of the country particularly include fermented fish (*pla-ra*) in their namphrik, and Bongkuch's preference for this type of namphrik distinguished him from other members of his family. For a reference to another type of namphrik, see the preceding case, that of Hair Kam Kanya.

and in 1966 was asking for this dish every time he went to a town where he could have it. He had not asked for tamarinds.

Chamrat's mother had also had an unusual craving for noodles with soup and tamarinds when she was pregnant with Chamrat. Sawayi Promsin said that Chamrat's father told her about this craving on the part of his wife. Achan Man Pooh Kio gave further details of this during my interview with him. He said that his wife, when pregnant with Chamrat, had a strong craving for white noodles. He was obliged to take her to the larger town of Tha Tako, where they could obtain white noodles. Siri Nuan ate a serving of them, but then vomited; for the remainder of the pregnancy she ate only her usual food.[13]

Achan Man Pooh Kio said that Chamrat's favorite foods were noodles, sticky rice, and fermented fish. His preference for eating sticky rice with fermented fish was unusual in his family: even though its members were Laotian, they ate mostly ordinary rice. I should mention here that Chamrat's younger sister, Sa Aht, said that Chamrat liked sticky rice, but preferred ordinary rice. However, she and Chamrat's older stepbrother, Moun Pooh Kio, both confirmed Chamrat's fondness for fermented fish.

Thai villagers usually keep water (obtained from wells or caught from the runoff of rain from roofs) in large earthenware jars. From these jars they then dip out with a bowl whatever they need for drinking and washing. They wash their hands by pouring some water on them, soaping, and then rinsing by pouring more water over them. Bongkuch washed his hands by putting them into the bowl of water, a habit considered dirty (and Laotian) by his family.

Bongkuch's sister said that he also ate in a dirty way. His father explained that Bongkuch ate with his hands, that is, that he took food directly to his mouth with his hand. Other members of their family used a spoon, as do most Thais. In contrast, Chamrat's family took food to their mouths with their hands.

Bongkuch's Laotian Speech. When Bongkuch was still quite young, his mother was startled to hear him referring to certain fruits and vegetables by words that she did not use herself or even recognize. She later learned that these were Laotian words.[14] She noticed also that he had a strange

---

[13]For other examples of altered appetites of subjects' mothers during pregnancy that corresponded to tastes shown later by the subjects, see the cases of Gopal Gupta, Kumkum Verma (first volume of this series), Gamini Jayasena, Sujith Lakmal Jayaratne (second volume), and Ornuma Sua Ying Yong (this volume). The present case is unique in my experience in that the previous personality's mother had also been affected during her pregnancy by a relevant dietary craving, as was, later, the subject's mother.

[14]Laotian is a Sinitic language closely related to Thai. On the criterion of mutual intelligibility, it may be regarded as a dialect of Thai rather than a separate language, but for purposes of the present case the important point is that speakers of Laotian have an accent quite distinct from that of speakers of Thai. Some differences of vocabulary also occur, and Table 8 provides examples of these.

accent in speaking Thai words. Bongkuch's parents remembered ten of the Laotian words used by Bongkuch, and I have listed eight of these in Table 8. (I set aside two of the words mentioned when further study of these words suggested that I might have noted down the words incorrectly.)

Laotian was the language usually spoken in Chamrat's family.

For two of the pairs of words (those for *buffalo* and *dirty*), the difference between Thai and Laotian is one of pronunciation only. For three other pairs, the difference consists only in a change of prefix from *Ma* to *Bug*. However, in three pairs, the words are quite different in the two languages.

Achan Man Pooh Kio told me that he had spoken Laotian with Bongkuch, and Bongkuch's mother said she heard him speaking Laotian with Chamrat's family when they came to see him. Chamrat's sister, Sa Aht, said Bongkuch spoke Thai mixed with Laotian. She said that he could speak Laotian well and that she "never saw a Thai child speaking as Bongkuch did; he had a definite Laotian accent."

Other informants were not so sure of Bongkuch's ability to speak Laotian fluently. One older woman, Tong You Srichot, who had stayed in northeastern Thailand and knew Laotian, said that she had spoken Laotian to Bongkuch. He looked at her as if he understood, but he did

TABLE 8. *Laotian Speech Used by Bongkuch*

	English	Thai Words Used in Bongkuch's Family	Laotian Words Used by Bongkuch	Comments
1.	Mister	Nai	Bach	The Laotian word has a slightly derogatory meaning. Bongkuch used it in referring to Chamrat's murderers.
2.	Eggplant	Makeua	Bugkeua	
3.	Guava	Farang	Bugsida	
4.	Buffalo	Kwy	Kuey	
5.	Papaya	Malagor	Bughoong	
6.	Dirty	Puwan	Piean	Bongkuch used the Laotian word for *dirty* when he told Chamrat's mother to "clean up the niece." (See item 36, Table 7.)
7.	Mango	Mamuang	Bugmuang	
8.	Lemon	Manow	Bugnow	

not reply in Laotian or, for that matter, in Thai. He seems to have been shy with her.

Chamrat's older stepbrother, Moun Pooh Kio, said that on the occasion when Bongkuch recognized him at Hua Tanon (item 39, Table 7), he asked him a question in Laotian. Bongkuch replied in Laotian, but indistinctly and with only two words. Moun Pooh Kio seems not to have made any further effort to test Bongkuch's knowledge of Laotian.

In summary, there is a little evidence that Bongkuch could speak Laotian with Laotian-speaking people, but no one ever systematically tested the extent of his knowledge of this language. There is further evidence from the concordant testimony of his parents that he had a definite preference for using certain Laotian words rather than Thai words, especially for some fruits and vegetables.

Could Bongkuch have learned these Laotian words from someone in his village? This seems improbable. His family were pure Thais, as were nearly all the villagers of Don Kha. There were, however, some Laotian-speaking Thais who had come from the northeast and settled in Don Kha. Bongkuch's older sister Supit Tha asked them about Bongkuch's speech. In particular, one Nai Dee helped the family to understand what Bongkuch was saying. There was no suspicion that Bongkuch had learned Laotian from him. (Nai Dee had left Don Kha before 1966, and so I did not interview him.) In 1969 Bongkuch's mother recalled that one Laotian had spent about a month in the village in 1967, but this was long after Bongkuch had been using Laotian words. Laotian-speaking persons would come into the village to sell cloth, but they would speak Thai with their customers.

In addition to the Laotian words listed in Table 8, Bongkuch used another phrase unfamiliar in his family. When Chamrat's parents first came to meet Bongkuch in Don Kha, they were invited to have a meal and Bongkuch was asked to join them. To this suggestion he replied: "Im lau," which means "I am full" in the sense of not being hungry. Sawayi Promsin, who was my informant for this item, learned that Chamrat had used this phrase. It is Thai, but evidently was not a phrase commonly used in Bongkuch's family.

In Table 9 I have summarized the correspondences observed between the behavior of Chamrat and that of Bongkuch.

Other Relevant Behavior of Bongkuch

Bongkuch's Intellectual Development. Bongkuch started attending school in 1968 at the age of six. In March 1969, his mother said he was clever at schoolwork and had already (after five months of school) learned to read well. He seems therefore to have been intellectually precocious.

TABLE 9. *Correspondences in Behavior between Bongkuch and Chamrat*

Bongkuch	*Chamrat*
1. Favorite foods: fermented fish, noodles, glutinous rice, shrimp paste	Favorite foods: fermented fish, noodles, glutinous rice
2. Expressed intention of becoming a monk	Often expressed intention of becoming a monk
3. Precocious attraction to older girls	"Flirted" with girls and was engaged to one
4. Washed self like an adult; brushed teeth (like an adult); expressed wish to be shaved; sat like an adult	Unverified specifically, but at eighteen was presumably shaving and carrying out personal cleanliness like an adult
5. Washed hands in bowl of water instead of pouring water over hands	Unverified specifically, but this habit was generally regarded as typical of poorer Laotian people as compared with Thai people
6. Took food to his mouth with his hand in contrast to other members of his family, who used spoons	Family members took food to their mouths with hands
7. Preference for use of certain Laotian words and reported ability to speak Laotian with Laotian-speaking persons	Parents came from northeastern Thailand and ancestors were Laotian; family spoke Laotian

Dr. Sophon and his colleagues took note of Bongkuch's superior intelligence in their report of the case in 1965. They were sufficiently impressed by his intelligence to consider it a point in favor of a normal interpretation of the case. They thought that Bongkuch might have remembered with unusual clarity information that he had acquired accidentally, but normally, about Chamrat; and that he might later have mistakenly presented what he had thus learned as if it had come from memories of experiences in a previous life.

Absence of a Phobia on the Part of Bongkuch. It is worth noting that Bongkuch had no phobia of knives, as do many subjects who remember a previous life in which the previous personality was killed by a knife wound.[15] Bongkuch was so far from being afraid of knives that he actually liked to play with them.

---

[15]For an example of a subject who remembered the life of a man who was killed with a bladed weapon (in this case, a spear) and who was said to have had a phobia of knives when he was a child, see the case of Charles Porter, a Tlingit of Alaska (*Twenty Cases*). Another Tlingit subject, Derek Pitnov (*Twenty Cases*), although he had no imaged memories of a previous life, was identified as the reincarnation of a Tlingit warrior who had been killed with a spear, and he (Derek Pitnov) also had a marked phobia of bladed weapons.

Absence of Evidence of Extrasensory Perception on the Part of Bongkuch.
Bongkuch's father told me that Bongkuch had told him lottery numbers,
and he had bought tickets for the lottery on the numbers Bongkuch had
mentioned. He had sometimes won with these numbers, but most of the
time Bongkuch was wrong. Bongkuch may have used extrasensory perception in recognizing Chamrat's young niece (item 36, table 7), but he
may also have inferred who she was. In short, Bongkuch showed little or
no evidence of extrasensory perception, apart from the memories of the
previous life he claimed to remember.

Absence of Birthmarks on Bongkuch

In many cases of the reincarnation type, the subject's parents report having noticed a birthmark on the body of the subject that is said to correspond in location and appearance with a wound on the related previous
personality. Such birthmarks are especially common when the previous
personality has been killed with a bladed weapon or firearm. Bongkuch
had no such birthmarks, or if he had, his parents did not notice them.
Birthmarks occur so commonly in cases like his that their absence in a
particular case arouses curiosity as to why one did not occur.

Before I try to answer this question, I should say that possibly
Bongkuch did once have birthmarks that had, however, faded by the
time of my first visit in 1966, when he was four and a half. At that time I
found one mark about a centimeter long just above the umbilicus, but
this seems not to have been noticed by his parents before, and it was not
in the (almost certain) location of the main stab wounds received by
Chamrat, which were in the lower chest and back. I believe the mark on
the abdomen that I noticed in 1966 was probably the scar of a postnatal
disease or wound, and not a birthmark. Birthmarks often fade as the subject grows older, but many do not, just as many acquired scars fade little
or not at all; and if Bongkuch had had any significant birthmarks, I think
it unlikely that they would have faded to nothing by the age of four and a
half. I believe, therefore, that he did not have any birthmarks.

Bongkuch's lack of birthmarks might be related to the rather long interval (for Asian cases) between the death of Chamrat and the birth of
Bongkuch. In most cases with birthmarks, the interval between death and
apparent rebirth is much shorter than it was in this case; but a full
discussion of this topic should await the book on cases with birthmarks
and cogenital deformities that I plan to publish soon.

Observations of the Behavior of the Adults Concerned in the Case

Chamrat's family fully accepted Bongkuch as Chamrat reborn. They
seem to have seriously considered selling some of their land in order to

"buy Bongkuch back." I heard of this from Bongkuch's father, not Chamrat's, and he had only heard of it indirectly. To Bongkuch's family, Chamrat's family said that Bongkuch would be better off with them (that is, Bongkuch's family) because they were more prosperous. Yet it seems likely that Chamrat's family had discussed such a proposal, at least with their friends. The report of Dr. Sophon and his colleagues mentioned that they had learned of an offer of 20,000 baht ($1,000.00) made by Chamrat's parents for the "buying back" of Bongkuch. This proposal, if ever seriously intended, was never presented formally to Pamorn Promsin. He said he had heard of it only from a fellow teacher in Don Kha. He assured me without hesitation that he would have refused if Chamrat's family had ever definitely proposed to take Bongkuch from his family.

Bongkuch's parents were undoubtedly enthusiastic about the case, but I think only because of the satisfaction they derived from its support of Buddhist teachings and the attention it brought them from newspapermen and visitors from outside their area, such as those who came from Nakhon Sawan or, like myself, from much farther away.

The report of Dr. Sophon and his colleagues mentioned that Bongkuch's parents were "apt to prompt the boy's answers." I myself did not observe such behavior on their part during my visits, but I do not question that it may have occurred at other times. If it did, I think the explanation a rather simple one. The parents themselves (or other persons who engage in such prompting) have told other persons what the child has said; they know his statements—often repeated many times—by heart. Then visitors come, and the child becomes shy and blocked in their presence. The adults, fearful that the visitors will think them exaggerators or even liars, cannot bear the child's silence and so prompt him with answers they know he has already given to them many times.[16] Such conduct naturally arouses the suspicions of even neutral observers, but I do not think that it alone should be allowed to damn a case. I do not approve of any prompting, but I think I can forgive the person who does it in cases, such as this one, in which the subject becomes taciturn when confronted by many strange people. Dr. Sophon and his colleagues in their report remarked that Bongkuch "was inclined to become reticent if questioned too much." He was always civil and interested during my visits, but never loquacious or even spontaneously talkative, as are some other subjects of these cases.

[16]For other examples of prompting that appeared to have the motive mentioned here, see the cases of Mounzer Haïdar and İsmail Altınkılıç (third volume of this series). For an allegation of prompting that probably did not occur as the accuser suspected, see the case of Lalitha Abeyawardena (second volume).

Comments on the Evidence of Paranormal Processes in the Case

This case seems to me one of the stronger ones I have studied with regard to the evidence of paranormal processes. Bongkuch's father, educated above the level of the average Thai villager, was in a better position than many parents of subjects of these cases to observe and remember accurately what his son had said and done. Circumstances enabled me to talk with his wife (for most of my first interview with her) independently of her husband, and their accounts were completely concordant on all important matters and on nearly all details. Two of Bongkuch's older sisters added additional confirmatory testimony, as did their neighbor, Kio Lipthep.

I could find no evidence that Bongkuch's parents had exploited his statements or behavior in any way, whether for fame or for money. If they had made any such attempt, it had certainly not succeeded in obvious financial gain. The house they occupied in 1971 was different from, but not distinguishably better than, the one they lived in when I first visited them in 1966. Their lack of interest in the proposal of Chamrat's parents to "buy Bongkuch back" seems further evidence of their incorruptibility. I do not think we should count their pleasure in the small publicity the case received as evidence that they contrived the case in order to obtain such notice.

Apart from the foregoing facts, one would have difficulty discovering any motive for a Thai family to invent, or wish to exploit, the claim of their child to have been a Laotian, especially one with the attitudes and habits shown by Bongkuch. Because of these, his family regarded him as something of a misfit, to put it mildly, in their circle. Furthermore, since the murderers of Chamrat were still in the area, Bongkuch incurred the risk of angering them, with some danger of retaliation.[17]

The theory of cryptomnesia has little more to recommend it than that of fraud. As in some other cases, there were at least two persons, and possibly more, who knew both families before the case developed. But there is no evidence that the families concerned ever had any direct contact with each other before Bongkuch made his more important statements about the previous life. In this case also, almost ten years had elapsed between the murder of Chamrat and Bongkuch's first utterances about

---

[17]In this respect, the case resembles that of Ravi Shankar Gupta (*Twenty Cases*), who also started talking of a murder at a time when the murderers of the previous personality were still in the area where he lived. If Ravi Shankar's case and those of Ramoo and Rajoo Sharma, Puti Patra (first volume of this series), İsmail Altınkılıç, Cevriye Bayrı (third volume), and the present one are interpreted as instances of reincarnation, they seem to provide exceptions to the aphorism that "dead men tell no tales." But tales of the kind they told would not be without risk of reprisals, which their parents would hardly find welcome. I should therefore be surprised if I found a case of this type in which the subject's parents encouraged him to make his accusations widely known.

Chamrat's life. Persons who had known about Chamrat's life and death would long since have stopped talking about him, and most of them (with the exception of such interested persons as the members of his family and the police officers concerned) had probably forgotten about him altogether. Furthermore, Bongkuch began talking about the previous life when he was just beginning to speak, that is, at the age of one year and eight months. It seems unlikely that anyone could have been in the house long enough to have communicated to such a small boy the information he showed about the life and death of Chamrat without his parents knowing who this person was and what he had said in front of Bongkuch. But even if such a person had existed and had talked at length in front of Bongkuch about Chamrat, that alone could not account for the remarkable correspondences between the behavior of Bongkuch and that of Chamrat.

Bongkuch's Later Development

Bongkuch's memories had begun to fade by the time of my second visit, in 1969. His parents said he was not then speaking of the previous life spontaneously but would talk about it when questioned. His "attacks of adulthood" were diminishing in frequency but had not ceased, and his sexual aggressiveness was still prominent. His diminished interest in visiting Hua Tanon was probably due to the deaths of Chamrat's parents rather than to the fading of memories.

In March 1971, Bongkuch was in the third class of school, and his father said that he was doing "very well." He was in good general health. According to his father, he was gradually forgetting the previous life. He had stopped talking about taking revenge on Chamrat's murderers, and he rarely made any mention of wishing to become a monk. However, just ten days before my visit that year, one of Bongkuch's aunts had died, and on that occasion Bongkuch again said that he wished to become a samanera (novice) in a wat.

Chamrat's family had continued to visit Bongkuch from time to time. Two of Chamrat's brothers and his sister occasionally came to see Bongkuch in Don Kha. A month or so before my visit in 1971, Chamrat's younger brother Somjit had visited Bongkuch and brought him a gift of tomatoes.

When I saw Bongkuch in November 1974, he was more than twelve and a half years old. He continued in good health and was attending school in the sixth class.

Bongkuch's father said that he no longer spoke spontaneously about the previous life. His reluctance to do so had been strengthened by teasing on the part of his brothers and sisters, who taunted him about being a Laotian. This was not easy for Bongkuch to deny, since he still preferred the Laotian diet, such as fermented fish and glutinous rice.

Bongkuch, in answer to a direct question, said that he no longer remembered the previous life, but then went on to show that in fact he still preserved at least some memories of it. He remembered that in the previous life he had owned a bicycle, and he correctly gave the names of Chamrat's parents and their family name. He knew that Chamrat had had a girl friend, but he could not recall her name. As we continued talking, Bongkuch admitted that he sometimes thought about the previous life when he was alone. On those occasions, his thoughts went back to the previous parents. He said that he no longer thought about the death in the previous life, although he remembered being stabbed in the neck and abdomen.[18] He denied harboring any thoughts of revenge against the murderers of Chamrat.

On the occasion of this meeting, Bongkuch was friendly and polite, as he had been at our earlier ones. It seemed to me, however, that he was even more shy and reserved than I had remembered him being on these previous occasions. If he was, the difference perhaps derived from the setting of our interview in 1974. On earlier visits, I had met Bongkuch at his home; but in 1974 he and his father came to Wat Don Kha, and we met them there. At the temple, monks and some persons Bongkuch did not know were present. Although by this time he might have become used to seeing me and the Ven. Sayadaw U Sobhana, Professor Kloom Vajropala and two women who accompanied us from Nakhon Sawan were all strangers to him.

On February 27, 1977, Professor Kloom and I returned to Don Kha, where we met Bongkuch and his parents, this time once again at their home in the village. Bongkuch was then fifteen years old. He was in the first class of secondary school and was described as doing average work there. Bongkuch spoke more freely at this meeting, and I was able to ask him about the persistence of his memories of the previous life. He still remembered the names of both Chamrat's parents and of both his presumed murderers. He also recalled the place where Chamrat had died, and that he had been stabbed. He remembered that Chamrat had had a girl friend, but he still did not recall her name. He said that he had forgotten other details of the previous life.

When I asked Bongkuch how he then felt toward Chamrat's murderers, he said: "I am not angry, but not pleased [with them]." He said that

[18] In commenting on item 25, Table 7, I mentioned that Dr. Sophon and his colleagues reported Bongkuch as having said when he was much younger that he had been stabbed in the abdomen. I also pointed out that the fatal wounds on Chamrat's body were almost certainly not in his abdomen, but higher up in his back and lower chest. These discrepancies could derive from faulty memories on the part of the informants or from difficulties in translating the Thai words for parts of the body.

he sometimes still thought spontaneously about the previous life; at such times his thoughts seemed to go back particularly to Chamrat's parents, who, he said, had been good to him. He added, however, that they had been no better than his own parents.

Pamorn Promsin said that Bongkuch no longer spoke about the previous life, but his wife, Sawayi, said that Bongkuch did sometimes speak to her about it. She confirmed that Bongkuch tended to think about the previous parents; he had told her this. She also reported that a new teacher at Bongkuch's school had asked him to tell her about the previous life; he had done this and had later told his mother about the schoolteacher's interest.

I enquired about the possible persistence of Laotian habits in Bongkuch. He was still more fond of glutinous rice (used as a general food, not just as a dessert) than were other members of his family. Bongkuch said that he now wished to become a policeman when he grew up. He was not thinking of joining the Sangha permanently, but did plan to enter a wat for several months, as many young Thai men do.

Bongkuch had not visited in Hua Tanon since Chamrat's father, Achan Man Pooh Kio, had died in 1967. Chamrat's younger brother—this was presumably Somjit, but I did not record his name this time—had last visited Bongkuch two or three years earlier. In effect, then, the two families concerned in the case had gone their separate ways. We cannot therefore attribute the persistence in Bongkuch of at least some residual memories of the previous life to repeated meetings with members of Chamrat's family.[19]

When I last met Bongkuch on March 9, 1980, he was eighteen and studying in a school in Nakhon Sawan at a level approximately equivalent to the third year of an American high school. (He would have to attend one more year in order to qualify for entrance to a university.) He said that he could still remember a few details of the previous life, such as the faces of Chamrat's parents. But he had forgotten most of the memories he had had earlier and attributed this to not having given them any attention recently. His father, Pamorn Promsin (whom I met earlier on the same day at Don Kha), said that he thought Bongkuch still remembered the previous life but preferred not to talk about it and did so only rarely. I was again told that teasing by fellow students, who sometimes referred to him as "the boy with two lives," had made Bongkuch reluctant to refer to the previous life.

---

[19]For an example of a subject in whom visits to the previous family appeared to sustain memories of the previous life, see the case of Gamini Jayasena (second volume of this series). For other possible examples and a discussion of the influence of meetings between the families on the memories, see the chapter on follow-up interviews in *Twenty Cases.*

Concerning his former Laotian habits, Bongkuch said that he still enjoyed glutinous rice and namphrik with fermented fish, and Bongkuch's mother, Sawayi Promsin (who was present when we met Bongkuch), confirmed that he was still more fond of this food than were other members of the family.

5.   The Case of Pratomwan Inthanu

Introduction

THIS CASE DIFFERS from the standard reincarnation case in Asia (or other parts of the world) in that the subject recovered her apparent memories not as a young child, but as a young adult of about twenty who was meditating in a Buddhist wat when she had her experience. All the memories concerned an infant who had lived in a distant village and died at the age of about three months. The memories came to the subject rather quickly and within a short period or periods.

Some readers may object immediately on the grounds that a three-month-old infant cannot remember anything, and therefore no one else could later have memories of its life. Such an objection arises from the fact that the brain of a young infant has not completely developed and from the assumption that memories exist only in brains and nowhere else. This assumption appears to be wrong. Some adult persons have re-covered verified memories of events that occurred to them, or around them, while they were infants, or even while not yet born, although con-ceived.[1] Investigations of these cases showed that the persons recalling

[1]The following articles report instances of a person's remembering events (many verified) that occurred before his or her birth (but after conception), during or immediately after birth, or during infancy (less than eighteen months of age): A. E. H. Bernstein and R. S. Blacher, "The Recovery of a Memory from Three Months of Age," *The Psychoanalytic Study of the Child* 22(1967):156–61; N. Fodor, "Cephalic Version—Diagnosed from a Free Dream," *International Record of Medicine* 173(1960):46–50; W. Frederking, "Intoxicant Drugs (Mescaline and Lysergic Acid Diethylamide) in Psychotherapy," *Journal of Nervous and Mental Disease* 121(1955):262–66; J. A. Hadfield, "The Reli-ability of Infantile Memories," *British Journal of Medical Psychology* 35(1962):31–46; R. J. Howell, "A Verified Childhood Memory Elicited During Hypnosis," *American Journal of Clinical Hypnosis* 8(1965):141–42; D. E. R. Kelsey, "Phantasies of Birth and Prenatal Experiences Recovered from Pa-tients Undergoing Hypnoanalysis," *Journal of Mental Science* 99(1953):216–23; L. M. LeCron, "A Study of Age Regression Under Hypnosis," in *Experimental Hypnosis*, edited by L. M. LeCron (New York: Macmillan Co., 1956), pp. 155–74; L. M. LeCron, "The Uncovering of Early Memories by Ideomotor Responses to Questioning," *The International Journal of Clinical and Experimental Hypnosis* 11(1963):137–42; T. Ribot, *Diseases of Memory* (London: Kegan Paul, Trench, Trübner and Co., 1906).

I have studied several cases of this type myself, but have not published reports of any.

For an example of the recovery in later childhood of a behavioral memory (without recovery of an imaged memory) of an event happening in early infancy, see P. F. D. Seitz, "Psychocutaneous Con-ditioning During the First Two Weeks of Life," *Psychosomatic Medicine* 12(1950):187–88.

these events almost certainly had not obtained their knowledge about them later—say from hearing their parents discuss the events.

Even if we discount all cases of this type already published, we should still approach the present case with an open mind concerning different interpretations of it. Whoever boggles at the question of whether a three-month-old infant can have imaged memories probably should not have picked up this book in the first place, since its main contribution to the study of human personality lies in raising the question whether in fact memories exist only in brains or may also exist "elsewhere" and consequently persist after the destruction of the brain following death. This suggestion does not deny that brains record memories, simply that they make the only records that exist.

Summary of the Case and Its Investigation

Pratomwan Inthanu was born on October 1, 1944, at Wat Doan in the village of Ban Chang (District Tarue), which is about 15 kilometers south of the city of Nakhon Sri Thammaraj in southern Thailand. Her parents were Pien Inthanu and his wife, Prim. They had a large family of six sons and five daughters, including Pratomwan, who was their third child.

Pratomwan's father told me that she had never mentioned memories of a previous life when she was a child. She did, however, develop an interest in religion at an early age and began meditating when she was ten. At twelve she expressed a wish to become a nun. She entered Wat Doan in Ban Chang as a nun and began to learn meditation. Later, she spent a year at another wat, Wat Makam, which is about 5 kilometers from Nakhon Sri Thammaraj. When she was about nineteen she moved to Wat Thao Kot, which is in the city of Nakhon Sri Thammaraj. The abbot of Wat Thao Kot, the Ven. Thammathero, was a well-known teacher of meditation. Under him Pratomwan studied the technique of meditation known as *Vipassana*.[2]

Pratomwan had been practicing meditation at Wat Thao Kot for about five months when (in 1964) she began to experience a series of images developing in her mind somewhat like a moving picture film shown on a

[2]Vipassana meditation emphasizes the induction of an altered awareness of oneself (and ultimately of everything else) by concentrating attention on physical processes of the body, for example, breathing and walking. For accounts by Western persons who have undertaken training in Vipassana, see E. H. Shattock, *An Experiment in Mindfulness* (London: Rider and Co., 1958); M. B. Byles, *Journey into Burmese Silence* (London: George Allen and Unwin, 1962); and J. Hamilton-Merritt, *A Meditator's Diary: A Western Woman's Unique Experiences in Thailand Monasteries* (Harmondsworth, Middlesex: Penguin Books, 1979).

Colleagues of mine in Bangkok expressed skepticism about Pratomwan's claim to have recovered memories of a previous life while practicing Vipassana meditation. I am not sufficiently expert to refute their objections on theoretical grounds, but merely report that Pratomwan told me she was practicing Vipassana meditation at the time she had the upwelling in her consciousness of the memories of the previous life.

screen. The images occurred over a period of several days, on one occasion apparently coming throughout a three-hour period of meditation.[3] In these images she seemed to relive the death of a baby in a village far removed from Nakhon Sri Thammaraj. She became aware of various details concerning the illness and death of this infant and the burial of its body, including the unusual circumstance that the undertaker assigned to bury the infant's body had deposited it, not in the cemetery, but in an area outside the cemetery. Pratomwan also became aware of at least one other event in the family's life that had happened after the infant's death, namely their move from Ban Huanon, where the infant had lived and died, to another, nearby village, Ban Naa. This removal took place a year or more after the infant's death.

During her experience of seeing these images, Pratomwan saw the faces of the parents and grandmother of the baby and also heard voices telling the names of persons and places. She did not learn the name of the infant itself, but knew that it was a girl. In fact, as I learned later, the parents of this infant had not yet given it a name. It was simply called "*Loogsao*," which means "daughter" in Thai.

In August 1965, Pratomwan took advantage of an opportunity to visit the village of Ban Naa. Another nun, Neio Niyomboon (of Wat Makam), wished to visit Ban Naa to study under a monk, the Ven. Achan Puruk, who had moved there recently. So she and Pratomwan went there together, although Pratomwan did not explain to Neio Niyomboon the main reason for her wish to go to Ban Naa. Neither of them had been to this village before. After going there myself by rail, bus, and Jeep, I had no difficulty believing this; it is one of the most inaccessible places I have ever reached. In Ban Naa, Pratomwan met Samran Wang Pri Chaa and Nang Chob, who were the parents of the infant girl she claimed to have been. She also saw the undertaker of the village and recognized him by name spontaneously. Pratomwan described some of the details of what she had remembered of the infant girl's death and burial, and her knowledge of these events quickly persuaded Samran Wang Pri Chaa and his wife that she was their deceased daughter reborn. This child had died as an infant of three months in 1943 (or possibly 1944). She was their first

---

[3]These reports of dates and time intervals derive from my interview with Pratomwan in 1966. In 1969 she gave somewhat different dates and times. She said then that she had only been practicing Vipassana meditation at Wat Thao Kot for one month when she had her experience and that all the images had come to her during one session of meditation lasting about an hour. Also in 1969, she calculated that she had come to Wat Thao Kot in 1963, although she had earlier said that she had had the images of the previous life memories in 1964 and had gone to Ban Naa in August 1965. I suppose that her earlier account in 1966, being closer to the actual experience than that of 1969, is the more accurate. Some of the discrepancies about dates and other details of this case may have arisen from difficulties with translation, especially in the transposition of dates from the Thai (Buddhist) calendar to the Western calendar. An interpreter may also have confused the length of time Pratomwan had studied at Wat Thao Kot with the length of time she had actually practiced the particular meditation technique that seemed to lead to the evocation of the memory images.

child. The undertaker could not at first recall this particular burial, but afterward he did remember it and admitted (to the surprise of the infant's parents) that he had not buried its body in the cemetery, but had placed it instead in the ground near the wat. (His excuse was that he was afraid of tigers at that time of day; the cemetery was more isolated and dangerous than the wat compound.)

Unfortunately, Pratomwan did not tell a single other person about her images until she went to Ban Naa. She later explained to Neio Niyomboon that she had not told anyone else about them because, before going to Ban Naa, she had no evidence of their correctness and was afraid people would say she was talking nonsense. We therefore lack corroboration of her experience from her family or friends at or near Nakhon Sri Thammaraj. Corroboration does, however, come from Samran Wang Pri Chaa, his wife, and the village undertaker, who remembered what Pratomwan had told them about her experience when she came to Ban Naa. They also provided the verifications of the details of her memories. Samran Wang Pri Chaa, who was a schoolteacher, wrote out an account of the meeting not long after it occurred in the summer of 1965. This important document, written in Thai, was loaned to me and subsequently translated for me, so that I have been able to draw on it in preparing the present report. This document has no date, but Samran Wang Pri Chaa said he wrote it in September 1965, that is, approximately a month after Pratomwan's first visit to Ban Naa. It gives a date for the first meeting between Pratomwan and Samran Wang Pri Chaa: August 20, 1965. This date accords fairly well with that given by Pratomwan in 1966: August 10, 1965. Pratomwan said she had been in Ban Naa a few days before she actually met Samran Wang Pri Chaa.

So far as I know, this case received no outside publicity of any kind until an article about it appeared in the Thai newspaper *Pim Thai* on June 19, 1966. This article appears to have been stimulated by news concerning a visit by myself to Thailand. The Secretary of the Thailand Society for Psychical Research, several of whose members have assisted me in investigations in their country, had released a report of my research to local newspapers. The article in *Pim Thai* gave a summary account of Pratomwan's case and invited me to study it. So in August 1966, I went to Nakhon Sri Thammaraj (accompanied by Francis Story) and spent three days investigating the case. During this time, I also made a visit to Ban Naa for interviews there. In March 1969, I returned to the area, rechecked certain details, and interviewed additional informants, particularly exploring all possibilities for Pratomwan to have heard normally about the infant girl in Ban Huanon.

Subsequently, I received news about Pratomwan from time to time through the assistance of Nasib Sirorasa, who had helped me as an interpreter during my earlier investigations of the case. I also met Pratomwan again in 1974 and in 1980.

Persons Interviewed during the Investigation

In Nakhon Sri Thammaraj I interviewed:

> Mae Chee Pratomwan Inthanu
> Pien Inthanu, Pratomwan's father
> Prim Inthanu, Pratomwan's mother
> Mae Chee Neio Niyomboon, nun of Wat Makam
> Ven. Thammathero, abbot of Wat Thao Kot

At Wat Doan, Ban Chang, I interviewed:

> Mae Chee Men, nun of Wat Doan
> Mae Chee Chang, nun of Wat Doan and distant relative of Pratomwan
> Mae Chee Ian, nun of Wat Doan
> Mae Chee Amnoi, nun of Wat Doan

In Sapang Chang Hoon I interviewed:

> Kamnan Pan Wichaibit, headman of that village and the area including
>   Ban Chang

In Ban Naa I interviewed:

> Samran Wang Pri Chaa, father of the infant girl, "Loogsao"
> Nang Chob, Samran Wang Pri Chaa's wife and "Loogsao's" mother
> Thad Somvong, villager and part-time undertaker of Ban Naa
> Mae Chee Rin, nun of Wat Ban Naa

In Ban Huanon I interviewed:

> Thua Thip Somvong, Thad Somvong's mother

In addition, Nasib Sirorasa interviewed Yai Men at Wat Thao Kot on my behalf. Yai Men was a distant relative of Samran Wang Pri Chaa and a friend of Pratomwan. Nasib Sirorasa also obtained for me additional information about details through correspondence with Samran Wang Pri Chaa.

*Relevant Facts of Geography and Possibilities for Normal Means
of Communication between the Two Families*

Ban Naa is in the district of Chang Klang, about 90 kilometers northwest of Nakhon Sri Thammaraj in a particularly remote part of southern Thailand. Ban Huanon is 1 kilometer from Ban Naa. Ban Chang, where

Pratomwan was born, is about 15 kilometers south of Nakhon Sri Thammaraj.

Pratomwan and the nun who accompanied her, Neio Niyomboon, both affirmed that they had never been to Ban Naa before 1965.

Samran Wang Pri Chaa said that his wife, Nang Chob, had never left the neighboring villages of Ban Naa and Ban Huanon. I think he should have added: "Since I have known her." In 1966 Nang Chob said she had never been to Nakhon Sri Thammaraj or Ban Chang. But in 1969 I learned in talking again with her and her husband that she had once been to Nakhon Sri Thammaraj before she married. And since her marriage she had been to Nabon, the nearest town to Ban Naa (about 30 kilometers distant), but never as far as Tung Song, the railway junction for this area, which is another 20 kilometers from Nabon. Neither as a child nor later had she ever been to Wat Doan, which is 15 kilometers from Nakhon Sri Thammaraj. Nang Chob also said she did not know anyone from Wat Doan. I think that we can confidently exclude her as a normal source of information reaching Pratomwan.

The movements of her husband, Samran Wang Pri Chaa, are more difficult to assess. He taught school and also owned a small rubber plantation. He had traveled to some extent in southern Thailand. He said that he had absolutely no knowledge of Pratomwan before her visit to Ban Naa in the summer of 1965. When they met for the first time, however, they exchanged information about backgrounds and possible mutual friends or acquaintances. In this way they learned that Samran Wang Pri Chaa had relatives at Ban Chang, the village where Pratomwan had been born and where she had lived until she was about nineteen. Some of Samran Wang Pri Chaa's relatives from Ban Chang came to visit him from time to time in Ban Naa. I interviewed two of his relatives, Mae Chee Men and Mae Chee Chang, at Wat Doan. (They were then elderly nuns.) Mae Chee Men said she was a cousin of Pratomwan and Mae Chee Chang said that she was a "distant relative" of Pratomwan. Both had known Pratomwan well when she had stayed at Wat Doan. They themselves had never been to Ban Naa. They said that earlier Samran Wang Pri Chaa used to visit Wat Doan often, but later discontinued his visits. He had visited Wat Doan during a period when he lived at a place called Kow Noi, which is about 30 kilometers from Nakhon Sri Thammaraj. In 1969 Samran Wang Pri Chaa told me he remembered these visits to Ban Chang. He had lived at Kow Noi before his second marriage, to Nang Chob, which took place in (approximately) 1941. But he had not returned to Ban Chang and Wat Doan from the time of the death of the infant girl in question until after Pratomwan began talking about her memories of the previous life.

Mae Chee Chang said that she had known Samran Wang Pri Chaa, or known about him, well enough to have once learned the names of his children, although in 1969 she could no longer recall these names. She said she had never heard of the death of his infant girl before she heard about Pratomwan's memories. (She had heard about these memories both from Pratomwan herself and from Samran Wang Pri Chaa, who visited Wat Doan again during this much later period.) Samran Wang Pri Chaa was a cousin of the Ven. Achan Puruk, the monk who was the object of Neio Niyomboon's visit to Wat Ban Naa when Pratomwan accompanied her to verify her memories. But Samran Wang Pri Chaa said that neither he nor his wife had ever had any contact with the Ven. Achan Puruk before the development of the case. It seems that the Ven. Achan Puruk had moved to Ban Naa in (about) the summer of 1964, a year before Neio Niyomboon (who was also his cousin) and Pratomwan went there to visit him.

Mae Chee Chang had a sister, Yai Men, with whom Pratomwan had once stayed. Pratomwan said (in 1965) that she also knew one Nang Yad, who, she thought, was Yai Men's daughter. Samran Wang Pri Chaa told Pratomwan (and mentioned in his report) that Nang Yad often came to see him. However, Pratomwan appears to have made a mistake here, because Yai Men had no daughter called Yad. I did not interview either Yai Men or Nang Yad, but in 1972 Nasib Sirorasa sought out Yai Men and interviewed her at Wat Doan, where she was then living.

Yai Men recalled having met Samran Wang Pri Chaa once at Wat Doan, when he had come there for the funeral of her oldest sister. Nasib Sirorasa did not learn the date of this meeting, but Yai Men told her that she and Samran Wang Pri Chaa had not talked about his dead baby. In fact, she had known nothing about this baby from any source before Pratomwan had her memories.

Samran Wang Pri Chaa had another relative, the Ven. Than Wan, who was a monk and abbot of Wat Doan. The Ven. Than Wan visited Ban Naa from time to time, and he had gone there twice in the five years between 1964 and 1969. I did not interview him in 1966 or 1969, and unfortunately, by the time it occurred to me that he might have been an important witness in the case, he had died. Samran Wang Pri Chaa, however, firmly denied that he had ever discussed the infant girl with him or with Mae Chee Chang prior to the development of the case. Nor did he know of anyone who could conceivably have been an intermediary for the normal transmission to Pratomwan of information about the infant girl.

As mentioned earlier, Neio Niyomboon said that she had never been to Ban Naa before the visit she made there with Pratomwan in 1965. And Samran Wang Pri Chaa said he had never met Neio Niyomboon before his meeting with her and Pratomwan at the time of their visit.

When I interviewed (in 1969) Pratomwan's father, Pien Inthanu, about acquaintance between the two families concerned, he said that he and

Samran Wang Pri Chaa were related, but that he had never known him personally until after Pratomwan had had her experience of apparently remembering a previous life. He had never heard of the death of the infant girl concerned and had never been to Ban Naa until after Pratomwan had been there to verify her memories. He accompanied Pratomwan to Ban Naa on a later visit there. I had earlier, in 1966, interviewed Pratomwan's mother, Prim Inthanu, on the same (and other) points. She had never been to Ban Naa or its district, or known anyone from there. She did not think her husband knew anyone from there either.

In summary, I could learn of no direct contact, before the case developed, between the immediate families concerned. And although it turned out that there were some (mostly distant) relationships between the two families, the testimony indicated that they had remained ignorant of each other and apparently did not even know they were distantly related until the case developed. In the written statement that I mentioned, Samran Wang Pri Chaa gave a detailed account of the conversation he had with Pratomwan at his house when they first met. This clearly shows that neither had known before this meeting that they had relatives in common. When Samran Wang Pri Chaa learned about the relationship, he characterized the persons known to Pratomwan at Ban Chang and Wat Doan as "close" relatives, but these persons, when I talked with them, regarded him as a "distant" relative.

In the end, I found no one with *both* knowledge of the long-deceased infant girl *and* acquaintance with Pratomwan who could have acted as the normal intermediary to her of the information about the girl that she obtained during meditation.

Statements and a Recognition Made by Pratomwan

In Table 10 I have listed the more important items that Pratomwan told me had emerged as memories during her meditation experience in 1964.

As I mentioned, no one in her family or at her wat corroborated what she said she had remembered before her visit to Ban Naa. However, Samran Wang Pri Chaa's written statement, as well as his testimony in 1966 and 1969 and that of other informants at Ban Naa, provide considerable corroboration that she had in fact learned about these details before she went to Ban Naa for verifications. No one corroborated the statements in Table 10 that show Pratomwan as the sole informant. Pratomwan made all but three of them to me in 1966, that is, about two years after her meditation experience in which she said she had learned the details of the previous life and about eighteen months after her first visit to the previous family. One must remember that in the interval she

TABLE 10. *Summary of Statements and a Recognition Made by Pratomwan*

Item	Informants	Verification	Comments
1. Her father was Samran Wang Pri Chaa.	Samran Wang Pri Chaa,* father of "Loogsao," a deceased infant girl Pratomwan (1966)	Samran Wang Pri Chaa	Samran Wang Pri Chaa did not state that Pratomwan had given his name, but simply that she had told him he was her father. According to Neio Niyomboon, whom Pratomwan accompanied to Ban Naa, Pratomwan began to make inquiries about Samran Wang Pri Chaa after they reached Ban Naa, and she expressed a wish to meet him. She evidently knew the name of the man she wanted to meet.
2. Her father was tall and thin.	Pratomwan (1966)	I verified this myself when I met Samran Wang Pri Chaa in 1966 and 1969.	
3. Her father was a teacher.	Pratomwan (1966)	Samran Wang Pri Chaa	
4. Her father had a hole in a tooth.	Pratomwan (1966)	I verified this myself in 1969. Samran Wang Pri Chaa had a rather prominent gap between his upper incisor teeth.	In reviewing this item in 1969, Pratomwan said the previous father had "one tooth that was rotten." This could have referred to Samran Wang Pri Chaa's having a tooth out of position. A blow he received when boxing at the age of about eighteen had displaced it. I think, however, that Pratomwan's statements of both occasions more likely refer to the definite gap between and slight deformity of Samran Wang Pri Chaa's upper incisor teeth, which

Item	Informants	Verification	Comments
			I saw and sketched myself in 1966. A slip in translation here might have led to "a gap between the teeth" being rendered in English as "a hole in a tooth."
5. Her father was a gambler.	Samran Wang Pri Chaa* (1966) Pratomwan (1966)	Samran Wang Pri Chaa	Samran Wang Pri Chaa had been inclined to gamble at the time the infant girl was living.
6. Her mother was Nang Chob.	Samran Wang Pri Chaa* (1966) Pratomwan (1966)	Samran Wang Pri Chaa Nang Chob, Samran Wang Pri Chaa's wife and "Loogsao's" mother	Samran Wang Pri Chaa did not state that Pratomwan had given Nang Chob's name, but that she had pointed to her and said she was her mother.
7. Nang Chob was small, fat, and fair.	Pratomwan (1966)	I met Nang Chob in 1969.	*Plump* describes her more fairly than *fat*. She was short and fair.
8. Nang Chob had a scar on the right side of her face.	Pratomwan (1966)	When I met Nang Chob, I saw that she had a prominent scar on the right side of her face.	Nang Chob had acquired this scar at the age of about five years.
9. Her grandmother was called Khling.	Pratomwan (1966)	Samran Wang Pri Chaa Thad Somvong, villager and part-time undertaker of Ban Naa	Samran Wang Pri Chaa's mother's name was Nang Khling.
10. She herself had no given name and was just called "Loogsao."	Pratomwan (1966)	Samran Wang Pri Chaa	*Loogsao* in Thai means simply "daughter" and could be applied to any still unnamed infant girl. Samran Wang Pri Chaa said that the baby had not been named at

Items marked with an asterisk(*) are included in Samran Wang Pri Chaa's written report of his meeting with Pratomwan when he questioned her about her memories of the previous life.

TABLE 10. (cont.)

Item	Informants	Verification	Comments
			the time of its death, and that he and his wife had called her "Loogsao."
11. She was the only child of the family.	Pratomwan (1966)	Samran Wang Pri Chaa	Six children were born to Samran Wang Pri Chaa and Nang Chob, but not until *after* the death of the infant girl. She was their firstborn child.
12. She was born at Ban Huanon.	Samran Wang Pri Chaa* Pratomwan (1966)	Samran Wang Pri Chaa Nang Chob	Although the baby was born and died in Ban Huanon, the family subsequently moved to Ban Naa, where I met them.
13. The house at Ban Huanon was in the jungle.	Pratomwan (1966)	I verified this myself in 1969, when I was shown the location where this house had formerly existed.	The house had been within 100 meters of the jungle, but not exactly in it. This and the following four items refer to the house where the infant girl was born and died.
14. The house at Ban Huanon was to the north of Ban Naa.	Samran Wang Pri Chaa	Incorrect	Ban Huanon is southeast, not north, of Ban Naa.
15. The house was raised up.	Pratomwan (1966)	Samran Wang Pri Chaa	Houses in or near the jungle are elevated on posts as a protection against tigers.
16. The house was made of bamboo.	Pratomwan (1966)	Samran Wang Pri Chaa	The floors of the house were of wood, but the walls were of bamboo.

17. The house had one story.	Pratomwan (1966)	Samran Wang Pri Chaa	
18. Her father had a musical instrument.	Samran Wang Pri Chaa* Pratomwan (1969)	Samran Wang Pri Chaa I saw the instrument in 1969.	This instrument was a type of xylophone. Samran Wang Pri Chaa said that Pratomwan had specified that the instrument was a bamboo xylophone. When Pratomwan made this remark, she was in the front room of the house and the xylophone was in the back room, out of her sight. Pratomwan remembered that Samran Wang Pri Chaa "loved" the instrument and had played on it to soothe the infant girl. I have been told that xylophones are rather uncommon in the private homes of the villagers in southern Thailand. This item, therefore, seems to me more specific than some others.
19. Her father had planned to take another wife.	Samran Wang Pri Chaa* Pratomwan (1966)	Samran Wang Pri Chaa	Samran Wang Pri Chaa had been thinking of taking a second wife at the time of the infant's death, but had not actually done so. He said he wanted someone to take care of his mother, Nang Khling. Second (simultaneous) wives are allowed among Buddhists of Thailand, and the first wife is usually much more accepting of the situation than her counterparts in the West would be.
20. She [the baby] was angry about this, and this was the reason she died.	Samran Wang Pri Chaa	Unverified	So far as Nang Chob could tell from the behavior of her infant daughter, she was *not* unhappy as a baby, and if we allow that a

TABLE 10. (cont.)

mother can tell much about how her baby feels, we should score this item as "incorrect," not merely "unverified."

Item	Informants	Verification	Comments
21. Her parents quarreled.	Pratomwan (1966)	Incorrect	Samran Wang Pri Chaa denied that he and Nang Chob had quarreled. Was this a projection of the baby's attitude onto the mother?
22. She died at the house in Ban Huanon.	Samran Wang Pri Chaa	Samran Wang Pri Chaa Nang Chob	
23. She was three months old when she died.	Samran Wang Pri Chaa* Pratomwan (1966)	Samran Wang Pri Chaa	Samran Wang Pri Chaa's written report quotes Pratomwan as saying she was three to four months old when she died.
24. She was ill one or two days before dying.	Pratomwan (1966)	Samran Wang Pri Chaa	Nang Chob said the baby had been ill three days before dying.
25. She died in her mother's arms.	Samran Wang Pri Chaa* Pratomwan (1966)	Nang Chob Samran Wang Pri Chaa	Since Samran Wang Pri Chaa was away from the house when the baby actually died, he was a secondhand witness for verification of this item. (See the following item.) Pratomwan added some incorrect details about the direction in which the baby was held in her mother's arms when she died.

Item	Informants	Verification	Comments
26. Her father was away from the house obtaining medicine from the hill when she died.	Samran Wang Pri Chaa (1966) Pratomwan (1966)	Samran Wang Pri Chaa	Samran Wang Pri Chaa had gone out to collect an herbal medicine to give the ill baby.
27. She died at night.	Samran Wang Pri Chaa* (1966)	Samran Wang Pri Chaa	
28. The undertaker, Thad, was called.	Samran Wang Pri Chaa* (1966) Pratomwan (1966)	Thad Somvong Samran Wang Pri Chaa	Pratomwan said she recalled both names of the undertaker, Thad Somvong. Samran Wang Pri Chaa said she referred to him as "Uncle Thad," but this may have been his own way of thinking about Thad Somvong. (See item 30.)
29. He was not a full-time [professional] undertaker.	Pratomwan (1966)	Thad Somvong	Thad Somvong was just a part-time undertaker who buried bodies to help neighbors and other villagers.
30. The undertaker was a cousin.	Pratomwan (1966)	Incorrect	When I was in Ban Naa and Ban Huanon, I noticed that Thad Somvong was referred to as "Uncle Thad." Samran Wang Pri Chaa referred to him thus. In Asian villages such usage does not necessarily imply a biological or marital relationship, but it does mean a sense of personal closeness to the person referred to.
31. A mattress was given to Thad Somvong.	Pratomwan (1966)	Nang Chob	The baby's mattress was buried with her body.
32. Thad Somvong buried her body and the mattress in the wat compound, not in the cemetery.	Samran Wang Pri Chaa Thad Somvong Pratomwan (1966)	Thad Somvong	

TABLE 10. (cont.)

Item	Informants	Verification	Comments
33. After her death, the family moved to Ban Naa.	Pratomwan (1969)	Samran Wang Pri Chaa	The family had moved from Ban Huanon to the almost adjoining village of Ban Naa about a year or two after the infant's death.
34. Samran Wang Pri Chaa moved three times.	Samran Wang Pri Chaa	Uncertain	Verification of this item remains doubtful. Samran Wang Pri Chaa had moved more than three times, but it is not certain that he moved three times *after* the death of his infant daughter. In 1966 he told me that he and Nang Chob had moved three times following the baby's death. But in 1972, in correspondence with Nasib Sirorasa, he wrote that they had moved (after the infant's death) directly from his house in Ban Huanon to one in Ban Naa, which they still occupied in 1972. According to his 1972 statement, he had moved three times, twice before the infant girl's birth and once afterward. I think slips in translation probably caused the discrepancies in the testimony for this item.
35. The second house [the one at Ban Naa] was wooden.	Pratomwan (1966)	I saw this house in 1969.	These and the following four items refer to the house in Ban Naa to which the infant's parents moved *after* her death.

No.	Item	Informants	Verification	Comments
36.	It had two stories.	Pratomwan (1966)	I saw this house in 1969.	
37.	It was close to the road.	Pratomwan (1966)	I saw this house in 1969.	The house was not more than 7 or 8 meters from the road.
38.	The kitchen of this house was downstairs.	Pratomwan (1966)	Samran Wang Pri Chaa	
39.	It was about 20 meters by 10 meters in size.	Pratomwan (1966)	I estimate that these are the approximate dimensions of the house I saw in Ban Naa.	
40.	Her father's name was on a piece of wood.	Pratomwan (1969)	In 1969 I saw a sign hung on the second floor of the house at Ban Naa that said: "House of Samran Wang Pri Chaa."	
41.	Recognition of Thad Somvong	Thad Somvong		According to Thad Somvong, this recognition occurred in 1965. Pratomwan was standing alone in front of the temple at Ban Naa. Thad Somvong came along, also alone, and Pratomwan said: "You are Uncle Thad, aren't you?" He said: "Yes, I am Uncle Thad." Pratomwan then went on to tell him that she had been born and died "here" and that he had buried her. She also said: "Why did you not bury me in the cemetery?" At that time he was nonplussed and could not remember the incident to which she referred. He recalled it afterward. Since this meeting occurred at Ban Naa, Pratomwan's use of the word *here* (as remembered by

TABLE 10. (cont.)

Item	Informants	Verification	Comments
			Thad Somvong) for the place of the infant girl's birth and death was, strictly speaking, incorrect. However, Ban Naa and Ban Huanon are only 1 kilometer apart and almost continuous, so use of the word *here* in a vague way does not seem to me unpardonably imprecise.

had made a number of other visits to Ban Naa, and I cannot exclude the possibility that she later thought she had remembered more details than she had in fact recalled earlier. I am suggesting not a conscious effort on her part to embellish the case with additional details, but only a natural fusion of the original memories with what she later saw and heard when she went to Ban Naa. However, even if she had recalled only those items for which we have independent corroboration, the list would still include sixteen statements that together sufficiently establish the correspondence of her memories to events in the life and death of the infant daughter of Samran Wang Pri Chaa and Nang Chob.

I have omitted from Table 10 a number of items about which inconsistent testimony made me unable to decide whether they had occurred to Pratomwan during the meditation when she first recalled the previous life. These doubtful items included statements that she had, in her meditation experience, remembered that the infant girl had died without fever and that the previous father had been a Christian, but not an ardent one. She also stated to me (in 1966) the names of the six children born after "Loogsao" died. Although Samran Wang Pri Chaa verified the correctness of these items, I have chosen, because of the inconsistencies, to delete them from the list of credited statements, and thus perhaps impoverish the case.

In 1966 Pratomwan herself said that she had remembered the names of the villages, Ban Naa and Ban Huanon, where the previous family had lived. In 1969, in going over this again, she at first said she had not remembered the names of the villages in her meditation experience, but then corrected herself to say that she had. Because the written report of Samran Wang Pri Chaa clearly states that Pratomwan told him that she recalled Ban Huanon as the birthplace of the infant girl, I have retained the items that include its name (items 12, 13, 14, and 22). And because Pratomwan must have known the name of the village, Ban Naa, that interested her in order to go there with Neio Niyomboon to verify her memories, I have felt justified in retaining item 33 also. Discrepancies occurred in the testimony connected with a few other items that I have listed in Table 10, but I have referred to these in the comments. As I mentioned earlier, I think at least some of the discrepancies in the testimony of this case are due to slips in translation by the interpreters, but others may just as certainly be due to faulty memory on the part of the informants or to defects in my own understanding and note-taking.

Pratomwan's Statements about Events Occurring after the Infant Girl's Death and before Her Birth

Items 28, 31, and 32 of Table 10 refer to events that occurred in the family *after* the death of the infant girl in question. Items 29 and 30 refer to related details. Of these, the most remarkable was Pratomwan's statement that Thad Somvong had buried the body of the baby girl outside the cemetery instead of within it. From my inquiries in Ban Naa, I am sure that Samran Wang Pri Chaa, his wife, and everyone else in the village (except Thad Somvong) knew nothing about this dereliction of duty until it came out at the time of Pratomwan's visit in 1966, when she challenged Thad Somvong with her memories. Thad Somvong said he had told no one where he had buried the baby's body, not even his wife. His mother, whom I interviewed, had not heard that he had buried the body outside the cemetery, although she said she remembered the death of the infant girl and that Thad Somvong had buried it. (She said his not having done the job properly did not surprise her, because he was young at the time and somewhat afraid of ghosts in the cemetery.)[1] However, she had no definite information that he had in fact ever buried anybody outside the usual place in the cemetery. Another informant, Mae Chee Rin, an elderly nun of Wat Ban Naa, also recalled the death of the infant girl and that Thad Somvong had buried its body. But she too did not know where he had buried it. She had heard some talk to the effect that the other undertaker of the area had sometimes buried bodies outside the cemetery, and she thought it possible that Thad Somvong had done so also. But she did not know where he had actually buried the body of Samran Wang Pri Chaa's baby.

We should next consider whether Thad Somvong confirmed burying the body outside the cemetery out of a wish to conform his memories to Pratomwan's statements. I asked him how he could be confident that he was remembering his burial of the infant in question and not that of some other child. He said that when Pratomwan had first confronted him with her memories, he did not recall the incident to which she was referring. But he thought about the matter later and eventually remembered that he had buried two bodies outside the cemetery at about the same time; one was the body of an adult woman and the other that of the infant girl of Samran Wang Pri Chaa and Nang Chob. It seems likely that the association of another improper burial temporally close to that of the infant could have enhanced the accuracy of his memory over many years. But we also need to know how often Thad Somvong buried bodies outside the cemetery, and on this point he gave conflicting testimony. In 1966 he said that he remembered burying other infant bodies outside the cemetery, but in 1969 he said that he could only remember placing the adult

---

[1]Thad Somvong said he had buried the body outside the cemetery because he was afraid of tigers, not of ghosts. According to a sketch I made of the area, including the location of the cemetery and the actual burial place of the infant girl, the cemetery was closer to the jungle and therefore more exposed to tigers than the place where he buried the infant's body. If my understanding is correct, tigers would only approach the village at times when they could not obtain food elsewhere. Thus the danger from them was periodic rather than continuous.

woman's body and the infant girl's body outside the cemetery. One point in favor of believing that he did remember the infant in question is that he was not the usual undertaker of the area and therefore would not have so many burials to perform and later to try to keep distinct among his memories as would someone who was burying bodies frequently. He did not immediately remember the episode and only recalled it afterward. Since he had once said that he did not remember it, he could easily have continued saying this even after he had, in fact, remembered the details. His confession evoked more amusement than criticism among the villagers of Ban Naa, but the admission cannot have earned him any merit in their eyes, and it would have been perfectly natural for him to have remained silent about the matter, as he had been already for many years. After considering all the available evidence, I have come to believe that Thad Somvong did bury the body outside the cemetery and did correctly remember that he had done so.

For similar reasons I think it unlikely that he ever told anyone else earlier that he had buried bodies outside the cemetery. To have admitted this would have involved painful alternatives. The villagers could have discharged him, an unpleasant prospect even though the work brought little or no remuneration; or he could have had to face the tigers. Far better, he must have thought, to dispose of an occasional body in a safe place and tell no one details they did not care to enquire about.[5]

I have given all the evidence I can provide concerning the burial of the infant, which I consider the most significant item in the case. For if it is true, as seems to me likely, that no one in the village except Thad Somvong knew about the burial of the baby in the wrong place, then this item at least could not have been picked up and passed on to Pratomwan by normal means. And if she did not learn about this item normally, I think the case for her having learned the other items as well by paranormal means becomes strengthened.

Readers may wonder why I have not included in Table 10 any recognition by Pratomwan of Samran Wang Pri Chaa at Ban Naa. Pratomwan, however, made no attempt to recognize him by herself. After she and Neio Niyomboon reached Ban Naa (I do not know how long after), she asked a nun at the wat about Samran Wang Pri Chaa and said she would

[5]In Thailand, about 85 per cent of the bodies of Buddhists are cremated; the remainder are buried. Burial rarely takes place on land owned by the family of the deceased. Usually land located near wats is designated for cemeteries. The cemeteries sometimes contain no gravestones or markers, as they usually do in the West and, for that matter, in Burma. It is not important from the point of view of a Buddhist for a person's body to be buried in a cemetery. The offense of Thad Somvong was not so serious in Thailand as it would have been in the West.

The ashes of a cremated person may be placed in a pagoda marked with a suitable inscription, and such pagodas are often placed together in an enclosed plot of land (in a wat) that is equivalent to a Western cemetery. For an example of such a cemetery with pagodas, see the case of Hair Kam Kanya (this volume).

like to meet him. The nun went to Samran Wang Pri Chaa and told him of Pratomwan's wish. He then came to the wat where the two nuns from Nakhon Sri Thammaraj were staying and introduced himself. After some preliminary talk he invited Pratomwan and Neio Niyomboon to his house. There Pratomwan met Nang Chob and began to narrate to her and Samran Wang Pri Chaa the details of her memories. Although she said, among other things, that Nang Chob was her (previous) mother, there was nothing paranormal about that, because she knew Nang Chob to be Samran Wang Pri Chaa's wife. Neither Pratomwan nor any other informant has claimed that she recognized Samran Wang Pri Chaa and Nang Chob paranormally.

Pratomwan's Statements about Events after the Burial of the Infant. Pratomwan said she remembered that, after the death of the infant girl, she was alone in the "spirit sphere" for three days. She then saw her (present) mother cooking fish and felt she liked her. She became attached to her, "entered her stomach," and remained for ten months until she was born. She remembered being born and was frightened by this process. Her mother, Prim Inthanu, said that although she was now a vegetarian, she had not become one until after Pratomwan's birth, and had, in fact, eaten fish before then. However, Pratomwan probably learned this normally.

Pratomwan said that her memories also included various details about the house the infant girl's parents later occupied in the village of Ban Naa, to which they moved one or two years after the infant girl's death. I have included these statements in Table 10. No one could corroborate that Pratomwan had recalled these details before she went to Ban Naa, but Samran Wang Pri Chaa verified their correctness for his house there.

An Allegation of Untrustworthiness against Samran Wang Pri Chaa

As I have explained in the General Introduction to this series of case reports (in the first volume), I have always tried to assess the reliability of the various witnesses for the information about which they testify. In accomplishing this, I have depended mostly on comparisons of what an informant said with what other informants said and of what an informant said at one time with what he or she said at other times. It has usually seemed to me inappropriate and unfair to invite one informant to comment on the reliability of another. I have nevertheless always listened attentively when someone has wished to make a remark—favorable or adverse—about the qualifications of another informant. Such an occasion occurred during the investigation of the present case in 1966. As the Jeep we were using was fording a river (not far from Ban Naa), it stalled, and we were obliged to pass several hours in the town of Nabon waiting for other transportation. During this wait, an official of the Department of Agriculture, Narooch Pratamol (pseudonym), struck up an acquaintance with us and learned of our investigation. He then volunteered that he personally would not believe 50 per cent of anything Samran Wang Pri Chaa would say. As evidence of the untrustworthiness of Samran Wang Pri Chaa, he alleged that he talked too much. (In fact, Narooch Pratamol far surpassed Samran Wang Pri Chaa in loquacity.) He also recounted an episode in which Samran Wang Pri Chaa had failed to deliver some honey that Narooch Pratamol had ordered and paid for in advance. It seems that he held Samran Wang Pri Chaa responsible for the delivery of this honey, although I did not learn whether he had actually paid his money to Samran Wang Pri Chaa, and Narooch Pratamol did not specifically accuse him of dishonesty. Narooch Pratamol knew nothing about the case of Pratomwan apart from what he had read in the newspapers. As our wait for other transportation became prolonged, he sank deeper into a state of inarticulate drunkenness, thus further eroding my confidence in the value of what he had to tell us. No other informant in Ban Naa or Ban Huanon impugned the honesty or credibility of Samran Wang Pri Chaa, although they had opportunities to do so during some interviews when he was not present.

I have nevertheless asked myself whether this case would collapse if Samran Wang Pri Chaa were in fact as undependable as Narooch Pratamol alleged. In that event, we would have to drop from consideration his corroborations of what Pratomwan had obtained in her memories, and the case would depend almost exclusively on what Pratomwan later told me she had recalled before going to Ban Naa. Most of the verifications would still stand, since Samran Wang Pri Chaa's wife, Nang Chob, was present during two of my three interviews with him. On these occasions she herself verified a few items and presumably assented to those confirmed by her husband. Maybe she did not dare to disagree with her husband; but I verified some items myself, either by direct inspection of the places involved or from other informants.

I could find no motive on the part of Samran Wang Pri Chaa to endorse falsely what Pratomwan had said about her memories. Most of his life he had been a lukewarm Buddhist. He had felt some attraction to Christianity and had actually attended a Christian church for a time, although he had never formally joined the Christian religion. He certainly could not be listed as a propagandist for Buddhism. He had gone to the trouble of typing out an account of his first meeting with Pratomwan almost a year before my first meeting with him in August 1966 and soon after his first meeting with Pratomwan in August 1965. But he seems to have done nothing with the report during the intervening year and certainly had not used it, so far as I could learn, to bring publicity to himself in any way.

Finally, by the criteria I consider most useful in assessing the value of testimony, Samran Wang Pri Chaa's accounts deserve credence; what he said (or wrote) on different occasions was satisfactorily consistent, and his testimony accorded (without more than the usual small discrepancies about details) with what other informants told me.

Another Life Remembered by Pratomwan

In November 1974, I went to Nakhon Sri Thammaraj (with Professor Kloom Vajropala and Nasib Sirorasa) in order to investigate some new cases there and also to meet Pratomwan again. During the course of our interview, Pratomwan mentioned that she had had memories of another life, again one as an infant girl, that she thought she had lived in Supanburi Province, far away from Nakhon Sri Thammaraj. (Nakhon Sri Thammaraj is in the southern peninsula of Thailand, more than 650 kilometers south of Bangkok; Supanburi is about 200 kilometers north and slightly west of Bangkok.) She offered information about these memories diffidently, in contrast to the confidence she had shown earlier concerning the life of the infant girl who died at Ban Huanon. I made notes of what she said about these memories and also met two persons who had accompanied her when she had gone to Supanburi to verify the details of the memories.

At that time I did not think I would ever learn more about these additional memories, but in March 1980 I did. I wished to meet Pratomwan again (for her latest news before I published this volume) and learned that she then was staying at a wat (with a meditation center) near Supanburi. Her teacher, the Ven. Thammathero, had founded this center in 1973, and he divided his time between it and Wat Thao Kot in Nakhon Sri Thammaraj. He had located the new wat, called Wat Sainam, about 1 kilometer from the village of Ban Don Masang, where the family of the second deceased infant girl lived. These circumstances enabled me to interview four members of this family on the same day (in 1980) on which I met Pratomwan. I thus find myself able to give more information about her second set of memories than I had earlier thought I would be able to.

Pratomwan's memories about the infant girl of Supanburi lacked the abundant detail of those she had about the girl of Ban Huanon. Also, I began my investigation of the Ban Huanon memories within a year (or two years at the most) of their occurrence, whereas I did not meet the family at Supanburi concerned in the second set of memories until many years after its members had met Pratomwan. For these reasons, I present only a summary of these memories and their verifications, not a detailed exposition of them.

Pratomwan said she had the memories of the life in Supanburi at about the time she had those of the life in Ban Huanon. Because she lacked confidence in their accuracy, she told no one—not even her teacher, the Ven. Thammathero—about the memories until she was about to verify them herself. And she did not do this until after the Ven. Thammathero had opened the new wat and meditation center in 1973.

In the second set of memories, Pratomwan seemed to recall the life of an infant girl who died of "vomiting" at the age of about ten months. She remembered the names of the child's parents: Kamwan Plad (the father) and Sri Nuan (the mother). A young man, Kinip Kesah, whom I interviewed in Nakhon Sri Thammaraj (in 1974) and who had accompanied Pratomwan when she first went to Supanburi, corroborated that she had mentioned these two names before they had gone to meet the family concerned. He did not say that Pratomwan also remembered the name of the village, Ban Don Masang, where they lived, and she may not have done so. When she reached Supanburi, she mentioned her memories of a life in the area to a man she met at the new wat. This was Op Champbaneung, who lived in a hamlet of Ban Don Masang. His wife, Nang Thoung, was a cousin of Kamwan Plad Pengkui, so he had no difficulty recognizing the names Pratomwan gave. He then accompanied Pratomwan to Ban Don Masang, where, according both to him and to Kamwan Plad's daughter Chamnong, she led the way to a house, which she entered. Inside, she pointed to a photograph on the wall and said that it was of her mother. The photograph was of Sri Nuan. This recognition impressed the witnesses favorably, because the house in question contained more than ten photographs.

Sri Nuan had died in about 1971, and Kamwan Plad was out of the village when Pratomwan came to it. When he returned, his daughter Chamnong told him of her visit, and he immediately went to the wat to meet her. Pratomwan came to him and called him "father." (No one claimed that she recognized him paranormally, because she must have expected him to come to the wat as soon as he heard about her claim to have been his daughter; Pratomwan's greeting, however, showed her confidence, at this time, in her memories.) Pratomwan was sad and cried. She and Kamwan Plad talked little that evening.

The next day, Kamwan Plad returned to the wat after having thought up four questions he intended to ask Pratomwan as a test of her claim. The questions were: How old had she been when she died? What was the cause of her death? Was the body buried or cremated? How long did they keep the body before cremation? Kamwan Plad said Pratomwan told him that she had died of "vomiting" at the age of one year and one month, and that her body had been buried. He said these were correct answers to his first three questions, although readers will remember that Pratomwan told me (in 1974) that she remembered the baby as having been only ten months old when she died. Kamwan Plad, recalling the conversation with Pratomwan seven years later, could not remember exactly what she had said in answer to the fourth question, but he thought she had been correct. (The family had first buried the baby and then, some months later, had dug up the body and cremated it.)[6] He declared himself fully satisfied with Pratomwan's answers. He recalled that Op Champbaneung had posed further questions to Pratomwan, but neither he nor Op Champbaneung could remember what further questions the latter had asked.

The details stated by Pratomwan corresponded to events in the life of an infant daughter, Chamnian, whom Kamwan Plad and Sri Nuan had lost in either 1942 or 1943. The infant became ill, vomited incessantly for about ten days, and then died—probably of dehydration.

According to what I learned of the probable dates of the two lives Pratomwan remembered, the infant girl at Ban Don Masang lived and died before the infant girl at Ban Huanon.

Chamnian was the second child of the family and the older sister of Chamnong, who witnessed Pratomwan's recognition of their mother's photograph. Many families of Thailand in those years lost a child in infancy, and we cannot give much credit to anyone for saying to middle-aged parents that this had happened to them. But Pratomwan had accomplished something more than this; she had correctly learned the names of a married couple living near Supanburi. (I mentioned earlier that a companion from Nakhon Sri Thammaraj, Kinip Kesah, corroborated that she had told him these names before they went to Ban Don Masang.) In addition, Pratomwan was credited with finding her way to a strange house and there pointing to a photograph of Sri Nuan and saying that it was of her mother.

Could persons at Wat Sainam have normally learned details about Kamwan Plad's infant daughter, which they might then have passed on inadvertently to Pratomwan? This seems unlikely. Kamwan Plad and his daughter Chamnong said they had never even visited the wat before learning about Pratomwan's claims. Op Champbaneung was a patron of the wat and a member of its governing committee, and so he went there often, but his wife went much less frequently; both denied that they had ever talked there about Kamwan Plad's infant daughter. Readers will

---

[6]Thai Buddhists believe that cremation provides a much more suitable means of disposing of a body than burial. Cremations, however, cost considerably more than burials; families therefore sometimes bury a body, or perhaps keep it preserved without burial, until they can afford to cremate it. I have heard of one case in which a family preserved and kept a body for more than sixteen years, so that they still had it when a child claiming to have lived in it visited them to assert his claim—not to the body, but to have been its tenant in his previous life.

find this easier to believe if they remember that Kamwan Plad had lost his infant about thirty years before Pratomwan came enquiring about her. In this connection, we should remember also that Pratomwan raised the question of verifying her memories on her first visit to the new wat at Supanburi; this means that she had fewer opportunities to pick up stray information from the villagers coming to the wat than she would have had if she had visited it often or for long before trying to verify her memories.

We should next consider the puzzling closeness of the new wat to the village that was the site for this set of Pratomwan's memories. Her teacher, the Ven. Thammathero, was born in Supanburi Province, and he had apparently wished to build a wat to serve his native community for many years before he could do so. When he acquired the means for a new foundation, he selected a site 10 kilometers from his birthplace, which happened also to be 1 kilometer from the village of Pratomwan's memories. Was this a mere coincidence? Could he have told Pratomwan anything about Kamwan Plad before she came to Supanburi? I asked him (in 1980) about this possibility. He recalled that Pratomwan had told him (in Nakhon Sri Thammaraj) that she remembered a previous life in Supanburi and that her (previous) father lived near the wat. But he also remembered that he had never met Kamwan Plad before the time when he came to the wat to meet Pratomwan; nor had the Ven. Thammathero ever heard before then that Kamwan Plad had lost an infant daughter. Furthermore, Pratomwan recovered memories of the life of this daughter when she was barely twenty, many years before the new wat was built. At that time she surely knew that her teacher came from Supanburi, but the wat could then have existed only in his mind as a project for the distant future. I am unable to think of any way in which Pratomwan could have obtained knowledge normally about Kamwan Plad's infant daughter.

Additional Details about Pratomwan's Meditation Experiences

In several conversations with Pratomwan, I tried to learn more about how the memories of the previous lives had come into her consciousness. She said the images occurred in black and white (as in her dreams) and not in color. She had not expected, much less sought, memories of a previous life in her meditation. They seem to have erupted into her consciousness without any effort on her part.

I regret to say that when I asked further questions about the process of her remembering, she gave answers that were inconsistent from one time to another. Again, some of this deviation may have derived from the trouble interpreters had in translating experiences that no one can communicate easily to another person, even without the barrier of a different language. Be that as it may, I received varying responses about whether or not Pratomwan seemed to relive the experiences of the infant girl, so that she felt as if she were in a body smaller than her own. And, as I mentioned earlier, she also seemed inconsistent in her statements concerning the length of the period of time during which the memories emerged.

From what Pratomwan said, it seemed that at least some of the time she inwardly "saw" the events of the previous life as in a moving picture. She said, for example, that in her meditation experience she could see the previous parents (of the infant "Loogsao") quarreling. And she seemed to see the previous father playing the musical instrument (xylophone) to soothe the infant. But she did not claim to have any auditory experience of the musical sounds.

In April 1981, Nasib Sirorasa had a further conversation with Pratomwan about her meditation experiences at the time she recalled the previous life in Ban Naa. She then mentioned that although she had had visual images of scenes at Ban Naa, the associated names had come to her as if spoken by (unidentified) voices. Pratomwan mentioned further that at the time of these experiences she was unusually calm and free from outside demands on her time and energy. She did not have to talk much. Later, she became involved in various other activities that required much of her attention.

Pratomwan may not have obtained all the correct information she had about the previous life during her meditation at Wat Thao Kot in Nakhon Sri Thammaraj. Samran Wang Pri Chaa described (both in his written report and during one of our interviews) how he had asked Pratomwan (in Ban Naa at the time of their first meeting): "At which house were you born?" Pratomwan then closed her eyes and after an interval said: "I was born at Ban Huanon. Is that right?" (His written and oral accounts of this episode differed in his estimates of the time it took Pratomwan to recover this detail. His written record, as translated, stated that she took a few seconds; but in his oral testimony to me he said she took ten minutes to come up with the answer.)

We cannot say definitely that Pratomwan recovered this detail first at Ban Naa. She may have done this; but it is also possible that she had recalled the detail at Wat Thao Kot and then later, in Ban Naa, needed some time to concentrate in order to remember it again.

In 1969 Pratomwan said that the images she had originally had were no longer so clear as they had been; some fading of memories had evidently occurred. She had not recovered any additional memories since my previous visit in 1966 or, so far as I know, since the above-mentioned episode in Ban Naa in 1965.

Other Relevant Observations

From 1966 on, during my interviews with Pratomwan, she has mentioned a vague impression she had of having lived as a monkey (in one or perhaps two lives) before the lives of the infant girls that she remembered.[7] She did not have any images of such a monkey life, and yet she asserted, as if from her own memories, that monkeys could talk. When someone— this could have been myself, but I did not make a note of it—asked her what they talked about, she replied: "Sex."

I questioned Pratomwan in 1969, and again in 1974, about paranormal experiences that she might have had apart from the memories of the previous lives. In 1969 she said that she had not had any such experiences, but in 1974 she said that she had had some, presumably in the interval since 1969. As an example, she mentioned an occasion when she became aware in advance that her father was coming to visit her at a time when she did not expect him to do so.

In 1966 I had asked Pratomwan's mother, Prim Inthanu, about her observations of such powers on the part of Pratomwan, and she said that she had never noticed any.

Persons who practice meditation recognize that they may have paranormal experiences during their practice or as a consequence of it, although no teacher recommends the cultivation of these. Perhaps Pratomwan's longstanding practice of meditation had led to some development in her of paranormal cognition.[8]

Comments on the Evidence of Paranormal Processes in the Case

If this case is a hoax, it is difficult to discern either the motives or the opportunities for its contrivance. Since the age of twelve, Pratomwan has meditated in order to attain Nirvana and escape from "the wheel of rebirth." The perpetration of a hoax would gravely violate all the rules of the Buddha, which she has ostensibly followed for many years. It would amount to much more than hypocrisy, because it would indicate that she had devoted these years of effort for nothing. Pratomwan had the confidence of her family, of her meditation teacher, the Ven. Thammathero, and of Neio Niyomboon, the nun whom she accompanied to Ban Naa.

[7]Although Hindus and Buddhists believe that human beings may be reborn as subhuman animals (and vice versa), they rarely put forward claims to remember such lives. For another example of such a claim, see the case of Warnasiri Adikari (second volume of this series).

[8]For further information about the expression of paranormal capacities during meditation, or as a result of it, see C. Honorton, "Psi and Internal Attention States," in B. Wolman, *Handbook of Parapsychology* (New York: Van Nostrand Reinhold Company, 1977), pp. 435–72.

One could suppose (because no one at Nakhon Sri Thammaraj could corroborate her statements) that she covertly gathered information on her first visit to Ban Naa. But she was with Neio Niyomboon on this visit, and they seem to have spent much of the time at Ban Naa together. Neio Niyomboon heard Pratomwan inquiring about Samran Wang Pri Chaa, but according to her testimony, Pratomwan's questions were designed to help her find and meet Samran Wang Pri Chaa, from whom she then wanted to verify her memories. Neio Niyomboon accompanied Pratomwan to the house of Samran Wang Pri Chaa and heard her claim to have been his infant daughter in a previous life. If she had any suspicions that Pratomwan had gained her information fraudulently, she did not communicate these to Samran Wang Pri Chaa then or to me later. She would certainly have known if Pratomwan had tried dishonestly to gather information about Samran Wang Pri Chaa and his family after she and Pratomwan reached Ban Naa. And so would all the local villagers; Ban Naa is small and the inquiries of strangers would immediately arouse curiosity and suspicion, if not resentment. Furthermore, it seems unlikely that anyone outside the immediate family knew some of the details in Pratomwan's information, such as that Samran Wang Pri Chaa had gone up the hill to get some medicine and was absent when the baby died. Nor could many persons have known that Samran Wang Pri Chaa had been considering taking a second wife when the baby died. He himself seems to have thought this one of the more impressive items Pratomwan told him. And as for the house in Ban Huanon, which Pratomwan accurately described (corroborated by Samran Wang Pri Chaa), it had been taken down within a year of the death of the infant girl and therefore approximately twenty years before Pratomwan had her meditation experience and apparently recovered memories of this house.

But an even greater difficulty for a hypothesis of normal communication comes from the testimony of Thad Somvong, the part-time undertaker of Ban Naa. As I mentiond earlier, the details of the infant girl's burial outside the cemetery seem by far the least likely of all to have been known to anyone else, in this instance to anyone other than Thad Somvong. And if a judge of the case agrees that Pratomwan could not have acquired this item of information by normal means, nor inferred it, he will probably also think that she derived knowledge about the other details of her memories paranormally as well.

Any paranormal interpretation of this case must explain how Pratomwan acquired information about events that had happened *after* the death of the infant girl whose life she claimed to remember. These later events divide into two groups. One cluster of details (items 28–32 of Table 10) concerns the undertaker and his burial of the infant girl, to which I have just referred. Another group (items 33–40) relates to the

removal of the family from Ban Huanon to Ban Naa and to the characteristics of the family's house there. The events of the first group
occurred within two days at most of the infant girl's death. Samran Wang
Pri Chaa said they kept the body of the dead infant in the house for a
night and then gave it to Thad Somvong for burial. Presumably he
buried it that day. If we accept Pratomwan's chronology, she went to her
"new mother" three days after the death of the infant girl; therefore,
memories of this burial could have been included, on the reincarnation
hypothesis, in the mind of the newborn infant, the daughter Pratomwan
of Pien and Prim Inthanu.

A year or two after the death of their infant girl, Samran Wang Pri
Chaa and his wife moved from Ban Huanon to a house in Ban Naa. They
still lived in the same house when I visited them in 1966 and 1969.
Pratomwan said that a number of details of this house had come into her
consciousness during her meditation (items 35–40 of Table 10). Unlike
the misbehavior of "Uncle Thad," which occurred just a day or two after
the deceased girl's death, these details of the new house could not have
formed part of the deceased girl's memories. They could not, that is, if
she went, as Pratomwan said she did, to her "new mother" three days
after her death. Pratomwan, however, may well have thought her measurement of elapsed time more accurate than it was. (The informants for
these cases show less exactitude in measurements of time than they do in
their memories of other details). If the infant girl of Ban Naa died in
1943 (instead of in 1944) and if the presumably surviving personality of
that baby did not go to her "new mother" until 1944, it might have remained near Samran Wang Pri Chaa and his wife and thus added knowledge about their new house in Ban Naa to its store of other memories. As
an alternative to this speculation, we could attribute to Pratomwan some
capacity for contacting the deceased infant's parents telepathically.[9]

In the foregoing remarks, I have considered only Pratomwan's memories of the previous life at Ban Huanon. Do the memories she said she
had of another previous life in Supanburi strengthen her claim that the
earlier memories (as well as the later ones) derived from a previous life
that she had lived? I think they do. When I first learned of the second
group of memories in 1974, I did not think them of more than marginal
importance, because at that time I did not imagine that I could ever in-

[9]For an example of a subject who had apparent paranormal knowledge of the details of the burial
of a person whose life she remembered, see the case of Disna Samarasinghe (second volume of this
series). For an example of a subject who showed apparent paranormal knowledge of events
occurring in the family of the concerned previous personality after that personality's death, see the
case of Veer Singh (first volume). For an example of a subject who had apparent paranormal knowledge of current events in the family of the concerned previous personality, see the case of Shamlinie
Prema (second volume).

vestigate them further. My inquiries of 1980, however, left me unable to account for the second set of memories along normal lines, with the consequence that I feel more confident in giving a paranormal interpretation to the first set.

Pratomwan's Later Development

When I met Pratomwan at Nakhon Sri Thammaraj in 1974, she seemed wan and somewhat downcast. She did not surprise me when she remarked that she wished to die. (For Western readers, I need to add here that such a remark by a Buddhist does not imply the malignant depression that it usually signifies in the West; devout Buddhists often express a sense of the futility of life, although not many say they wish to die.) Perhaps some of Pratomwan's distaste for life came from true physical lassitude. She suffered from anemia that probably resulted from the deficiencies of her diet.

In 1980, when I last met Pratomwan, I noticed with pleasure a marked improvement in her mood. She radiated cheerfulness and expressed satisfaction with the life she was living—still that of a nun able to meditate about six hours a day. Although her health had not become robust, her contentment made her seem less frail than she had appeared in 1974.

Pratomwan said (in 1980) that she still remembered the previous life—the one at Ban Huanon is meant here—but acknowledged some fading of her memories of it. She rarely thought spontaneously about it anymore.

The building of modern roads into the area of Ban Huanon and Ban Naa had reduced their inaccessibility, and Samran Wang Pri Chaa or other members of his family came to visit Pratomwan (when she was in Nakhon Sri Thammaraj) two or three times a month.

6.

The Case of the Ven. Chaokhun Rajsuthajarn

Introduction

ALTHOUGH THIS CASE was already quite old when first investigated in 1963 by Francis Story and later, in 1969, by me, it contains several exceptional features that justify its publication despite a paucity of supporting independent testimony, a weakness that may have resulted from the delay in starting the investigation. The subject of the case, the Ven. Chaokhun Rajsuthajarn (who died in 1976), was a much respected abbot in Thailand. He had from infancy some memories of a previous life, including rather detailed ones of the death in that life. He also claimed to recall events during the "intermission" after that death, and some pertinent details of his infancy. Furthermore, he stated that his birth occurred one day *before* the death of the previous personality whose life he said he remembered.

Summary of the Case and Its Investigation

Chaokhun Rajsuthajarn was, when I first met him in 1969, abbot of Wat Wachiralongkorn near Pakchong (Nakhon Rajsima Province) in central Thailand. He was born in Ban Nabua (Surin Province) on October 12, 1908. (Ban Nabua is 20 kilometers from Surin, the provincial capital.) His parents were Nai Pae and his wife, Nang Rien. His childhood name was Chote.

When Chote was a small boy, he startled his parents by addressing his relatives by the names of relationships that would have been appropriate for his mother's brother, Nai Leng, who had died just after Chote was born in the nearby village of Ban Kratom. (It is only 200 meters from Ban Nabua.) For example, he called his grandmother "mother" instead of "grandmother," and he addressed his mother by a familiar term that one might use for junior persons. (Chote's mother, Nang Rien, had been a younger sister of Nai Leng.) During these early years, Chote also recognized various persons and objects familiar to Nai Leng, of which Chote, according to the informants, could have had no normal knowledge.

Although the case was well known in the area where Chote grew up, the subject himself had never mentioned it outside village circles until he was a monk in his forties at Wat Bavornnives in Bangkok. (Readers will learn later how his family had made strenuous efforts when he was a child to make him forget the memories of the previous life, but had merely succeeded in having him stop talking about them.) At that time, the Ven. Krom Luang Wachirayanwongse, who was lord abbot of the wat and also Supreme Patriarch of the Buddhist Sangha in Thailand, asked him if he knew anyone who could recall a previous life, and he said that he himself could. Thereafter, he began again to talk about his memories. Later, Krom Luang Wachirayanwongse persuaded him to write an account of his experiences as he remembered them. This was published in Thailand in January 1969; in March 1969, when I first met Chaokhun Rajsuthajarn, he gave me a copy of the booklet.[1]

Francis Story first learned about the case in January 1963, when he was in Thailand to investigate other cases. Informants introduced him to Chaokhun Rajsuthajarn, who happened to be in Bangkok, and Francis Story interviewed him there. Subsequently, he went to Surin Province, where Chaokhun Rajsuthajarn was then a monk at Wat Pa Yodhaprasiddhi, in Changwad. He also interviewed, at Ban Kratom, all three of Nai Leng's daughters: Pa, Poh, and Pi, and Nai Leng's sister Nem. They were all by then elderly people. Pi, the youngest, was sixty-five, and Nem, the oldest, was eighty-one. They seemed, however, to remember well some of the pertinent details of the case, especially Chote's familiar conduct with them when he had been a young boy, and his ability to recognize persons known to Nai Leng. Francis Story also talked with several older persons of the area who confirmed that Chaokhun Rajsuthajarn's case had been well known and fully accepted in the area from the time of his childhood.[2] Nang Rien (Chaokhun Rajsuthajarn's mother and Nai Leng's sister) had died a few years before 1963.

In 1969 I took up the investigation of the case. I went to Surin Province, where I found one of Nai Leng's daughters, Pi, still living, although his other two daughters and his sister had died. I interviewed Pi at Ban Nikom, and at Ban Kratom I talked with two of Chaokhun Rajsuthajarn's surviving cousins. The main result of my efforts in Surin Province to confirm the testimony given earlier to Francis Story was the development in

---

[1]The title in English of this booklet is *Removing Doubts about the Next Life or the So-called Next World.* The booklet was published in Bangkok in 1969 by the Religious Affairs Publishing House. An English translation was made at the University of Virginia by Chantima Ongsuragz in 1971. This remains in typescript form, and extracts have not been published before. Chaokhun Rajsuthajarn gave me permission to include quotations from his booklet in my report of his case.

[2]Francis Story's account of the case of Chaokhun Rajsuthajarn was included in his posthumously published book *Rebirth as Doctrine and Experience: Essays and Case Studies* (Kandy: Buddhist Publication Society, 1975).

it of a rather important discrepancy. This concerned the date of birth of Chaokhun Rajsuthajarn in relation to the date of Nai Leng's death. I shall discuss this discrepancy more fully and give my explanation for it later. Also in 1969, I had the first of two rather long interviews with Chaokhun Rajsuthajarn, whom I met on both occasions at Wat Wachiralongkorn. He said that his memories of the previous life had not faded, although he was then sixty-one years old. The second of these two interviews took place in 1973.

In compiling this report, I have used the notes that Francis Story made in 1963 and the autobiographical account written by Chaokhun Rajsuthajarn. (I have depended so greatly on these sources that I would not object to being characterized more as an editor than an investigator for this report.)

In presenting the remainder of this case report, I shall first furnish some information about Nai Leng, the previous personality of the case. I shall then give Chaokhun Rajsuthajarn's account of his memories as described in his autobiographical booklet and in his interviews with Francis Story and me. After that, I shall present corroborating testimony from other informants and, finally, some comments about unusual features of the case.

The Life of Nai Leng

Readers should understand that nearly all my information about Nai Leng comes from statements made by Chaokhun Rajsuthajarn himself and was not independently verified.

Nai Leng was born in Ban Kratom in about 1863. His parents were Wa Sawa and Ma Chama. He was the eldest of their seven children. At the age of sixteen he became a samanera of the Buddhist Sangha. He remained in the Sangha until the age of twenty-five, when he withdrew. The monastery that he joined—Wat Nahaew, 10 kilometers northwest of Ban Kratom—had a set of Buddhist scriptures written in Khmer,[3] and Nai Leng learned to read these. In fact, he learned to read them so well that he taught others how to do this.

After he left the monastery, Nai Leng became a farmer, married, and had children. He remained a devout Buddhist and practiced Vipassana meditation every night.

---

[3]Khmer (Cambodian) is the language of the Khmer or Cambodian people. The frontier between Cambodia and the neighboring provinces of Thailand, such as Surin, has often changed. In modern times new international boundaries were drawn during and after the French control of Cambodia, which began in 1863. Consequently, a considerable number of Khmer-speaking people lived, and still live, within the Thai borders in areas adjoining Cambodia. This bears on the evaluation of the feature of xenoglossy in the present case.

In addition to working as a farmer, Nai Leng also traveled each year with an oxcart to other provinces of Thailand for trading at the end of the monsoon season. During these excursions, he visited parts of Thailand where Laotian is spoken, and he also visited Laos itself. In the course of these journeys he became fluent in Laotian.

Of importance in what follows is Nai Leng's strong attachment to Nang Rien, the eldest of his younger sisters, who later became the mother of Chote (Chaokhun Rajsuthajarn).

At the age of forty-five, in 1908, Nai Leng developed a fever, not otherwise diagnosed, and died after an illness of six days.

Chaokhun Rajsuthajarn's Memories of Nai Leng's Death and Chote's Birth and Early Life

I shall next quote a long extract from Chaokhun Rajsuthajarn's autobiographical account. This account (published in 1969) differs in no important respects from what he told Francis Story in 1963 and me in 1969. But as it contains more details than he narrated to either of us, I think it best to include here a relevant section from the translation of this report. Readers will understand the first parts of this narration better if they remember that Nai Leng was mortally ill and semicomatose during the period described; at the same time he appears to have had paranormal experiences, perhaps facilitated by the enfeeblement of his body.

> In the year 1908, when I [as Nai Leng] was forty-five years old, and had already had three children, Nang Rien was in the seventh month of her pregnancy. It was the eighth month of that year. I, Nai Leng, had already been sick off and on for several months. During that period of time, this brother and sister [Nai Leng and Nang Rien] recurrently saw each other in their dreams. On Nang Rien's part, ever since the conception, she had had an extraordinarily passionate faith in Buddhism, especially with regard to meditation. She had been devoting more and more time to praying and meditating. Instead of craving sour fruits or other foods that she had wanted while expecting her other children, she preferred to go to the wat for religious exercises. Indeed, she even wanted to become a *bhikkhuni* [a nun]. So on the eve of the Buddhist Lent of that year, still being pregnant of course, she left her mother and husband for a monastery. She shaved her head, put on a white robe, and became ordained. From the beginning of the Buddhist Lent in 1908, she joined those who shared her interest in praying and meditation at the Ven. Plaek's school. This school was located at Wat Takien—about 1 kilometer to the east of Lam Chee Railway Station and 7 kilometers to

the west of *Amphur*[4] Muang, Surin Province. It was approximately 15 kilometers from Ban Kratom [Nai Leng's village].

While Nang Rien was at the wat praying and meditating, I, Nai Leng, was lying sick at home. However, I felt as if I was well aware of Nang Rien's activities at the wat. After having left the house and arrived at the wat, she and a group of relatives and friends went up to the venerable monk [the Ven. Plaek] to receive a special sermon. The monk then asked the rest of the group to prepare the flowers, meals, candles, and altar as was customary in those days. All the while that Nang Rien was praying and meditating, I not only knew it, but saw it too. As it appeared to me, I was always about one *wa* [approximately 2 meters] behind her. I never did talk to her. Nor did I ever help the others with the preparations. My eyes never seemed to blink at all. I was merely staring at her, so constantly that I forgot to take notice of my own state of being, that is, how I was able to move along with her . . . . Even while she was praying before the Buddha's image, I was still looking at her from behind. Then she lit the main pair of candles and three joss sticks [incense sticks]. Below this was a container of blessed water. Sticking to the rim of this container were five candles, each weighing 1 baht [a weight equivalent to approximately 15 grams]. Stuck to each candle, I also recalled, were three pieces of metal [that were used as money]. (These were called "look sakod," [not translatable].) After having lit all the candles, she started to pray again. As soon as the flame reached the "look sakod," the latter would fall into the blessed water container, producing a soft sound like "tom." At this moment, she would raise her hands up to the level of her face and gently press them against each other, while uttering the word *saatu* [a word said at the end of.an act of worship]. Then she would put her hands down, close her eyes, and continue praying until all the joss sticks and candles were burnt away. At dawn, she would go to visit the venerable monk to relate what she had experienced. She practiced this regularly until the night of the half-moon in the eleventh [lunar] month. They then had a celebration to mark the end of the ceremony.

All along, I knew and saw her activities. But, on the day of her return [from the wat to Ban Kratom], I felt somewhat confused and could not remember anything. It was not until the third day of the waning moon, at three o'clock in the afternoon, that I felt fresh again. I then recalled that I was sick. One day, there were four persons in the house—three female relatives and Nai Leng's wife. I opened my eyes and saw and heard what they were saying to each other: "At nine o'clock last night Nang Rien delivered a cute little boy. . . ." I was thinking that if I were normal, I would have gone to visit her also. But here I was, lying sick. All I could do was merely listen to their conversation.

At the moment I felt anguish, and wanted to change from the lying position to a more comfortable one. Seeing that they [the other persons

[4]An amphur is an administrative subdivision of a province in Thailand.

present] were busy talking to each other, I did not ask for their help. Besides, I could not even make my voice heard. Therefore, I tried to turn toward the side wall by myself. I succeeded, but could not retain my balance in that position. So once again, I was lying on my back. I told myself to be content for a while with that degree of comfort. Thinking that I might be better off if I went to sleep, I then sighed deeply a few times and closed my eyes. At this very moment, I felt as if I was back to normal again. I felt stronger and could move much more rapidly from place to place. My body was light, as if it had no weight. I was so glad that I rushed up to join the conversation of my relatives. But no one noticed me. I grabbed this one's hand and pulled that one's arm, to draw their attention. Still, no one did anything.

The time came to prepare another meal of the day. My relatives were getting ready to leave. One of them felt Nai Leng's feet. I was then behind her, trying to seize her hand and shoulder. I yelled out: "I am here. I am no longer sick; I have recovered already. Do not be afraid or frightened. Do not panic, I am all right." However, I could not make them understand.

They were crying and moaning. Some of them went to tell other relatives and friends in the neighborhood. The latter were now pouring into the house. At that moment, I felt as if I were omnipresent: I could simultaneously see people coming in from two or three different directions. Moreover, I could be there to receive them all at the same time. I could also hear their voices as well as see things quite clearly.

Far distant places appeared to be near, because I could move very rapidly from place to place. I could immediately be there to hear or see. There seemed to be no obstacle [to movement or vision] at all.

At the same time I was thinking: "I am an appointed head of the hosts; I am great. I am the master of ceremonies who has the final word on all matters. I have so great an authority that none can possibly obstruct or encroach upon it." However, I was satisfied with what my relatives had done so far. I was so deeply grateful that I did not feel hungry or thirsty. I was so carried away in this enchanting state of emotion that I forgot to sleep and to eat. Nor did I ever feel tired.

During the whole period of the funeral ceremony (I learned later on that it was three days), I felt somewhat elevated—[by] about the height of an average person—above the others. In other words, if the others sat, I felt as if I were standing; if they were standing or walking, I felt as if I were standing or walking on something the level of which was higher than theirs. While the funeral procession was on its way to the cremation, I was sitting on the cart's curve, the highest part of the cart. That cart, to be sure, did not have a curve; it was merely my feeling that I was at that level. [This refers to a curved frame that could be attached to the cart to hold in materials, such as sacks of rice that were being carried in it, but that would be removed during transport of a body in a coffin.]

After the cremation, my relatives gathered the remains. Then they invited monks for the "remains ceremony," which was the last phase [of the funeral]. It was about eight o'clock in the evening when the monks finished chanting. My preoccupation with the reception of the guests was somewhat reduced by then. The women who came to help went up to sleep in the house, while the men slept in a disorderly group in a building constructed especially for the ceremony. On the porch of this building, three elderly men were sitting around a stove. They were either chewing Thai gum or smoking cigarettes. They might be considered night watchmen of a sort. All of a sudden, a thought of Nang Rien flashed into my mind. "I heard that she had just given birth to a child. I have not yet paid her a visit, because I was so busy receiving guests. Now I am free to go."

At the time, I was at the place where the monks were sitting [in the wat where the cremation was held]. With the said idea in mind, I turned in the direction of Nang Rien's house, which was 5 *sen* [approximately 200 meters] away to the west. No sooner had I decided to move than I was there.

The child, as my relatives had said, was really cute and adorable. I thought to myself: How could I possibly have a chance to touch him and to give him my heartfelt kiss? Nang Rien was then sleeping with her right hand over the child. Before long, she opened her eyes, [saw me], and said: "My dear brother, you have already departed for another world. Please go to that place which will offer you happiness. Please do not make any more appearances to your brothers and sisters, nor feel concern about them." (This was the only time that people ever noticed me and talked to me.) I felt so awkward that I went and hid. I was leaning on the wall in front of her room, facing north.

After a while, thinking that she was again asleep, I came out to get another glimpse of the child. She again opened her eyes and said the same thing to me. I went back to hide. I told myself that the time had come for me to decide once and for all. I was torn between two feelings. Although I would like to stay, yet I should go; indeed, I must go. Before leaving, however, I wished to get another good look at the child. This time I dared not approach so close lest she reproach me once more. Thus, I poked only my head out. After obtaining a good look, I started to go away again. As soon as I turned, my body began spinning like a top. I could not regain my balance. I tried to cover my head, face, and ears with my hands before I fell unconscious. At that point I thought I was dead.

I did not know how long it was before I regained consciousness. I was wondering where I was. Concentration and recollection told me that not long before this I was Nai Leng. I felt myself full of vigor. Recalling all of the past, I often wondered why I was in such a helpless condition. I felt somewhat frustrated.

Later on, I was very glad I could turn to lie on my stomach. Even more so when I could recognize everyone who came to see me. I remembered their names. I waved my hands and tried to call them. However, only guttural sounds, normal to babies, came out. Some one noticed my gesturing and held me up. I was very glad, and I laughed heartily. During this period, there were more joyful moments than sorrowful ones.

Then came another period during which I learned to walk and talk. One day when my grandmother [Ma Chama] came, instead of calling her that, I used the word *mother*. I was governed by past acquaintance and my own memory. She then pointed at Nang Rien and asked: "Well, if I am your mother, who is that?" I answered: "That is my *Ee Mah*" [literally, "Puppy," an intimate and affectionate way of addressing one's junior]. "Well, what is *your* name then?" she asked further. "It is Leng," I replied. I . . . wondered why they could not recognize me.[5] I was Nai Leng right then and there.

Suddenly, Nang Rien exclaimed: "No wonder. I saw brother Leng sometimes during the postpartum period. He must have been reborn." She then asked: "If so, son, what is your name again? What about your wife's? Where did you live?" And so on and so forth. I gave correct answers to all questions. They gave up and concluded that Nai Leng had truly been reborn.

Additional Information about the Early Life of Chaokhun Rajsuthajarn

I noted earlier that the infant whose birth the just-cited report described was named Chote. I shall now supplement Chaokhun Rajsuthajarn's report with some additional information about Chote's experiences as an infant, child, and young man that is not included in the section of the report that I have quoted. The following information comes from the interviews Francis Story and I had with him in 1963 and 1969.

When Chaokhun Rajsuthajarn "came to" in the infant body of Chote, the newborn son of Nang Rien, he tried to think what he (Nai Leng) had done the day before and what had happened to him before he had lost consciousness as he felt himself spinning. Then he remembered the past up to that time, but felt that his body was stiff and that he could not move easily. He almost felt as if he were tied up. He could not turn or sit up. He tried to turn over onto his stomach. He did not know the difference between day and night. He thought of himself still as Nai Leng, but disliked his situation, feeling helpless and unable to speak. Moreover, when he was on his back, he could not recognize the people around him. But when he turned over on his stomach, the confusion ceased, and he knew everyone in the house. He was about five months old before he attained clarity of memories in all bodily positions. As he became more mobile and could sit and then walk and move around the house, he became aware that he was in a baby's body, that of Nang Rien's baby. He comprehended that he

---

[5]For other examples of subjects who felt frustrated because relatives and friends of the deceased person whose life they remembered did not recognize them, see the cases of Rabih Elawar, Zouheir Chaar, İsmail Altınkılıç (third volume of this series), and Hair Kam Kanya (this volume).

had been given the name Chote, yet he still thought of himself as Nai Leng. Before this realization, he had had two states of consciousness: either he thought of himself as Nai Leng (when on his stomach) or he was in a state of confusion without clear identity or recognition of the people around him (when on his back). At the stage now reached, he had a sense of continuity between the life of Nai Leng and the life of Chote, the still very small, but now more mobile, son of Nang Rien.

When Chote learned to speak, his mother explained to him who his uncles and aunts were; but he insisted on identifying them as brothers and sisters. His own report, already cited, described how he had called his grandmother "mother"; identified his mother, Nang Rien, by her nickname, Ee Mah; said that she had been his younger sister; and said that he was Leng. When questioned about the names of members of Nai Leng's family, such as those of his wife and three daughters, he gave them all correctly. He also correctly named places Nai Leng had visited and other people he had known. In tests of his knowledge about Nai Leng, Chote could separate articles that had belonged to Nai Leng from others that had not. (I did not learn any details of these recognition tests.)

The conviction of being Nai Leng remained with Chote through childhood, and he resisted his family's efforts to teach him relationships different from those to which, as Nai Leng, he felt himself accustomed. The story of his family's efforts to suppress his memories is best continued in the words of Chaokhun Rajsuthajarn himself, and so I shall quote another extract from his autobiographical account:

> The people of that area had one time-honored belief: the parents of a child who could recall his former life must do everything to have him forget it, lest he become a stubborn child, hard to handle, and short-lived. I was, therefore, on the rack. [No physical torture is meant; the word *rack* is a metaphor for the nonviolent and largely symbolic means used to suppress Chote's memories.] Once they covered my head with a woman's garments and then they made me walk under the ladder. At one time they held me by my feet; at other times they pushed me about in a wooden basket. Every time I identified myself as Nai Leng, they would do something of this sort. No matter how hard I cried, they would not stop. Sometimes I even called them names, but they ignored me.
>
> I felt extremely uneasy. To adapt to their way was against my own conscience, but to do what I wished was against their feelings. I was frustrated and could not really decide what to do.
>
> It was not until I had learned a harsh lesson that I finally decided to keep quiet. One day, they turned me round and round. I felt so dizzy that I did not dare to open my eyes. The earth looked as if it was about to fall down on me. I fell down and vomited . . . . While I was lying down, an idea flashed into my mind: "If I keep on insisting on identifying myself as Nai Leng and talking about him, they will put me on the rack

again. They have probably done this in order to make me forget it. Therefore, even if I do not really forget, I must so act. From now on I would not accept [openly] that I was Nai Leng."[6]

From that time I did not identify myself [publicly] with Nai Leng. Nor did I ever talk about his story again [during early childhood.] At times, I was teased by people who knew that I was Nai Leng and decided to make fun of me. They would come up to me and say: "Hi, Nai Leng." I would avoid them. This tactic was of great help to me. From then on, I kept quiet, and others thought that I had forgotten. The story of Nai Leng was rarely referred to again.

I also tried to adapt myself to their [the adults'] ideas of the family hierarchy. I went along with their wishes, except with regard to forgetting my former life; they could not make me forget that.

In his early teens, Chote recovered the memory of an incident that had occurred in the life of Nai Leng when he (Nai Leng) was only fifteen. The incident had therefore happened some forty-three years earlier.[7] Chaokhun Rajsuthajarn included the episode in his autobiography, which he wrote in about 1968, ninety years after the remembered incident. I cite below the pertinent passages. Chaokhun Rajsuthajarn said that he verified the incident he remembered from his mother, Nang Rien, who had been present at the incident. His memory of it occurred long after he had deceived his family into thinking that he had forgotten the previous life.

> I was Nai Leng at the age of fifteen. It was an evening at the beginning of the planting season. After finishing the day's work, my sister [Nang Rien] and I walked home as usual. On our way back, we came across a woman who was resting after having just delivered a child on the road. The road was located near the swamp called "Nong Ya Ka" or, as the local people preferred to call it, "Jarb Saboaw." To the northwest of this swamp there was a sort of trench. The couple [the mother of the baby and her husband] had arrived there. The husband was a native of Ban Nua, but his wife came from Ban Tai. His wife had wanted very much to deliver her child at her mother's place. As the time for her delivery approached, she insistently asked her husband to take her there. Her husband finally agreed, but not until she was almost due to deliver her baby. By the time their cart reached the place in question, her labor had

---

[6]For another example of a subject whose parents tried to suppress memories of a previous life with nonviolent methods, see the case of Puti Patra (first volume of this series).

[7]The subjects of these cases tend to remember most easily events in the concerned previous personality's life that happened within a few months of that personality's death. Occasionally, however, one remembers some event that happened in the early life of the concerned previous personality. For other examples, see the cases of Kumkum Verma (first volume of this series), Lalitha Abeyawardena (second volume), Zouheir Chaar, Rabih Elawar (third volume), Ratana Wongsombat, and the Ven. Sayadaw U Sobhana (this volume).

started. Her husband stopped the cart, untied the oxen, and prepared a place for his wife to rest there. This was something I had never seen before. It was strange to me, and as a consequence, it deeply impressed me.

Here Chaokhun Rajsuthajarn interrupted his account of this episode in order to summarize briefly the later life of Nai Leng, which I have already mentioned. He then resumed his account and described how the memory of the above incident came to him.

During all those thirty years [remaining in the life of Nai Leng] and another thirteen in my following life [that is, as Chote], I had never had another chance to visit that location [where he had seen the woman who had given birth to a child on the road].

One day, however, almost at noontime, the cattle that I had to take to pasture led me to this location. On arriving at that place a thought flashed into my mind: "There must have been some people who came here, delivered a child, and spent some time here afterward. But I have never been here before. Why do I have such a clear idea of this?"

Then I recalled that the oxen had been untied. The cart was blocking the way. Its front was facing north, with its rear to the south. It had a roof built onto it, and the woman was resting inside the cart. Underneath the cart there was a fire in which three or four big pieces of firewood were burning. The husband had set up a stove in front of the cart, and on this there was a big pot of traditional medicine [apparently of a kind appropriate for women who had just delivered babies]. About 5 yards away there was another stove for preparing meals. The two oxen were deep yellow in color with a few spots. Both of them had bells hanging from their necks, and they were tied to a Chuak Rok Fa tree, which was about 12 yards to the east. (I could still recall the sight and sound of the fire under the cart.) The rice was boiling on the stove and making a sound as it did so. The fire for the medicine pot, however, was by this time rather low. The husband, holding a big spoon, was watching the rice pot. Then he turned to look at the things he had set up. The two oxen were licking each other; they seemed to be in a friendly mood. They perhaps hoped to rely on each other, since there were only two of them. As they moved their necks, the bells tinkled "ding-ding." The tinkling of the bells added another sound to those of the fire and the rice pot.

This picture was in my mind as I—the thirteen-year-old Chote—stood there. However, at that time there were no such things there. I was surprised and decided to remain for a while, hoping that I might discover some clues to the experience. After about half an hour I left in order to find my cattle. For the rest of the day my mind was full of doubts.

As soon as I arrived home that evening, I asked my mother whether any woman had ever delivered a baby at that place. She said: "Yes, but that happened when I was fourteen years old and was returning from the field with my fifteen-year-old brother." The brother was I, who had become the youngest son of the sister.

When he was twenty-six years old, Chote, who by this time was a full monk known as Phra Samuha Chote, had another déjà vu experience. It remains unverified as deriving from the previous life of Nai Leng (as Chaokhun Rajsuthajarn himself fully admitted), and yet because it illustrates the clarity with which apparent memories of the previous life came to him, I think it valuable to quote from his own account of the episode:

> I was then [in 1934] twenty-six years old, and was spending my sixth year as a monk at Wat Buraparama, in Amphur Muang, Surin Province. One day in the dry season, a group of people had organized a celebration at Wat Kae Yai. They had also invited a number of monks from Amphur Muang, including myself, to lunch there. It was about ten o'clock that day and we were at the northern side of Huey Tuppol. I was walking behind the rest of the group. On my arrival at the said place, I recalled that I was once a caravan merchant who used to camp here. A scene of that time flashed back into my mind. I could even hear the tinkling sound of the oxen's neck bells as well as the boiling rice pots. Unfortunately, I could not share it with the others. I walked about the place for almost half an hour, hoping to find some clues to understand my experience. My feeling told me that sometimes the fire was placed inside the carts. The others' carts were joined to each other in circular form. The sun had not set as yet. Some workers were in a hurry preparing the meal, while the others were untying the oxen and the buffaloes. The animals were grazing and drinking at leisure nearby. The tinkling sound of their neck bells was impressive. I was then on my way to get some water with the bamboo-trunk container. Having gotten it, I came back and hung it on the lefthand side of the cart yoke. It swung as I let it go. The rice pots on the stove were boiling and making a sound.
>
> Though the scene and sounds of this event had occurred thirty-three years earlier, that is, the period covering seven years prior to my last death plus twenty-six years in the present life, I felt as if it were only yesterday. I have also visited the place several times in the ensuing years; each time has brought back the feelings and memory of that event. Sometimes, being carried away by this fascinating recollection, I have even missed my lunch.
>
> Unfortunately, there are no witnesses left to verify this memory. I regret to say that all my traveling companions of those days are already deceased.

Comment. I do not understand how Chaokhun Rajsuthajarn can have dated the episode of the above memory as occurring seven years before Nai Leng's death. Indeed, since he stated that Nai Leng used to camp at the site where he (Chaokhun Rajsuthajarn) had the memory, a scene similar to the one recalled must have occurred on a number of occasions, perhaps even often. Readers may note the similarities between some of the details of this remembered scene and those of his earlier memory of an episode in which a woman who had just delivered a baby figured: tinkling neck bells on untied oxen and rice boiling in a pot, for example. Such scenes would have been commonplace in rural Thailand during the period of the events remembered and for the times when Chaokhun Rajsuthajarn had his memories of them, and they still occur in many areas away from the highways.

Both the memory of the episode with the woman who had delivered a baby and that of the caravan camp occurred when Chaokhun Rajsuthajarn visited the site of the remembered event.[8]

The Knowledge of Khmer (Cambodian) and Laotian Shown by Chaokhun Rajsuthajarn

The village of Ban Kratom, where Nai Leng died, and the nearby village of Ban Nabua, where Chote (Chaokhun Rajsuthajarn) was born, lie in the southern part of Surin Province, close to the Cambodian border. The people of that area mostly speak Khmer, the language of the Cambodians, but the school instruction in reading is given in the Thai language with Thai characters, which are quite different from those of Khmer. At the age of sixteen, Chaokhun Rajsuthajarn became a samanera in Wat Nahaew. At that time he could read only Thai characters. Although he spoke Khmer, he knew nothing of the Khmer alphabet, in which many of the Pali Buddhist manuscripts of Thailand were then written. He had had no instruction in reading Khmer. He noticed the monks of the monastery reading the palm-leaf manuscripts written in Khmer and decided to see if he could do this also. He took some of the manuscripts to his room and tried to decipher them. He found that "on the third attempt" he could read Khmer characters perfectly.

The following passage from Chaokhun Rajsuthajarn's autobiographical account describes how he first learned to read Khmer:

> The book [written in Khmer that he started reading by himself] had ten leaves. I went through it within an hour or so. Being afraid that the first reading might not be correct, I began all over again. This reading also took me about an hour. I was not quite satisfied yet, so I read it for the

[8]For examples of other subjects who have had additional memories of a previous life when they visited places familiar to the concerned previous personality, see the cases of Swarnlata Mishra (*Twenty Cases*), Gopal Gupta, Bishen Chand Kapoor (first volume of this series), Gamini Jayasena, Disna Samarasinghe (second volume), Suleyman Andary, and Necati Çaylak (third volume).

third time. I was very glad as well as surprised that I could read it without having had any lessons before. A lot of people had put great effort
into it year in and year out, yet only a few succeeded. Later on, I began
to write as well as read [Khmer] . . . . From then on I could read any ca-
nonical work, be it in Thai or in Khmer. The reason is simple: I was already quite well-versed in it [Khmer] since I had been a monk as Leng.
To be sure, part of it was forgotten, but this is only natural.

When Chaokhun Rajsuthajarn was a young man in his village (Ban
Nabua) in southeastern Thailand, he had had no opportunity to learn
Laotian. Thai and Khmer (Cambodian) are the languages of southern
Surin Province; Laotian is the language of Laos and of some inhabitants
of northeastern and eastern Thailand. But Laotian speakers often mi-
grate to central Thailand, as I mentioned in the report of Bongkuch
Promsin's case. Around the age of nineteen, when Chaokhun
Rajsuthajarn was still a samanera, he went to live at Wat Suthachinda in
Rajsima, which is west of Surin and a little north. At the wat he spoke
Thai with the other monks, but he noticed that many of the peasants and
other villagers of the area spoke Laotian. He thought he would try to
speak Laotian with them and found that he could immediately speak it
fluently. He wondered about his ability to speak Laotian although he had
had no previous training or experience in the language. The next night,
he closed his eyes, and memories of the previous life came into his consciousness. He remembered that as Nai Leng he had traveled with an
oxcart for trading into other provinces of Thailand where Laotian was
spoken and that he had learned to speak Laotian during the course of his
trading journeys. Nai Leng's daughter Pi told me that Chote did not
speak Laotian as a child, although he talked of having traveled to Laos as
Nai Leng. The ability to speak Laotian did not emerge, therefore, until
Chote was actually among Laotian-speaking people at Wat Suthachinda.

Corroborations of Chaokhun Rajsuthajarn's Account of His Memories

As I mentioned earlier, Francis Story interviewed (in 1963) Nai Leng's
three daughters, Pa, Poh, and Pi, and his surviving sister, Nem.

Pa (who said she was seventy-four years old) stated that she was about
twenty-two years old when her father, Nai Leng, died.[9] She remembered

---

[9]If Nai Leng died in 1908 and Pa was then twenty-two years old, she was born in 1886. This would
have made her seventy-seven years old in 1963, not seventy-four.

A discrepancy occurred also in the ages Pi gave for herself in 1963 and 1969. Probably she was
sixty-five in 1963 and therefore seventy-one, not seventy-three in 1969.

Chaokhun Rajsuthajarn was an educated man, and he almost certainly knew the correct year of his
birth and therefore also that of Nai Leng's death. But Nai Leng's daughters were simple village folk
whose memories of their own ages would not be reliable to within more than a few years.

that Chote (Chaokhun Rajsuthajarn) had recognized her when he was about four and had said to her: "I am your father." He addressed her by her name before anyone had told him what it was. He also said what her baby nickname had been. This at first annoyed her, but later she became convinced that Chote was her father reborn.

The second daughter, Poh (who said she was about sixty-seven years old), gave much the same account and said that the boy, Chote, had referred to incidents in the life of her father that he could not have learned normally. He recognized persons her father had known and called them by name at sight.

The third daughter, Pi (who said she was sixty-five years old), confirmed the accounts of her sisters. She added that her father had been ill for about six days with fever before he died and that he had died the day *after* the baby who was later named Chote was born. She remembered that Chote had become angry when Nai Leng's daughters did not address him as "father."

Nai Leng's sister Nem said that Chote had recognized her by name as soon as he could speak. According to her, he used to signal with his hand that he recognized her and other persons in the family even before he could express himself in words.

By the time I visited Surin in 1969, Pa and Poh had died, but Pi was still living and gave her age then as seventy-three years. I interviewed her in Ban Nikom in Surin Province. She confirmed to me that Chote had had detailed memories of Nai Leng's life when he was young, and she mentioned one episode not previously brought out. She said that when Nang Rien brought Chote, who was between four and five years old, to Nai Leng's house at Ban Kratom, he commented that the house had been finished, meaning after Nai Leng's death. According to Pi, the house had not been finished when Nai Leng died, a fact that he (Nai Leng) regretted. (Chaokhun Rajsuthajarn diminished the value of this item by telling me, in 1972, that Nai Leng's house *had* been finished when he died; this discrepancy may have occurred from his misremembering or from an error in translation.)

The Temporal Relation between the Death of Nai Leng and the Birth of Chaokhun Rajsuthajarn

When I met Nai Leng's daughter Pi in 1969, she reversed the testimony she gave Francis Story concerning the sequence of the birth of Nang Rien's baby and the death of Nai Leng. She told me that Nai Leng had died *before* Nang Rien's baby was born. (Pi also changed her testimony between 1963 and 1969 regarding another, much less important detail, that of how long her father, Nai Leng, had been ill before he died.) At Ban Kratom (also in 1969) I interviewed two cousins of Chaokhun Rajsuthajarn (without Pi being present), and both of them also stated that Nai Leng had died one or two days before Nang Rien's baby was born. (I do not believe errors of translation can account for these discrepancies, because my interpreter, Dr. Thavil Soonthararaksa, had studied in the United States and spoke English quite well; he had also assisted Francis Story as an interpreter for the investigation in 1963.)

I discussed this discrepant testimony with Chaokhun Rajsuthajarn at Wat Wachiralongkorn when I met him after my interviews in Surin Province. He insisted on the accuracy of his own memory of events and said that Pi had simply become forgetful. (I discount the testimony of Chaokhun Rajsuthajarn's two cousins, which supported Pi's 1969 opinion, because in the first place they were cousins, not members of the immediate family, and in the second place they were not even born until six and fifteen years after Nai Leng's death; therefore, anything they claimed to know about the sequence of events around that time must have been secondhand evidence.) In 1963 Francis Story had interviewed all three daughters of Nai Leng together in the presence of Chaokhun Rajsuthajarn. No one present then had questioned Chote's having been born the day *before* Nai Leng died, a detail that Pi herself had specifically asserted. Since she was six years older at the time of my interview than she had been when Francis Story talked with her, and had become rather elderly, I believe Chaokhun Rajsuthajarn is right in stating that her memory had failed her at the time she reversed her earlier testimony.

Pi's later statement that Nai Leng died before Chote's birth would—if we accept it instead of her earlier statement—discredit Chaokhun Rajsuthajarn's claim to remember seeing (in Nai Leng's postmortem condition) Nang Rien and her baby, Chote, whose body, according to his account, he entered to be reborn.

Cases in which a child subject remembers a previous life as someone who died after the subject's birth occur with exceeding rarity in Buddhist countries. I have investigated one such case in Burma, one in Sri Lanka, and one in Thailand; and I have learned of a few others in these countries. They occur more often in India, but are also rare there.[10] Buddhists tend to regard these cases as suspect and even inauthentic because they do not harmonize with the Buddhist concept of rebirth. If we wish to find a motive for Pi's apparent forgetfulness concerning the chronology of Nai Leng's death and Chote's birth, we could attribute it to a wish on her part to have the facts of the case conform to orthodox Buddhist teachings.

[10]I have published one other example of such a case, that of Jasbir Singh *(Twenty Cases)*.

The Resemblances between Chaokhun Rajsuthajarn and Nai Leng

The informants for the case mentioned some resemblances between the personality of Chaokhun Rajsuthajarn and that of Nai Leng. Nai Leng's daughter Pa said that when Chaokhun Rajsuthajarn was young, he, like her father, had preferred to go about naked above the waist. He was also, she said, fond of visiting the temple, as her father had been. Nai Leng had spent nine years in the Sangha. Chaokhun Rajsuthajarn entered the Sangha at sixteen, the same age as Nai Leng. (There is nothing unusual about this correspondence, however, since sixteen is a common age for boys to become samaneras.) Nai Leng had remained in the Sangha until the age of twenty-five, when he left the monastery and became a farmer. According to Chaokhun Rajsuthajarn, economic factors played no part in Nai Leng's decision to leave the Sangha; he simply thought that he would like to be a layman. Chaokhun Rajsuthajarn, on the other hand, spent his entire adult life in the Sangha and rose in the order to become one of the most respected abbots in Thailand.

Although the personalities of Chaokhun Rajsuthajarn and Nai Leng had, according to the informants, important resemblances, their physiques did not. Chaokhun Rajsuthajarn said that Nai Leng was tall, strong, and robust, perhaps because of his work as a farmer. In contrast, Chaokhun Rajsuthajarn was short and thin, and to me he appeared quite frail. Apart from some tendency to fevers when younger, his health had been good. (In 1969 Nai Leng's daughter Pi denied that the physiques of her father and Chaokhun Rajsuthajarn differed, but I consider this additional evidence that at that time her memory was failing.)

The Significance of the Chronological Order of Death and Birth in This Case

I have already indicated my reasons for believing that Nai Leng died about a day after Chaokhun Rajsuthajarn's birth; but even if his death occurred a day or two before the birth of Nang Rien's baby, the case would still conflict with traditional Buddhist beliefs about the formation of a new physical body. Buddhists, as I have mentioned previously, do not believe in a continuing entity that endures from one terrestrial life to another. They believe rather in a stream of changing personalities that are, however, causally linked. The actions (karma) of one personality in a series influence the circumstances, including the physical body, of the successor personality in the same series. Furthermore, Buddhists believe that the influence of the previous personality's karma begins at the time of conception of a new physical body.[11] Whether Nai Leng died a day before or after the birth of Chaokhun Rajsuthajarn, it is certain that the physical body of Chaokhun Rajsuthajarn had developed during an apparently normal gestation in Nang Rien's uterus over a period of seven months or more. During all this time Nai Leng was living and presumably not influencing the development of the embryo in his sister's body. If he had been influencing its development then, according to this view, Chaokhun Rajsuthajarn should not have been short and frail, but tall and strong, as Nai Leng had been.

The question then arises of whether the baby's body had been influenced by another personality who was, so to speak, planning to occupy it after birth. But this also is not harmonious with Theravada Buddhist concepts concerning the relationship between one personality and its body and another personality and its body. According to Theravada Buddhism, no personality can exist apart from either a physical body or a body of some other kind, such as one in the heavenly realms. I asked Chaokhun Rajsuthajarn if he considered that he had "pushed out" another tenant of the body of his sister's baby, and he replied that he did not think so. Even though this baby had left Nang Rien's womb several days earlier, and was ostensibly born and living, he evidently did not believe that its life actually began until he (that is, the discarnate Nai Leng) activated its body. Nor did he think that the baby had any mind before that of Nai Leng became associated with it. Yet by our usual criteria it was obviously living before that time.

Because Chaokhun Rajsuthajarn's case is incompatible with Buddhist concepts of the relationship between one life and another, I think it much to his credit and to that of the Ven. Krom Luang Wachirayanwongse, who encouraged publication of this case, that it was first published in Thailand and that they then endorsed enthusiastically an investigation and publication of it by Westerners. They had a sufficiently high regard for the facts of the case to wish them publicly known, even though they had no way of accommodating all these facts within their beliefs.

Chaokhun Rajsuthajarn's Explanation for the Persistent Strength of His Memories

Both in 1969 and in 1972 Chaokhun Rajsuthajarn told me quite firmly that his memories had undergone no fading whatever from the time he

[11]To show the strength of this belief among some Buddhists, I shall mention another case, this one in Burma, in which the interval between the death of the presumed previous personality and the birth of the subject was less than six months. (The subject's mother was already pregnant when the previous personality died.) I more or less stumbled on this case during a search for the subject of another case. I stopped at a house with the man who was then assisting me, and our hostess, learning of our work, told me about the case. The man assisting me told me later that he had known about the case beforehand and said that he had not told me about it because the anomalous dates did not harmonize with Buddhist expectations. From his point of view, the case had an irremediable flaw, and he did not think it worth mentioning, much less worth investigating.

was a child. (He did not claim that he had total recall of Nai Leng's life.) Few subjects claim in adulthood that childhood memories of a previous life have not faded. For this reason and also because of the unusual memories Chaokhun Rajsuthajarn had of the period after Nai Leng's death but before he (as Nai Leng) occupied the infant Chote's body, I think it worth considering the factors that may have contributed to the long persistence of his memories.

When I asked Chaokhun Rajsuthajarn about his understanding of why his memories of the previous life had been and continued to be so strong, he credited this to the intense practice of meditation in the previous life that he remembered. Nai Leng had meditated during his period as a monk, and he continued doing so after he became a layman and until his death. If he was too busy to meditate during the day, he would do so at night before sleeping, even when traveling. He had thus acquired considerable control over his mind by the time of his death, and this facilitated the preservation of Chaokhun Rajsuthajarn's memories of Nai Leng's life. Nai Leng had also followed closely the five main rules—the pancha sila[12]—of Buddhism. Occasionally he had killed something, but he had strictly followed the other four rules.[13]

Comments on the Evidence of Paranormal Processes in the Case

Since both personalities in this case were members of the same family and lived in villages only 200 meters apart, the case would not have provided strong evidence of paranormal processes even if it had been studied much earlier. By the time the outside investigators did arrive, many of the key informants had died. The main interest of the case, therefore, lies in Chaokhun Rajsuthajarn's account of his memories of the transition from death to apparent rebirth. This does not mean, however, that the case never had any meritorious evidence of paranormal processes. If an investigator had witnessed the interrogation of the young Chote by his relatives, that child's detailed knowledge of Nai Leng's life might well have impressed him as much as it evidently did his relatives. Their knowledge of the answers to the questions posed does not mean that they unwittingly gave him this information, either normally or by telepathy, although they may have done so.

Nai Leng seems to have been a person of excellent character, and Nang Rien's love for him might have provided a motive for her to have

---

[12]For details concerning the pancha sila, see note 20 in the case of Ratana Wongsombat (this volume).

[13]This case provides a further example of the remembrance by a subject of the life of a person who was pious and who died naturally. In these respects it resembles the cases of Disna Samarasinghe (second volume of this series), Ratana Wongsombat, Hair Kam Kanya, and the Ven. Sayadaw U Sobhana (this volume).

imposed his personality on Chote. Yet it must have been somewhat irritating to her and other members of the family to have this small boy behaving toward them as if he considered himself their equal or, for some of them, their senior. Moreover, if she and other members of his family shaped Chote's personality to resemble that of Nai Leng, why did they attempt with rather strong measures to suppress his claims to be Nai Leng reborn? For me, the interpretation of these cases as being due to the influence on a child of grieving parents trying to recreate a deceased loved person seems particularly inappropriate for the present case.

7. The Case of Ornuma Sua Ying Yong

Introduction

NO PERSON CORRESPONDING to the statements made by the subject of this case has been traced, and so her statements about a previous life remain unverified. That, however, is my reason for presenting the case in this volume. Although the majority of Asian subjects of cases of the reincarnation type state sufficient detail to permit identification of a person corresponding to their statements, some of them do not.[1] In this and previous volumes I have presented other examples of such unverified cases.[2] I think it important for students of cases of the reincarnation type to appreciate the wide range in both the number and the specificity of statements that the subjects make about the previous lives they seem to recall. Some of them have abundant and detailed memories, others—like the subject of the present case—mere fragments.

Summary of the Case and Its Investigation

Ornuma Sua Ying Yong was born in Dhonburi (the twin city of Bangkok) on July 28, 1972. Her parents were Aht Sua Ying Yong and his wife, Sampan. Ornuma was their only child, but she had a half brother, Anupan Sripayak, who was her mother's son by a previous marriage. Ornuma was given the pet name Nok. Her father was a photographer, but he later worked in a variety of other jobs, mostly in service occupations at a hotel. Her mother was employed (in 1975) as a clerical worker at the Ministry of the Interior of the government of Thailand.

Ornuma's mother had a possible announcing dream in 1971, about two months before she became pregnant with Ornuma. At the time of this dream, she and her husband were living temporarily in Paknam, a town

---

[1]The proportion of unverified cases among all cases I have investigated varies widely in different cultures. For example, among the cases in Thailand only 8 per cent are unverified and among those in Burma only 20 per cent; in contrast, 74 per cent of the cases in Sri Lanka and 78 per cent of those in the United States (nontribal cases) are unverified.

[2]For other examples of cases that have not been verified, see those of Ranjith Makalanda (*Twenty Cases*), Wijanama Kithsiri (second volume of this series), and Ma Tin Aung Myo (this volume).

south of Bangkok. She subsequently forgot the dream, but later remembered it and connected it with Ornuma's statements about a previous life.

Ornuma made her first reference to a previous life when she was just beginning to speak, at about the age of one year. At that time she uttered the single word *Paknam* under circumstances that I shall describe later. Subsequently, she narrated some details of the life of a young child who had accidentally drowned while in a boat with another child. She said this accident had occurred near the pagoda at Paknam.

Ornuma spoke insistently about the previous life between the ages of two and three. Eventually Sampan Sua Ying Yong reported what she had been saying to Achan Boonmee, a teacher of Buddhism at Wat Pho, in Bangkok. He arranged for a tape recording to be made of what Sampan remembered of Ornuma's statements and behavior up to that time, and this was done at a public meeting in September 1975. The tape recording was transcribed and printed in Thai in the form of a pamphlet.[3] Prof. Kloom Vajropala gave me a copy of this pamphlet when I was in Thailand soon after its publication, in November 1975. At that time I was able to meet Ornuma and her father; her mother was not available. I did, however, learn everything Ornuma's father could remember about the case.

During subsequent visits to Bangkok in 1977 and 1978, I was unable to find Ornuma's parents again because of insufficient detail in the address I had for them.

In 1977 Professor Kloom and I went to Paknam and enquired there of the monks at Wat Prasamutchedi about children who had drowned near the pagoda, which is close to the wat. None had heard of a drowning corresponding to Ornuma's statements.

In 1979 John McCracken, a graduate student at the University of Virginia who was then working with me, met Sampan Sua Ying Yong at Wat Phra Keo in Bangkok. Although he was unaware of my previous inquiry into the case, he interviewed her and made notes of her testimony to him. He recorded an address for Ornuma's parents, but this also proved inadequate when, in March 1980, I tried again to trace Ornuma's family.

In the meantime, Nasib Sirorasa translated the transcription of the statements by Ornuma and her mother that had been recorded and printed (in Thai) in 1975. I have made use of this translation in the present report.

---

[3]The English translation of the title of this pamphlet is *Memory of Rebirth*. Authorship is credited to Sampan Sua Ying Yong and also to Ornuma, which is quite correct, because some statements from Ornuma herself were recorded and included in the transcription. The pamphlet states that the transcribed interview took place at the Monkalatip School of the Abbidhamma Foundation at Wat Phra Chatupon (in Bangkok) on September 14, 1975. The pamphlet itself was published in Bangkok on October 17, 1975. Nasib Sirorasa translated parts of the pamphlet into English for me.

In the summer of 1980 Nasib Sirorasa succeeded in tracing Ornuma and her family, so I was able to meet Sampan Sua Ying Yong and had one long interview and another short one with her in the late autumn of 1980. I also met Ornuma once more. I obtained the testimony of two former neighbors of the Sua Ying Yongs who recalled some of the statements Ornuma had made when she was younger. In addition, I renewed and extended my inquiries at Paknam in an effort to find evidence of a child corresponding to Ornuma's statements, but without success.

I took much longer to complete the investigation of this case than I think desirable, but the prolongation brought one advantage: I could compare the three statements about the case that Sampan Sua Ying Yong made to Achan Boonmee in 1975, to John McCracken in 1979, and to me in 1980. Although these different statements showed some variation in a few details, which I shall mention later, the account of the case that Sampan gave remained stable in its main features over the five-year period of the interviews.

Persons Interviewed during the Investigation

In Bangkok I interviewed:

Ornuma Sua Ying Yong
Sampan Sua Ying Yong, Ornuma's mother
Aht Sua Ying Yong, Ornuma's father
Chaeng Chu-asawa-banchong, former neighbor of the Sua Ying Yongs
Anu-pan Sripayak, Ornuma's older half brother
Surang Sripayak, Anu-pan Sripayak's paternal grandmother and Sampan Sua Ying Yong's former mother-in-law

In Paknam I interviewed:

Ven. Phra Pramod, monk of Wat Prasamutchedi
Ven. Phra Kru Paisarn Samutprakhun, abbot of Wat Prasamutchedi
Somboon Pasawachayun, proprietor of the Charoen Suk Hotel
Master Sergeant Law Ma-mak, police officer of Paknam
Capt. Sontaya Sangphow, officer in charge of the police station at Ban Plakot
Chaiyut Tangnu, headman of Ban Plakot

At Laemphapa I interviewed:

Chamnong Sithiphan, merchant of Laemphapa

I have not listed a number of other policemen, villagers, and merchants of the area around the pagoda at Paknam of whom I enquired concerning a child corresponding to Ornuma's statements.

Relevant Facts of Geography

Paknam is a town of several thousand persons located about 25 kilometers south of Bangkok near the mouth of the Chao Phraya River. The area included in the designation *Paknam* (which means "mouth of the river") lies on both sides of the river, which is about 1.5 kilometers wide at that point.

The larger part of Paknam lies on the east side of the river, where are located a modest hotel (the Charoen Suk Hotel), a substantial police station, a wat, and the academy of the Royal Thai Navy. On the west side of Paknam are located a small police post (at a place called Ban Plakot), Wat Prasamutchedi, and the tall pagoda, or *stupa*, that dominates the skyline of that side. Both sides have wharves, and there is a certain amount of boat traffic between them, although the ferries for automobiles cross the river farther north, nearer Bangkok. In the area of the west side of Paknam there are a number of small villages on klongs that run into the river. I made inquiries in one of these, Laemphapa, to which we had been directed by an informant who remembered having heard of a boy and girl who had drowned in that area many years earlier. The west side of Paknam appeared to me to be much less densely populated than the east side, and the area within the jurisdiction of the police post at Ban Plakot extended along the river for several kilometers.

Statements Made by Ornuma

According to Sampan Sua Ying Yong's statements of 1975, Ornuma had said that in the life she was remembering she had been in a boat with a boy named Ai Kai[4] on the river near the pagoda at Paknam. Ai Kai sat carelessly,[5] it capsized, and they both drowned. Ornuma further stated that she had with her a satchel of schoolbooks that went into the water with her. She said that Ai Kai's body drifted away, but that hers sank and her head struck a pillar. (This was presumably the pile of a wharf.) Ornuma also said that she drowned because she could not swim well and no one came to help her.

[4]This boy's proper name, if we assume that such a person existed, would have been Kai. The word *Ai* is a colloquial form of address. It might be considered a kind of honorific. It does not here have the somewhat pejorative tone that it had when used by Bongkuch Promsin (see the report of his case in this volume).

[5]The details of Ai Kai's culpability varied in different statements by Ornuma and her mother. He was said to have sat carelessly, to have rowed badly, and to have stood up in the boat.

Ornuma said that she had been a girl four years of age when she drowned in the previous life. (This raises the question of whether a child so young would have had a satchel of schoolbooks; but this would be possible for a Thai child sent a little early to kindergarten.)

In the interviews of 1979 and 1980, Sampan Sua Ying Yong stated that Ornuma had also mentioned the names of the parents of the child whose life she claimed to remember: Ah Keh (the father) and Boon Ruen (the mother). Up to the time of the tape-recorded interview in September 1975, Ornuma had not stated these names. A questioner in the audience specifically asked Sampan Sua Ying Yong whether Ornuma had given the names of the parents of the previous life, and she said Ornuma had not. Ornuma must therefore have added these names to her memories between the autumn of 1975 and the spring of 1979, when John McCracken made notes of his interview with Sampan.

Sampan also said in 1980 that Ornuma had talked of a third child, Odd, who had been with her and Ai Kai in the boat and who had drowned when they did.

Sampan Sua Ying Yong tended to refer to her daughter as "Nok," which was a pet name Ornuma's stepgrandmother had given her before she spoke of the previous life. She also said (in 1979 and 1980, but not in 1975) that Ornuma had said she was called "Nok" in the previous life she claimed to remember. When I asked Sampan whether she could explain how Ornuma and the presumed previous personality happened to have been called by the same name, she said only that she thought it was a coincidence and offered no further explanation. Perhaps none was needed. In Thai *nok* means "bird," and the name is not uncommon in Thailand.

No other informant for what Ornuma has said, including her father, remembered nearly as many details as Sampan Sua Ying Yong did. Ornuma's father said that he had never heard Ornuma say anything about the previous life, although he had learned about her statements from his wife. Sampan Sua Ying Yong explained this as due to her husband's having been working away from the home during much of the period when Ornuma spoke about the previous life. Similarly, Ornuma's older half brother had heard her say nothing about it, because his parents had separated when he was six months old, and he had been raised by his father and paternal grandmother.

Surang Sripayak (Sampan Sua Ying Yong's former mother-in-law) recalled having heard Ornuma say that she had lived at Paknam and had drowned. She also remembered Ornuma's references to a friend named Kai. A former neighbor of the Sua Ying Yongs, Chaeng Chu-asawabanchong, recalled hearing Ornuma say that she had lived at Paknam and that she had gone to play with two friends and had drowned.

Despite the scantiness of the corroboration by other adults of Sampan's memories of what Ornuma said, the case does not rest solely on Sampan's statements, unless one believes that she trained Ornuma to speak freely about the previous life with similar details, which Ornuma did at the time of the tape-recorded interview of September 1975. Ornuma said much less when I met her two months later, but she may then have been inhibited by the other adults who were with me in my small hotel room, to which we had brought her and her father. (In 1980, when she was with only her mother, Nasib Sirorasa, and me, Ornuma was more relaxed; but although she spoke more then, she remembered less than she had five years earlier.)

Sampan Sua Ying Yong said that Ornuma had once recognized a picture of the pagoda at Paknam on a calendar. This had occurred in the home of a neighbor who had not previously heard about Ornuma's references to a previous life, so she was quite baffled by Ornuma's statement: "This is Paknam. I died there." Unfortunately, when I met this neighbor, Chaeng Chu-asawa-banchong, she recalled nothing of the episode, although she did remember Ornuma's having mentioned to her at one time the details about the previous life that I have noted above.

Ornuma's Statements about Events Occurring after Death.   In 1980 Sampan Sua Ying Yong said Ornuma had told her that after she had drowned she had stayed with a nun in a wat at Paknam. As I mentioned earlier, there are wats on both sides of the river at Paknam, and Ornuma had indicated that she had stayed at the one near the pagoda, that is, Wat Prasamutchedi.

An Announcing Dream

In 1971 Aht and Sampan Sua Ying Yong were living temporarily in Paknam at the Charoen Suk Hotel (on the east side of the river). Aht Sua Ying Yong was working in Paknam, but Sampan worked in another town, Lopburi. On the first day of their residence at the hotel in Paknam, Sampan returned tired from Lopburi and went to bed early. She then dreamed that two children—a boy and a girl—came to her walking hand in hand. They called her "auntie" and asked for something to eat. She told them to go downstairs and help themselves to food. They disappeared, but then came back and said that they had eaten two platefuls of Chinese noodles. Sampan said that in that case they could go on home, but they replied that because she was so kind they would stay with her. Sampan said that their parents would not allow this. They then said: "We have no parents. We were drowned at the pagoda in the middle of the river." At this, Sampan—still dreaming—protested and said: "No. No. I will not take you. You are dead." The children, however, insisted that they would stay with her. At this point, Sampan awoke frightened and told her husband the dream. Although the dream impressed her forcefully at the time she had it, she apparently did not identify it as foretelling the birth of a child. She later said that she had forgotten the dream entirely until after Ornuma began to refer to a previous life, at which time she suddenly remembered it and thought that it had some connection with Ornuma's statements.

Aht Sua Ying Yong in 1975 recalled the main outlines of this dream, but not all its details, which I have taken from the interview with Sampan that was tape-recorded in September of that year.

Sampan and her husband remained in Paknam only two or three months; they then moved to Dhonburi and later to Bangkok. Sampan was pregnant by the time she and her husband left Paknam.

Sampan Sua Ying Yong's Experiences during her Pregnancy with Ornuma

Sampan Sua Ying Yong observed three unusual changes in herself during her pregnancy with Ornuma.

First, she had a marked—I could say extreme—craving for Chinese noodles. She found that she could eat no other food throughout the entire pregnancy. When she tried to eat other food, she vomited it.

She found also that she could no longer indulge in gambling in card games, an activity she had previously enjoyed. When she tried to play cards, she developed a headache and even vomited.

She also noted an increase in piety during her pregnancy. She liked to listen to sermons on the radio and to give food to monks.[6]

Since Sampan had already had one other child, Anu-pan, she was able to contrast her feelings and behavior during the two pregnancies, and she said that she had not had the cravings and aversions that I have mentioned during her pregnancy with Anu-pan. While she was pregnant with him, she loved playing cards and could eat anything she wished.

A Physical Abnormality of Ornuma's Head Possibly Related to Her Statements

Ornuma was born with an area of concavity in the parietal (upper back) region of her head. Her skull is depressed there in an (approximately round) area about 1 centimeter in diameter to a depth of about 2 millimeters below the adjoining area of the skull. I palpated this area and made notes and a sketch of it in 1975. I examined the same area again in 1980, and at that time the concavity seemed to be even deeper than I had thought it had been before. It then seemed to me at its greatest depth to be about 4 millimeters below the adjoining area of the skull.

---

[6]For other examples of unusual pregnancy cravings and aversions in the mothers of children remembering previous lives, see the cases of Gopal Gupta, Kumkum Verma (first volume of this series), Gamini Jayasena, Sujith Lakmal Jayaratne (second volume), and Bongkuch Promsin (this volume).

Sampan Sua Ying Yong asked Ornuma why she had this concavity in her head, and Ornuma replied that she had bumped her head there on a pillar, meaning in the previous life when she had drowned.

Ornuma's Behavior Related to the Previous Life

Circumstances and Manner of Ornuma's Speaking about the Previous Life. In 1975 Sampan Sua Ying Yong recalled the startling effect that Ornuma's first reference to the previous life had had on her. This occurred when Ornuma was about a year old and just beginning to talk. Sampan and Aht were in bed, and the infant Ornuma was with them or nearby. Sampan remarked to Aht that they had traveled much around Thailand and had no idea where the baby had come from, meaning where it had lived in the previous life that every Thai Buddhist would assume it to have had. She had barely finished saying this when Ornuma distinctly pronounced the word *Paknam*. Sampan then remembered the dream she had had when they were staying at the Charoen Suk Hotel in Paknam about two years earlier. She asked Ornuma how many persons had come with her and Ornuma replied: "One." Then she asked what she had done at Paknam, and Ornuma said that she had fallen into a river and drowned. Sampan asked Ornuma why the two children (of her dream) had not come to be born together, presumably as twins. Ornuma's answer to this was: "Ai Kai is seeking a place to be reborn."

Sampan was surprised at the extent of Ornuma's answers, because Ornuma had only recently learned to say the words for father and mother.

When she was about two years old, Ornuma described the drowning in the previous life and attributed it to Ai Kai's sitting carelessly in the boat they were in. Sampan asked Ornuma to show how the boat had sunk, and Ornuma squatted on the floor and demonstrated the rolling motion of a boat and then—by falling over—its capsizing.

Ornuma needed little stimulation (during this period) to talk about the previous life. The pagoda at Paknam (like others of Thailand and Burma) is broadly conical, but the upper part extends in a tall, thin spire, not unlike the spires of some Christian churches. The sight of such a spire—for example, one on a spirit-house of a type found in the compounds of most houses in Thailand—would stimulate Ornuma to talk about the previous life.

Paknam (on the eastern side of the river) has a clock tower, and whenever Ornuma saw a picture of a clock tower, she would point to it and say: "This is Paknam." A picture of a boat or water would also stimulate her references to the previous life.

Between the ages of one and two, Ornuma spoke about the previous life nearly every day. She then began to speak about it less and had stopped mentioning it spontaneously by the age of about four, when she began attending school.

Ornuma's mother noted (in her interview in 1975) that Ornuma would not talk about the previous life whenever it suited someone to ask her about it, but she was inclined to talk about it at bedtime.[7]

When Ornuma was between two and three years old, Sampan observed her sometimes speaking to herself. She discovered then that Ornuma seemed to see and hear Ai Kai, whose presence, completely undetectable to Sampan, was obvious to Ornuma. Sampan, entering into Ornuma's experience, asked questions directed at Ai Kai and received sensible answers (through Ornuma) in reply. (These exchanges appear to have resembled those of a Western séance between a sitter and a mediumistic communicator.)[8] Communications thus received purportedly from Ai Kai gave, for example, the age at which the child whose life Ornuma was seeming to remember drowned and an intimation that Ai Kai was trying to be reborn. Ornuma continued to sense the presence of Ai Kai up to the time of my interviews in 1980. Sampan said that Ornuma would sometimes draw pictures of a boy and say: "This is Kai."

Other Behavior of Ornuma Possibly Related to the Previous Life. Following Ornuma's birth, Sampan Sua Ying Yong resumed mild gambling in card games at a neighbor's house. She found, however, that Ornuma (whom she took with her) strongly objected to this. Ornuma cried so much when her mother tried to play cards with neighbors that the other players asked her to leave and take the baby with her. Later, Ornuma became less noisy in her protests, but she would still try to get her mother to leave any place where she was playing cards.

Ornuma's attitude toward cardplaying was that of a typical devout Buddhist, and her mother credited her with precocious piety in other respects as well. She liked to go to wats and listen to sermons. (We have to assess this report in the light of Sampan's own considerable religiousness; Ornuma's interest in wats and religious observances may have derived from her mother's example, although her antagonism to cardplaying did not.)

Sampan told me that Ornuma, between the ages of three and five, had a greater than average fondness (compared with other Thai children) for

---

[7]For other examples of subjects who have spoken about the previous lives more at certain times of the day than at others, see the cases of Prakash Varshnay (*Twenty Cases*), Kumkum Verma (first volume of this series), Shamlinie Prema, Gamini Jayasena, Indika Guneratne, Disna Samarasinghe, Wijanama Kithsiri (second volume), Suleyman Andary (third volume), Ratana Wongsombat, and Bongkuch Promsin (this volume).

[8]Ai Kai's existence is no more verified than that of the child Ornuma claimed she had been. Ai Kai thus had the status of an imaginary companion for Ornuma. For another possible example of a subject of one of these cases who had an imaginary companion, see the references to Jyotsna in the case of Rajul Shah (first volume of this series); but Jyotsna may have been a real child companion of Gita (the concerned previous personality) whom we could not trace.

Chinese noodles. After the age of five, her liking for this food diminished and became average.

Ornuma had a marked phobia of open water, such as that of the River Chao Phraya. She had an interest in boats, but would not approach them closely. Asked, when she was three (in 1975), whether she would like to go swimming, she refused, saying that she was afraid of drowning.

Attempts to Verify Ornuma's Statements by Inquiries at Paknam

In 1977 Professor Kloom and I went to the west side of Paknam and made inquiries in the area of the pagoda to try to learn if a child had drowned in the river there under circumstances corresponding to Ornuma's statements. We included among the persons we asked a monk of the nearby Wat Prasamutchedi. Unfortunately, the abbot was away on the day of our visit, and the monk we interviewed had only been at the wat for five years. Neither he, nor any of a group of younger monks who were present when we talked with him, could recall a drowning of a child such as Ornuma had described.

An informant at the wharf near the pagoda remembered having heard about a boy and a girl who had drowned "many years ago" while boating at Laemphapa, a village about 6 kilometers south of Paknam. We made extensive inquiries in that village without finding anyone who could recall this drowning. One longtime resident of Laemphapa, Chamnong Sithiphan, was quite sure that he had never heard of the drowning of a pair of children in a boat accident.

In 1980 I decided that, even though three more years had passed, I should make another effort to trace a child at Paknam corresponding to Ornuma's statements. This time I extended the inquiries.

Nasib Sirorasa and I asked for information, both at the main police station on the east side of the river and at the smaller police post on the west side, about children who had drowned while boating in the area. Master Sergeant Law Ma-mak (of the police station on the east side) remembered some drownings of children, but not the names of the children.

We talked with the proprietor of the Charoen Suk Hotel, Somboon Pasawachayun, who had owned it for thirty-six years. She could remember no children called "Nok" and "Kai" who had drowned at Paknam. (Both the police station on the east side of Paknam and the hotel are near the river, and persons living or working in either place would be particularly likely to hear about drownings in the river.)

Capt. Sontaya Sangphow of the police post at Ban Plakot (on the west side of the river) had been stationed there only for a year and a half; so he could contribute information about the keeping of records of drownings, but none about specific drownings relevant to Ornuma's case.

We also interviewed the headman of Ban Plakot, which includes the area around the pagoda at Paknam on the west side of the river. The headman, Chaiyut Tangnu, had lived at Ban Plakot all of his forty-eight years, and he had been headman for seven years. Earlier, he had been away from the village while serving in the navy, but he had come home from time to time on leave, and he was sure that he would have learned from other persons in the village about any drowning of a child such as that described by Ornuma. He had not.

In 1980 I also returned (accompanied by Professor Kloom and Nasib Sirorasa) to Wat Prasamutchedi and this time was able to meet the abbot, the Ven. Phra Kru Paisarn Samutprakhun, who had been at the wat since 1968. He had heard of a girl drowning in the area three or four years earlier, but not of any drowning in the period before Ornuma's birth.

Comment. These inquiries seem rather thorough, and I hope they were. But they by no means exclude the possibility that Ornuma was talking about a real previous life. Children drown frequently in the river at Paknam, as elsewhere in the rivers and klongs of Thailand. Master Sergeant Law Ma-mak said this happened "often," and when I asked him to put a figure on his estimate, he said that between ten and twenty children drowned in the area each year. Evidently more children drown on the east side than on the west side of the river, perhaps because it is more densely populated, as it seemed to me. Chaiyut Tangnu said that in his area of (west) Paknam one or two children drowned each year; and he had learned of two such drownings during 1980 by the time we interviewed him early in December of that year. Capt. Sontaya Sangphow pointed out that cases of children drowning are unlikely to come to the attention of the police, as would, for example, the murder of an adult. The drowning should, in principle, be reported to the headman of the area or to the governmental office of the amphur. But this does not mean that all drownings are reported. I came away from these inquiries with the thought that the loss of a child through drowning near Paknam would be a devastating sorrow for the child's parents, but might attract little attention outside the family concerned and their neighbors.

Comments about the Interpretation of the Case

I cannot discuss the evidence of paranormal processes for this case, because we have found none. Ornuma's statements about a previous life remain unverified, and they are not likely to be verified in the future. The case nevertheless contains all the ingredients but one—that of verifiable statements—of what I consider the standard case of the reincarnation type: an announcing dream (although it was not recognized as such when it occurred), cravings and aversions during pregnancy, a congenital deformity related to the subject's statements, an account of a violent death, and unusual behavior (particularly a phobia) on the part of the subject corresponding to her statements.

The case differs from standard cases in the occurrence of quasi-mediumistic communications through the subject from a supposedly discarnate personality. It is worth noting that Ai Kai's existence was fully accepted not only by Ornuma but also by her mother and by Achan Boonmee, who conducted the tape-recorded interview of September 1975. Achan Boonmee even expressed the opinion (during that interview) that the discarnate Ai Kai had impressed memories on Ornuma that she would not otherwise have had; in short, he favored interpreting the case as one of partial possession.

Because Ornuma's mother is the principal informant for Ornuma's statements (although her account has some corroboration from other witnesses), one may properly ask whether she might have imposed on the case the form it took and even its details. That question occurred to me, and I asked Sampan about her knowledge of other cases prior to the development of Ornuma's. She said that no one had ever spoken to her about another case and that she had never read a report of one in a newspaper. She may nevertheless have read accounts of cases of the reincarnation type in newspapers and forgotten that she had done so. In the 1960s a number of cases were reported in the newspapers of Thailand, and it was from such reports that I first learned about the cases of Ratana Wongsombat, Ampan Petcherat, Bongkuch Promsin, and Pratomwan Inthanu.

If we accept Sampan Sua Ying Yong's denial of knowledge of other cases, we confront the question of how she could have managed so neatly to have imitated standard cases, if she was, perhaps quite unconsciously, trying to mold her daughter's behavior toward seeming to remember a previous life. One would need to add also that such guidance as she may have imposed on Ornuma had no obvious motivation. As a Thai Buddhist, Sampan believed in reincarnation as unquestioningly as scientists believe that the earth is round; she had nothing to gain by developing a case within her family. When her son, Anu-pan, once suggested that she had tutored Ornuma to make statements about a previous life, she retorted that if she had wanted to do that, she could have started with him. Sampan said that her reply satisfied Anu-pan. I did not learn why he thought she might have coached Ornuma to say that she remembered a previous life when she did not. Possibly he suspected her of seeking a little publicity for having a child with such memories.

Cases of the reincarnation type for which we can find no deceased person corresponding to the subject's statements bring no comfort to those who like settled answers for questions. It is difficult to show that such a case does not arise exclusively from fantasies on the part of the subject, perhaps encouraged by indulgent and too credulous parents. On the other hand, cases with unverified statements often show remarkable similarities— Ornuma's case being an example—to those having verified ones. It is therefore worth remembering that several factors may prevent a case that is not a fantasy from being verified: the subject may fail to give sufficient or sufficiently detailed proper names; slight mistakes in the proper names given may divert the search toward the wrong place or persons; when excessive time elapses between the death of the presumed previous personality and the subject's birth, informants knowledgeable about the former may have moved away or died by the time verifications are attempted; or informants who do not believe in reincarnation, or who for other reasons find a case distasteful or disturbing, may suppress information. To this inventory we may add another item—one that is perhaps relevant to the present case: an obscure existence (that of a young child, for example) on the part of the concerned deceased person.

Ornuma's Later Development

When I met Ornuma in November 1980, she was then not quite eight and a half years old. She was attending a school at a wat in Bangkok and doing well in the second grade. She was also learning classical Thai dancing.

Ornuma went from time to time to Wat Pho with her mother and meditated there. She also sometimes meditated at home. She said that during her meditations she could still contact Ai Kai, hearing his voice, but not seeing him. When I asked her why she still wished to communicate with Ai Kai, she said that she missed him, a reasonable reply for an only child.

Sampan said that Ornuma did not talk about the previous life unless someone asked her questions, but if asked, she still seemed to remember some of what she had said earlier. Ornuma herself at first said that she remembered nothing about the previous life, but then said that she did not remember much. I asked a few questions, and from her replies about details I concluded that some of the earlier memories still persisted.

She still had a fear of deep water, but had learned to swim a little.

The Cases in
Burma

Introduction to Cases in Burma

B UDDHISM FIRST CAME to Burma during the reign of the Emperor
Asoka of India in the third century B.C. (Htin Aung, 1967). During
the next few centuries it spread through Burma until it became, as it has
remained, the religion of the majority of Burmese. The Buddhists of
Burma belong to the Theravada branch of Buddhism, as do those of Sri
Lanka and Thailand. I have already given some account of the belief in
reincarnation (or rebirth, as Buddhists prefer to call their concept)
among Theravada Buddhists of Sri Lanka and Thailand.[1] Since the Buddhism of Burma resembles in many respects that of those two countries,
especially Thailand, I can make briefer remarks concerning the concept
of rebirth in Burma. In this chapter I shall therefore restrict myself
largely to special features of the Burmese ideas about rebirth.[2]

Although the Pali Canon forms the basis of Theravada Buddhism, the
religion of everyday life in Burma includes features not having scriptural
authority. Some of these derive from ancient beliefs that preceded Buddhism in Burma and have persisted since its advent.

The Concept of Reincarnation among Burmese Buddhists

The most important tenet of Buddhism states that life cannot occur without suffering. Buddhists therefore believe that the radical cure of suffering requires that life itself cease through the abolition of the cravings that
lead to rebirth. Buddhism is thus, in the words of Parrinder (1954/1970,
p. 138) "world-renouncing." This does not mean that the Burmese (and
other Buddhists of Southeast Asia) are gloom-ridden people; on the con-

---

[1]For information about the belief in reincarnation among the Buddhists of Sri Lanka, see
Stevenson (1977); for information about the belief in reincarnation among the Buddhists of
Thailand, see the Introduction to Cases in Thailand (this volume).

[2]For further information about Burmese Buddhism, see Fielding Hall (1898), King (1964, 1976),
Ling (1979), Mendelson (1975), Nash (1965), Shway Yoe (1882/1910), Slater (1951), and Spiro (1967,
1970, 1977). All of these authors (except Mendelson) mentioned the belief in reincarnation among
the Burmese Buddhists, but only Fielding Hall and Spiro (1970) treated the subject at any length.
Fielding Hall, who wrote at the end of the nineteenth century, gave short accounts of several Burmese cases of the reincarnation type having characteristics similar to the modern cases I have investigated.

trary, from my observations they seem often smilingly insouciant, and they certainly wear less dour expressions than the average Westerner. I do not imply that this difference—if it really exists—derives only from the Buddhist's detachment from life, which contrasts with the grim search for a meaning to life apparent in many Westerners. A sense of the futility of life may add something to the cheerful and carefree, but not careless, attitude shown by many Burmese. Yet other factors also contribute to the character of the average Burman. Although Buddhism is the most important single element in the culture of Burma, that culture includes numerous other ingredients as well.[3]

The Buddhists of Burma, like those of Thailand, believe that human beings undergo a cycle of terrestrial lives separated by periods of discarnate existence until they achieve Nirvana. The word *Nirvana* means literally "extinction" with reference to the loss of the cravings that, according to Buddhism, comprise our familiar personalities and lead to rebirth again and again. Although some exceptional persons may attain Nirvana quite rapidly, the usual aspirant reaches it only after a slow amelioration through many lives. Meritorious actions and the practice of meditation, both of which, in different ways, increase detachment from the usual desires of incarnate existence, help the seeker to attain Nirvana.

Burmese Buddhists, like those of Thailand, believe (in principle) in the doctrine of anatta, or "no soul," which I discussed earlier in this volume in the Introduction to Cases in Thailand. In their ordinary discourse and behavior, however, they often depart from the ideal concept of their scriptures. Spiro (1970) found that, although most of the villagers in Burma with whom he talked about Buddhism had heard of the doctrine of anatta, few knew what the term meant. The Burmese often speak and act as if a deceased person continues to exist in the discarnate realm more or less as he was when alive. And they have kept the pre-Buddhist concept of the *leikpya* or "butterfly spirit," which corresponds, at least to some extent, to Western ideas about the soul (Shway Yoe, 1882/1910; Spiro, 1970). The leikpya is thought to leave the body temporarily during sleep and permanently at death, after which it continues to exist in a discarnate state. The idea of the leikpya as a persisting entity contradicts the Buddhist concept of anatta. But the doctrine of anatta itself seems discordant with that of karma regarded as the results of actions in one life mani-

---

[3]Burma contains important minorities of Christians (especially among the Karens) and Moslems (most of whom are descended from Indians who emigrated to Burma during the British period). The Christians and Moslems of Burma do not believe in reincarnation doctrinally, although some of them appear to have been influenced by Buddhism and accept the possibility of reincarnation. A small number of cases have occurred among these groups and have been studied by U Win Maung and me. These few cases will not, however, be considered separately in this chapter, although they have been included in the analysis of the data from all the Burmese cases, which, with these few exceptions, have occurred among Buddhists.

fested in a later one. Without an enduring entity, the idea of karma loses most of its moral force. If the sower cannot reap, it makes no sense to sow.

In fact, most Burmese do sow as if they expected to reap. Because Nirvana appears almost hopelessly remote—something attainable only after many lifetimes—the average Burman concerns himself more with his near future state: what he will likely encounter in his next few lives. This provides his motive for merit-making through charity—as in giving food and robes to monks, building monasteries and pagodas, or otherwise supporting Buddhism. Uninformed Westerners sometimes think that the Burmese "squander" their money on such institutions when they could and should "invest" it in a company, land, or project that will bring a financial return for the investment. But Western investments are short-term ones compared to those of the Burmese pagoda builder. He expects his returns not in the future years of this life necessarily, but in future lifetimes (Spiro, 1966). The belief in the leikpya, an entity persisting from life to life, assures him that he can enjoy in a later life the benefits of good actions in the present one.

The word *karma* subsumes all the forces and processes by which the influence of moral conduct in one life affects the events of a later one. The effects may not occur in the immediately following life; indeed, they may not manifest until many lives later. They are, however, conceived as comprehensive. They determine such matters as the parents of the next terrestrial rebirth in a series, the order of birth in the family, and the physical body the next personality will have, including its sex.

Burmese Buddhists (like other Buddhists and Hindus) believe that the last thoughts of a dying person particularly influence the circumstances of the next life. Thus,if a person thinks noble thoughts as he dies, he may create for himself better conditions for his next life than a person who occupies his last moments with sensuous and selfish ones. A person's last thoughts before dying express or illustrate the character he has made for himself during the life terminating. One might suppose, therefore, that the last thoughts before dying would *indicate* the character that might be carried over into another life but not necessarily *form* that character. Buddhists believe, however, that thoughts just before dying have a special causative power not possessed by thoughts at other times of life. Thus, a villain who reforms on his deathbed may modify the circumstances of his next life compared with what they might have been if he had not repented.

Burmese Buddhists believe that death initiates a new birth into one of thirty other (nonhuman) realms. The most probable first birth after death is as a *preta,* the concept of which corresponds rather closely to that of the "earth-bound ghost" in Christianity.

The preta remains tied to earth, usually in the area where the deceased person lived, until he is released by a *paritta* ceremony,[4] in which monks chant verses from Buddhist scriptures. This ceremony is generally held on the seventh day after the death. The paritta usually frees the preta for a wider life in the discarnate realm or for rebirth as a new terrestrial personality. But serious misconduct during a human life may lead to a longer period of detention as a preta before such release.

The period lived as a discarnate personality cannot lead to moral progress, but it is not necessarily one of stagnation. On the contrary, discarnate personalities may be assigned some task such as that of guarding temples or treasures; or they may occupy themselves in mild amusements such as frightening incarnate persons. They may, it is said, create physical disturbances among the living of the sort that a Western parapsychologist would attribute to a poltergeist; or they may manifest as apparitions to living persons. Subjects of rebirth cases sometimes claim that they were agents for events of these types during the period between death and rebirth.

The interval between one terrestrial life and its successor may vary greatly. It may extend over many years or less than one year, but it should never be less than the normal period of human gestation. This restriction follows from the Buddhist belief that the new physical body derives its characteristics from the influence of the concerned previous personality, and that the latter cannot modify a new physical body until it has died. I have found that Theravada Buddhists, not only in Burma but in Thailand and Sri Lanka as well, view with skepticism cases in which the subject was born, or even conceived, before the death of the concerned previous personality. No matter how impeccable the informants, how precise and authentic the documentation of dates, or how impressive the information known to the subject about the previous personality's life, they may judge the case to have "something wrong" with it. The speaker may not diagnose the trouble more exactly, but his uneasiness appears nevertheless. Such cases offer a sensitive challenge for persons devoted both to Buddhist teachings and to facts.[5]

Burmese subjects sometimes say they remember being guided to the home of the next rebirth by an elderly sage dressed in white, similar to

---

[4]A paritta ceremony may have different objectives, varying from warding off evil discarnate entities and averting misfortunes to merit-making for the living or the dead. It is perhaps best known as a means of conferring merit on a recently deceased person and freeing him from the preta state for a rebirth in another realm.

For further information about paritta ceremonies (in Sinhalese Buddhism), see Gombrich (1971) and Piyadassi Thera (1975).

[5]Hindus and northern or Tibetan Buddhists can assimilate such cases more easily because they do not expect them to conform to the concept of anatta. There is even a word in Hindi—*prakayapravesh*—for cases in which the previous personality dies *after* the birth of the subject. For examples, see those of Jasbir Singh (Stevenson, 1974) and Chaokhun Rajsuthajarn (this volume).

the "men in white" described by many subjects in Thailand.[6] And as in Thailand, the Burmese "men in white" usually act as guides who only indicate the place for rebirth already selected by other processes and do not influence the selection.

Sometimes a "man in white" seems to keep in touch with a person whose rebirth he has guided after the person has been reborn and even throughout the rest of his life. The "man in white" may sometimes appear in dreams or apparitions to the subject, especially at times of crisis or danger.[7]

The habit of viewing dead bodies seems more widespread in Burma (and other Asian countries) than it is in the West. The Burmese are apparently quite willing to examine the bodies of persons who have died violently or otherwise suddenly and unexpectedly. (Such bodies may be exposed where the person died for some hours or longer before being taken away for burial or other disposition.) This practice may bring unexpected consequences for women of childbearing age. The parents of several subjects of Burmese cases had gone—alone or in a throng—to inspect the body of a person whose life their child later claimed to remember. My informants implied that the deceased previous personality had remained near its discarded physical body and then had attached itself to the first available potential parent. If this was a man, the discarnate aspirant for rebirth followed him home and there "got inside" his wife. If it was the woman herself, association and entry were simpler.

A new incarnation initiated by a discarnate personality through karmic processes may be that of a subhuman animal, and indeed Burmese Buddhists consider it more likely that a person will be reborn as a subhuman animal than as a human. They say this happens because few humans demonstrate the elevated conduct that leads to rebirth as a human; most pay the penalty for their vices by being reborn in a lower form of life. But they may later return to human existence after expiating the wickedness that earned rebirth in that form.

The first intimation of a rebirth may occur in an announcing dream had by a married woman or sometimes by other members or friends of a family. In these dreams, a deceased person seems to inform the dreamer of his wish to be reborn in a particular family, usually that of the dreamer.

The habitual politeness of the Burmese people manifests in a feature of their announcing dreams. The dreamers often describe the presumed

---

[6]As I explained in the Introduction to Cases in Thailand, these sages dress in white because that is the traditional color of a Buddhist layman; the next world has no monks in ocher robes. The Thai and Burmese words for these sages mean literally "man in white." The Burmese (but not the Thais) sometimes identify the "men in white" as spirits who dwell in big trees.

[7]For an example of this, see the case of the Ven. Sayadaw U Sobhana (in this volume).

previous personality as requesting permission to be reborn to the parents
he has chosen. The discarnate personality does not assert that he is coming to them, as do those who appear in announcing dreams among the
Tlingits (Stevenson, 1966); instead, he seems to supplicate a place in the
family he desires to enter. This petitionary type of announcing dream is
not a new development found only in recently investigated cases.
Fielding Hall (1898) referred to it as a feature of the cases he studied at
the end of the nineteenth century. But he believed, incorrectly I think,
that such a dream often occurred to pregnant women near the time of
their deliveries; we[8] have found that the announcing dreams of recently
investigated cases occur more often before the pertinent pregnancy than
during it. (I give figures for their times of occurrence below.)

The Burmese accept the idea that a person can change sex from one
life to another; indeed, they seem to expect that this will happen often,
and as I shall show later, the case material seems to support their belief.

Burmese women enjoy social and legal equality with men, and their
freedom contrasts markedly with the status of women in such neighboring countries as India and Thailand. Nevertheless, both sexes regard being a woman as less desirable than being a man. Spiro (1970) found, in a
small survey he conducted in a village of upper Burma, that the women
often expressed a desire to become men in another life, whereas no man
said that he wished to become a woman. In a later book, Spiro (1977)
stated that "all women recite, as part of their Buddhist devotions, the following conventional prayer: 'Before attaining Nirvana, I pray that I may
be reborn as a male in a future existence' " (p. 260). According to a Burmese fable, if a woman and a male dog are placed before a certain magic
mirror, only the image of the dog will appear in it. The Burmese consider
the dog the lowest form of all animals, and the fable implies that a woman
ranks even below a male animal.

Some aspects of Buddhist beliefs and practice also make a man's life
more desirable than a woman's. It is possible for women to attain Nirvana
(contrary to a mistaken idea some persons have about this), but men have
more opportunities for advancing toward Nirvana through being able to
join the Sangha, which provides freedom and encouragement for meditation and other meritorious actions. Convents exist for nuns, and the
rules of conduct for nuns are less rigorous than those for monks. Yet
women enter convents much less often than men enter monasteries, perhaps because they have deeper emotional ties to their families and

---

[8]I deliberately use "we" here, because I myself have only investigated about two-fifths of the cases
in Burma, and these with varying degrees of thoroughness. For all but a few of the cases I have
studied, U Win Maung has assisted me as interpreter. He has investigated most of the cases himself,
again with varying intensity. I have also included in the total a small number of cases about which we
have received reports from trustworthy informants.

stronger wishes to have children than do men. These restraints increase the longing to become a man that most Burmese women have. This preference has not arisen recently, because a prayer for women who wish to be reborn as men is found among the inscriptions of Pagan, which was an important center of Buddhism and the capital of Burma from the eleventh to the thirteenth centuries (Pe Maung Tin, 1935). In the late nineteenth century Fielding Hall (1898) wrote: "Some Burmans have even supposed that a woman must be reincarnated as a man to gain a step in holiness" (p. 172).

For these reasons, part social and part religious, the Burmese consider a man's rebirth as a woman to be a demotion. Such a change of sex from one life to another may have various causes, but I heard about two of these more often than others. First, informants most commonly attributed a change of sex from man to woman to the deceased man's moral misconduct in a previous life. This theory is difficult to refute, since one can easily find blemishes in the life of anyone; and if there was no evidence that the deceased person has committed some major crime, informants might conjecture some unknown wickedness that he had managed to keep secret during his lifetime; or he may be said to have committed some crime in a more anterior previous life. Second, informants frequently attributed a man's becoming a woman to the deceased man's having thought about his girl friend or wife just before he died. The fixation of the mind on a woman during these few moments before death—the importance of which in Buddhism I have already emphasized—would suffice, many Burmese believe, to draw the deceased person into a female body at his next rebirth. In those last moments before death, to think is to become.

Characteristics of Cases of the Reincarnation Type in Burma

Although we have now investigated nearly 400 cases of the reincarnation type in Burma, I shall confine the summary of this section to the first 230 cases for which we have adequate data. We do not have complete data for all of these 230 cases, and so I shall mention a smaller number when considering some of their characteristics.[9]

The cases have occurred in nearly every section of Burma proper. In using the word *proper* here, I exclude some of the outer states, such as the Kachin state and the Shan states, which form, with Burma proper, the

---

[9]Partly because of local difficulties in conducting investigations in Burma (which I shall briefly describe below), we have investigated few Burmese cases with the thoroughness that I have found possible for many cases that I have studied in other countries. The comparative shortness of the lists of informants for cases in Burma reflects this difference.

Union of Burma. These states are much less accessible than central Burma, and although I have studied a few cases in the Southern Shan States, U Win Maung and I have not traveled much for these cases to areas outside central Burma.

Here I think it appropriate to mention some of the difficulties of investigating cases in Burma compared with other countries where I have studied them. My visits to Burma have never lasted more than one week at a time. Long distances and undeveloped transportation systems led to our often consuming precious time in traveling to the sites of the cases. We could not go at all to some areas that insurgents and *dacoits* still infested. We have occasionally found another difficulty, that of movements of persons from one place to another, so that we have sometimes learned at the end of a long journey that the target witness had moved away from the village where we thought we would find him.

We have learned about the cases in a variety of ways. An informant (that is, a firsthand witness) for one case may tell us about another, or several others, that he knows about. Some informants have even diligently sought out numerous cases in their regions and informed us of them. This has resulted in our knowing about large groups of cases in some areas; but there are many other areas where we have no informants at present, and therefore we know little or nothing about cases in such places. The difficulties of traveling to certain parts of Burma and the somewhat accidental distribution of our informants make it unwise to state anything firmly about the real incidence of cases, or their distribution, in Burma. We can only say at present that they appear to occur frequently and to show no special pattern of geographical distribution.

We have also not discerned any tendency for the cases to occur more frequently in one socioeconomic group than in another.

Among the 230 cases I am summarizing here, 128 (56 per cent) of the subjects were male and 102 (44 per cent) were female.

The presumed previous personalities of the cases show a more biased distribution between the sexes. In 221 cases the sex of the previous personality was definitely known (because a person corresponding to the subject's statements had been identified) or could be reasonably conjectured from the subject's statements. In nine unverified cases, the sex of the previous personality could neither be determined nor conjectured. Among the 221 cases in which this was possible, 150 (68 per cent) were male and 71 (32 per cent) were female. These differences reflect both the high incidence of cases in which a subject remembers a previous life as a member of the opposite sex and the greater frequency, among cases of the "sex change" type, of the male-to-female "change" compared with the female-to-male "change." Of the 230 cases, 65 (28 per cent) were of the "sex change" type. And among these 65 cases, 18 (28 per cent) of the subjects were males who recalled a previous life as a female, while 47 (72 per cent) were females who recalled a previous life as a male. I shall comment on this difference below.

Informants reported announcing dreams for 107 (47 per cent) of the 230 cases and did not report them for 123 (53 per cent). We obtained information with regard to the person having the announcing dream, or the person having what we considered the main dream (if more than one person reported an announcing dream), for these 107 cases. Among them, the subject's mother had the dream in 75 cases (70 per cent), the subject's father in 12 (11 per cent), both parents in 8 (7 per cent), a member of the previous personality's family in 6 (6 per cent), and some other person, such as a neighbor or relative, in 6 (6 per cent). For 84 of the dreams, we obtained information about the time of the dream's occurrence in relation to the pregnancy from which the subject was born. Among these 84 dreams, 54 (64 per cent) occurred before the pregnancy and 29 (35 per cent) occurred during it; only one occurred after the baby was born.[10]

The subjects of Burmese cases usually remember proper names, including the name of the person whose life the subject claims to remember. This facility with names has resulted in a high proportion of "solved" cases, by which I mean those in which we have identified the presumed previous personality with satisfactory assurance. But this remark applies only to "pure Burmese" cases, that is, those in which both the subject and the presumed previous personality lived in Burma. Among the 230 cases, the previous personality has been identified in 185 (80 per cent) and not identified in 45 (20 per cent) cases.[11]

Among the cases for which we do not have a satisfactorily identified previous personality, many (76 per cent) belong to the group of "international cases" that I shall consider below. In these international cases, the subject claims to have been someone other than a Burman in his previous life. For none of these cases have either we or the families concerned found a person corresponding to the subject's statements. This failure is at least partly due to the inability of the subjects of these cases—in strik-

---

[10]Announcing dreams among the Tlingits of southeastern Alaska tend to occur during the later weeks and days of the pregnancy and much less often before the pregnancy has begun than in Burmese cases. For further information about announcing dreams occurring among the Tlingits, see Stevenson (1966, 1974); for examples of such dreams among the Alevis of Turkey, see the cases of İsmail Altınkılıç, Cevriye Bayrı, Erkan Kılıç, and Nasır Toksöz (Stevenson, 1980).

[11]We have found a similar high proportion of solved cases in India. Among 172 cases in India, I consider that a person satisfactorily matching the subject's statements has been found in 135 (78 per cent) and not found in 37 (22 per cent). In contrast, the cases in Sri Lanka have a high incidence of unsolved cases. Among 102 cases in Sri Lanka, I consider 27 (26 per cent) solved and 75 (74 per cent) unsolved. For further information about unsolved cases in Sri Lanka, see the Introduction to Cases in Sri Lanka (Stevenson, 1977).

ing contrast to the pure Burmese cases—to state proper names of places and persons. (The subjects usually gave the name of the country of the previous life, but, with rare exceptions, no other proper names.)

In the majority of Burmese cases in which a previous personality was adequately identified, the two families concerned were related or at least acquainted. Among 154 verified cases for which this information was available, in 83 cases (54 per cent) the subject and previous personality were related closely or distantly; in another 48 cases (31 per cent) the two families were not related but had been acquainted before the case developed; the two families were strangers before the case developed in only 23 (15 per cent) of the cases.

Because we have not verified a single one of the international cases, their main interest lies, not in verified statements, but in the unusual behavior that the subjects of these cases almost always show. The subject of such a case usually claims that in his previous life he was a Japanese, an American, an Englishman, or an Indian. (Occasionally the subject makes no claims to have imaged memories, but his parents identify him with someone of a foreign group on the basis of a dream or perhaps because of his unusual behavior.) Although these subjects behave in ways that are unusual for their families, their behavior is typical for persons of the country where they claim to have lived in their previous lives.

I shall not enlarge here upon the cases whose subjects claim to have been Americans or Englishmen in previous lives; they are extreme blonds—albinos, almost or actually—and their striking appearance (for Burma) makes the interpretation of their cases unusually difficult. (I hope to give some further account of these cases in a later work.) And the cases having presumed previous personalities who were Indians are too few in number to justify any generalization or special attention here.

A third group of international cases, however, deserves some further discussion in this chapter. I refer to those with subjects who claim to have lived previous lives as Japanese soldiers killed in Burma during World War II. Their cases comprise a substantial subgroup (sixteen) of the subjects we have studied in Burma. The children subjects of these cases have shown several behaviors that are strange for normal Burmese children but typical of many Japanese persons. Not all the children show all the traits that I shall list, and they vary greatly both in the strength with which they manifest the traits and in the tenacity with which they resist their elders' attempts to replace the behaviors with conventional Burmese attitudes and habits. Among the traits that we identify as Japanese are:

  a) Complaints about the heat in Burma
  b) Preference for Japanese clothes, especially heavy belts and trousers (instead of the light Burmese *longyis*)

   c) Complaints about the spicy food in Burma and preference for eating instead raw or half-cooked fish, black tea, and sweet foods

   d) Ability to work hard without fatigue and to endure physical pain without complaint

   e) Tendency toward insensitivity, and even harshness, toward other persons

   f) Resistance to the rituals of Burmese Buddhist worship and tendency toward Japanese styles of religious worship

   g) Tendency to expression of vexation, and even rage, when British and American people are mentioned

   h) Difficulty in learning the Burmese language and some tendency to speak Burmese—even in adulthood—with a trace, or more than a trace, of a foreign accent.

Concerning the last trait, informants for several of these cases reported having heard the subject speaking (when he was young) a language that they could not understand. They assumed, from the child's behavior or statements, that the language he was speaking was Japanese. Unfortunately, these cases all occurred in areas where, at the time the cases developed, there were no Japanese-speaking people who might have positively identified the child's strange language.

The listed traits are by no means specific for Japanese people. Other persons may show them, while Japanese people may not. In particular, the trait of insensitivity and harshness toward other people is certainly not a general characteristic of the Japanese people, but it was noticed by Burmese informants as common among Japanese soldiers during World War II; and all the subjects being considered here claimed to have been such soldiers in their previous lives. In the study of these cases, therefore, we should emphasize no single trait, but rather the prominence of the traits in these subjects and the occurrence of a group of them in one child.

No one would suppose that Burmese parents would intentionally influence their children to develop character traits they regarded as typically Japanese. Although the Burmans who aspired to independence from Great Britain initially welcomed the Japanese when they invaded Burma in 1942, they quickly saw that the Japanese came to Burma as an occupying and exploiting power rather than a liberating ally. By the time (in the spring of 1945) that the Japanese were finally expelled from Burma, they had, with exceptions, become thoroughly unpopular. I do not mean to suggest that Burmese parents, once they realized that a child was claiming to have been a Japanese soldier in his previous life, would suppress any Japanese tendencies the child might show. The great tolerance of the Burmese people might even lead some parents to encourage the child to express himself as he wishes, even as a Japanese. But I do not think we should assume any stronger influence from the parents that would initiate the development of Japanese traits in their children. In the present volume, the case of Ma Tin Aung Myo provides illustrations of several of the "Japanese" behaviors I have listed above.

Burmese cases show a high incidence of violent death among the related previous personalities. We obtained adequate verification of the previous personality's mode of death for 168 cases. Among these persons, 76 (45 per cent) died violently, the majority through homicide and war; 92 (55 per cent) died natural deaths.[12]

Informants reported that in 82 (36 per cent) of the 230 cases here considered, the subject bore birthmarks or congenital deformities apparently corresponding to wounds or lesions in the related previous personality. The majority of the wounds had been fatal, but a small number had been holes pierced for earrings, and a few birthmarks corresponded to nonfatal injuries and other marks, such as tattoos, on the body of the related previous personality.

For 152 cases, we obtained data that I consider sufficiently accurate concerning the related previous personality's age at death; the median age at death for these cases was thirty-five years. For 122 cases, we obtained data concerning both the related previous personality's date of death and the subject's date of birth that were sufficiently accurate to allow us to compute the interval between them. The median interval for these cases was twenty-one months, but the interval varied widely—as the cases in this volume show. For them the interval extends from nine months in the case of the Ven. Sayadaw U Sobhana to more than eight years in that of Ma Tin Aung Myo.

I mentioned earlier that Burmese Buddhists would not normally believe that a subject who remembered the life of a deceased person could have been conceived, much less born, before that person died. Nevertheless, I have studied two exceptional cases of this type for which I am confident concerning the accuracy of the relevant dates of death and birth.

I shall now take up again the topic of the high incidence of cases of "sex change" among the Burmese. The incidence (28 per cent) is—with the exception of the Kutchin of the Canadian Northwest Territories (Slobodin, 1970)[13]—the highest of any culture in which I have investi-

---

[12]I have not obtained any figures for the incidence of violent death among the general population of Burma. We can safely assume, however, that the incidence of violent death among the concerned previous personalities of these cases far exceeds that among the general population.

For figures of the incidence of violent death among the concerned previous personalities in cases of other cultures, see Table 15 of the third volume of this series (Stevenson, 1980).

[13]Slobodin (1970) found twenty-two cases of "sex change" among forty-four Kutchin cases, an incidence of 50 per cent.

During a short visit to the Canadian Northwest Territories in 1977, I was able to investigate briefly seven Kutchin cases, and in six of these the subject was identified as having been a person of the opposite sex in the previous life.

gated these cases. I cannot account for the comparatively high frequency of cases of the sex change type in Burma. Buddhism teaches detachment from one's earthly condition, including one's sex, so that if reincarnation occurs, Buddhists may be more ready to give up one sex and assume another than would persons of other cultures whose members give greater importance to the sex one has. The complete absence of cases of the sex change type in Lebanon and Turkey harmonizes with this interpretation, but cannot tell the whole story. Among 102 cases in Sri Lanka (another Buddhist country), only 9 cases (9 per cent) of the sex change type occurred.

Apart from the foregoing problem, the cases of the sex change type in Burma present a distinctive feature within themselves that also calls for explanation. I refer to the much higher frequency of women who remember previous lives as men than of men who remember previous lives as women. Among 75 Burmese cases of the sex change type,[14] in 56 (75 per cent) the subject was a female and in 19 (25 per cent), a male. (I have confidence in these data: first, because the ratio of about three to one appeared in the early days of my investigations in Burma and has persisted since then, so it is not due to some sudden addition of deviant cases; and second, because we have also found a higher proportion of female subjects than of male subjects in the cases of the sex change type of other cultures in which such cases occur.)

I believe that, if reincarnation occurs, one would be more likely to remember a violent death than a natural one. A violent attack on someone (or a violent accident) usually arouses strong emotions in the victim, and also usually entails great physical suffering, each of which may enhance memories.[15] Since men die violently more often than women, one would expect to find more men's lives remembered than women's lives. We can test this conjecture with the cases of sex change in Burma. Among the 168 cases (mentioned above) for which we obtained adequate verification of the mode of the concerned previous personality's death, there were 51

---

[14]The number of Burmese cases of the sex change type given here (75) exceeds that mentioned earlier in this chapter (65) because we have analyzed more cases solely for features related to sex change than for other characteristics of the cases.

[15]Other factors beside the effect of suffering on memory may account for (or contribute to) the high incidence of violent death among these cases.

A normal explanation is that cases that include violence are more likely to be remembered and reported by informants to investigators than are cases in which death occurred naturally.

A violent death is usually also sudden, unexpected, and premature with regard to the victim's natural expectation of life. Consequently, the victim is likely to have left behind "unfinished business," and this, if reincarnation occurs, may lead to an earlier reincarnation than would occur at the end of a longer life whose cravings—for that particular life—had been satisfied. However, an earlier empirical test of this hypothesis on cases in India failed to show a statistically significant difference between cases with violent deaths and those with natural deaths with regard to the median interval between death and presumed rebirth. (See Stevenson [1975], p. 96.) This analysis examined only a small number of cases, and I intend to repeat it with the larger number of cases now available.

instances of the sex change type. Among the 36 of these cases having a female subject, the related (male) previous personality died violently in 13 (36 per cent). In contrast, among the 15 cases having a male subject, the related (female) previous personality died violently in 2 (13 per cent). We cannot interpret these figures, however, without comparing them with those for same sex cases. Table 11 gives the data for the causes of death for males and females in sex change and same sex cases. The data show that the incidence of violent death among previous personalities (of both sexes) in the same sex cases actually exceeds that in the cases of the sex change type. Table 12 presents the same data arranged to emphasize the previous personality's mode of death. It shows that among sex change cases, males preponderate by far over females among the previous personalities in the cases involving a natural death as well as in those involving a violent death. It also shows that the proportion of violent death (compared with natural death) is actually considerably lower among sex change cases than among same sex ones. From these data I conclude that violent death, although playing an important part in the generation of memories in cases of both sex change and same sex types, does not explain the lopsided ratio of male-to-female compared with female-to-male cases of the sex change type in Burma. Considering the prospects of a man who was going to die and reincarnate in Burma, one might say that he had a somewhat greater chance of reincarnating as a female if he died naturally than if he died violently.

These data may have one or more normal explanations. Girls are more willing in Burma to say that they were men in a previous life than boys are willing to say that they were women. According to U Win Maung, a Burmese boy who says that he was a woman in a previous life might be mercilessly teased by his peers, although adults would accept the boy's claim as a matter of fact. We should remember, however, that the Buddhist judgment of male-to-female change as a demotion tends toward the opposite bias, since girls and women might be reluctant to make a claim that would involve an avowal of wrongdoing in a previous life and the consequent loss of status by being reborn as a girl.

A bias in the collection of data might occur also if cases in which male previous personalities figured received more attention first within the families of the subjects and then from local informants who notify us about cases. Despite the near social and legal equality of men and women in Burma, men play a much larger part in public affairs; their lives may therefore be considered more significant and thus be more memorable to others.

We need also to consider interpretations of the data if reincarnation does occur. The suggestion emerges that "maleness" somehow generates

TABLE 11. *Incidence of Modes of Death of Previous Personalities in Verified "Sex Change" Cases of Burma (Data Organized to Compare Sexes of Previous Personalities)*

Sex of Previous Personality	"Sex Change" Cases	"Same Sex" Cases	Total Verified Cases
Male			
Violent	13 (36.1%)	50 (65.8%)	63 (56.3%)
Natural	23 (63.9%)	26 (34.2%)	49 (43.7%)
Total	36	76	112
Female			
Violent	2 (13.3%)	11 (26.8%)	13 (23.2%)
Natural	13 (86.7%)	30 (73.2%)	43 (76.8%)
Total	15	41	56

TABLE 12. *Incidence of Modes of Death of Previous Personalities in Verified "Sex Change" Cases of Burma* (*Data Organized to Compare Modes of Death of Previous Personalities*)

Mode of Death	"Sex Change" Cases	"Same Sex" Cases	Total Verified Cases
Violent			
Male	13 (86.7%)	50 (82.0%)	63 (82.9%)
Female	2 (13.3%)	11 (18.0%)	13 (17.1%)
Total	15	61	76
Natural			
Male	23 (63.9%)	26 (46.4%)	49 (53.3%)
Female	13 (36.1%)	30 (53.6%)	43 (46.7%)
Total	36	56	92
Percent of violent deaths / total deaths of known cause in cases	29.4	52.1	45.2

memories of a previous life.[16] It seems to me that although women's lives have many moments of excitement, they are not, on the whole, as various and as exciting—hence as memorable—as men's lives. I think this may be particularly true of societies, such as that of the Burmese villages, where life goes on in a routine way for decades—unless disrupted by war—and where men have more opportunities for traveling outside the area of the home than do women. This greater variety of a man's life compared with a woman's might lead to a greater fixation of memories in the mind of a person who had been a man, died, and reincarnated—whether as a man or a woman.

I venture to offer another explanation that is more conjectural. Given the prevailing attitude in Burma that to become a woman means that one has been demoted—socially (to a slight extent) as well as in opportunities for spiritual advancement—the awareness by a girl of having been a man may bring some shock and thereby stimulate memories more than would the awareness on the part of a boy that he had been a woman in a previous life.[17]

Our data permit us to advance no further. I am even afraid that I have speculated too far ahead of the facts already. The development of further data may aid arbitration among the rival interpretations, or may help us to think of even better explanations. Unfortunately, at this time we have studied many more cases of the sex change type in Burma than elsewhere; but as the numbers of such cases investigated in other countries increase, so will our ability to draw firmer conclusions from all such cases.

Although, as I mentioned earlier, the Burmese show considerable concern about their future lives, as evidenced by the importance they attach to charity and other acts of merit-making, few of them express openly a wish for a *particular* change of status in the next incarnation, except for a change of sex. They hope for better circumstances in general, but rarely attempt to specify—at least publicly to other people—what these circumstances should be. For example, I know of only a few instances in which the related previous personality selected premortem his parents for his next life or expressed other wishes about it.[18]

[16]"Maleness" does not supersede "violent death" as a factor facilitating memories of a previous life; the life most likely to be remembered in Burma seems to be that of a man who died violently, and so these two factors may supplement each other.

[17]We have found a preponderance of male previous personalities also in the cases of Alaska (Tlingit), Turkey, and Lebanon. In these countries there are more male than female previous personalities in cases of violent death, natural death, and unknown causes of death. Since there are no "sex change" cases in these three cultures, males also outnumber females among the subjects of the cases.

[18]One of these is the case of Ma Tin Tin Myint in this volume; the concerned previous personality of her case expressed a wish to have in her next life a better education, including an opportunity to study abroad.

I shall conclude this section by mentioning the high incidence of an additional feature of the cases in Burma: claimed memories of experiences between death and presumed rebirth.

Claims to remember events occurring between the death of the concerned previous personality and the subject's birth occurred in 52 (23 per cent) of 230 cases. The subjects who claim to remember experiences during the interval between death and rebirth describe a variety of them. Some of them, as I mentioned earlier, say they recall intervening in the lives of living persons to whom they manifested as poltergeists. Some speak about the disposal of the concerned previous personality's body after its death. And some describe experiences in another realm of existence, such as those in which the "men in white" figure. And an appreciable number say that they recall "sending" a petitionary announcing dream in which they asked to be allowed to be reborn as a child of their parents.[19]

Occasionally, a discarnate personality manifests to another person when that person is awake—in short, as an apparition.[20]

Parental Attitudes and Other Circumstances Related to Cases of the Reincarnation Type in Burma

Children who remember previous lives appear to be quite common in Burma—common enough, at least, to have gained a name for themselves: *luwinza*.[21] Burmese parents seem to me generally neutral with regard to memories of a previous life stated by one of their children. They do not give eggs to young children because of a widespread belief that eggs somehow block memories of a previous life from coming into consciousness and being expressed (Foll, 1959; Mi Mi Khaing, 1962). On the other hand, some Burmans believe, as do many Indians, that children who remember previous lives will die young, and for this reason parents sometimes discourage a child from expressing any memories he may have; but they rarely resort to more than mild discouragement in such efforts at suppression. If feeding the child boiled duck eggs does not suf-

---

[19]The case of the Ven. Sayadaw U Sobhana (in this volume) includes the features of a "man in white" and announcing dreams.

[20]The case of the Ven. Chaokhun Rajsuthajarn (in this volume) provides an example of this in Thailand and that of Maung Yin Maung (also in this volume) an example in Burma.

[21]The word *luwinza* is usually reserved for someone who claims to have memories of a previous life, although Burmans may apply it loosely to persons who give other indications of a previous life—for example, in unusual behavior—without claiming to remember one. The word literally means "reborn human," since in Burmese *lu* means "human" and *winza* means "reborn." A subject claiming to remember the previous life of a subhuman animal would be referred to differently. If he was thought to have been a dog in his previous life, he would be called *khwaywinza* (the Burmese word *khway* means "dog").

fice, they may make gestures of beating him with a broomstick, although without actually hurting him.

I have studied several cases in which informants attributed a fading, or even a total loss, of memories to the subject's having been burned accidentally; according to their testimony in such cases, the subject recalled many details of the previous life until, at a certain age, he was burned by boiling water or in some other way.

I know of one Burmese case in which memories of a previous life first occurred, at least substantially, during an illness. In another case, that of Maung Yin Maung (this volume), the subject's memories became intensified during an illness. There are also cases in which an illness has weakened memories of a previous life; the case of the Ven. Sayadaw U Sobhana (also this volume) provides two instances of that.

Informants for Burmese cases frequently state that the subject, as a young child, spoke about his memories of a previous life only or especially on "dark and gloomy days." I have heard (or learned of) this observation in every part of Burma where I have studied cases. It occurs so commonly in connection with Burmese cases and so rarely in those of other cultures that I have come to regard it as perhaps a "culture-bound" feature of Burmese cases. But I do not understand how this can be; although the informants for one case had often heard of other cases, it does not seem likely that information about a "typical case" could have diffused to so many informants with the result that they developed a model of a typical case to which they, perhaps unconsciously, made other cases conform. The simplest explanation of this observation may also be the best. "Dark and gloomy days" are cloudy ones on which it is raining or likely to rain. Children are therefore detained indoors, either by the bad weather or by their parents. Restrained from their outdoor play, their thoughts turn inward and backward and so toward the memories of previous lives, which they then talk about with the adults and other children who are equally housebound at such times. Perhaps we need to seek no more complicated interpretation than this. But I remain puzzled by the much greater frequency with which Burmese parents make this observation about the subjects than do parents of subjects in other countries, including those with as many clouds and as much rain as Burma has.

I have already mentioned the high incidence among the cases in Burma of those in which the two personalities concerned belonged to the same family or the two families concerned were acquainted before the development of a case. These are, in fact, a large majority (85 per cent) of the cases. Burmans are no freer than other peoples from the desire to have reality conform to their wishes and from hope that deceased loved ones have not been lost forever. The familial and social relationships between the concerned personalities weaken the evidence of paranormal processes in many Burmese cases. (In addition, Burman informants share with those elsewhere the other causes of fallibility in oral testimony.) And yet against this possible flaw—that of wishing to see a deceased loved person return—it is only fair to mention two ways in which Burmese cases differ from those of some other countries, notably India; these are features that reduce or eliminate errors of testimony that sometimes create difficulties in the assessment of cases in these other countries.

The first of these derives from newspaper publicity. Cases of the reincarnation type are rather often reported in the newspapers of India, Sri Lanka, and Thailand. With one exception, of which I plan to publish a short report later, I have never learned of a case in India, Sri Lanka, or Thailand that seemed to be developed, or exploited in a major way, solely for the sake of such publicity as newspapers could offer. At the same time, I have suspected that a few informants enjoyed the publicity of the newspapers and could not free themselves of temptations to round off the jagged edges of facts in order to present a smooth account of events, which a journalist might expect. How much such adaptations might have affected the testimony given to me I have always tried to assess and describe in my case reports. This has never been necessary in considering Burmese cases, for the simple reason that Burmese newspapers rarely publish reports of cases. Burma has fewer newspapers than India, Sri Lanka, and Thailand; and those there are show comparatively little interest in rebirth cases. Apart from this, Burmese parents of subjects (and the subjects themselves) seem to gain little or nothing, even among their own circle of acquaintances, from the development of a case. This, however, is a matter for judgment in each individual case and not a feature in which Burmese informants for a case differ from those in other countries of South Asia.

Burma also lacks another factor that sometimes provides in India a motive for impeding the flow of information to investigators: it has no castes. Moreover, although some Burmans obviously have more wealth than others, especially in the cities, most of the people of the villages and the smaller towns live on the same socioeconomic level or on similar levels. These factors probably account for the paucity in Burma of cases of a type observed rather often in India, those in which a vast difference in social and economic status separates the two families concerned. As I have mentioned in connection with the reports of some Indian cases, such as those of Sunil Dutt Saxena and Dolon Champa Mitra (first volume of this series), disparities of this kind may provoke in the family of the previous personality a suspicion that the subject's family is trying to exploit them. Groundless as these conjectures are, they can nevertheless seriously interfere with an investigator's work. Such difficulties rarely occur in cases in Burma.

Note on Burmese Names and Honorifics

A Burmese boy is given the honorific *Maung* and a girl the honorific *Ma*. Upon attaining a certain adult status, men are given the respectful honorific *U* and women the corresponding *Daw*. These adult honorifics have nothing to do with marital status. Thus a mature woman may be called "Daw" although she remains single; and some married women, usually ones of inferior social status, may continue to be addressed as "Ma." Similarly, a man of inferior status may continue to be called "Maung" even though he has married.

Ko is an honorific used among men who are equal in status and familiar with each other.

Most Burmese do not have or use family names, but usually have two or three given names. Moreover, a woman retains her given names after marriage and does not modify them or adopt her husband's name. Occasional exceptions to this general rule occur when a daughter takes her father's name or a wife her husband's. But such exceptions occur, in my experience, only among the more Westernized Burmese.

References

Fielding Hall, H. 1898. *The soul of a people.* London: Macmillan and Co.

Foll, C. V. 1959. An account of some of the beliefs and superstitions about pregnancy, parturition and infant health in Burma. *The Journal of Tropical Pediatrics* 5:51–59.

Gombrich, R. 1971. *Precept and practice: Traditional Buddhism in the rural highlands of Ceylon.* Oxford: Oxford University Press.

Htin Aung. 1967. *A history of Burma.* New York: Columbia University Press.

King, W. L. 1964. *A thousand lives away: Buddhism in contemporary Burma.* Cambridge, Mass.: Harvard University Press.

_____. 1976. Contemporary Burmese Buddhism. In *Buddhism in the Modern World,* edited by H. Dumoulin. New York: Macmillan Publishing Co.

Ling, T. 1979. *Buddhism, imperialism and war: Burma and Thailand in modern history.* London: George Allen & Unwin.

Mendelson, E. M. 1975. *Sangha and state in Burma: A study of monastic sectarianism and leadership.* Ithaca, N.Y.: Cornell University Press.

Mi Mi Khaing. 1962. *Burmese family.* Bloomington: Indiana University Press.

Nash, M. 1965. *The golden road to modernity: Village life in contemporary Burma.* New York: John Wiley and Sons.

Parrinder, E. G. 1970. *African traditional religion.* Westport, Connecticut: Greenwood Press. (First published in 1954 by Hutchinson's University Library, London.)

Pe Maung Tin. 1935. Women in the inscriptions of Pagan. *Journal of the Burma Research Society* 25:411–21.

Piyadassi Thera. 1975. *The book of protection: Paritta.* Kandy: Union Printing Works.

Shway Yoe (J. G. Scott). 1910. *The Burman: His life and notions.* London: Macmillan and Co. (First published in 1882 by Macmillan and Co., London)

Slater, R. H. L. 1951. *Paradox and Nirvana: A study of religious ultimates with special reference to Burmese Buddhism.* Chicago: University of Chicago Press.

Slobodin, R. 1970. Kutchin concepts of reincarnation. *Western Canadian Journal of Anthropology* 2:67–79.

Spiro, M. E. 1966. Buddhism and economic action in Burma. *American Anthropologist* 68:1163–73.

———. 1967. *Burmese supernaturalism.* Englewood Cliffs, N.J.: Prentice-Hall.

———. 1970. *Buddhism and society: A great tradition and its Burmese vicissitudes.* New York: Harper and Row.

———. 1977. *Kinship and marriage in Burma.* Berkeley: University of California Press.

Stevenson, I. 1966. Cultural patterns in cases suggestive of reincarnation among the Tlingit Indians of southeastern Alaska. *Journal of the American Society for Psychical Research* 60:229–43.

———. 1974. *Twenty cases suggestive of reincarnation.* Charlottesville: University Press of Virginia. (First published as *Proceedings of the American Society for Psychical Research* 26:1–362, 1966.)

———. 1975. *Cases of the reincarnation type. Vol. 1, Ten cases in India.* Charlottesville: University Press of Virginia.

———. 1977. *Cases of the reincarnation type. Vol. 2, Ten cases in Sri Lanka.* Charlottesville: University Press of Virginia.

———. 1980. *Cases of the reincarnation type. Vol. 3, Twelve cases in Lebanon and Turkey.* Charlottesville: University Press of Virginia.

8. The Case of Ma Tin Aung Myo

Introduction

THE SUBJECT OF this case, Ma Tin Aung Myo, is a Burmese girl who claimed to remember a previous life as a Japanese soldier killed in Burma during the Second World War. She made no verifiable statements, and so the interest of her case lies almost entirely in her unusual behavior. In important respects she has shown the behavior that one would expect of a Japanese man and not that of a typical Burmese girl.

Summary of the Case and Its Investigation

Ma Tin Aung Myo was born in Nathul, a village of Kyaukse District, Upper Burma, on December 26, 1953. Her parents were U Aye Maung and Daw Aye Tin. They had three other daughters, all older than Ma Tin Aung Myo, and one son, younger than she. U Aye Maung died in 1963, when Ma Tin Aung Myo was still a child and long before the investigation of this case began. He had been a railway porter. After his death, his widow worked as a hawker of meals and fruits at the nearby railway station in Kume.

In 1972 Daw Aye Tin told me that when she was several months pregnant with Ma Tin Aung Myo she dreamed repeatedly that a stocky Japanese soldier wearing short pants and no shirt followed her and said he would come and stay with them. She recognized him as an army cook with whom she had become friendly during the Japanese army's occupation of Nathul, which I shall describe. In the dream Daw Aye Tin was afraid of the soldier and told him not to follow her. The same dream occurred three times at intervals of five to ten days.[1]

---

[1] In the interest of accuracy, I must note that when I asked Daw Aye Tin in 1975 if she remembered any dreams that she had had during this pregnancy, she said that she did not. Since her testimony that year was otherwise quite consistent with what she had said in 1972 (I did not see her when I was in Nathul in 1974), I think this discrepancy is due either to forgetfulness on her part or possibly to her failure to understand in 1975 what I (through U Win Maung) was asking her. In 1981 (in a conversation with U Win Maung) she again remembered the dream. She did not explain why she had forgotten it earlier.

Ma Tin Aung Myo's mother and older sisters differed in their memories of when Ma Tin Aung Myo first spoke. One of her older sisters, Ma Nyunt, said that she began to speak when she was two years old, but another, Ma Shwe, said that she did not speak before she was three. And her mother, Daw Aye Tin, said that she did not speak normally until she was about five.[2] (She was slow to learn Burmese, a feature of the case to which I shall return later.)

Our informants also differed about when Ma Tin Aung Myo first referred to a previous life. According to Ma Shwe, Ma Tin Aung Myo made her first reference to a previous life when she was about four. She was walking with her father one day when an airplane flew overhead. She began to cry and seemed frightened. When her father asked her what the matter was, she replied: "I want to go home. I want to go home." Thereafter she cried every time an airplane flew over. Her father asked her why she was afraid of them, and she said that they would shoot her. Her father answered that people on the ground had been shot at from airplanes but this would not happen now. His reassurance, however, had no effect, and Ma Tin Aung Myo continued to show an extreme fear of airplanes for many years.

At about this time, or perhaps a little later, Ma Tin Aung Myo was noted to be depressed and weeping. Asked to say what was troubling her, she answered: "I am pining for Japan." Thereafter she gradually began to tell what she remembered of how, as a Japanese soldier stationed in her family's village, she had been strafed and killed by an (Allied) airplane.

At this time also Ma Tin Aung Myo's family noted that she resisted wearing girls' clothes; instead, she dressed invariably in a boys' style.

In September 1972, U Win Maung learned about this case from U Hla Baw, a prominent resident of Nathul. U Win Maung took down a statement from Ma Tin Aung Myo and sent this to me along with some other pertinent information about the case.

On November 4, 1972, U Win Maung and I went to Nathul and talked with Ma Tin Aung Myo's mother and her oldest sister, Ma Shwe. But Ma Tin Aung Myo was not in the village that day. Our luck improved two years later when we returned to Nathul. We then met Ma Tin Aung Myo, another of her older sisters, Ma Nyunt, and her younger brother, Maung Sein Maung. (Her mother was away that day.) U Hla Baw furnished some

---

[2]Unfortunately, we did not have the opportunity of obtaining the information on this point (and others) from the informants at the same time. For this reason I cannot be sure that each informant was asked the same question in the same way. Parents and other informants are apt to interpret in different ways the question "How old was the child when he or she first began to speak?" Here it seems obvious that Ma Tin Aung Myo's sisters were trying to remember when she first began to speak and Daw Aye Tin was trying to fix a date for her finally attaining satisfactory competence in speaking Burmese.

helpful information about the Japanese occupation of Nathul. In 1975 U Win Maung and I returned again to Nathul and talked further with Ma Tin Aung Myo and her mother.

In January 1977 and in May 1981, U Win Maung visited Nathul again and obtained additional information about the case from Ma Tin Aung Myo, her mother, two of her older sisters (Ma Nyunt and Ma Myint), and U Hla Baw.

Persons Interviewed during the Investigation

In Nathul I interviewed:

Ma Tin Aung Myo
Daw Aye Tin, Ma Tin Aung Myo's mother
Ma Shwe, Ma Tin Aung Myo's oldest sister
Ma Nyunt, Ma Tin Aung Myo's second oldest sister.
Maung Sein Maung, Ma Tin Aung Myo's younger brother
U Hla Baw, village elder of Nathul

The Japanese Occupation of Nathul

In the 1940s and later, U Hla Baw was Nathul's most important resident. The Japanese evidently thought so, because they used his house as their headquarters when a unit of their army occupied the village in 1942. Allied fliers contested their presence, mainly because of the important railway station at Kume, which is nearby. Allied fighter-bombers came over—for a time, twice daily—and bombed the area. They would also make runs as needed to machine-gun any person they saw on the ground. To avoid these attacks, the Burmese regularly left the village in the morning and returned only at night.

The bombing and strafing of Nathul and Kume continued until the Japanese were finally driven away by the advancing British and American armies in the spring of 1945.[3]

Daw Aye Tin had not learned of the death of any Japanese soldier under circumstances corresponding to those mentioned by Ma Tin Aung Myo, which I shall describe below. But we should feel no surprise at this. Burmese villagers traded with the Japanese soldiers without becoming much acquainted with them, except in special circumstances. On the con-

---

[3]For information about the fighting in Burma during the spring of 1945, see J. Masters, *The Road Past Mandalay: A Personal Narrative* (London: Michael Joseph, 1961); R. McKelvie, *The War in Burma* (London: Methuen and Co., 1948); W. Slim, *Defeat into Victory* (New York: David McKay Company, 1961); E. D. Smith, *Battle for Burma* (New York: Holmes and Meier Publishers, 1979).

trary, the tendency toward rudeness, and sometimes cruelty, shown by many of the Japanese soldiers led most of the Burmese villagers to avoid them as much as they could.

When I talked with Daw Aye Tin in 1975, she could not remember that she had had a special relationship with any of the Japanese soldiers who occupied Nathul. She treated them like any other customers and carried on her modest business with as little interruption as the unusual circumstances permitted. However, in her interview with U Win Maung in 1981, she said that she had become friendly with a Japanese army cook during the Japanese occupation. Because they were both interested in foods, they had exchanged ideas about foods and methods of cooking in Japan and Burma. This army cook was the soldier Daw Aye Tin recognized in the dreams that she had when she was pregnant with Ma Tin Aung Myo.

Statements Made by Ma Tin Aung Myo

I shall divide Ma Tin Aung Myo's statements about the previous life into those remembered by members of her family (as having been said when she was young) and those few additional items that she told to U Win Maung and me when we met her.

Ma Tin Aung Myo's Statements Made When She Was Young.   Members of Ma Tin Aung Myo's family remembered that when she was young she said that she had been a Japanese soldier who came from the northern part of Japan. He had been married and had had children. He had been stationed at Nathul.

Ma Tin Aung Myo remembered the soldier's being near a pile of firewood and about to cook a meal when an airplane came over. She recalled that, at that moment, he was wearing short pants and a big belt, but had taken off his shirt. The firewood pile was near an acacia tree, about 75 meters from the house where Ma Tin Aung Myo's family lived. The pilot of the airplane spotted the Japanese soldier and dived at him, spraying machine gun bullets. The soldier ran around the pile of firewood in an effort to escape, but a bullet struck him in the groin. He died immediately.

Ma Tin Aung Myo included no other names (other than that of Japan) in her statements—neither those of the Japanese soldier and his family nor that of the community in Japan where he had lived.

Ma Tin Aung Myo's Later Statements.   In 1974 Ma Tin Aung Myo told U Win Maung and me that in the previous life she had had five children, of which the oldest was a boy. She thought that she had had a small shop in Japan before joining the army. She also said that she had been a cook in the Japanese army and had died during the period when the Japanese were evacuating Burma.[4] She remembered the airplane that shot the soldier as having had two tails, but could not say whether it was a British or an American airplane.[5]

Ma Tin Aung Myo said nothing about events between the death of the Japanese soldier and her own birth.

Ma Tin Aung Myo's Behavior Related to the Previous Life

Circumstances and Manner of Ma Tin Aung Myo's Speaking about the Previous Life.   Ma Tin Aung Myo had a severe phobia of airplanes and would cower and cry whenever one flew over.[6] When reproached about this, she said: "What do you know? I was shot and killed." Once when Ma Tin Aung Myo was about nine years old (that is, in about 1963) a helicopter landed in a field at Nathul. Most of the villagers wanted to see the helicopter, but Ma Tin Aung Myo fled crying into the house and said she was frightened.

Apart from airplanes, the chief stimulus of Ma Tin Aung Myo's talking about the previous life was cloudy weather. On cloudy days she was likely to hide herself behind a door or in a pile of clothes and say that she wanted to go to Japan, where she had children.

Ma Tin Aung Myo's Attitudes toward Burma and Burmese Customs.   Ma Tin Aung Myo did not like the hot climate of Burma. Nor did she like its spicy food; on the contrary, she preferred sweet foods. She wanted the family's curries to be cooked with juggery, a preparation high in sugar content obtained from certain types of coconut palms.

When she was a young child, she liked to eat fish, especially half-raw fish. (She did not care for completely raw fish as do some Japanese people.) One day a fish bone stuck in her throat, and after this unpleasant experience, she acquired a dislike for fish.

Ma Tin Aung Myo did not clamor for, or even request, strange foods

---

[4]The British army captured Kume from the Japanese on March 23, 1945. There would have been no Allied overflights for bombing and strafing after that date, so we can assume that the Japanese soldier Ma Tin Aung Myo claimed to remember would have died before then. Thus, if she was remembering events that actually happened, the interval between the soldier's death and her birth would be at least eight and a half years.

[5]The United States Army Air Force used two-tailed airplanes, such as the P-38 and the P-61, during the campaigns of World War II in Southeast Asia.

[6]For other examples of subjects who have shown phobias related to the death of the person whose life they claimed to remember, see the cases of Parmod Sharma, Ravi Shankar Gupta, Sleimann Bouhamzy, Derek Pitnov (*Twenty Cases*), Shamlinie Prema, Ruby Kusuma Silva, Sujith Lakmal Jayaratne (second volume of this series), Necati Çaylak, Cevriye Bayrı, Erkan Kılıç, Süleyman Zeytun (third volume), and Ornuma Sua Ying Yong (this volume).

that her family had never heard of. Nor did she summarily reject the food offered her; she only complained about its spiciness.[7] Her mother yielded and gave her blander food such as eggs. In view of her claim to have been a cook in the previous life she remembered, one might have expected her to have participated actively in the cooking at her home. She told me, however, that because of her aversion to spices and chilis, she omitted them when she cooked, and other members of the family therefore forbade her to cook for them. She had, and voiced, an equally low opinion of the competence at cooking of others in the family.

She frequently expressed a longing to return to Japan and said she would go there when she grew up. Sometimes she lay on her stomach and cried for homesickness. In addition to Japan as a whole, she seemed to miss the children of the previous life; or perhaps her memories of them made her wish to return to Japan. Her enthusiasm for Japan led her family to give her the nickname Japangyi. (The word *gyi* in Burmese means "big" and is sometimes applied half jocularly at the end of a word used to characterize a person. Thus *Japangyi* could be rendered in American slang as "the Japanese guy.") Ma Tin Aung Myo did not like being called "Japangyi," and when her family realized that the nickname disturbed her, they stopped using it.

When Ma Tin Aung Myo was quite young, her family noticed that she talked to herself and to other children with words they could not understand. No attempt was made to understand this language or even to learn whether it was a definite language, such as Japanese, and not mere childish chatter. Ma Shwe said that Ma Tin Aung Myo learned Burmese readily, but Daw Aye Tin had a different opinion. She said that Ma Tin Aung Myo was slow to learn Burmese words and that when she was young she often mispronounced certain words. According to her, Ma Tin Aung Myo could not speak Burmese normally until she was about five.

Ma Tin Aung Myo's Sexual Orientation.   From an early age, Ma Tin Aung Myo insisted on wearing boys' clothes and refused to wear girls' clothes.[8] When her mother tried to put girls' clothes on her, she threw them aside. She told me, almost boastfully, in 1974 that she did not own a single item

[7]For examples of children who have rejected their families' foods or asked for special foods not ordinarily eaten in their families, see the cases of Jasbir Singh *(Twenty Cases)*, Jagdish Chandra, Veer Singh (first volume of this series), Shamlinie Prema, Gamini Jayasena, Mahes de Silva, Wijanama Kithsiri (second volume), and Bongkuch Promsin (this volume). In each of these cases, the food in question either was not eaten by the person the subject claimed to have been or was particularly relished by that person.

[8]For other examples of children who have remembered previous lives as persons of the opposite sex and who have shown cross-dressing and other behavior appropriate for the concerned previous personalities, see the cases of Gnanatilleka Baddewithana, Paulo Lorenz *(Twenty Cases)*, Dolon Champa Mitra (first volume of this series), Ruby Kusuma Silva (second volume), and Ampan Petcherat (this volume).

of Burmese women's clothes. The photograph that she has allowed me to publish (see figure) shows the masculine style of her dress as compared with that usual for Burmese women.

Both men and women in Burma wear, from the waist down, an ankle-length garment called a longyi. The women wear longyis having (nearly always) floral designs, although sometimes they are of a solid color; the men wear longyis nearly always having check patterns. The women tuck the upper edge of the longyi into itself at the left side of the waist, without a knot; in contrast, the men pull the longyi tight with a rather conspicuous knot that protrudes outward in the middle. For upper garments the women usually wear delicate blouses, whereas the men wear shirts somewhat like those worn by Western men. Burmese women wear their hair long, often drawn into a bun or queue at the back of the head. Most Burmese men wear their hair rather short. In the photograph that I took, Ma Tin Aung Myo stands in the center flanked by her younger brother and one of her older sisters. Readers can readily see that her dress and general appearance resemble those of her brother much more than those of her sister.

Ma Tin Aung Myo would actually have preferred a style of dress closer to that of the Japanese. She said at one time that she wanted a big belt to protect her stomach against the cold. (Nathul is somewhat elevated, and although it has withering heat in summer, it can be extremely cold in winter.)

When she was a young child, Ma Tin Aung Myo played with boys and particularly liked to play at being a soldier. She asked her parents to buy her toy guns and said that she wanted to be a soldier. Whenever U Aye Maung went to Mandalay, Ma Tin Aung Myo asked him to buy toy guns for her, and he did. No other children of the family, including Ma Tin Aung Myo's younger brother, ever played at being a soldier or asked their parents to buy them toy guns. She continued playing at being a soldier until the age of about ten.[9] She also played football and caneball[10] as a boy would.

Ma Tin Aung Myo's menarche did not occur until she was 15, almost 2 years later than the mean age in Burma, which is 13.2 years.[11] Her menstrual periods were regular, but she suffered from dysmenorrhea that

[9]For other examples of subjects who have expressed in their play the occupation of the person whose life they remembered, see the cases of Sukla Gupta, Parmod Sharma (*Twenty Cases*), Lalitha Abeyawardena, Wijanama Kithsiri (second volume of this series), and Erkan Kılıç (third volume).

[10]As the name suggests, the ball used in caneball is a light one made from strips of cane stalks woven together in a spherical form. The players endeavor to keep the ball in the air as long as possible with the use of their feet only. Although caneball is mainly a boy's game, girls do sometimes play it.

[11]C. V. Foll, "The Age at Menarche in Assam and Burma," *Archives of Disease in Childhood* 36(1961):302–4.

lasted two or three days each month and was severe enough to require medical attention. This disability was still persisting in 1981. She was then affected with pain and other discomfort for three days each month. Ma Tin Aung Myo hated menstrual periods, which she thought "unbecoming for a man." (Other women in the family occasionally suffered from dysmenorrhea, but not to anything like the same degree as Ma Tin Aung Myo.)

In her late teens, Ma Tin Aung Myo began to associate more with girls, and she was well accepted by them. They tended, however, to address her as "Ko" (a male honorific), because of her masculine traits.

Ma Tin Aung Myo's family did not passively accede to her wish to wear boys' clothes. Her mother told me that she used to scold Ma Tin Aung Myo about her male style of dress and frequently told her to wear girls' clothes. In resisting these admonishments, Ma Tin Aung Myo claimed that when she wore girls' clothes she got a headache and was otherwise uncomfortable. She said such clothes irritated her skin. (This was almost certainly a rationalization, although Burmese women do wear their clothes somewhat more tightly fitting than Burmese men wear theirs.)

The struggle over Ma Tin Aung Myo's dress reached a crisis when she was in the sixth class at school. The school authorities began to insist that she come to school dressed as a girl; she refused, they remained adamant, and so she dropped out of school. (She was eleven when this happened.) Eventually, her family capitulated in the matter of clothes and made no further objections to her masculine style of dress.

Ma Tin Aung Myo's family originally gave her just two names: Tin Aung. This pair of names may be used by persons of both sexes. (Some names in Burma are epicene; others are used by persons of one sex only.) Ma Tin Aung Myo attached *Myo* to her name in order to make it more masculine. She became annoyed at her sisters if they addressed her simply as "Tin Aung."

When I first met Ma Tin Aung Myo in 1972, she was overtly masculine in her sexual orientation. She said that if conventions permitted she would associate only with boys. She had no wish to marry a man and expressed instead a desire to have a woman as a wife. In 1977 she had even taken to having steady girl friends.

I asked her to perform the extended Draw-a-Person Test.[12] For her two free choices she drew masculine figures, in accordance with the other indices of her male sexual orientation.

[12]L. Whitaker, Jr., "The Use of An Extended Draw-a-Person Test to Identify Homosexual and Effeminate Men," *Journal of Consulting Psychology* 25 (1961):482–85. For other applications of this test to subjects who remembered previous lives as members of the opposite sex, see the cases of Paulo Lorenz *(Twenty Cases)*, Ruby Kusuma Silva (second volume of this series), and Ampan Petcherat (this volume).

Ma Tin Aung Myo standing between her older sister Ma Nyunt and her younger brother, Maung Sein Maung.

Other Relevant Observations.   Ma Tin Aung Myo is left-handed, and she thought that the Japanese soldier whose life she remembered had been left-handed. This, like all her other statements about the previous life, remains unverified. I mention it here, however, because of the occurrence of left-handedness in other subjects who remembered the lives of left-handed persons.[13]

Ma Tin Aung Myo's Birthmark

I myself have not seen Ma Tin Aung Myo's birthmark, and so I hesitate to offer a description of it. Moreover, I obtained somewhat discrepant accounts from the informants who had seen the birthmark. Nevertheless, it has a bearing on one possible explanation for why Ma Tin Aung Myo remembered a previous life as a man.

Daw Aye Tin said that she had noticed a birthmark on one of Ma Tin Aung Myo's thighs immediately after her birth. She did not remember on which thigh the birthmark had been, and I did not elicit a fuller description of the birthmark from her. Ma Shwe, Ma Tin Aung Myo's oldest sister, said that she had noticed a birthmark on her immediately after her birth. She said it was not open or discharging. Ma Nyunt, another older sister, gave a different description. She said that Ma Tin Aung Myo had had a "sore in the groin," which itched and which she used to scratch. According to her, the lesion persisted until the age of two or three, when it closed up. When U Win Maung interviewed Ma Nyunt again in 1977, she gave a further description of the birthmark. It was, she said, "just over her sexual organ. It was a brownish patch, the size of a thumb, that was an inch by an inch and a half in area."

U Hla Baw (when he was interviewed again by U Win Maung in 1977) also remembered seeing Ma Tin Aung Myo's birthmark, and he said that it was "a darkish patch, the size of a thumb, on her groin."

The Attitude of Ma Tin Aung Myo's Family
toward Her Memories and Behavior

When Daw Aye Tin became pregnant with Ma Tin Aung Myo, she had already given birth to three girls. She said that she and her husband both wished that their next child would be a boy, and so they were disappointed when another daughter was born. As I have already mentioned, however, Daw Aye Tin expressly denied that she had in any way encour-

---

[13]For an example of left-handedness in a subject and a related previous personality, see the case of Corliss Chotkin, Jr. *(Twenty Cases).*

aged Ma Tin Aung Myo to dress as a boy. She dressed in this manner entirely on her own and against her mother's protests and rebukes. Her father, however, had been more indulgent; he allowed her to wear boys' clothes and even to crop her hair short like a boy's.

U Win Maung is an educated Burmese who has lived many years in the West and also has a profound knowledge of the customs and attitudes of his own people. He told me that although Ma Tin Aung Myo's family, at the time she was born, would have preferred to have a son, they would never have dressed her in boys' clothes or imposed a male role on her just to suit themselves. The Burmese people like the first child to be a boy; but they do not object to girls, and women generally prefer them because they are easier to manage and they stay around the home more to help their mothers.

Ma Tin Aung Myo's Explanations for her "Sex Change"

The Burmese people, nearly all of whom are Buddhists, need no explanation for cases like Ma Tin Aung Myo's. It suffices for them to subsume the case under the law of karma. From their point of view, Ma Tin Aung Myo simply remembers the life of a Japanese soldier who happened to be killed near their house and got himself reborn among them. Further and more specific interpretations, of the type I am constantly seeking, seem to them a somewhat odd Western craving. Afflicted as I am with this, however, I put to the informants various questions that I thought might satisfy my curiosity on the matter. But readers should weigh the answers without forgetting that they came in response to my inquiries and not spontaneously. To questions about why, as she saw herself, she had changed sex from one life to another, Ma Tin Aung Myo gave different answers on different occasions.

In 1972 Ma Shwe said that Ma Tin Aung Myo explained her condition by saying that the fatal shot from the airplane had hit the Japanese soldier whose life she remembered in the genitalia and thereby induced "sex change" in the next life. (I did not meet Ma Tin Aung Myo that year.) Ma Shwe said that Ma Tin Aung Myo had normal female genitalia.

When I asked Ma Tin Aung Myo about this in 1974, she conjectured that perhaps the Japanese soldier had wished to change sex and that this had caused her condition. In 1975 she advanced a third explanation. She suggested that the Japanese soldier had molested girls and had been punished for that by becoming a girl himself in his next life.

Comment. The last two explanations put forward by Ma Tin Aung Myo form part of the repertoire of interpretations usually deployed by the few Burmese who trouble themselves with such questions. As I explained in the chapter introducing the cases of Burma, Burmese women have a somewhat inferior status to that of men. Therefore, being born a woman usually implies some misconduct in a previous life that has earned such a demotion. Any kind of misbehavior may produce such an effect; it does not need to be maltreatment of women, although it may be.

Ma Tin Aung Myo's Later Development

Fading of Ma Tin Aung Myo's Memories.   In 1974 Ma Tin Aung Myo told me that she had forgotten most of what she had formerly remembered about the previous life. And yet she seemed to remember much of what members of her family said that she had stated as a young child. I infer from this that perhaps she had earlier remembered more about the previous life than she had expressed to her family. Or possibly they and she remembered, of all she had earlier said, only the more emotion-laden events of the previous life, such as the fatal shooting of the Japanese soldier by an Allied airplane. Still another possibility is that Ma Tin Aung Myo had forgotten all the original imaged memories of the previous life that she had had when young and only remembered what she had later been told she had said; such secondhand memories would accord with what members of her family remembered.

Modifications of Ma Tin Aung Myo's Behavior.   Ma Tin Aung Myo was already nineteen years old when U Win Maung and I first began to study her case. I have tried to describe her behavior, as I learned about it from the informants, during the peak of its abnormality as compared with what is expected of Burmese girls. As she grew older, she modified her behavior in certain respects, but not with regard to her sexual orientation.

Ma Tin Aung Myo lost her phobia of airplanes when she was in her late teens. As late as 1972, however, U Win Maung learned that she was still "rather nervous" whenever an airplane flew over her village, although she no longer became immobilized with fear as she had earlier.

She also gradually adapted to the spicy Burmese food. She told me in 1975 that she was then eating Burmese food "normally."

In general she was happy in Burma and had lost the desire to go to Japan. The intense heat in summer of Upper Burma's plain still bothered her, but she obtained some relief by visiting one of her sisters, who lived in the upland town of Taunggyi.

In her sexual orientation, however, Ma Tin Aung Myo remained intransigent. She continued to dress in the male style and completely rejected a female position in society. U Win Maung had once written to her and in addressing his letter had used the female honorific *Ma*. She wrote back saying that this had made her sad and that she wished to be called either *Maung* Tin Aung Myo or, if her friends would not make this concession, just plain Tin Aung Myo. In 1975 she again brought up this matter of her preference for the male honorific at the time of signing our release form for the use of her real name and photograph in a report of her case.

When we met Ma Tin Aung Myo, her father was dead and her three older sisters were married. She said then that she would never marry. She was partly dependent on her mother, although she helped the latter in her little trade as a hawker of meals and fruits at the railway station. I raised the question of what would happen to her after her mother's death. They had already considered that. She had told her mother not to worry about her fate after she died, and Daw Aye Tin had accepted her decision to remain single.

Perhaps I communicated some incredulity about the flintlike hardness of Ma Tin Aung Myo's position concerning the sex she wished to be. She evidently felt the need for a stronger statement to overcome my skepticism, and so she told U Win Maung and me that we could kill her by any method we chose under only one condition: that we guarantee she would be reborn as a boy. But we had no wish to carry out her suggestion and no power to implement her stipulation.

In May 1981 when U Win Maung visited Nathul again, he learned that Ma Tin Aung Myo had a steady girl friend with whom she was living in another town. Her mother and two of her older sisters (Ma Nyunt and Ma Myint on this occasion) said that she was as firmly masculine in her attitudes as ever. She talked of joining the army to live and fight with the men, and she said that if she ever married she would marry a girl. She was still wearing men's shirts and longyis and keeping her hair close-cropped like a man's.

9. The Case of the Ven. Sayadaw U Sobhana

Introduction

THE INVESTIGATION OF this case did not begin until the subject was in his forties. This fact, together with the remoteness of the region of Burma from which he came and where the concerned previous personality had lived, has limited the corroboration and verification of the subject's memories. (I have, nevertheless, obtained some support for them.) The case derives its interest principally from the subject's statements about memories of experiences during the unusually short interval between the death of the previous personality and his birth.

Summary of the Case and Its Investigation

Maung Htwe Nyein, later known as the Ven. Sayadaw U Sobhana,[1] was born on November 5, 1921, in the village of Htanaungdaing, Myingyan District, Upper Burma. His parents were U Chan Tha and Daw Lay Khin. They had four other children. Of these, two brothers and one sister, all older than the Ven. U Sobhana, survived infancy, but a younger sibling died as an infant. U Chan Tha was a farmer and also worked as clerk to the village headman for some years. The Ven. U Sobhana told me that his father was acting headman of the village at the time of his (Maung Htwe Nyein's) birth. Toward the end of his life U Chan Tha became permanent headman himself.

The Ven. U Sobhana told me that he had had memories of a previous life at an early age, even before he could express in words the images of the memories. When he was a young child, he spoke about the previous life to his parents and sometimes to his siblings. And he went often to visit the home, nearby in his village, where the widow and children of the man whose life he remembered continued to live.

---

[1]These are the subject's name and titles as a senior Buddhist monk. *Sayadaw* is an honorific given to abbots and other monks who are distinguished teachers of Buddhism in Burma. *U* is the ordinary honorific for adult men in Burma and corresponds to the English *Mr*. The subject's parents gave him the name Maung Htwe Nyein. When he became a monk, he assumed instead the Pali name Sobhana, and I shall usually refer to him in this report by that name.

When the Ven. U Sobhana was about sixteen years old, he left his village to become a novice at a monastery in Myingyan. Later, he became fully ordained. As a monk he gained recognition as a scholar and teacher of meditation. The Burma Buddhist Sasana Council sent him to Thailand as a teacher, and since 1959 he has lived and taught at Wat Bodharama, Nakhon Sawan, Thailand.

In Janury 1963, Francis Story went to Nakhon Sawan to investigate a case about which I had received some preliminary information. While he was there, he met the Ven. U Sobhana and recorded a long statement from him. (The Ven. U Sobhana, who speaks English, said that his memories had not then faded.) In July 1966, I was in Nakhon Sawan (with Francis Story) and had a long interview with him. He largely repeated what he had told Francis Story three years earlier; but some supplementary details also emerged. During the next eight years (between 1966 and 1974), I returned three times to Nakhon Sawan. I went there mainly to continue my investigation of the case of Bongkuch Promsin (in this volume); but on each occasion the Ven. U Sobhana accompanied me to Bongkuch's village, and we often talked about his own experiences. In this way, I gained a friend and also an appreciable amount of additional information about his case.

The Ven. U Sobhana encouraged me to visit his village in Upper Burma, where, he said, some persons still living could at least partially corroborate and verify his statements. The remoteness of his village made this appear a wildly unrealistic suggestion. And yet in November 1974 I found myself, somewhat astonished, actually in the village of Htanaungdaing, to which I had been transported through the resourcefulness of U Win Maung. I was able to talk there with two persons who provided some corroboration and verification for the Ven. U Sobhana's statements.

During all these years I corresponded with the Ven. U Sobhana, and as I continued to study his case, he graciously answered questions for me. I was able to meet him again on later visits to Thailand in 1978, 1979, and 1980. In 1978 he read and approved, after correcting two details, a draft of this report.

The Ven. U Sobhana's Statements of 1963

I shall give first the statement that the Ven. U Sobhana made to Francis Story in January 1963. (In 1974 the Ven. U Sobhana read the text of his remarks and approved it as accurate; I have edited it slightly for easier reading.)

From my earliest years I have remembered my previous life. I was a land surveyor named Maung Po Thit. My wife's name was Ma Shwe Thin and we had one son, Maung Po Min, whose age was three at the time of my death. We lived in Htanaungdaing village, Myingyan, in Upper Burma. When I was thirty-six, I contracted a severe fever and was sent to Myingyan Hospital. I distinctly remember going to the hospital by oxcart. It was toward the end of the monsoon and raining. I remember arriving at the hospital and being admitted and examined. The doctors said that I would have to have an operation. After that I remember nothing more of the time I spent in the hospital.

I then found myself in the jungle,[2] alone. I was feeling sorrow, hunger, thirst, and great distress, but did not know that I was dead. I was dressed in my usual clothes, that is, longyi, *aingyi* [a short Burmese jacket], and sandals—with long hair and a towel around my head.[3]

I seemed to wander about in the jungle for two or three hours. Then I met a very old man dressed in white with a white beard and moustache and carrying a staff. He was dressed like an Upasaka [Buddhist lay devotee] with a white shawl over his shoulder.[4]

When I saw the old man, all my distress vanished. He called me by my name and told me I must follow him. I did so for about an hour, walking. We reached a place I knew near my village. Then we entered the village and went to my house. In front of it there was a fence and a tree. The old man told me to wait there under the tree while he went into the house. I can remember this and can see it all in my mind's eye even now. The memory is very vivid.

The old man went into my house and emerged again after five minutes. He said: "You must follow me to another house."

We went in a westerly direction. About seven houses distant from my house was the house of the village headman. In front of that house, the old man again told me to wait for him. He went inside and returned to me after about five minutes. He called me into the house, and when I was inside he said to me: "You must stay here. I shall go back." He then disappeared.

I saw people in the house, but after that I remember nothing until I came to consciousness in my present existence.

---

[2]This "jungle," described by the Ven. U Sobhana (in 1971) as containing trees and beautiful flowers, did not correspond to the vegetation around Htanaungdaing. I myself saw the arid landscape of the area—not completely devoid of trees, but not having many either. The Ven. U Sobhana himself realized and mentioned to me, in a later interview, the inapplicability of the word *jungle* to this terrain. The surroundings that he remembered for the discarnate Maung Po Thit were therefore not those of the region where he had lived before his death.

[3]A long piece of cloth, here called a towel, wrapped around the head forms a common turbanlike headdress for men in Upper Burma.

[4]For further information about the "man in white" in Thai and Burmese cases of the reincarnation type, see the Introduction to Cases in Thailand and the Introduction to Cases in Burma. For other accounts of experiences between the death of the related previous personality and the subject's birth, see the cases of H. A. Wijeratne, Jasbir Singh *(Twenty Cases)*, Gopal Gupta, Veer Singh, Puti Patra (first volume of this series), Disna Samarasinghe (second volume), Nasır Toksöz (third volume), Ratana Wongsombat, Ampan Petcherat, Bongkuch Promsin, Hair Kam Kanya, and the Ven. Chaokhun Rajsuthajarn (this volume).

At the age of about two years I was able to tell all these things. I used to go sometimes and stay in my old home. I remembered all my previous relations, friends, property, and even old debts.

Two Announcing Dreams

In his 1966 statement to Francis Story, the Ven. U Sobhana gave an account of two dreams that occurred, one to Daw Lay Khin and one to Ma Shwe Thin, after the death of Maung Po Thit. In the part of his statement that follows, he drew on memories of what he had learned from his parents in childhood; he did not claim any paranormal knowledge of these dreams.

> My dead body of the previous life was removed from the hospital and buried. Seven days later a number of monks were given food and recited paritta[5] according to custom. The same night my wife [that is, Ma Shwe Thin, Maung Po Thit's wife] dreamed that she saw an old man in white who appeared to her and said: "I am sending your husband to the village headman's house." Then he vanished.
>
> In the early morning she [Ma Shwe Thin] got up and ran to the village headman's house and told the headman's wife [Daw Lay Khin] about her dream. The headman's wife told her that she too had had a dream of the [apparently] same old man; he had come to her the same night and told her that he was entrusting Maung Po Thit to her family as a member. He then went out of the house and returned with Maung Po Thit, after which he vanished.
>
> From that day my present mother became pregnant,[6] and I was reborn as the headman's son.

Additional Details Elicited in Later Interviews

Before giving the details that the Ven. U Sobhana added in later interviews, I should mention that he had returned to Htanaungdaing in 1964 for one of his infrequent visits there. He would then have had a chance to

---

[5]For further information about the paritta ceremony, see the Introduction to Cases in Burma in this volume.

The Ven. Sayadaw U Sobhana credited the paritta ceremony with contributing to the shortness of the interval between Maung Po Thit's death and his (the Ven. U Sobhana's) birth. He said that the shortness of the interval was also due to Maung Po Thit's merit.

[6]Subjectively, the discarnate Maung Po Thit passed only "two or three hours" before the "man in white" took him in hand. Yet seven days (of terrestrial time) appear to have elapsed between Maung Po Thit's death and the paritta ceremony on his behalf. Persons who have apparently died and have then revived often report a similar, greatly altered sense of the passage of time.

We may doubt whether Daw Lay Khin actually became pregnant on the day of her dream. I think it unlikely that either she or her son would know the day of conception precisely. As I have mentioned in the Introduction to Cases in Burma, Burmese Buddhists believe that an announcing dream should not occur *after* conception. Some informants may conjecture dates to harmonize with this belief.

refresh his memory about the details of his experiences and of the life of
Maung Po Thit. I am not suggesting that he did this systematically, and
certainly not that he did it deliberately; but some discussions between him
and members of his family or other villagers may have touched on matters relevant to his memories.

In his statement of 1966, the Ven. U Sobhana said, or implied, that his
last memories of the previous life were of being admitted to the hospital
in Myingyan and of then being examined and told that he needed an operation. He also said that he could remember being on the table in the
operating room of the hospital, but nothing of the operation itself. About
Maung Po Thit's illness, he remembered the symptoms of vomiting, pain
in the abdomen, and fever. From this I conjecture that Maung Po Thit
may have had appendicitis with rupture of the appendix and peritonitis.

In 1966 and 1971 the Ven. U Sobhana's memories seemed still remarkably clear, and he said that they had not faded in any respect. He said that
he could easily see inwardly the memory image of the febrile Maung Po
Thit's ride to the hospital in the rain, in an oxcart with no cover. In 1966
he remembered the clothes that he (Maung Po Thit, after his death) had
worn in the jungle. But, contrary to his claim of not having forgotten any
memories, he could not then remember the beard worn by the "man in
white" (that he had described in 1963), although his description of the
"man in white" in other respects repeated what he had said earlier, except for the addition (in 1966) that the man was tall and had a knot of
hair at the top of his head. At that time, the Ven. U Sobhana also revised
his earlier statement about "wandering about in the jungle" and said that
he had remained leaning against a tree in the jungle until he met the old
"man in white." And in 1971 he slightly modified what he had said in
1963 about the sensations the discarnate Maung Po Thit had when he
was alone in the jungle. He said that he had felt thirsty, weak, discour-
aged, and lonely, but *not* hungry, as he had earlier stated.[7]

Subjects who have survived close brushes with death sometimes report
experiencing panoramic memory.[8] However, the Ven. U Sobhana did
not recall any such experience in connection with Maung Po Thit's death.

He said that his memories of the previous life extended back to the pe-

---

[7]In the traditions of Burmese Buddhism this distinction about hunger is not a quibble. Lower-
rank pretas (ghosts) suffer from hunger, but those graded in the middle and upper ranks do not.
The Ven. U Sobhana considered that Maung Po Thit had become a middle-rank preta at his death,
so that he did not have to endure a long period as a preta, and could therefore be reborn within a
year after dying.

[8]I. Stevenson and B. Greyson, "Near-death Experiences: Relevance to the Question of Survival
After Death," *Journal of the American Medical Association* 242(1979):265–67; B. Greyson and I.
Stevenson, "The Phenomenology of Near-death Experiences," *American Journal of Psychiatry*
137(1980):1193–96.

riod when Maung Po Thit was about twelve or thirteen years old.[9] He remembered that Maung Po Thit was educated up to the seventh class of school, after which he attended for two years a school for training government surveyors. He also recalled that Maung Po Thit had studied English in school and spoke English during his work as a government surveyor (in the days of British rule in Burma). The Ven. U Sobhana thought that he had learned English rather easily when he was young, but he did not claim to have had as a child any paranormal knowledge of English.[10] He recalled also that he had married at the age of thirty-two or thirty-three, and he remembered the wedding ceremony. He said that his wife, Ma Shwe Thin, had been the daughter of U Nyunt.

According to the Ven. U Sobhana, Maung Po Thit was shorter and darker in complexion than he is.

Maung Po Thit had been a novice in a Buddhist monastery for three months in his youth,[11] but he never became fully ordained. Nor did he meditate much. He was, however, a pious person. He gave food every day to the monks at the Shwe Oo Hmin Monastery in Htanaungdaing. Their scholarly work interested him, and about a year before his death he contributed 1,000 *kyats*, an enormous (for him) sum of money, to their monastery. Maung Po Thit had a monthly salary of only 45 kyats, so the gift required a major financial sacrifice. He made it with his wife's approval. The money was to be used to provide a copy of the *Tipitaka* (the three parts of the Pali Canon) for the use of scholars at the temple. Maung Po Thit had wished to be a scholar, and the Ven. U Sobhana thought that the merit Maung Po Thit had earned by this generosity had enabled him (the Ven. U Sobhana) to become a scholar.

In his statement of 1962, the Ven. U Sobhana said that he had begun to tell his parents about the previous life at about the age of two. As I mentioned earlier, he said that he had imaged memories of the previous life before he could verbalize them. He was certain that he had spoken about the previous life to his mother before she had said anything to him about Maung Po Thit. Soon after he began to talk about the previous life, he became seriously ill with smallpox. (This illness followed a vaccination

---

[9]The subjects of these cases do not often say that they recall events that occurred long before the death of the person whose life they remember. For other examples of subjects who did recall such events, see the cases of Kumkum Verma (first volume of this series), Lalitha Abeyawardena (second volume), Zouheir Chaar, Rabih Elawar (third volume), Ratana Wongsombat, and the Ven. Chaokhun Rajsuthajarn (this volume).

[10]The Ven. U Sobhana's English is surprisingly good considering how little opportunity he has to exercise it in Nakhon Sawan. But it is imperfect, and some discrepancies in his statements may have derived from his difficulty in finding the right words to express his thoughts in English.

[11]This in itself does not denote unusual piety. In Burma, as in Thailand, nearly every man spends at least a few weeks or months in a monastery.

that led to a full-blown attack of smallpox.) He was then ill, or an invalid, for about two years, and during this period he could not remember the previous life. He recovered from the illness when he was about four, and at the same time regained his memories of the previous life; he has retained them since. But he has no memory of events during the approximately two years (between the ages of two and four) when he was ill or debilitated.

When he was a young child, he often went to Maung Po Thit's house, where he played familiarly with the two children of Maung Po Thit and Ma Shwe Thin. (There were two children—a boy and a girl; Ma Shwe Thin had been pregnant at the time Maung Po Thit died.) He addressed these children directly by their names as a parent would, without the honorifics *Maung* and *Ma* that Burmese usage would expect between children of different families. The Ven. U Sobhana recalled that, as a young child, he considered the children of Maung Po Thit "inferior" to him, even though they were actually older than he was. (Maung Po Thit's posthumous daughter, however, was just a few months older.) The Ven. U Sobhana said that he felt just as fond of Ma Shwe Thin as he did of his mother, Daw Lay Khin. The house of the previous family seemed familiar to him, and he sometimes slept there.

The two families in this case were fairly close neighbors and had been good friends before the case developed. But they were not related. The Ven. U Sobhana did not recall that Maung Po Thit had had a special attachment for Daw Lay Khin.

He did not think his memories of a previous life had influenced him to become a monk. He thought that the presence of many monks in the village of Htanaungdaing, which was (at least) a minor center of Buddhist learning, was a more probable stimulus for his decision to join the Sangha.

On two occasions since his birth, the Ven. U Sobhana has seen the same, or presumably the same, old "man in white" that he described encountering after his death as Maung Po Thit. The first of these was in 1955, when he found himself in a personal situation that evoked distress and perplexity. It appears that he had arrived at one of those moral crises of life in which one feels unsure about what to do and yet certain that what one decides will later prove important. In this condition, he saw an apparition of the old "man in white." The Ven. U Sobhana described his experience as half vision, half dream. The "man in white" said: "You must speak the truth at all costs." This advice applied appropriately to the circumstances; the Ven. U Sobhana followed it, and the crisis resolved in a completely satisfactory manner. He told me that he had not tried to call upon the "man in white" or in any way evoke him consciously; the apparition (or appearance in a dream, as the case may be) occurred quite spontaneously.

In 1974 the Ven. U Sobhana told me that two years earlier, that is, in 1972, during another somewhat similar crisis, he had again had a vision (or dream) of the same old "man in white." He did not give me further details of this experience, and I did not press him to do so.

Results of Interviews at Htanaungdaing in 1974

My main informant at Htanaungdaing was U Aye Thein, an older brother (by three years) of the Ven. U Sobhana. Daw Phwa Thet, a cousin and niece by marriage of Maung Po Thit, also furnished a small amount of information.

Corroborations.   Daw Lay Khin had told U Aye Thein about the dream she had had before she became pregnant with the Ven. U Sobhana. (I cannot say precisely when she told U Aye Thein about her dream, but, as she died when he was fourteen, she must have told him before then.) According to U Aye Thein's memory, Daw Lay Khin had dreamed that an old "man in white" with a staff had brought Maung Po Thit to her husband (not directly to her) and said: "This Maung Po Thit wants to live with you, so I am bringing him along. Please accept him." He repeated the last phrase three times. U Aye Thein did not know anything about a dream had by Ma Shwe Thin on the same night as Daw Lay Khin's dream.

U Aye Thein said that he did not become aware of his brother's memories of a previous life until he (the Ven. U Sobhana) was about eight years old. At that time, they were coming home from school together when the Ven. U Sobhana stopped at Maung Po Thit's house and went in. Then he returned to his own house and announced that Ma Shwe Thin was dead and had had a happy release, adding: "The crazed woman is released." (Ma Shwe Thin had become mentally ill after Maung Po Thit's death and remained so until she died; the boy's remark alluded to this tragedy.) It was then that U Aye Thein learned that his brother had been talking about a previous life for some years. He had begun, U Aye Thein said, at about the age of three. He had said that he was Maung Po Thit and that he had been married to Ma Shwe Thin and had had a son, Maung Po Min. U Aye Thein also remembered his brother's saying that his (previous) wife had been pregnant when he (as Maung Po Thit) had died. (The Ven. U Sobhana did not include this item in his own account of his memories.)

U Aye Thein recalled that the Ven. U Sobhana as a young child had behaved familiarly with persons known to Maung Po Thit and had addressed them without honorifics, as Maung Po Thit would have done. He remembered in particular that his brother omitted the honorific in talking with Ma Sein Shwe, Maung Po Thit's posthumous daughter. The Ven. U Sobhana often went to visit at Maung Po Thit's house. Other children of his family also went there—it was close by and on the way to school—but not so frequently as the Ven. U Sobhana did.

Ma Shwe Thin had mixed some of Maung Po Thit's belongings, such as clothes and jewelry, with other similar objects and had asked the Ven. U Sobhana to select the objects that had belonged to Maung Po Thit. (U Aye Thein did not say what the results of this test had been; it should be regarded only as evidence that the Ven. U Sobhana's claims were taken seriously in the village, not that he did in fact have paranormal knowledge of the objects shown to him.)

Verifications.   U Aye Thein verified the following details of the life of Maung Po Thit. He had been a land surveyor who had married Ma Shwe Thin, the daughter of U Nyunt, and they had had two children, Maung Po Min and Ma Sein Shwe. Maung Po Thit had been quite prosperous. He had married Ma Shwe Thin just a few years before his death. He had died of an illness that had developed while he was on survey work. U Aye Thein said that he himself was born in 1918 and was between one and a half and two years old when Maung Po Thit died; this would place Maung Po Thit's death in about 1919–20.

In the 1920s U Chan Tha's house was the seventh one down the road from Maung Po Thit's house. (However, it was *east* of Maung Po Thit's house, not west, as the Ven. U Sobhana had stated in describing his experiences following death in the previous life.) U Chan Tha was a cultivator who in his early life had been a clerk and assistant to the headman and, toward the end of his life, himself headman of the village. U Aye Thein did not think he had been headman at the time the Ven. U Sobhana was born; he became headman in about 1925 and died in about 1930. But U Aye Thein thought that his father might sometimes have been acting headman before he was appointed to the position formally.

When U Win Maung and I were in Htanaungdaing, we visited the Zetawain Monastery and talked with an elderly monk, the Ven. U Ogekantha. He had taught the Ven. U Sobhana many years before at Myingyan. He did not, however, know anything about his memories of a previous life, and he could not recall Maung Po Thit. He said that there was a monastery called Shwe Oo Hmin in Htanaungdaing, but the abbots there had changed and he did not think anyone at this monastery would remember any gift that Maung Po Thit may have made to it.

The children of Maung Po Thit, who had become U Po Min and Daw Sein Shwe, had both died before my visit to Htanaungdaing. U Tin, the Ven. U Sobhana's other older brother, was living in 1974 in another town (Yezagyo), but it was even more inaccessible than Htanaungdaing, and I was unable to meet him. There were no other informants in Htanaungdaing able to contribute further information about the case.

Comments on the Evidence of Paranormal Processes in the Case

No one regrets more than I that this case was not fully investigated when the subject was a young child. Even if it had been, however, its evidence of paranormal processes would have remained somewhat weak because the two families concerned were near neighbors and good friends before the case developed. On the other hand, it has the strength of being a "private case," as I call those that are observed only in a family circle, or within a village, and never receive any outside publicity. Cases that do receive such publicity are sometimes damaged by informants' needs (or wishes) to accommodate their statements to fit the expectations of a larger circle of interested persons.

The case also has a remarkable and particularly trustworthy subject. Judgments about cases of this type almost always reduce to assessments of the honesty and competence of the informants. I try to check the informants' testimonies against each other so as to provide some objective assistance for the otherwise subjective appraisals of these qualities that we must make. I do not like any case to rest solely on my opinions about the informants' capacities for reliable witnessing; yet I know that the cases I have published often do depend largely, and sometimes entirely, on my judgments thereon. I think that of all the cases I have studied, the present case and that of the Ven. Chaokhun Rajsuthajarn, are the ones about which I am least uncomfortable in this situation. As a Buddhist monk, the Ven. U Sobhana has to observe ten precepts, one of which is: "I shall refrain from telling lies." He is therefore unlikely to tell falsehoods, which would make a mockery of his profession. I believe that he is a completely trustworthy person, and I am quite content to present his case depending, as it now must, largely on his own statements.

Further Observations on Fluctuations in the Clarity of the Ven. U Sobhana's Memories

I mentioned earlier that the Ven. U Sobhana said he had been unable to remember anything about the previous life during approximately two years of a severe illness (smallpox) and convalescence when he was between two and four years old. He underwent a similar temporary attenuation of his memories in the 1970s. He told me (in 1978) that a (possibly) rabid dog had bitten him at some time between 1972 and 1975. (He did not remember the year exactly.) He underwent the usual antirabies treatment, but had a bad reaction (evidently serum sickness) and remained depleted in strength for a time. He found that his memory—both for events of his (present) life and for those of the previous life—was impaired and remained so for a year or more. As an example of the deficiency of his memory, he mentioned that before the antirabies treatment he could remember that Maung Po Thit had given a gift of 1,000 kyats to the Shwe Oo Hmin Monastery for providing a copy of the Tipitaka. During the year or two after he was bitten by the dog and treated, he could still recall that Maung Po Thit had made a gift to the monastery, but could no longer remember the exact amount of the gift. Later, he again recalled the exact amount. The Ven. U Sobhana appears to have had some reduction of his memories even before the dog bit him; he told me in 1971 that Maung Po Thit had given the monastery 100 kyats, whereas on every other of the four occasions when we have discussed this gift (before and after 1971), he mentioned the figure of 1,000 kyats.

In 1979 the Ven. U Sobhana told me that he could then recall as the last event of Maung Po Thit's life his seeing the surgeon in the operating room with his mask on. (He had not mentioned this detail earlier.) After that Maung Po Thit was "in the jungle."

I think these variations in the Ven. U Sobhana's memories worth noting. They illustrate an aphorism of Ballard: "We not only tend to forget what we have once remembered but we also tend to remember what we have once forgotten."[12]

When I first met the Ven. U Sobhana in 1966, he said that he thought his memories of the previous life were then just as clear as they had been when he was a young child. In the years 1978–80, however, he said that some fading of his memories had occurred. This diminution of his memories was not part of that which followed his being bitten by a dog and the subsequent antirabies treatment that he received. The Ven. U Sobhana thought that he had eventually recovered fully from the impairment that he attributed to these events.

[12]P. B. Ballard, "Oblivescence and Reminiscence," *British Journal of Psychology Monograph Supplement* 1(1913):1–82.

10.   The Case of Ma Than Than Sint

Summary of the Case and Its Investigation

MA THAN THAN Sint was born in Rangoon on September 10, 1965. She was the fourth daughter and fifth (and youngest) child of her parents, U Pe San and Daw Hla Sein. U Pe San was an electrical engineer. His father was Spanish and his mother Burmese; he belonged to the Roman Catholic Church. Daw Hla Sein was wholly Burmese and a Buddhist.

Ma Than Than Sint started to speak when she was between one and two years old, and at about the same time she began to refer to a previous life. Thereafter, she talked about it until she was between five and six years old, at which time her remarks diminished. She did not make many statements about the previous life, and she made most of them when she noticed some object that had belonged to the person whose life she was remembering. That person was Daw Ma Ma May, who had been the first wife of U Ba Kan, a lawyer of Rangoon. U Ba Kan's second wife was Daw Nu Nu May, who was Daw Hla Sein's sister and thus Ma Than Than Sint's maternal aunt.

This was one of the first Burmese cases that I investigated. I heard about it in March 1971 during my second visit to Burma. At that time I was able to meet Ma Than Than Sint and to interview five informants for the case.

In March 1978 I had further interviews with U Ba Kan, Ma Than Than Sint, both her parents, and her older sister Ma Aye Aye Kyaing.

In April 1979 I met Ma Than Than Sint and her parents again. I also had further interviews with U Ba Kan and Daw Nu Nu May, and I talked for the first time with Ma Than Than Sint's oldest sister, Ma Than Than Nu.

In November 1980 I visited U Ba Kan and Daw Nu Nu May again, mainly for the purpose of checking further some details of the case.

Persons Interviewed during the Investigation

In Rangoon I interviewed:

Ma Than Than Sint
U Pe San, Ma Than Than Sint's father

Daw Hla Sein, Ma Than Than Sint's mother
Daw Htwe, Daw Hla Sein's mother and Ma Than Than Sint's maternal
    grandmother
Ma Than Than Nu, Ma Than Than Sint's oldest sister
Ma Aye Aye Kyaing, one of Ma Than Than Sint's older sisters
U Ba Kan, Daw Ma Ma May's husband
Daw Nu Nu May, Daw Hla Sein's sister and U Ba Kan's second wife

It may be inaccurate to use the word *interviewed* in connection with my
meetings with Ma Than Than Sint. She was present during several interviews, but she said little. She was friendly, however, and appeared to enjoy my visits.

Relevant Facts of Geography and Possibilities for Normal Means of Communication between the Two Families

I have already mentioned that the two families were related by marriage.
Daw Ma Ma May had been U Ba Kan's first wife; and he had married as
his second wife Daw Nu Nu May, who was Ma Than Than Sint's maternal
aunt.

U Pe San and his wife, Daw Hla Sein, married in 1956. U Pe San had
known U Ba Kan slightly during the years before Daw Ma Ma May died
(in 1962), but neither he nor his wife had ever met Daw Ma Ma May. U
Ba Kan married Daw Hla Sein's sister, Daw Nu Nu May, in 1963; this was
about a year after Daw Ma Ma May's death. From the time of U Ba Kan's
second marriage, the two families were naturally well acquainted. This
means, therefore, that they had known each other more or less intimately
for about three years before Ma Than Than Sint began to speak about
the life of Daw Ma Ma May. It would be best to regard nearly all of Ma
Than Than Sint's statements about the life of Daw Ma Ma May as being
within the knowledge of her parents. But there were a few exceptions to
this general rule.

Readers will find the remainder of this report easier to follow if I mention now that at the time the case developed U Ba Kan and his second
wife lived on Pongyi Street (in Rangoon), whereas Ma Than Than Sint
and her family lived on Tarok Kyaung Street, which is about 3 kilometers
distant in a quite different quarter in Rangoon.

The Life, Death, and Character of Daw Ma Ma May

Daw Ma Ma May was born in 1898 in Yandoon, which is located in the
Moulmein District of Lower Burma. She married in 1941. Her husband,
U Ba Kan, was a lawyer and, for a time, a successful businessman. He had

an import business, and he and Daw Ma Ma May also owned some land. They were quite successful financially and became prosperous. They had no children.

Piety was the outstanding trait in Daw Ma Ma May's character. She was a devout Buddhist and meditated for one or two hours a day over many years. She was active in Buddhist charities and gave generously to monks and monasteries. Toward the end of her life, she and her husband created a trust to which they gave their property, with the eventual proceeds assigned to charities.

Daw Ma Ma May suffered from hypertension and, ultimately, from heart disease, of which she died in 1962. She was about sixty-four years old when she died.

A Possible Announcing Dream

Before she became pregnant with Ma Than Than Sint, Daw Hla Sein dreamed that an old woman came to her and presented her with a *gouer* (a kind of fruit that grows in Burma). She interpreted the dream to mean that she would conceive, and because the fruit was round like a ball (which she associated with boys), she thought she would have a boy. When I asked Daw Hla Sein whether the old woman in the dream resembled Daw Ma Ma May, she could not say because she had never met Daw Ma Ma May. She conceived soon after the dream, and Ma Than Than Sint was born about nine months later.

Statements and Recognitions Made by Ma Than Than Sint

In Table 13, I have listed the statements and recognitions attributed to Ma Than Than Sint. Daw Nu Nu May said that Ma Than Than Sint usually talked about the previous life when she saw some object or person that had been familiar to Daw Ma Ma May. This is reflected in Table 13. It lists twelve statements and eleven recognitions; three of the statements (items 5, 10, and 14) occurred at the time of a recognition. Item 10 could also have been listed as a recognition, because Ma Than Than Sint first recognized the bottle with coins in it and then gave the correct number of coins it contained. If, as I believe, she could not have seen the coins inside the bottle, her correct description of them is impressive.

Two more of Ma Than Than Sint's recognitions were also noteworthy, because the persons observing them did not know the identity of the person or object that Ma Than Than Sint recognized, but only confirmed her correctness later. Ma Than Than Sint recognized a longyi that Daw Ma Ma May had owned and did so when no one else present knew its former ownership (item 19, Table 13). On another occasion, Ma Than Than Sint spontaneously recognized Ma Khin Mya Mya, one of Daw Ma

TABLE 13. *Summary of Statements and Recognitions Made by Ma Than Than Sint*

Item	Informants	Verification	Comments
1. Her name was Ma Ma May.	Daw Hla Sein, Ma Than Than Sint's mother	U Ba Kan, Daw Ma Ma May's husband	
2. U Ba Kan was her husband.	U Pe San, Ma Than Than Sint's father	U Ba Kan	
3. Her hair was good when she was young, and she cut it off.	U Ba Kan	U Ba Kan	Daw Ma Ma May had had good hair, which she cut off from time to time and kept.
4. Her money was still in the safe.	U Ba Kan	U Ba Kan	
5. She had given clothes to a *pongyi* [monk].	U Ba Kan	U Ba Kan	The clothes were actually monks' robes. At a temple to which U Ba Kan took her, Ma Than Than Sint indicated a pongyi and said she had given clothes (robes) to him. She did not give the monk's name. Daw Ma Ma May had given Thai silk robes to this monk.
6. She was using her aunt's property [at present], and her aunt was using hers.	U Ba Kan	U Ba Kan	Ma Than Than Sint's parents were occupying a house that belonged to Daw Nu Nu May. At the same time, Daw Nu Nu May, as U Ba Kan's second wife, was living in the house that Daw Ma Ma May had formerly occupied. Ma Than Than Sint made a similar remark to her father. Once he smacked her for some misdeed and she said: "This is not your house. It is my aunt's house. My house is on Pongyi Street and I will go back there."

Item			Comments
7. She owned two big buildings.	U Pe San	U Pe San U Ba Kan	These were substantial residential buildings on Pongyi Street. U Ba Kan lived in one of them with his (successive) wives, Daw Ma Ma May and Daw Nu Nu May. This is the house on Pongyi Street that figures in item 18.
8. She owned a small black car.	U Pe San U Ba Kan	U Ba Kan U Pe San	Ma Than Than Sint further commented correctly that the car U Ba Kan had (at the time she made these remarks) was not the one he had had before, that is, when his first wife, Daw Ma Ma May, was living. He had owned a black Ford, which he had sold in 1958, before Daw Ma Ma May died.
9. She had seven boxes for clothing.	Daw Nu Nu May, U Ba Kan's second wife and Ma Than Sint's maternal aunt	Daw Nu Nu May	
10. She had put nine 25-*pya* pieces in a small bottle.	Daw Nu Nu May	Daw Nu Nu May	Ma Than Than Sint made this remark when she noticed the bottle standing on a shelf at U Ba Kan's house. The shelf was rather high, and as the coins were at the bottom of the bottle, they could not be seen from below. When the bottle was taken down and the coins counted, Ma Than Than Sint was found to be correct. (There are 100 pyas in a kyat.)
11. She had plenty of money.	U Pe San	U Ba Kan	U Ba Kan and his first wife were quite prosperous. They owned two houses and 300 acres of land.

TABLE 13. (cont.)

Item	Informants	Verification	Comments
12. Recognition of buttons that had belonged to Daw Ma Ma May	Daw Nu Nu May		This was one of the first expressions by Ma Than Than Sint of her memories of the previous life. Daw Nu Nu May went to visit her sister (Ma Than Than Sint's mother) wearing some buttons that had belonged to Daw Ma Ma May. Ma Than Than Sint examined the buttons intently and then asserted that they were hers.
13. Recognition of a purse that had belonged to Daw Ma Ma May	U Ba Kan U Pe San Daw Nu Nu May		This item was another of Ma Than Than Sint's first expressions of a previous life. Daw Nu Nu May went to visit Ma Than Than Sint's family and carried a purse that had belonged to Daw Ma Ma May. Ma Than Than Sint noticed the purse and said it was hers.
14. Buttons were in a tin inside the purse.	Daw Hla Sein U Pe San Daw Nu Nu May U Ba Kan	Daw Nu Nu May	Following her recognition of Daw Ma Ma May's purse (described in item 13), Ma Than Than Sint was shown a tin that was in the purse and was asked what it contained. She replied, correctly: "Buttons." According to Daw Hla Sein, Daw Nu Nu May teased Ma Than Than Sint a little by suggesting that the tin contained medicinal lozenges, but Ma Than Than Sint insisted that it contained buttons. She had never seen the tin before this episode.

Item	Informants	Comments
		The buttons, made of gold and diamonds, are more accurately described as studs, because they could be transferred from one blouse to another. U Ba Kan was a secondhand witness for this item.
15. Recognition of Ma Khin Mya Mya, one of Daw Ma Ma May's nieces	Daw Nu Nu May	Ma Khin Mya Mya came unexpectedly to U Ba Kan's (and Daw Nu Nu May's) home one day when Ma Than Than Sint was there. Ma Than Than Sint rushed to her and greeted her by name. She said the girl was her niece. Daw Nu Nu May did not know who Ma Khin Mya Mya was and asked her. She said that she was a daughter of Daw Ma Ma May's sister-in-law and hence her niece by marriage. She lived in Yandoon.
16. Recognition of a photograph of Daw Ma Ma May	U Ba Kan Daw Nu Nu May	U Ba Kan had two photographs hanging on a wall at his house. They were of himself and his first wife, Daw Ma Ma May. Pointing at the first one, he asked Ma Than Than Sint whose photograph it was. Ma Than Than Sint said: "Mine."
17. Recognition of a photograph of U Ba Kan	U Ba Kan Daw Nu Nu May	This item occurred immediately after the preceding one. U Ba Kan pointed to this photograph and asked Ma Than Than Sint whose it was. She replied: "Baba's." At this time Ma Than Than Sint was calling U Ba Kan "Baba" as a

TABLE 13. (cont.)

Item	Informants	Verification	Comments
			kind of pet name. The word means "grandfather" in Burmese. Although U Ba Kan was not Ma Than Than Sint's grandfather, but rather an elderly uncle, she thought the word right for him. Daw Ma Ma May had not called U Ba Kan "Baba." She called him "Maung." (See the discussion of this in the text.) In 1980 I examined the photographs concerned in this recognition and that of item 16 more carefully than I had done on earlier visits. They were taken when U Ba Kan and Daw Ma Ma May were in their early forties, therefore in about 1940. Ma Than Than Sint was about four when she made the recognitions. These therefore occurred toward the end of 1969, or nearly thirty years after the photographs had been taken. Although U Ba Kan had changed in appearance during these years, I think he could be recognized in the photograph. If Ma Than Than Sint had done this, then she could have inferred that the photograph hanging beside that of U Ba Kan was that of his first wife. These recognitions are therefore not impressive.

18. Recognition of the house on Pongyi Street	U Ba Kan	This item consisted only of Ma Than Than Sint's saying that the house was hers.
19. Recognition of one of Daw Ma Ma May's longyis	Daw Htwe, Ma Than Than Sint's maternal grandmother Ma Aye Aye Kyaing, one of Ma Than Than Sint's older sisters U Pe San U Ba Kan	When Daw Htwe was staying with her daughter Daw Nu Nu May, she asked her to give her a longyi to wear as an undergarment. Daw Nu Nu May gave her one of Daw Ma Ma May's longyis without telling her that it had belonged to Daw Ma Ma May. Daw Htwe then went to visit her other daughter, Daw Hla Sein. At this second house, she took a bath while wearing the longyi. Afterward she asked one of the daughters of the family to "go and dry my longyi." Ma Than Than Sint noticed the longyi and said it was not Daw Htwe's, but hers. Ma Aye Aye Kyaing and U Pe San gave substantially similar accounts of this episode, although both varied the details slightly. In 1978 U Pe San said that the recognition had occurred at U Ba Kan's house on Pongyi Street; but this disagreed with what other informants said and with what he himself had said in 1971: that it had occurred at his (U Pe San's) house on Tarok Kyaung Street. U Ba Kan was a secondhand informant for this item. This was an exceptionally impressive recognition, because Daw Htwe did not know that the

Table 13. (cont.)

Item	Informants	Verification	Comments
			longyi she had been given had belonged to Daw Ma Ma May, and she was unable to confirm that Ma Than Than Sint's statement was correct until she went back to U Ba Kan's house on Pongyi Street and asked Daw Nu Nu May.
20. Recognition of Daw Ma Ma May's blanket	Daw Htwe Daw Nu Nu May		Ma Than Than Sint could barely speak when she made this recognition. A servant had spread an old blanket (which had belonged to Daw Ma Ma May) on the floor in order to put on it some clothes that she was ironing. When Ma Than Than Sint saw it, she said: "This is my blanket."
21. Recognition of Daw Ma Ma May's diamond pin	U Ba Kan		Ma Than Than Sint saw one of her aunts putting on a diamond

		stud pin that had belonged to Daw Ma Ma May and said that the pin was hers.
22. Recognition of Daw Ma Ma May's hair	U Ba Kan	Some of the hair that Daw Ma Ma May had cut off and kept (see item 3) had eventually come into the possession of U Ba Kan's second wife, Daw Nu Nu May. One day, when she was trying the hair on her head, Ma Than Than Sint saw her and said: "That is my hair."
23. Recognition of some of Daw Ma Ma May's longyis	Daw Nu Nu May, Ma Than Than Nu, Ma Than Than Sint's oldest sister	On an occasion when Ma Than Than Sint was about four, some longyis and dresses had been washed and dried, before being folded and put away. Ma Than Than Sint was observed picking out longyis that had belonged to Daw Ma Ma May. She started folding these, but left the others. Ma Than Than Nu heard Ma Than Than Sint claim that the longyis she was folding belonged to her. Daw Nu Nu May said that Ma Than Than Sint correctly selected Daw Ma Ma May's longyis.

Ma May's nieces, in the presence of Daw Nu Nu May, who herself did not know either the niece's name or her relationship to Daw Ma Ma May (item 15, Table 13).

I did not learn where Ma Than Than Sint had made several of the recognitions credited to her, for example, those of items 20, 21, 22, and 23. Since either U Ba Kan or his second wife, Daw Nu Nu May, were informants for these items, I believe they occurred at U Ba Kan's house on Pongyi Street. If so, they have somewhat less value than they would have had if they had occurred elsewhere; when visiting U Ba Kan, Ma Than Than Sint might have expected to see some of Daw Ma Ma May's possessions at his house.

U Ba Kan said that Ma Than Than Sint was able to recognize some of his relatives from Yandoon, but that she was unable to call any of them by name. I did not learn the details of how, in his opinion, Ma Than Than Sint had implied that she had recognized these people if she had not given their names; but presumably she had given some indication of their relationships to U Ba Kan. U Ba Kan appears not to have been a witness of Ma Than Than Sint's recognition of Ma Khin Mya Mya, whom she *did* call by name (item 15, Table 13).

U Ba Kan also said that Ma Than Than Sint could not give the names of his neighbors on Pongyi Street; she said she remembered them, but could not give any details about them.

Ma Than Than Sint's Behavior Related to the Previous Life

Circumstances and Manner of Ma Than Than Sint's Speaking about the Previous Life. I have already emphasized that Ma Than Than Sint made more than half of her recorded references to the previous life she was remembering when she saw some object or person that had been familiar to Daw Ma Ma May.[1]

Ma Than Than Sint did not like to be called by her given name. She would point to herself and say that she was Ma Ma May and would insist on being called by that name. However, she did not refuse to respond, as

---

[1]Many other subjects have shown a similar tendency to utter remarks about a previous life when they happen to encounter a person or object that had been known to the related previous personality in their cases. Mallika Aroumougam (*Twenty Cases*) is a subject whose remarks about a previous life occurred *only* at such times.

In my report of the case of Zouheir Chaar (third volume of this series), I noted that when the two families concerned in a case know each other before its development or meet soon afterward, the case will include (generally) fewer statements and more recognitions than we find in cases in which the families do not know each other initially and do not meet until the subject is older, say four or five years old. The delay in meeting gives more time in which the subject can make statements about the previous life, but during the same time his memories may fade somewhat, so that when the families do meet, he can make fewer recognitions. The present case belongs to the former group.

have some children, unless she was called by the name of the person whose life she claimed to remember.[2] Perhaps this was because no one seems to have fallen in with her wishes; members of her family referred to her as Ma Than Than Sint, and presumably they addressed her by that name only.

Ma Than Than Sint said repeatedly—in her younger years—that U Ba Kan was her husband. She addressed him directly as "Baba," which means "grandfather." (He was, in fact, her uncle by marriage, not her grandfather.) However, when other persons asked her what relationship U Ba Kan had to her, she would say: "Maung." This word had a special significance for the relationship that Daw Ma Ma May had to U Ba Kan. Ordinarily in Burma a wife addresses her husband, who is usually older, as *"Akogyi,"* which means "older brother." But it happened that Daw Ma Ma May was two years older than U Ba Kan; so instead of calling him "Akogyi" she addressed him as "Maung," a word that means "younger brother."

Other Behavior of Ma Than Than Sint Related to the Previous Life. No informant for the case said, or implied, that Ma Than Than Sint preferred U Ba Kan to her own family. On the contrary, she was affectionate toward her family; and she intended to use the resources of the deceased Daw Ma Ma May to assist them. She said that when her father became old she would support him. She claimed to have adequate funds for this. When he happened to mention that he could not afford something, she told him that he could get the necessary money from "Baba." And to give that suggestion extra authority she added: "That money is my money."

Ma Than Than Sint showed a strong attachment to U Ba Kan. She was much fonder of him than were the other children of her family, despite his having favored one of her older sisters over her. Ma Than Than Sint was jealous of U Ba Kan's second wife, Daw Nu Nu May. When they first became acquainted, she regarded her disapprovingly. She would not go to her, but punished her with aloofness. Later, when she was about four, she became aware that Daw Nu Nu May was her aunt and could be loved in that capacity. This sentiment overcame her dislike for Daw Nu Nu May as U Ba Kan's second wife, and so they became friends. More than the other children of her family, Ma Than Than Sint liked to visit the home on Pongyi Street where U Ba Kan and Daw Ma Ma May had lived and

---

[2]For examples of other subjects who demanded to be called by the name of the person whose life they remembered, see the cases of Prakash Varshnay *(Twenty Cases)*, Mounzer Haïdar, Rabih Elawar, and Cevriye Bayrı (third volume of this series).

For an example of a child who refused to respond to his given name and whose name was eventually changed officially to that of the person whose life he claimed to remember, see the case of İsmail Altınkılıç (third volume).

where U Ba Kan later lived with Daw Nu Nu May. She once remarked that it would be much more convenient if her entire family would move to the house on Pongyi Street. This would enable them to avoid the coming and going between the two houses, which Ma Than Than Sint evidently found tedious.

Once U Ba Kan fell down some stairs. When Ma Than Than Sint heard of this, she instructed her father to look after him, saying that if anything happened to him "we will be separated."

Ma Than Than Sint never said anything spontaneously about experiences between the death of Daw Ma Ma May in 1962 and her birth in 1965. However, U Ba Kan once asked her a leading question about this period of "intermission," and she then said that she had asked the devas to send her back to him (U Ba Kan).

Ma Than Than Sint showed a precocious interest in religion and knowledge of Buddhist practices. U Ba Kan said that she had understood how to worship properly in a Buddhist temple before she had been instructed; she knew how to fold her hands, put a handkerchief on the floor, and kneel correctly. He said she had done this the first time she went to a temple, between the ages of three and four.[3] Daw Nu Nu May said that she had observed Ma Than Than Sint prostrate herself before a monk in the usual manner of Buddhists before she had been instructed to do so. (I did not learn why Daw Nu Nu May was sure that Ma Than Than Sint had not earlier received some instruction—from precept or model—in the manner of prostrating before monks; but because she spoke with conviction, I assume that she had asked Ma Than Than Sint's parents about the matter.)

U Pe San said that when Ma Than Than Sint was about two years old, she sat with her legs folded and her hands together while she muttered something that he could not understand. Her posture resembled that of a Buddhist meditating. She did this every night for about two weeks and then stopped, probably because she became self-conscious about this behavior. U Pe San does not and did not meditate, and Daw Hla Sein, although she took up meditation later, was not meditating at that time. Her mother (Daw Htwe) went regularly once a week to a temple, but Ma Than Than Sint did not go with her. In short, U Pe San was confident that Ma Than Than Sint had had no model whom she might have been imitating in this unusual behavior. As I mentioned earlier, U Pe San was a Roman

---

[3]For examples of other subjects who were precociously religious and were said to have known some of the forms of Buddhist worship before they were instructed in them, see the cases of Disna Samarasinghe, Lalitha Abeyawardena (second volume of this series), and Ratana Wongsombat (this volume).

Several other subjects showed precocious knowledge of other forms of worship. Among these are Kumkum Verma (first volume of this series), Gamini Jayasena, and Wijanama Kithsiri (second volume). They showed knowledge of (respectively) Hindu, Christian, and Moslem practices.

Catholic; he was attempting to bring his children up as Christians. But his wife, Daw Hla Sein, remained a Buddhist and their home had a small Buddhist shrine. U Pe San had observed that Ma Than Than Sint had less interest in Christianity than his other children had. In contrast to them, she was indifferent in church, but worshiped fervently in the pagoda. He also noticed that when she passed a Christian church she would make no special sign of reverence as many Roman Catholics do; but when she passed a pagoda she would briefly make a gesture of worship with the palms of her hands together. (Many Buddhists do this when they pass a pagoda, just as many Roman Catholics cross themselves when they pass a Catholic church.)

Ma Than Than Sint did not confine her religiousness to ritual. She was notably generous and shared willingly with other persons. Her father said that she was more gentle and sedate than his other children.

I learned of one trait in which the two personalities of this case did not resemble each other. Ma Than Than Sint's father said that she was rather fussy about food and would not eat food that she regarded as inadequate. But U Ba Kan said that Daw Ma Ma May had not been particular about her food. This difference may derive from the different circumstances of the two personalities concerned in the case. U Ba Kan and his first wife were prosperous and would never have had to eat inferior food; but U Pe San had a more modest income, and probably the food served in his home was at times mediocre compared with that to which Daw Ma Ma May had been accustomed.

Comments on the Evidence of Paranormal Processes in the Case

Because the two families knew each other before the case developed, we cannot positively attribute to paranormal processes any of Ma Than Than Sint's statements about the previous life she said she remembered. It seems to me, however, that we could not reject several of her statements, such as that about the bottle with small coins (item 10, Table 13), and her recognitions of Daw Ma Ma May's niece (item 15) and one of Daw Ma Ma May's longyis (item 19), without impugning the competence of several apparently reliable witnesses. Some of Ma Than Than Sint's other recognitions may have had equal value, but there may also have been more opportunities at the times they occurred for normal sensory cues to have stimulated her remarks. Unfortunately, I did not learn as much detail about the circumstances under which they occurred as I did for the three items just mentioned.

Ma Than Than Sint's piety and her strong and somewhat jealous attachment to U Ba Kan harmonized with her claim to be Daw Ma Ma May reborn, although they cannot be regarded as evidence of this by themselves.

It is worth noting again that U Pe San was a practicing Roman Catholic. According to his understanding of his religion, reincarnation cannot occur. And yet he found himself believing in it from the evidence provided by this case in his own family.

Ma Than Than Sint's Later Development

When I met with Ma Than Than Sint in March 1978, she was twelve and a half years old. She had just completed the fourth class of school. She was therefore a little behind her contemporaries, but I do not know why.

Daw Hla Sein said (at this meeting) that Ma Than Than Sint no longer talked about the previous life she had remembered earlier. She attributed the cessation of spontaneous remarks to shyness on the part of her daughter. When I asked Ma Than Than Sint directly whether she still remembered the previous life, she replied that she remembered it when she went to visit U Ba Kan (at the house on Pongyi Street where Daw Ma Ma May had lived). But U Ba Kan (whom I interviewed separately, at his home) said that Ma Than Than Sint was shy about talking of the previous life with him also. U Pe San said that she was still attached to U Ba Kan and was more fond of him than his other children were. She had met U Ba Kan just the day before our visit to her home.

In U Pe San's opinion, Ma Than Than Sint had, at this time, no obvious inclinations toward either Christianity or Buddhism. She was attending Mass with her father on Sundays; and she was also going with her mother to a Buddhist temple. U Pe San was willing to allow his children to select their own religion when they grew up. U Ba Kan, however, had a different perspective on Ma Than Than Sint's religious preference. He thought she was merely obliging her father by attending the Roman Catholic church with him. He said that she had told him that she intended to become a Buddhist later.

When I met Ma Than Than Sint and her family again in April 1979, she was thirteen and a half years old. She had completed the fifth class of school and expected to enter the sixth when her classes resumed. She said she remembered the previous life only vaguely. She could still recall putting up a building for the ordainment of monks. (U Ba Kan had described how Ma Than Than Sint had recognized two monastery buildings that he and Daw Ma Ma May had erected; but I did not include this item in Table 13 because he had stimulated her recognition with a leading question.) She said that she also remembered the diamond buttons that she (meaning Daw Ma Ma May) had kept in a tin box, and further recalled having recognized these buttons (item 14 of Table 13).

11.   The Case of Ma Tin Tin Myint

Introduction

THIS IS ANOTHER case in which the subject recalled the life of a member of her immediate family, in this instance that of her father's first wife, who was also her mother's older sister. I did not reach the case until the subject was almost eighteen years old, and I did not then learn of many statements that she had made. However, I think the case deserves recording because I believe it is typical of many other Burmese cases in which the personalities concerned belong to the same family. Many such cases, like this one, receive no attention (much less publicity) outside the immediate circles of the family and friends who observe them. This isolation may give such a case an additional value compared with other cases that do receive such publicity.

Summary of the Case and Its Investigation

Ma Tin Tin Myint[1] was born in Pyinmana on June 6, 1960. She was the first child of her parents, U Hla Pe and Daw Thoung. Subsequently, two younger daughters were born in the family. U Hla Pe was a businessman and had also spent a period of his life employed by the government.

Before Ma Tin Tin Myint's birth, Daw Thoung had two dreams, of which the second particularly gave an indication that her deceased sister, Daw Htwe, intended to reincarnate in her family. I shall describe these dreams later. I should also mention here that both of Ma Tin Tin Myint's younger sisters claimed to remember previous lives. The first remembered the previous life of her (and Ma Tin Tin Myint's) maternal grandmother, Daw Shwe Naing, who was the mother of Daw Htwe and Daw Thoung. The younger daughter recalled, in a fragmentary way, the life of an Indian (male) friend of the family. Hers was therefore a case of the "sex change" type.

Ma Tin Tin Myint was about two years old when she began to speak

---

[1] I have used pseudonyms for the names of persons and places concerned in this report, except for U Tin Tut (who informed me about the case) and Rangoon.

coherently. When she was between three and three and a half, she began to make allusions to a previous life. These continued until she was about eight. During this period, Ma Tin Tin Myint also showed some unusual behavior that accorded with her memories of the life of Daw Htwe.

I first learned of this case in April 1972 from a friend in Rangoon, U Tin Tut, whose sister had been friendly with Daw Htwe. But it was almost six years before I met Ma Tin Tin Myint and her parents in 1978. This was partly because of the comparative inaccessibility of the town, Pyinmana, where they lived. (It is about 200 kilometers north on the main road and railway line between Rangoon and Mandalay.) And it was partly due to my having given a higher priority in my investigations to other cases in Burma, especially some whose subjects had birthmarks and congenital deformities.

I was able to travel to Pyinmana in March 1978, and there U Win Maung and I had interviews with Ma Tin Tin Myint and her parents. When we returned to Rangoon, we interviewed several relatives and friends of the family who, we had been told, could furnish further first-hand testimony. It turned out that only one of these persons, Daw Aye Ohn, could remember statements and recognitions that Ma Tin Tin Myint had made when she was a young child.

In March 1979 U Win Maung traveled again to Pyinmana and obtained the answers to some questions that had occurred to me after our visit the previous year. Then in March 1980 he and I went to Pyinmana together for further (brief) interviews with Ma Tin Tin Myint's parents. Ma Tin Tin Myint was present then, but could contribute no further information.

Persons Interviewed during the Investigation

In Pyinmana I interviewed:

Ma Tin Tin Myint
U Hla Pe, Ma Tin Tin Myint's father
Daw Thoung, Ma Tin Tin Myint's mother and Daw Htwe's younger
   sister

In Rangoon I interviewed:

U Bo Sein, Ma Tin Tin Myint's maternal uncle and Daw Htwe's
   younger brother
Daw Tin Kyi, friend of Daw Htwe and U Hla Pe
Daw Aye Ohn, U Hla Pe's first cousin and friend of Daw Htwe
Daw Aye Myint, friend of Daw Htwe

In 1978, when I first investigated the case, Ma Tin Tin Myint said that she no longer remembered the previous life. My only informants in her family were therefore her parents.

Of the persons who had known Daw Htwe and whom I interviewed in Rangoon, only Daw Aye Ohn contributed information about Ma Tin Tin Myint's statements and behavior. The others, however, furnished some information about Daw Htwe.

Daw Aye Ohn proved to be an excellent informant; a graduate of Rangoon University, she had studied abroad and had become a much respected civil servant. Her frank and direct responses to our inquiries gave the case important support from outside the subject's immediate family.

The Life, Death, and Character of Daw Htwe

Daw Htwe was born in 1916 in the town of Meiktila. She was the second child and oldest daughter among seven children in the family. Her parents were U Po Gyi and Daw Shwe Naing. She had little education and left school at about the age of nine or ten, when she had reached the fourth class. Because she was the oldest daughter of the family, she was given considerable responsibility for the management of the household. In 1938 she married U Hla Pe, a businessman and later a government official of Pyinmana. She and U Hla Pe were married for twenty years, but they had no children.

Daw Htwe worked for a time as a volunteer social worker or aide in the area of Pyinmana. Although she had little formal education, her equable temper and sociability qualified her for such work.

She died in Pyinmana in about 1959. I was not able to learn the exact cause of her death. She seems to have been ailing somewhat for a year or two. A doctor had recommended a hysterectomy, which she had refused. In the end, she died rather suddenly after a brief illness. Indeed, her final illness was so short that her younger sister Daw Thoung said that she died within a few days of becoming overtly ill. About a year after Daw Htwe's death, her husband, U Hla Pe, married Daw Thoung.

Daw Htwe appears to have been a person of exemplary character— kind and friendly. She was considerate to her brothers and sisters, of whom her favorite was Daw Thoung, the youngest child in their family. Yet Daw Htwe was no puppet and showed an independence and assertiveness that others afterward remembered.

She knew that her inadequate education had handicapped her, and she prayed that in her next life she would have a greater ability to learn and that she would obtain a higher education. She also expressed the hope that she could go abroad to study in her next life.

Two Announcing Dreams

Within a few weeks of Daw Htwe's death, Daw Thoung dreamed about her. By this time Daw Thoung had returned from Pyinmana, where she had gone to be with her dying sister, to the school in Rangoon that she was attending at the time. In the dream Daw Htwe said to her sister: "I am following you." (This phrase, in Burmese, also carries the meaning "I am coming to you.") The remark implied that the discarnate Daw Htwe had selected her sister as a vehicle for her rebirth; but at that time Daw Thoung was still unmarried. However, within about a year she and U Hla Pe married. Soon after her marriage, Daw Thoung again dreamed that Daw Htwe came to her and said that she was "following" Daw Thoung and U Hla Pe. In the dream, Daw Thoung remonstrated with her sister and said that under the circumstances—she having married Daw Htwe's widowed husband—it would be improper for Daw Htwe to "follow" them. To this Daw Htwe replied: "It is a different matter altogether now. I am going to stay with you anyway." She then seemed to insinuate, or rather to push, herself between Daw Thoung and U Hla Pe. From the dates given to me, I think that Daw Thoung was already pregnant with Ma Tin Tin Myint when she had this second dream.

Statements and Recognitions Made by Ma Tin Tin Myint

I only learned of a small number of statements that Ma Tin Tin Myint had made about the previous life. The paucity of the statements mentioned by her parents was at least partly due to the lapse of time—about twelve years—between the period when Ma Tin Tin Myint spoke most about the previous life and my investigation of the case. But it was also due to the tendency of Ma Tin Tin Myint and one of her younger sisters to talk between themselves about the lives that they each remembered; when adults questioned them about these they became silent.

The statements I learned about are so few in number that I will not arrange them in tabular form.

On one occasion Ma Tin Tin Myint remarked: "Now that I am the oldest I am managing the house again." This was not a complaint, but rather a pleased allusion to her situation as the oldest daughter in her family. Her use of the word *again* showed that she compared it to Daw Htwe's position as the oldest daughter in *her* family.

Ma Tin Tin Myint never claimed to her mother that she was Daw Htwe, but Daw Thoung sometimes overheard her saying this to other persons. And when Ma Tin Tin Myint was between two and three years of age and still learning to speak, two daughters of a friend mentioned to Daw Thoung that Ma Tin Tin Myint had told them she was Daw Htwe. The friend's daughters who reported this to Daw Thoung were themselves still children at the time, but older than Ma Tin Tin Myint; they were nine and ten years old. They mentioned Ma Tin Tin Myint's claim to be Daw Thoung soon after she made it to them.

Ma Tin Tin Myint once recalled an episode that had occurred about nine years before Daw Htwe's death. Some relatives in Pyinmana had lost their house in a fire and had had to disperse. During this crisis, a nursing baby of this family was left in the care of Daw Htwe's and Daw Thoung's family. Ma Tin Tin Myint recalled that an Indian wet nurse had been engaged, and that the nurse's breast was so dirty they had to wipe it off before she could be allowed to suckle the baby. This memory appears to have been stimulated by Ma Tin Tin Myint's meeting a member of the family of relatives to whom the baby belonged.

When Ma Tin Tin Myint was between three and four years old, Daw Thoung decided to test her by asking her to pick out Daw Htwe's longyis and jewelry after she had mixed these with similar objects belonging to other persons. Ma Tin Tin Myint could tell which longyis and pieces of jewelry had belonged to Daw Htwe.

Daw Thoung also credited Ma Tin Tin Myint with being able to recognize a number of friends of the family whom Daw Htwe had known, but whom Ma Tin Tin Myint had not met before. She said that when visitors came to their home, Ma Tin Tin Myint would peek around the edge of an open door, examine the visitors from a distance, and sometimes identify them as from the life of Daw Htwe. I suppose she would whisper the recognition to Daw Thoung when she (Daw Thoung) would leave the living room and go into the kitchen.

Daw Thoung mentioned Daw Tin Kyi and Daw Aye Myint as being among the persons Ma Tin Tin Myint had recognized; however, when I interviewed them in Rangoon, neither could remember having been recognized by Ma Tin Tin Myint.[2] Daw Tin Kyi was in fact quite sure that Ma Tin Tin Myint had *not* recognized her. She said that she had not visited Pyinmana (where she had lived for a time when Daw Htwe was alive) during Ma Tin Tin Myint's early childhood, when, according to Daw Thoung, this recognition had taken place; and there had been no occasion at some other place during the same period when Ma Tin Tin Myint could have recognized her. It appeared then that, for this item, either Daw Thoung or Daw Tin Kyi had a defective memory.

Daw Aye Ohn, another informant whom I interviewed in Rangoon, did confirm some statements and recognitions that Ma Tin Tin Myint made when she came to her house. Ma Tin Tin Myint was then six or

---

[2]I have noted in earlier reports the failure of a second informant to confirm the occurrence of a recognition with which a first informant had credited the subject of a case. In such instances, the first informant may have made a mistake; but the second may also have done so. For other examples of this possibility, see the cases of Sunil Dutt Saxena (first volume of this series) and Shamlinie Prema (second volume).

seven years old at most, and possibly younger; Daw Thoung thought she was only five at the time. When Ma Tin Tin Myint reached Daw Aye Ohn's house, she said: "I know this house. There is a lavatory upstairs with a big bathtub." This was correct.[3] She further remarked that there was a big lake "over there." (Inya Lake is a substantial lake within the Rangoon city limits; it is near Daw Aye Ohn's house, but not visible from it.) Ma Tin Tin Myint was able to point out the bed in which Daw Htwe had slept when she had stayed with Daw Aye Ohn about two years before her death. Daw Aye Ohn said she had initially been skeptical when she learned that Ma Tin Tin Myint was said to be Daw Htwe reborn; but she was much impressed by the precise remarks Ma Tin Tin Myint made about her house, which she had never before visited.

U Bo Sein (Daw Htwe's brother) said that when he first met Ma Tin Tin Myint (when she was about eight years old), she did not recognize him, although he had expected that she might. (Daw Thoung had not said that Ma Tin Tin Myint had recognized U Bo Sein.)

Ma Tin Tin Myint's Behavior Related to the Previous Life

Circumstances and Manner of Ma Tin Tin Myint's Speaking about the Previous Life.   I have already mentioned that Ma Tin Tin Myint tended to make statements about the previous life, or recognitions related to it, when she saw someone whom Daw Htwe had known. Ma Tin Tin Myint spoke rather freely with one of her younger sisters about the previous life; this sister also recalled a previous life, that of Daw Htwe's (and Daw Thoung's) mother. But neither of the girls would respond when adults questioned them about details.

Other Behavior of Ma Tin Tin Myint Related to the Previous Life.   When she was young, Ma Tin Tin Myint addressed her father by his name instead of as "father," as a polite Burmese child would do. (She did, however, address her mother as "mother" and not by her name.) She showed considerable jealousy of her mother. When her parents were sitting together, she would come and sit between them. According to U Hla Pe, Ma Tin Tin Myint showed this jealous behavior between the ages of two and seven or eight. It ceased at about the time she stopped talking spontaneously about the previous life. It was still sufficiently obvious for Daw Aye Ohn to notice it when Ma Tin Tin Myint and her parents visited Daw Aye Ohn's house in Rangoon, at which time Ma Tin Tin Myint was between five and seven years old.

---

[3]Western readers will consider this remark more significant if I mention that in Burma most houses have the bathroom downstairs and few bathrooms have bathtubs. These are mainly found in hotels and in the more elaborate and expensive houses.

Ma Tin Tin Myint was notably considerate of her younger sisters. In this she resembled Daw Htwe, who, as I mentioned, had shown a similar thoughtfulness toward her brothers and sisters. Ma Tin Tin Myint also evoked memories of Daw Htwe's assertiveness; she learned to drive an automobile without her parents' knowledge.

Comments on the Evidence of Paranormal Processes in the Case

This case is not rich in details. Moreover, I did not learn about any statement or recognition attributed to Ma Tin Tin Myint that included information unknown to her parents. The case cannot therefore be said to contain any features that require some paranormal process for their explanation. This does not mean, however, that no paranormal elements were present.

There seem to be no explanations obviously preferable to that of reincarnation. The case is certainly not a hoax. There was a gap of six years between the time I first learned of the case and my investigation of it, and there is no evidence that during this period the family gave it any publicity or otherwise tried to exploit it; nor have they done so since. Even if, against this lack of evidence, we assumed that Ma Tin Tin Myint's family were trying to obtain some gain from the case, we should have to name Daw Aye Ohn in Rangoon as a coconspirator prepared with the proper answers when U Win Maung and I arrived unexpectedly to interview her in Rangoon. I find this suggestion laughable.

A more serious one is the conjecture that Ma Tin Tin Myint's parents subtly influenced her to assume the personality of Daw Htwe and then, quite unconsciously, attributed to her statements and recognitions that she did not make. Since they had been the husband and sister of Daw Htwe, each of them had a motive for hoping that Daw Htwe had been reborn in the family. The dreams of Daw Thoung seemed to suggest this development. And yet for each of them such a return of the deceased Daw Htwe would have added an awkward complication to their relationship with each other. However much she loved her sister, Daw Thoung could not have welcomed her back after she (Daw Thoung) had assumed her position as the wife of U Hla Pe. And U Hla Pe himself would have been exceedingly tactless, to say the least, if he had tried to introduce his first wife into his relationship with his second one. In short, for this interpretation of the case, one has to suppose rather contorted and indeed self-destructive motives on the part of Ma Tin Tin Myint's parents.

The most plausible explanation of the case other than reincarnation seems to be that Ma Tin Tin Myint herself contributed all the motivation needed for it. By presenting herself as Daw Htwe, she could, in principle, have pleased both her father and her mother, each of whom, in different ways, had loved Daw Htwe.

Western psychiatrists determined to find a psychological explanation for the case that would be familiar to them might attribute its production to Ma Tin Tin Myint, but assign her a less worthy motive than the one I have just mentioned. They might suggest that her conduct of putting herself between her parents expressed hostility toward both of them in a manner that made retaliation difficult. What, after all, could embroil them with each other more effectively than a representation of Daw Htwe as still being with them?

To the people immediately concerned in this case, such an interpretation would seem absurdly contrived. I would think this also. I am far from being an expert in the psychology of the Burmese people, but I can say that the good relationships between parents in Burma and their children might surprise most Westerners and shame many. I see no reason to attribute hostility toward her parents to a small child in the absence of any evidence for it. Perhaps Ma Tin Tin Myint gained something with her parents by her claim to have been Daw Htwe. But there were complexities also, as we have seen. And one may reasonably ask whether, when Ma Tin Tin Myint wedged herself in between her parents— physically as well as emotionally—she did not incur risks, especially from her mother, that outweighed any possible advantage to her of assuming the role of Daw Htwe.

Ma Tin Tin Myint's Later Development

I can add little under this heading. In view, however, of Daw Htwe's expressed wish to have a better education in another life, I shall record that Ma Tin Tin Myint had continued her education successfully up to 1980. She was then in the second year of a junior college at Pyinmana. She was planning to continue on to a university, perhaps in Rangoon, and she hoped ultimately to study abroad.

12. The Case of Maung Yin Maung

Summary of the Case and Its Investigation

MAUNG YIN MAUNG was born in Rangoon on August 3, 1960. He was the fourth child of his parents, U Ba Hein and Daw Kyin Htein. One older brother died before Maung Yin Maung was born; and he had two older living brothers. Later, a younger sister was born. U Ba Hein and Daw Kyin Htein are both Sino-Burmese. In addition, U Ba Hein's mother had some Mon ancestry as well as Burman. U Ba Hein was a store manager of the Forest Department of the government of the Union of Burma.

Before Maung Yin Maung's birth, his mother had an apparitional experience in which she saw an old friend of the family in her house. He was U Pe Tin, a pilot officer of the Burmese Air Force, who had been killed in an airplane crash some months earlier. I shall describe Daw Kyin Htein's vision later, and also some announcing dreams bearing on the case.

Maung Yin Maung began to speak coherently at the age of between fourteen and eighteen months. When he was about two and a half years old, he was still lisping and not pronouncing words correctly. He was then heard to be saying: "U Po Taik. U Po Taik." His parents recognized this as his mispronunciation of the name U Po Saik.[1] U Po Saik was the father of U Pe Tin, the deceased airplane pilot mentioned above. They assumed that Maung Yin Maung was beginning to remember a previous life, and when they asked him who his (previous) mother was, he said: "Daw Shwe Chote," which was the name of U Pe Tin's mother. When they asked who he was, Maung Yin Maung said: "Ah Maung," which had been a pet name of U Pe Tin.

Over the next few years, Maung Yin Maung made a few statements about the previous life that he claimed to remember. He also showed an unusual attachment for Daw Shwe Chote, U Pe Tin's mother, and he

---

[1]For other examples of subjects who, when they were just beginning to speak, mispronounced proper names figuring in the lives they remembered, see the cases of Imad Elawar (*Twenty Cases*), Bishen Chand Kapoor (first volume of this series), Sujith Lakmal Jayaratne, Mahes de Silva, Shamlinie Prema, Lalitha Abeyawardena (second volume), Cevriye Bayrı, Erkan Kılıç, and Necati Caylak (third volume).

manifested some other behavior that harmonized with relationships and attitudes U Pe Tin was known to have had or might be conjectured to have had.

I should mention here that Maung Yin Maung's claim to remember a previous life did not surprise anyone in his family. Four other members had already had some memories of previous lives; and later, Ma Myint Myint Aye, the youngest child and only daughter of the family, added her claim to remember a previous life to those already noted.

I first learned of this case in 1972, when U Win Maung sent me a summary of a preliminary interview he had (in February of that year) with Maung Yin Maung's parents. In November 1972 I met and interviewed Maung Yin Maung and his mother, Daw Kyin Htein. Two years later, in November 1974, I was able to interview his father, U Ba Hein, and had another short talk with Maung Yin Maung. In the same month I also interviewed U Htun Hlaing, an older brother of U Pe Tin. In 1975 I briefly interviewed Ma Than Tin, one of his older sisters. In March 1978 I had further interviews with Maung Yin Maung and his parents, and in November 1978 U Win Maung asked U Htun Hlaing some further questions about details. At that time, U Htun Hlaing read a draft of this report, made a few corrections, and offered some clarifications for it.

In March 1979 U Win Maung and I had a second interview with Ma Than Tin, mainly about a loan (or gift) that U Pe Tin had made to her, which figures in the case as the most evidentially important item of information Maung Yin Maung knew about the life of U Pe Tin.

In November 1980 U Win Maung and I had a further meeting with Maung Yin Maung and his mother, Daw Kyin Htein. We also had a second interview with U Pe Tin's older brother U Htun Hlaing.

In July 1981 U Win Maung visited Daw Kyin Htein to enquire about several details on which I needed more information.

Persons Interviewed during the Investigation

In Rangoon I interviewed:

Maung Yin Maung
U Ba Hein, Maung Yin Maung's father
Daw Kyin Htein, Maung Yin Maung's mother
U Htun Hlaing, U Pe Tin's older brother
Ma Than Tin, one of U Pe Tin's older sisters

Other potential informants among members of U Pe Tin's family were either dead or otherwise unavailable by the time of my investigation of the case. Most regrettably, I did not meet Daw Shwe Chote, U Pe Tin's mother, who died in 1973, or U Po Saik, his father, who died in 1974.

Acquaintance between the Two Families Concerned in the Case

Because of his employment in the Forest Department of the Burmese government, U Ba Hein lived in a house within the department's timber depot in Rangoon. U Pe Tin's older brother U Htun Hlaing also worked for many years in the Forest Department, and he had a house in the same compound of the timber depot. At one time he and U Ba Hein occupied adjoining houses in the compound, and they shared an outhouse. U Pe Tin stayed with his brother at the timber depot during much of the time (at different periods) when he lived in Rangoon. The two families were well acquainted. U Pe Tin spent more time at the home of U Ba Hein than at his brother's home; he ate, bathed, and slept there often. It could be said with some truth that, in the years before U Pe Tin's death, U Ba Hein and his family knew U Pe Tin better than his own family knew him. Be that as it may, Maung Yin Maung's family knew U Pe Tin so well that almost nothing Maung Yin Maung said about the previous life was new to them. There was one noteworthy exception: a loan of money U Pe Tin had made to one of his older sisters, which I shall mention later.

The Life, Death, and Character of U Pe Tin

U Pe Tin was born in 1931 in Kamawet, which is 43 kilometers south of Moulmein. His parents were U Po Saik and Daw Shwe Chote. They were Mons, members of a minority group, most of whom live in southeastern Burma and adjoining regions of Thailand. U Pe Tin was the youngest child in a family of seven children.

When U Pe Tin was about five years old, his parents moved from Kamawet to Kwan Klar, which is 14 kilometers farther south. They had a rubber plantation there. U Pe Tin stayed with his parents until his teens, when he came to Rangoon for a better education. In Rangoon he stayed with his older brother U Htun Hlaing.

In 1949, when U Pe Tin was about eighteen, U Htun Hlaing helped him to obtain a position with the Forest Department of the government of Burma. Two years later, in 1951, U Pe Tin was selected for training as a radio operator in the Burmese Air Force. His training included two years in the United Kingdom, from which he returned to Burma in 1956. He then stayed in quarters at an army base, while U Htun Hlaing continued to live in the compound of the timber depot.

In the late 1950s U Pe Tin was selected for further training, first as a glider pilot and then as an airplane pilot. He had completed his training and been commissioned as a pilot just two months before the accident in which he was killed.

U Pe Tin was flying solo in a Sea Fury airplane when he crashed during a takeoff at Mingaladon Airport, near Rangoon. When the accident occurred, his airplane caught fire, so that his body was badly burned. He probably died just before that, immediately after the impact. The accident occurred on August 20, 1959. (U Pe Tin's brother U Htun Hlaing remembered in 1974 only that it had occurred in August 1959; I have adopted the more precise date given in a detailed report of the accident published on August 21, 1959, in *The New Light of Burma,* a daily newspaper of Rangoon.) U Pe Tin was twenty-eight years old and unmarried when he died.

I did not learn much about U Pe Tin's personality. His older brother described him as a brilliant student and superior to other members of the family in many respects. He seems to have been his mother's favorite son. He was much attached to an older sister, Ma Than Tin, and they loaned money to each other. However, some strain occurred between them when Ma Than Tin married a man of whom U Pe Tin did not approve. U Pe Tin was extremely friendly with U Ba Hein and his family, in whose home, as I have mentioned, he was often a visitor and always welcome.

An Apparition and Two Announcing Dreams

Three or four months after U Pe Tin's death, Daw Kyin Htein had occasion during the night to go to the outhouse behind the house at the timber depot where she, U Ba Hein, and their children lived. As she was returning toward the house, she heard the gate to the inner compound creaking, and she then saw the gate open and U Pe Tin enter. He wore a white, short-sleeved shirt and a pink longyi. He came and stopped near her. She waited for him to come closer. He seemed like a real person, and she momentarily forgot that he was dead. She asked him what he was doing there. He did not reply, and suddenly she remembered that he was dead. Then she told him that she would share her merits with him so that he could go to a "good and proper place."[2] To this he did not reply, and so, thinking that something more was needed, she added: "If you have a fixation and have so much attachment to us, you can be born into our family; but please do not come back to us disfigured and deformed. Come physically whole."[3] As soon as she said this, the apparition disappeared.

[2]This is an example of the Buddhist belief that merit acquired by good conduct, meditation, ritual observances, or otherwise can be beneficially shared with other living persons and also with discarnate ones. For a further discussion of this topic, see the section on the paritta ceremony in the Introduction to Cases in Burma (this volume); for another example of the transfer of merit to discarnate persons in order to release them for an improved existence, see the case of the Ven. Sayadaw U Sobhana (this volume).

[3]The subjects of cases who remember previous lives that ended violently often have birthmarks and deformities that correspond to the fatal wound or wounds of the related previous personality. In Buddhism, all birth defects are attributed to some cause in the subject's previous life. Daw Kyin Htein's remark implies that a discarnate person may have some control over the occurrence of birthmarks and birth defects in his next physical body. I know of one other case in which a mother-to-be urged a discarnate person who had appeared to her in an announcing dream not to be born with deformities, which the discarnate person appearing in the dream had had when alive.

In the paragraph above, I have given the account I received from Daw Kyin Htein during my first interview with her in November 1972. However, in an interview with U Win Maung in February of the same year she had given some additional and different details. She said that she had told the apparitional U Pe Tin: "We promise to treat you well." Her conversation was vocal and was heard by U Ba Hein, who was inside the house. He called out: "With whom are you speaking?" When she replied: "Ah Maung" (U Pe Tin's pet name), her husband remarked: "You must be mad." Daw Kyin Htein showed him where the apparition stood, but he did not see it. Then it disappeared.[4]

This did not end Daw Kyin Htein's experiences concerning U Pe Tin that night. When she went to sleep, she dreamed of him. He was sleeping in the bed she and her husband occupied, while they were sitting nearby. She then saw U Pe Tin's mother and one of his sisters enter the room and ask him to go with them; but he declined. Later, in the same dream, she saw U Pe Tin pushing a deed box and a small steel trunk under another bed. He was trying to open up one of the boxes in the room in order to take out some bars of chocolate. When he got these out, he gave them to the children of the family who were present. Daw Kyin Htein remembered that in the same dream U Pe Tin told her and her husband that he was going to stay with them.

Maung Yin Maung was conceived soon after the night when Daw Kyin Htein had her apparitional experience and dream. He was a full-term baby and was born slightly less than a year after U Pe Tin's death.

The above experiences occurred during the period when U Ba Hein and U Htun Hlaing were living in adjoining houses at the timber depot and sharing an outhouse.

Daw Kyin Htein learned later from Daw Shwe Chote that she too had dreamed her son was going to live with their old friend and neighbor U Ba Hein. (U Win Maung and I heard of this second dream only from Daw Kyin Htein; we did not interview Daw Shwe Chote, who had died in 1973.)

Statements and Recognitions Made by Maung Yin Maung

If Maung Yin Maung made many statements about the previous life when he was young, his parents had forgotten most of them by the time I began to investigate the case. I have summarized those that I learned about, along with two recognitions attributed to Maung Yin Maung, in Table 14. I have grouped the statements together first, followed by the recognitions.

---

[4]This apparition has two important features often found in apparitional experiences reported in the West. First, it seemed so life-like that the percipient at first thought she was meeting the living man; and second, the apparition did not speak.

TABLE 14. *Summary of Statements and Recognitions Made by Maung Yin Maung*

Item	Informants	Verification	Comments
1. He was named Ah Maung.	Daw Kyin Htein, Maung Yin Maung's mother U Ba Hein, Maung Yin Maung's father	U Htun Hlaing, U Pe Tin's older brother	*Ah Maung* was a pet name of U Pe Tin.
2. Daw Shwe Chote was his mother.	Daw Kyin Htein U Ba Hein	U Htun Hlaing	
3. U Po Taik [name mentioned by Maung Yin Maung]	Daw Kyin Htein	U Htun Hlaing	*Taik* was Maung Yin Maung's first babyish mispronunciation of *Saik.* When he became older, he pronounced the name correctly. U Po Saik was U Pe Tin's father. Daw Kyin Htein did not say that Maung Yin Maung had said that U Po Taik (or Saik) was his father, although this was understood. In 1974 I recorded U Ba Hein as saying that Maung Yin Maung had identified the father of the previous life as U Po Sein (not Saik). U Win Maung, however, assured me that I had made a mistake in hearing the name, not U Ba Hein in remembering it.
4. He had a bicycle.	Daw Kyin Htein	U Htun Hlaing	Maung Yin Maung asked Daw Shwe Chote what had happened to the bicycle that he remembered having had in the previous life. He seemed reassured when she said that she had given it to U Pe Tin's older brother U Tun Kyi.

282

5. Ma Than Tin was his favorite sister.	Daw Kyin Htein, Ma Than Tin, U Pe Tin's older sister	Ma Than Tin, U Htun Hlaing	Daw Kyin Htein said that Maung Yin Maung was about four or five years old when he made this remark. Ma Than Tin was a secondhand informant for the item. Of U Pe Tin's three older sisters, Ma Than Tin was the one next in age to him.
6. He had loaned 1,000 kyats to his sister Ma Than Tin.	Daw Kyin Htein, Ma Than Tin	Ma Than Tin	Ma Than Tin said that U Pe Tin had sent her 1,000 kyats when he was in England. The money was to help her start a business as a seamstress. Ma Than Tin regarded the money as a gift by which her brother repaid her for what she had done for him earlier. Maung Yin Maung considered the money a loan. He seems never to have mentioned it directly to Ma Than Tin, so that she was a secondhand informant for the item. According to Maung Yin Maung's parents, the loan of 1,000 kyats was confirmed to them by Ma Thoung Kyi (whom I did not interview), who said that she had seen U Pe Tin hand over 1,000 kyats to Ma Than Tin. (This does not accord with Ma Than Tin's saying U Pe Tin had sent the money to her from England, but there may have been more than one transaction.) The loan (or gift, as the case may be) appears to have been a private affair; Maung Yin Maung's parents said it was known only to U Pe Tin, Ma

TABLE 14. (cont.)

Item	Informants	Verification	Comments
7. He was sent to England and Czechoslovakia for training as a pilot.	Maung Yin Maung (1972)	Partly verified, partly incorrect	Thoung Kyi, and Ma Than Tin. They themselves knew nothing about it until Maung Yin Maung first spoke of it. According to U Htun Hlaing, U Pe Tin had been sent to England for training as a radio operator and subsequently to Yugoslavia for training as a glider pilot. He had trained to be an airplane pilot at Meiktila, in Burma.
8. He had come from Hmawpi to Mingaladon in his airplane.	Maung Yin Maung (1972)	Article in *The New Light of Burma* for August 21, 1959	The newspaper article does not state that U Pe Tin had just come from Hmawpi; but it does say that he was stationed there, so it is a reasonable inference that he had flown to Mingaladon from Hmawpi.
9. He landed successfully.	Maung Yin Maung (1972)	Unverified	
10. Then he had a meal of Burmese spaghetti.	Maung Yin Maung (1972)	Unverified	
11. After the meal he started to fly back to Hmawpi.	Maung Yin Maung (1972)	Daw Kyin Htein	
12. His commanding officer recalled him, and he returned.	Maung Yin Maung (1972)	Daw Kyin Htein	
13. He landed and then took off again.	Maung Yin Maung (1972)	Daw Kyin Htein	

Item	Informants	Verification	Comments
14. The commanding officer called him back again.	Maung Yin Maung (1972)	Daw Kyin Htein	
15. On the third takeoff the landing gear hit a ditch by the side of the runway.	Maung Yin Maung (1972)	Unverified	Maung Yin Maung mentioned only two takeoffs from Mingaladon, but there were (at least) three takeoffs altogether, counting U Pe Tin's flight to Mingaladon from Hmawpi. Daw Kyin Htein said she had learned that U Pe Tin had taken off three times from Mingaladon and had been recalled each time.
16. The landing gear broke and flew off.	Maung Yin Maung (1972)	Unverified	
17. The airplane did not take off, but veered into the officers' quarters.	Maung Yin Maung (1972)	Article in *The New Light of Burma* for August 21, 1959	
18. The airplane crashed.	U Ba Hein	U Htun Hlaing Article in *The New Light of Burma* for August 21, 1959	The airplane in which U Pe Tin crashed was a Sea Fury single-engine fighter of the Burma Air Force.
19. It caught fire.	U Ba Hein	U Htun Hlaing Article in *The New Light of Burma* for August 21, 1959	
20. A fountain pen he had borrowed from Ma Thoung Kyi was destroyed in the crash of his airplane.	Daw Kyin Htein	Daw Kyin Htein	When Maung Yin Maung was still very young, Ma Thoung Kyi (who had been a friend of U Pe Tin) asked him what had become of a pen that U Pe Tin had borrowed from her. Maung Yin Maung said that it had been destroyed in the airplane crash. Ma Thoung Kyi (whom I did not interview) told Daw Kyin Htein that she had been at Mingaladon Airport to see U Pe Tin off on his

TABLE 14. (cont.)

Item	Informants	Verification	Comments
			flight back to Hmawpi. Just before he departed, he borrowed a pen from her, and it was presumably destroyed in the crash that occurred soon afterward.
			U Win Maung and I heard what are probably variant accounts of this episode. For example, in 1972 Maung Yin Maung's parents told U Win Maung that Maung Yin Maung had asked Ma Thoung Kyi what had happened to a pen that U Pe Tin had loaned *her*.
			In 1972 Daw Kyin Htein and in 1979 Ma Than Tin separately recounted to me two other seemingly different incidents in which a pen had figured and of which Maung Yin Maung had apparent paranormal knowledge. These may have been badly remembered versions of the same incident, but it is also possible that two or more pens figured in different episodes remembered by Maung Yin Maung.
			Daw Kyin Htein was a witness of Maung Yin Maung's remark to Ma Thoung Kyi. She said that until she heard him make it, she had known nothing about U Pe Tin's having borrowed a pen from Ma Thoung Kyi.
21. Recognition of Ma Than Tin, one of U Pe Tin's older sisters	Ma Than Tin		Maung Yin Maung's mother asked him if he knew Ma Than Tin, and he replied: "Yes, that is my older sister." He did not give her name.

22. Recognition of Daw
Than Kyi, one of U Pe Tin's
older sisters

U Ba Hein
Ma Than Tin

U Ba Hein reported two occasions of Maung Yin Maung's meeting Daw Than Kyi. On the first occasion, Maung Yin Maung and his father were walking in the compound of the timber depot when they met Daw Than Kyi, who had come from Moulmein to visit her brother U Htun Hlaing. Maung Yin Maung seemed to recognize her, because his eyes filled with tears; but he did not greet her. When his father asked him whether he knew her, he said that he did, and when his father then asked him why he did not greet her, he replied: "I don't because they do not believe me." (This last remark referred to the skepticism concerning his claim to be U Pe Tin reborn that some members of U Pe Tin's family had expressed.)

Ma Than Tin gave me a secondhand account of what I assume was the same meeting. She had heard about it from Daw Than Kyi. According to her version, U Ba Hein had asked Maung Yin Maung if he knew Daw Than Kyi, and he had replied: "Yes, that is my older sister."

On a later occasion Maung Yin Maung (again walking in the compound with his father) met Daw Than Kyi again, and she asked him if he knew her. He said: "Yes, you are Ma Than Kyi." He said nothing more and walked past her as if displeased to see her.

I have included in Table 14 a number of items stated to U Win Maung and me by Maung Yin Maung himself in 1972. Because he was then more than twelve years old, these statements have no value as evidence of any paranormal knowledge of the life of U Pe Tin that he may have had earlier; also, some of them remain unverified. Their usefulness therefore lies in showing the persistence of Maung Yin Maung's claimed memories of the previous life and his continuing strong identification with U Pe Tin.

Two informants attributed to Maung Yin Maung recognitions that I have not listed in Table 14. For example, U Ba Hein said that he recognized and called by name other sisters of U Pe Tin, but I did not learn details of these recognitions. U Htun Hlaing said that his (and U Pe Tin's) mother, Daw Shwe Chote, had shown Maung Yin Maung photographs of U Pe Tin and had also shown him some clothes that U Pe Tin had worn. According to U Htun Hlaing, Maung Yin Maung had recognized these appropriately. But, as I mentioned above, I was unable to meet Daw Shwe Chote, and so I could not obtain firsthand testimony for these recognitions. Therefore, I have not listed them in Table 14.

At the time Maung Yin Maung first alluded to the loan of 1,000 kyats to Ma Than Tin (item 6, Table 14), his family knew nothing about it. Nor did most members of U Pe Tin's family. They did know about his claim to be U Pe Tin reborn, and they had divided opinions about the case; U Pe Tin's mother, Daw Shwe Chote, readily accepted his claims, but his sisters remained skeptical. According to Maung Yin Maung's parents, his knowledge of this loan diminished the sisters' disbelief, because only U Pe Tin, Ma Than Tin, and one of her friends, Ma Thoung Kyi, had known about it. U Htun Hlaing recalled that U Pe Tin had sent Ma Than Tin 500 kyats from England, but he knew nothing about the loan of 1,000 kyats.

Maung Yin Maung's Statements about Events Occurring after U Pe Tin's Death and before His Birth.   In 1972 Maung Yin Maung said that after U Pe Tin's death he became a ghost "running around Mingaladon at the western end of the airport by the officers' quarters." He thought he had lived this existence for about two years. (In fact, the interval between U Pe Tin's death and Maung Yin Maung's birth was just under one year.)

Maung Yin Maung further recalled that he (still as a discarnate personality) had somehow got into the compound of the timber depot. He recalled that someone—he thought this was probably his mother—had come out of the outhouse near the house of his (previous) brother (U Htun Hlaing). He then "showed himself" as an apparition. The person who saw him asked him who he was and where he had come from. He did not reply, but kept on approaching the person until he was unable to come nearer. He remembered the person saying to him: "If you have such a fixation [on us], why don't you become my child?"

Maung Yin Maung also said that he recalled communicating (still as a discarnate) with U Pe Tin's mother and older sister. They asked him in the Mon language to be reborn with them. But he replied, in Burmese, that he was going to be reborn into the family of U Ba Hein and Daw Kyin Htein. He then asked his mother and sister to "please go back." He did not "show himself" to them as an apparition; and he said that they did not hear his reply.

Comment. I find it difficult to assess Maung Yin Maung's statements about his claimed existence during the interval between U Pe Tin's death and his birth. He spoke quite naturally, as if he were remembering these events just as clearly as he appeared to remember the details of U Pe Tin's death. And what he said corresponded—in general, if not in all details—to the apparitional experience of Daw Kyin Htein and to the dream of Daw Shwe Chote, as reported by Daw Kyin Htein. However, Maung Yin Maung was twelve years old when U Win Maung and I first met him, and he must have heard these experiences described often before that time. We cannot therefore give them the credit we would if his parents had said that he had described them when he was younger, before he could have listened to them talking about the adults' experiences to which they seemingly correspond.

Maung Yin Maung's Behavior Related to the Previous Life

Circumstances and Manner of Maung Yin Maung's Speaking about the Previous Life. I know of only one special circumstance related to Maung Yin Maung's speaking about the previous life. His mother said that once when he was ill and delirious, he said repeatedly: "I want my money back." His father asked him: "What money?" Maung Yin Maung replied: "The 1,000 kyats that I gave my sister Ma Than Tin."[5] (See item 6, Table 14.)

Maung Yin Maung showed no aversion to his given name, but he liked to be called "Ah Maung," which had been a pet name of U Pe Tin.

---

[5]Some other subjects of these cases have remembered events of a previous life with particular vividness during illnesses with fever. Children develop fever readily, and the delirium that often accompanies high fever appears to facilitate the upwelling into consciousness of memories of a previous life in persons otherwise predisposed to have such memories. I plan to publish reports of two other cases showing this feature, those of Vinita Jha (India) and Ma Mu Mu (Burma).

In a few other cases a subject's illness (or injury) appears to have induced a partial or complete fading of memories of a previous life. The case of the Ven. U Sobhana earlier in this volume provides an illustration of this effect.

Maung Yin Maung's Relations with the Adult Members of Both Families.   I
have already mentioned that the two families concerned in this case were
neighbors and close friends, and that U Pe Tin was perhaps even more
friendly with U Ba Hein and his family than he was with his own family.
Furthermore, when Maung Yin Maung was an infant, Daw Shwe Chote
lived nearby and spent much time looking after him. Under these circumstances, it is scarcely surprising that Maung Yin Maung and Daw
Shwe Chote developed a strong attachment to each other. It is more difficult to explain the prolongation of their mutual affection. During Maung
Yin Maung's later childhood, Daw Shwe Chote no longer lived at the timber depot next to U Ba Hein's family. And sometimes she was away from
Rangoon. But when she returned to Rangoon, she would visit U Ba
Hein's home and stay there for several nights in order to visit Maung Yin
Maung. She was a notably thrifty person, but she generously gave Maung
Yin Maung substantial pocket money when she visited him. She called
him by U Pe Tin's pet name, Ah Maung. She continued to visit him about
once a month up to the time of her death in 1973.

This was no one-sided attachment. Maung Yin Maung, without re-
jecting Daw Kyin Htein, stated that Daw Shwe Chote was his mother.
Whenever he saw Daw Shwe Chote, he would say: "You are my mother."
Unlike some mothers of subjects who have made such statements, Daw
Kyin Htein took no offense at her son's fondness for Daw Shwe Chote.
The families had been good friends before the development of the case,
and they remained friends afterward.

I mentioned earlier that U Pe Tin's sisters expressed some doubts
about Maung Yin Maung's claim to be their brother reborn. Maung Yin
Maung objected to this incredulity.

On the occasion of Maung Yin Maung's first meeting with Daw Than
Kyi (see item 22, Table 14), he did not greet her, and when his father
asked him why he had not done so, he replied: "I do not because they
[meaning U Pe Tin's family] do not believe me." This comment, perhaps
warranted for most of U Pe Tin's family, was unjust as applied to Daw
Than Kyi; she lived in Moulmein and had never met Maung Yin Maung
before. It is unlikely that she had formed any opinion about his case at
that time, and even more unlikely that, if she had done so, he knew what
it was.

Toward U Pe Tin's favorite sister, Ma Than Tin, Maung Yin Maung
was, according to her, "very affectionate." His belief that she owed him
money—in repayment of the loan U Pe Tin had made to her— apparently did not impair his friendliness toward her.

When he was young, Maung Yin Maung called U Ba Hein and Daw
Kyin Htein by their given names, just as U Pe Tin had done. This was
grossly familiar and impolite conduct for a Burmese child addressing his

parents. (Maung Yin Maung's parents tolerated this behavior when he was young, but corrected him as he became older.)

Other Behavior of Maung Yin Maung Related to the Previous Life.   When Maung Yin Maung was young, he showed a strong interest in airplanes. His parents remarked that when he was just a few months old, he seemed to respond to the sound of an airplane flying overhead and would turn his head in the direction from which the sound came as if he was trying to see the airplane. This was not all. Daw Kyin Htein told me that when Maung Yin Maung was about six or seven months old and just able to sit up, he asked somehow—perhaps just gestured—for the comb that Daw Shwe Chote (who was visiting) wore in her hair. After she gave her comb to him, he somehow asked for another one. Then he put the two combs together in the shape of an airplane—with wings and fuselage—and made a buzzing sound that seemed to imitate the noise of an airplane. This startled and impressed Daw Shwe Chote so much that she burst into tears and said to Daw Kyin Htein: "Look at what he is doing. He is really my son." (This conviction of her son's rebirth as Maung Yin Maung occurred, according to Daw Kyin Htein, before Maung Yin Maung had begun to speak, but after both the apparitional experience of Daw Kyin Htein and the dreams that she and Daw Shwe Chote had had.) I find it difficult to give credit to the incident, because of the extreme young age attributed to Maung Yin Maung when it happened. But he may have been older; informants accurate in other details of events often make mistakes about their temporal placement.

During the time of my first interviews with him in 1972–74, Maung Yin Maung wished to become a pilot when he grew up.[6] But later he lost this interest.

Maung Yin Maung was cautious about fire, but this was not unusual among members of his family. During the years of their early married life, U Ba Hein and Daw Kyin Htein had lived in no fewer than three

---

[6]Maung Yin Maung's having, not a phobia, but—on the contrary—a philia for airplanes deserves comment. In the report of the case of Ma Tin Aung Myo (earlier in this volume) I mentioned the frequency with which the subjects of these cases show phobias related to the concerned previous personality's mode of death; and I cited there some other examples.

Airplanes figure in the deaths that Maung Yin Maung and Ma Tin Aung Myo claimed to remember. The obvious difference between them is that Ma Tin Aung Myo recalled being killed *by* an airplane and Maung Yin Maung recalled being killed *in* one. On the other hand, Erkan Kılıç (third volume of this series) recalled the life of a man who was killed in an airplane, and he (Erkan) had a phobia of airplanes. If Maung Yin Maung is the reincarnation of U Pe Tin and carried into his life U Pe Tin's fondness for airplanes, this might have neutralized the shock of having been killed in one.

For other examples of subjects who did *not* show phobias related to the previous personality's mode of death, see the cases of Mounzer Haïdar (third volume) and Bongkuch Promsin (this volume).

houses that burned down. They had therefore become unusually prudent about fire and warned their children about its dangers.

Ma Than Tin had given Maung Yin Maung some of the clothes that had belonged to U Pe Tin. These included neckties, shirts, and longyis; some of them were shown to me in 1978. Maung Yin Maung sometimes wore these clothes.

Birthmarks on Maung Yin Maung

When Maung Yin Maung was born, the skin of his body was unusually red and entirely covered with numerous small vesicles, from some of which a fluid oozed. His skin was dusted with talcum powder, and after about a month the vesicles dried up. The skin then shed flakes. After that, it became normal and remained so. (This dermatitis was related by observers of the case to the burns of the body of U Pe Tin when the airplane in which he crashed caught fire.)

Maung Yin Maung had a prominent pigmented nevus near the midline of his lower neck, where it joins his back. No other member of his family had a nevus in the same place. (I examined both his parents, his two older brothers, and his younger sister; and I satisfied myself that this was so.) According to U Ba Hein, U Pe Tin had had a nevus at exactly the same place on his lower neck. U Pe Tin's nevus had been slightly bigger than Maung Yin Maung's. U Ba Hein said that he had often had occasion to notice it because U Pe Tin frequently bathed at his house. I asked U Htun Hlaing and Ma Than Tin whether they could confirm that their brother had had a nevus at the back of his neck; but neither remembered whether he had.

Comments on the Evidence of Paranormal Processes in the Case

The close acquaintance between the families concerned in this case meant that they knew much about each other before its development. Maung Yin Maung made few statements (when he was a young child) about the previous life, and these contained little that his parents did not already know. His only statement of matters both unknown to them and verifiable concerned U Pe Tin's loan of 1,000 kyats to his sister Ma Than Tin. However, Maung Yin Maung's knowledge of this loan had a profound impression on some members of U Pe Tin's family, because only two persons still living had known about it.

The most remarkable feature of Maung Yin Maung's behavior was his strong attachment to Daw Shwe Chote. I have already shown that we could account for this by the closeness of the two families and by Daw

Shwe Chote's care of Maung Yin Maung when he was an infant. But I do not think these circumstances will account for Maung Yin Maung's repetitive statements to the effect that Daw Shwe Chote was "my mother."

I have emphasized the extent to which U Pe Tin had become effectively a member of U Ba Hein's family before his death, so that he was in some respects closer to them than he was to his own family. Under these circumstances, U Ba Hein and Daw Kyin Htein could have wished for him to be reborn into their family just as much as if he had been one of their own children who had died. Daw Kyin Htein's apparitional experience and subsequent dream might be regarded as arising from such a wish and certainly as strengthening her own expectations that U Pe Tin would be reborn as her child. Maung Yin Maung's parents were, therefore, excellently placed, both by their knowledge of U Pe Tin and by their wish for him to return, to impose the role of U Pe Tin on Maung Yin Maung. This interpretation does not appeal to me, however, mainly because I do not think children are as malleable as the suggestion implies.

Maung Yin Maung's Later Development

I saw Maung Yin Maung again in March 1978. He was then seventeen and a half years old. He was in the seventh class of school, a little behind his peers because he had missed one year when he was ill.

He was still interested in airplanes, but becoming a pilot now had less appeal to him than it had had earlier. He liked the idea of flying, but was somewhat apprehensive about crashes. (He had not yet been in an airplane.) He was favoring medicine as a profession to enter when he went to a university.

Maung Yin Maung no longer spoke spontaneously about the previous life; he had not done so since my previous visit in 1974. But his memories of the previous life had not entirely faded. He still remembered the loan that U Pe Tin had given to his sister Ma Than Tin, although he was no longer asking for the return of this money. Maung Yin Maung explained that he had not wanted the money for himself, but to give to Daw Shwe Chote.

U Htun Hlaing came to visit his old friend U Ba Hein from time to time; but he did not make these visits especially to see Maung Yin Maung. Maung Yin Maung had preserved a friendly attachment to Ma Than Tin. He was still visiting her and had done so last (before this interview) in January 1978.

I met with Maung Yin Maung again in November 1980. He was then a little more than twenty years old. He had continued in school up to the eighth class and then had left without completing secondary school. He was working as a laborer in the Furniture Industries Department of the government of Burma, while trying to find a better job.

At this time his memories of the previous life had largely faded, and he said that he could recall it only vaguely. He still continued to visit Ma Than Tin from time to time; and he also saw U Htun Hlaing every few months, when the latter came to the timber depot to collect his pension.

Glossary

Index

Glossary

WORDS DEFINED IN *this glossary have been given an initial capital letter even when they would not be in the original Asian languages. Words of these languages have been romanized without diacriticals.*

ACHAN. Teacher. Sometimes used as an honorific or form of address for teachers in Thailand.

AINGYI. A short jacket with cloth buttons worn in Burma.

AMPHUR. Administrative district; subdivision of a province. (Thailand)

ANAGARIKA. Literally "a homeless one." It refers to Buddhists who adopt many or most of the rules of the monks without formally entering the Sangha, the order of Buddhist monks.

ANATTA. *Buddhism:* No soul. The doctrine that no enduring entity or soul exists either during one life or persisting from one life to another. *Cf.* ATMAN.

ATMAN. *Hinduism:* The transcendent principle in man. The atman endures from one terrestrial life to another in successive incarnations. *Cf.* ANATTA.

BAHT. Principle monetary unit in Thailand. Also called "tical." Worth approximately U.S. $.05. Also a unit of weight equal to about 15 grams.

BAN. Village. (Thailand)

BHAWANA. Mind development, especially by meditation and concentration.

BHIKKHU. An ordained monk in Buddhism; a member of the Sangha, the order of monks founded by the Buddha. (Fem. BHIKKHUNI.)

BO TREE. Short or corrupt form of *Bodhi tree.* The pipal tree *(Ficus religiosa).* The type of tree under which the Buddha attained Enlightenment at Buddh Gaya (now in Bihar, India). Ultimately from the Sanskrit word *budh,* meaning "to wake."

CHAOKHUN. An honorific given to a senior monk or abbot of a wat (monastery) in Thailand.

DACOIT. Armed brigand. (Burma; also India)

DANA. Giving to the poor and needy and also to monks. The benevolence of dana may be distinguished from moral conduct indicated by the word *sila* (q.v.).

DAW. Honorific given to older women. Although they are usually married, women who are addressed as "Daw" are not necessarily married. They are women of a recognized seniority. (Burma)

DEVA. A discarnate personality; generally of a beneficent nature. *Cf.* PRETA.

DHARMA. (Sanskrit); DHAMMA (Pali). Doctrine, especially the teachings of Buddhism considered as a whole.

DUM HUA. Literally "head washing." The name of a ceremony in which children pay respects to their elders by giving them perfumed water with which they (the parents) should wash their hair. It occurs during the Songkran Festival. (Thailand)

DURIAN. Fruit of the tree *Durio zibethinus,* which is found in Southeast Asia.

GATHA. A set of verses, especially ones based on Buddhist scriptures.

GOUER. A type of fruit found in Burma.

GYI. Big or great. Often found as a suffix. (Burma)

HINAYANA. Literally "Lesser Vehicle" (of salvation). The term was developed by members of the Mahayana school to distinguish those who departed from their teachings. Most of the early Hinayana sects ceased naturally or were suppressed when the Moslems controlled India. The only surviving group is better known as the Theravada. *Cf.* MAHAYANA; THERAVADA.

JOSS STICKS. Incense sticks.

KARMA. (Sanskrit); KAMMA (Pali). Literally means "action," but has come to refer more narrowly to actions the effects of which are experienced later, often in another incarnation. The word should not be used to describe the effects of karma.

KHANOM KROK. A preparation of coconut with flour, sugar, milk, and salt. (Thailand)

KHUN. Honorific; more polite than *Nai* and corresponds to *honorable sir* or *honorable madam;* it is used in addressing persons of both sexes. (Thailand)

KLONG. A canal or other connecting body of water with sluggish currents; klongs are still much used for transportation in southern Thailand.

KO. Honorific used by men who are approximate equals to address each other. (Burma)

KUTI. A hut, especially one used for meditation and also as a dwelling place for one or two monks or nuns. (Thailand)

KYAT. Burmese unit of currency. In 1982 a kyat exchanged for approximately U.S. $.15; U.S. $1.00 was worth about 6.6 kyats.

LEIKPYA. The "butterfly spirit," which Burmans believe is able to leave the body during sleep and to survive its death with persistence in a discarnate state.

LIKAI. (also LIKEH.) Thai musical folk drama. (Thailand)

LONGYI. A cloth garment worn in Burma around the lower part of the body. Women's longyis are usually of solid colors or have colored floral patterns; men's longyis nearly always have check patterns and are usually brown or gray.

LUWINZA. A person who remembers a previous life as a human being.

MA. Honorific given to girls and young women. Some women are still called "Ma" when older and married if they are of inferior status. (Burma)

MAHAYANA. The Buddhist school of the "Great Vehicle" (of salvation). Sometimes also called the northern school because its adherents are mainly found in Tibet, Mongolia, China, Korea, and Japan. *Cf.* HINAYANA; THERAVADA.

MAUNG. Honorific given to boys and young men. Some men are still called "Maung" when older. (Burma)

MERIT-MAKING. Activities, such as moral conduct (sila), benevolence and generosity (dana), and meditation (bhawana), which assist a person toward the goal of Nirvana. (Buddhism)

NAI. Honorific corresponding to "Mr." (Thailand)

NAMPHRIK. A spicy sauce, especially for dipping certain foods in before eating. There are many varieties of namphrik in Thailand. Namphrik pla-ra (preferred by the people of northeastern Thailand) contains fermented fish paste.

NANG. Honorific corresponding to "Mrs." (Thailand)

NIRVANA. (Sanskrit); NIBBANA (Pali). The extinction of personality through the loss of all cravings for existence. It means a cessation of rebirth and of all independent existence; a union with Ultimate Reality (Buddhism). (The concept in Hinduism is somewhat different.)

PAGODA. A sacred building or monument; the term is often used more narrowly for a type of monument in which relics or the ashes of deceased persons are interred. In parts of Southeast Asia similar monuments may be called stupas and dagobas.

PALI. Originally, "text." The word was applied to the scriptural text of the Theravada Buddhist Canon and then later to the language in which the text was written. The language was originally a Prakrit (vernacular dialect) contemporary with Sanskrit.

PANCHA SILA. "Five precepts." The five most important precepts taught by the Buddha and observed by devout Buddhists.

PARITTA. A prayer ceremony that includes the recitation of Buddhist texts. It may be used for warding off unwelcome discarnate persons, for sharing merit with discarnate persons in order to release them for rebirth, and for other aims.

PHRA. A Buddhist monk in Thailand. Corresponds to *bhikkhu* in Sri Lanka and *pongyi* in Burma. *Phra Kru* is an honorific for a monk of more senior standing, but of less seniority than one addressed as "Chaokhun."

PONGYI. Literally, "the great glory." A monk in Burma. Equivalent to *bhikkhu* in Sri Lanka and *phra* in Thailand.

PRETA. (Sanskrit); PETA (Pali). Supernatural entity inhabiting a nonterrestrial realm, but capable of interacting with living humans and manifesting to them. Pretas are said to result from strong, unfulfilled cravings that lead to rebirth after death in this form instead of in a higher realm as a deva (q.v.).

PSYCHOMETRY. As used in psychical research and parapsychology, this term refers to the practice in which a sensitive or a medium holds an object that belonged to a deceased person from whom it is desired to receive a communication. Handling the "psychometric object" is supposed to facilitate the contact with the deceased person. In principle, a living person could be a psychometric object. This would not mean that the sensitive or medium would have to handle the person tactually; some other sensory contact might suffice.

PYA. Burmese unit of currency. There are 100 pyas in a kyat (q.v.).

REBIRTH. *Buddhism:* The activation of a new physical body by effects or residues of a personality that had previously been associated with another (now deceased) physical body. *Cf.* REINCARNATION.

REINCARNATION. *Hinduism:* The union of a soul with a new physical body after the death of the physical body with which it was previously associated. *Cf.* REBIRTH.

SAATU. Expression spoken at the end of an act of worship. Corresponds loosely to *amen.* (Thailand)

SAMANERA. Novice monk of the Buddhist Sangha (order of monks).

SANGHA. The order of Buddhist monks considered collectively.

SASANA. Doctrine, particularly that taught by the Buddha. (Burma)

SATANG. A Thai coin worth one hundredth of a baht (or tical).

SAYADAW. Honorific given to senior Buddhist monks. They are usually abbots, but a distinguished teacher may receive the title also. (Burma)

SEN. A unit of measurement equivalent to approximately 40 meters. (Thailand)

SILA. Moral conduct. *See also* PANCHA SILA.

SONGKRAN. An important annual festival in Thailand held in April each year. It is an occasion when children pay special respects to their parents and try to visit them.

STUPA. A burial mound. Stupas usually contain the ashes or relics of an important person. Similar monuments are sometimes called pagodas and dagobas. (Sanskrit)

THERAVADA. Literally "doctrine of the elders." The branch of Buddhism based on the teachings in the Pali Canon. It is the principal sect of Buddhism in Sri Lanka, Burma, Thailand, Laos, and Cambodia. Sometimes called "Hinayana" (q.v.).

TICAL. Older name for the principal monetary unit in Thailand. It is now more often called "baht." Worth approximately U.S. $.05.

TIPITAKA. Literally "three baskets." The three divisions of the Pali Canon. (Pali)

TULKU. A lama identified as the reincarnation of a particular deceased lama. Tulkus are said to be the reincarnations only of "high lamas," that is, of spiritually developed lamas who have attained the ability, more or less, to control the time and circumstances of their next incarnations. (Tibet)

U. Honorific given to older men in recognition of their seniority. It corresponds loosely to *Mr.* (Burma)

UPASAKA. A Buddhist layman committed to following the Buddhist precepts as fully as he can without entering the Sangha, or order of Buddhist monks. (Fem. UPASIKA.)

VIPASSANA. A Buddhist system of meditation practiced by members of the Theravada school. It is based on the system of "mindfulness" given in the Satipatthana Sutta of the Pali Canon.

WA. A unit of measurement equivalent to approximately 2 meters. (Thailand)

WAT. A Buddhist temple (and associated buildings) in Thailand.